PROGRESS IN LINGUISTICS

JANUA LINGUARUM

STUDIA MEMORIAE
NICOLAI VAN WIJK DEDICATA

edenda curat

C. H. VAN SCHOONEVELD
INDIANA UNIVERSITY

SERIES MAIOR
43

1970
MOUTON
THE HAGUE · PARIS

PROGRESS IN LINGUISTICS

A COLLECTION OF PAPERS

selected and edited by

MANFRED BIERWISCH

and

KARL ERICH HEIDOLPH

1970

MOUTON

THE HAGUE · PARIS

LIBRARY OF CONGRESS CATALOG CARD NUMBER: 78-123127

Printed in The Netherlands by Mouton & Co., Printers, The Hague.

PREFACE

The form of the present collection of papers, its constructive intention as well as its unavoidable gaps, is motivated objectively and subjectively. What objectively gave rise to this publication was the Tenth International Congress of Linguists in Bucharest, while the subjective element arises from the attempt of the editors to find out those papers in the programme of the Congress which are most relevant to the present state and the development of linguistics.

The picture of linguistics presented by the Congress was necessarily so comprehensive and internally so heterogenious that it was virtually impossible to recognise any general pattern or orientation. Communication with numerous collegues convinced us that this was not only our own impression. This encouraged us to attempt to select a number of papers which seemed to us to be of particular importance to the progress of linguistics and to incorporate them into a single volume. This aim was met with a gratifying response: nearly all the twenty or so colleagues we invited to contribute have done so. The restrictions on the length imposed by the Congress now no longer held and most of the papers have been revised and expanded. We have also included some contributions which were prepared for but not presented at the Congress.

We do not claim that the selection we have made gives an uncontroversial picture of the state and development of linguistics — as evident at the Bucharest Congress. Such a claim would be untenable for the following three reasons. Firstly, our aquaintance with the material was inevitably limited, since the number of lectures we were able to attend and the amount of information contained by the abstracts were relatively small. Secondly, the size of the present selection had to be restricted if it was to have any meaning at all. And thirdly, the selection to be made under these conditions necessarily depended on what we understand to be the progress of linguistics.

The particular standpoint which largely determined our choice cannot be formulated precisely in a few words. We hope that the present volume will give some implicit indication. What was important, we felt, was that work on semantic, syntactic, morphological and phonological problems should at least be capable of integration into a general theory of language, and should if possible improve on such a theory. The question of how semantic phenomena should be represented and how this representation should be brought into relation to syntactic structure, and how syntactic structure itself may be represented in such a way as to account for this relation, is in our view a central problem at the present time.

It includes — with a considerable degree of variation in all the specific aspects — the actual fields of syntax and semantics, the thorny problems of word formation, and extends to the syntactic-semantic motivation of morphological phenomena such as aspect, tense, number, etc.

With regard to the nature of the integrating theory we have imposed no particular conditions. At the same time it is, in our view, no coincidence that a large number of papers relevant to our aims are written in the framework of generative grammar.

Finally, we have selected some papers which do not specifically deal with theoretical integration within linguistics but which contribute to the study of the relation between linguistic theory and other disciplines such as poetics and psycholinguistics. Papers on phonology do not form part of the present volume since the programme of the Bucharest Congress, which almost coincided with the International Congress of Phonetic Sciences in Prague, scarcely contained any such papers.

MANFRED BIERWISCH
KARL ERICH HEIDOLPH

CONTENTS

8   CONTENTS

IRENA BELLERT

ON THE SEMANTIC INTERPRETATION OF SUBJECT-PREDICATE RELATIONS IN SENTENCES OF PARTICULAR REFERENCE*

At the outset I wish to point out that the notions of subject and predicate used in this paper pertain neither to the grammatical categories as defined for hierarchical surface structures of utterances, nor to the relations definable in terms of the deep structures of a transformational grammar [*cf.* Chomsky (1965:23) for his notion of logical subject], for neither of these two terms could then be assigned an invariant semantic interpretation.

Most linguists agree that a more abstract level of representation than a hierarchical surface structure tree should be assumed as a basis for the semantic interpretation of utterances in natural language. However, the problem of how deep structures should be represented still remains open, even for those linguists who are known as adherents of a transformational generative grammar.

Without considering the general and complex problem of how deep structures could be represented as to constitute an adequate basis for the semantic interpretation, I will discuss here only one problem which seems to me quite essential with respect to the search for a possible deep structure representation, namely, the problem of how to determine the notions of subject and predicate in such a way that their semantic interpretation be invariant from utterance to utterance and compatible with the linguistic intuitions of a competent speaker.

It appears that the notion of subject — which we will refer to as logical subject[1] —

* This paper was in part delivered at the Meeting of the Polish Linguistic Society in Kraków, March 1967, and in part at the International Congress of Linguists, Bucarest, August, 1967. It is a largely extended version of the two reports.
[1] The notion of logical subject as used here should not be confused with the notion of 'topic', 'datum' or 'logical subject' as used in different versions in the literature. This notion is used here to a certain extent analogically to the notion of referring phrase, with the difference that it does not apply only to those phrases which actually occur on the surface. Thus it differs from the above mentioned notions in essentially two respects: (1) it appears that a different assignment of the function of logical subject in this sense of the term corresponds to semantic oppositions, rather than to pragmatic ones, and (2) such a notion cannot be determined in terms of surface structure alone, as will be shown in this paper. In a further paper of mine, in which I extend the present discussion to related topics (Bellert, to appear), I dropped altogether the confusing term 'logical subject' and replaced it by ARGUMENT OF TYPE 1.

may have an invariant semantic interpretation if it is related to Peirce's notion of designation.[2] It is hard to disagree with Peirce's statement that

designations are absolutely indispensable both to communication and to thought. No assertion has any meaning unless there is some designation.

Accordingly, it seems plausible to assume that the function of logical subject should be assigned to such a linguistic device which serves as an index pointing to some 'object' or particular of the universe of discourse to which a given predicate applies. The notion of logical subject would then be related to that of designation.

It seems reasonable to assume that in the deep structure description no distinction should be made between indices used in everyday or scientific discourse and those used in literary discourse (fiction). The name *John* in the utterance *John was a physicist* cannot be represented differently depending on whether the utterance belongs to one or another type of discourse. We may say then that the object, purported object or quasi object to which an index is intended to refer should be conceived of merely in the same sense as the possible value of a variable, with no ontological implications as are usually associated with the term 'object'. Thus an 'object' is meant here as anything namable.[3]

We will assume that by using a sentence as an utterance, the speaker expresses at least an elementary proposition. An elementary proposition may be represented by a predicate and its argument, or arguments, with a modal frame or pragmatical qualification being added concerning the speaker's attitude with respect to the given predication, that is, assertion, denial, belief, doubt, will (as in orders or questions), *etc.*[4] In this paper we will consider only sentences of particular reference, by which we mean those which a speaker can use in order to point at least to one 'object' and apply to it a predicate. Moreover, the discussion will be limited only to those utterances which express an elementary proposition.[5]

---

[2]   One of the trichotomies most frequently discussed by Peirce is that between Icon, Index and Symbol. Peirce distinguished two classes of indices. One of them is "a class of indices which merely stand for things or individual quasi things with which the interpreting mind is already acquainted" (Peirce). Such indices are called by Pierce designations. Linguistic designations are, then, personal or demonstrative pronouns, proper names, words such as *here, there, now, then, etc.*, in general all such signs which, when used in an utterance, purport uniqueness of reference.

[3]   In the sequel, I will use simply the short term 'OBJECT' in quotation marks as an equivalent of 'purported object', which in fact renders the intended concept more adequately.

[4]   Some authors use the term 'propositional attitude' (Russell, Quine). I will use here the term MODAL FRAME.

[5]   I wish to clarify some points concerning my use of the terms 'utterance', 'sentence' and 'proposition'. I follow here, in the essential points, the view expressed in this connection by Y. Bar-Hillel (1967). Generally, I use the term UTTERANCE with respect to observable entities and the term SENTENCE with respect to abstract entities (which when used become observable entities — utterances). An utterance is, accordingly, an actual or potential realization of its underlying string of formatives (abstract units, such as, for instance, morphemes) which is a theoretical construct of the category of sentence, to which a structure is assigned. Each utterance corresponds to the PROPOSITION (or propositions) which it expresses (to different ones in case of ambiguity), and which is common to all utterances that are close paraphrases of each other. A proposition is obviously an abstract entity. Its structure — which some linguists call the semantic structure of an utterance — is precisely what

When discussing a possible abstract representation of utterances, we will be refer-ring to the logico-semantic structure (LS structure),[6] rather than to the deep structure, because the latter term (although used in many senses by different linguists) to remain unambiguous should in fact be reserved only to the transformational generative grammar; however, it is hard to tell how the presently discussed notions could be related to that grammar.[7]

Obviously several designations may occur in an utterance, or else there may be none at all on the surface, but our problem is to postulate such a description which would account for the fact that a competent speaker always infers from the surface structure what is the subject (subjects) of predication, that is, he must understand which expressions or which linguistic devices have an identifying function and which have a predicating function. One thing is clear: there are no formal exponents on the surface which would suffice to determine once for all that a specific word or phrase is to be assigned the function of logical subject or predicate of the utterance in which it occurs. Actually, formal exponents do play a role in determining such functions, but only as signals of the contrastive semantic oppositions between the discovered LS structures in terms of which such functions can be adequately assigned.

Consider the simple example in Polish of a sentence with a proper name in the nominative case, which in general is the best candidate for logical subject:

(1) *Jan przyjechał* 'John has arrived'

The written form (1) represents two different propositions which correspond to two different utterances in speech; they differ from one another only in stress assignment, the word *Jan* receiving an extra stress in (1b):

(a) *Jan przyjéchał* 'John (= the one who I am referring to by *John*) has arrived here'
(b) *Ján przyjechał* 'The one who has arrived here is John'[8]

We may paraphrase (1b) by *To Jan przyjechał* 'It is John who has arrived', *Ten kto przyjechał to Jan* 'The one who has arrived is John', or by inverting the word order *Przyjechał Jan*; none of these utterances is a paraphrase of (1a).[9]

---

is being sought for here and referred to as the LS structure. Following Bar-Hillel, I do not identify the difference between 'utterance' and 'sentence' with the difference between 'token' and 'type', for we may speak about several tokens of the same utterance, when it is repeated. When I say in the paper that an utterance implies a proposition, I use the term 'proposition' because whatever is implied by an utterance is not actually uttered, and thus is not an observable entity. But such an implied proposition may be expressed by a corresponding utterance, and this is a way in which a proposition may be referred to.

[6] I use the term LOGICO-SEMANTIC STRUCTURE in Bellert (1968, 1969).

[7] Some recent papers (Bach, mimeographed, and McCawley, mimeographed) suggest an approach to the deep structure description which could be compatible with my proposals.

[8] For the sake of simplicity, I shall not always explicate an occurrence of a proper name as *the one who is being referred to by* '...', where in the place of dots the given proper name occurs, but such an explication is assumed for all the examples here. The adverb *here* would be replaced in some contexts by *there*.

[9] The utterance (1b) is ambiguous. For the purpose of the present analysis I am considering only that one of its readings which is paraphrasable in the way indicated here.

Since we assume that the LS structure of an utterance is to be compatible with its semantic interpretation, the function of logical subject can only be assigned to an expression (or expressions) capable of functioning as an index, independently of whether such an expression actually occurs on the surface or is somehow signaled and implied by the utterance in question. Such expressions can then either be designations, or at least contain designations.

Consider from this point of view the utterance (1a) and (1b). If the LS structures are to be in accordance with the semantic interpretation connected with the syntactical features present in these utterances, then they should account for the evident difference discussed above. The indices — either explicitly occurring on the surface, or implicit and only implied by certain signals on the surface — are *Jan* 'John' and the implicit *tu* 'here' in (1a), while *Jan* and the implicit *ten kto tu przyjechał* 'that one who has arrived here' in (1b). Moreover, the two utterances differ in their semantic structures in another respect which should be disclosed in their LS structure representation: (1a) is an ordinary statement, whereas (1b) is an identification statement; thus (1b) will be used in a situation when it is known that somebody has arrived and the speaker intends to identify that person as John.

In order to show that such an interpretation is not arbitrary, let us test its validity in the following way. For two different propositions we should have two corresponding propositions one of which will be a negation of (1a), the other of (1b). In fact we do have two utterances which represent such propositions:

(1)(a′) *Jan nie przyjéchał* 'John has not arrived'
   (b′) *To nie Jan przyjechał* 'It is not John who has arrived', or *Ten kto przyjechał to nie Jan* 'The one who has arrived is not John'

The LS structure representation of these negations should correspond to their respective paraphrases in which the modal frames are explicitly expressed:

   I deny that John has arrived (for 1a′)
and
   I deny that the one who has arrived is John (for 1b′)

It is evident that (1a) with (1a′), and (1b) with (1b′), form pairs which in the symbolic of truth functional calculus can be represented by S and $\sim S$, whereas neither (1a) with (1b′), nor (1b) with (1a′), form such pairs. Moreover, notice that a proper assignment of LS structures consistent with our analysis would account for the fact that the negative particle which is attached on the surface to the term *Jan* functions in fact as a negation of the identification statement. As is well known, there is no reasonable interpretation for 'not x_1', where x_1 functions as an argument or name.[10]

The fact that (1a) and (1b) represent two different propositions cannot be accounted for by any semantic ambiguity of the segmental morphemes involved, for they have

---

[10] A possible interpretation, which, however, obviously cannot be accepted here would be: the complement of x_1 with respect to a given universe.

exactly the same meaning. This fact can only be accounted for by the assignment of two different structures, which are signaled on the surface by the opposition of stress.

Examples can be multiplied endlessly. For a better illustration consider the sentence *Jan ożenił się z Anną*, for which in spoken language there are three variants which differ in the place of the main stress:

(2)(a)   *Jan ożenił się z Anną* 'John has married Ann'
   (b)   *Ján ożenił się z Anną* 'The one who has married Ann is John'
   (c)   *Jan ożenił się z Ánną* 'The one whom John has married is Ann'

Consider also the corresponding negations:

(2)(a′) *Jan nie ożenił się z Anną* 'John has not married Ann'
   (b′) *To nie Ján ożenił się z Anną* 'It is not John who has married Ann'

or its paraphrase

     Ten kto ożenił się z Anną to nie Jan 'The one who has married Ann is not John'
   (c′) *Jan nie ożenił się z Ánną*

or its paraphrase

     Ta z którą Jan się ożenił to nie Anna 'The one whom John has married is not Ann'

The LS structure representation of these negations should correspond to their respective paraphrases in which the modal frames are explicitly expressed:

    I deny that John has married Ann
    I deny that the one who has married Ann is John

and

    I deny that the one whom John has married is Ann

Notice that whatever content is conveyed by (2a′) is also conveyed by (2b′) and (2c′), but the converse does not hold. The proposition

    Somebody has married Ann

is implicitly conveyed or implied by (2b′), whereas the proposition

    John has married somebody

is implied by (2c′), and they should be accounted for by the corresponding LS structure representations. On the other hand, none of these propositions is conveyed by (2a′). An analogous semantic surplus is contained in (1b′) with respect to (1a′). This follows from the fact that (1a′) and (2a′), similarly as (1a) and (2a), are ordinary statements, whereas all the remaining utterances are identification statements which contain implicit definite descriptions.

The fact that certain propositions are implied by the use of definite descriptions is related to several other linguistic facts which can be accounted for by rules of linguistic quasi implications (which I have dealt with in Bellert, 1968). I will not enter into a detailed analysis concerning the problem of linguistic quasi implications, but I will briefly sketch here the reasons for which we can establish a quasi implication on the grounds of which certain propositions are implied from utterances with proper names or definite descriptions used as indices.

In logic, a propositional function φ is defined as a unit function if it satisfies two conditions, one which guarantees the existence of an 'object' which is φ, the other one the uniqueness of such an 'object'. A unit function can thus be prefixed by the iota operator[11] to form an expression $(\iota x)\varphi(x)$, which can be interpreted roughly as 'that object which is φ'. It seems that an analogous representation of proper names and definite descriptions used as indices would be compatible with several facts pertaining to the semantic interpretation of indices by competent users of language, and would account, among other facts, for the above discussed implications. Although definite descriptions and even proper names, as such, do not normally satisfy such conditions, yet for reasons which are quite convincing with respect to the role of proper names and definite descriptions in the process of linguistic communication, we have to admit that whenever they are used in normal discourse (not in sentences used as examples), they cannot be interpreted otherwise than as being intended to point to one and only one 'object', and thus they purport uniqueness of reference. The conditions of existence and uniqueness are then, even for a literary discourse, assumed as if they were satisfied in a specific sense, both in the intention of the addresser and the interpretation of the receiver. It is an empirical fact that a speaker or author will not use a sentence, say, *John lived in Paris*, or *The little boy lived in Paris* without believing, pretending to believe,[12] or assuming (as in a novel) that the given index (*John, the little boy*) as used in the given utterance is applicable to one and only one 'object', or in other words, that there is one and only one 'object' which is being referred to by such an index. With the term 'object' as used in this paper in the sense of purported object, the statements *there is an 'object' which is such and such* are obviously not meant to constitute existential statements in the ontological sense of the term, for they are devoid of ontological commitments. We may assume that independently of its modal frame (see examples below), an utterance which contains an explicit or implicit index φ — which is always interpreted roughly as 'that x which is referred to by φ — implies, among other propositions, one of the form: *The speaker believes or assumes that an x is φ*, for such a proposition is a necessary condition of the appropriate use of indices.

---

[11]   The IOTA OPERATOR was first used by Peano, then by Russel, Reichenbach, Mostowski and several other logicians.

[12]   From the point of view of the semantic interpretation, which is concerned with the information conveyed by utterances as such, not with the states of minds of the speakers, it makes no difference whether the speaker actually believes or only pretends to believe that such and such is the case. In our further discussion, the phrase *the speaker's belief* will always be intended to mean exactly 'the speaker's purported belief'. Similarly, I understand that a speaker uses an expression or an utterance appropriately, if he uses it consistently with the rules of language and with his purported beliefs. And it is in this sense of the term that I will speak of the appropriate use.

We can thus establish a corresponding quasi implication: *For any linguistic index* φ, *the speaker uses appropriately an utterance containing a linguistic index* φ, *only if he believes or assumes that there is an x which is* φ. In the case of any utterance which contains a linguistic index, we can accept a statement corresponding to the antecedent as holding true, by a very general assumption that people use their utterances appropriately, such an assumption being indispensable for any consistent semantic interpretation. We therefore can always infer the corresponding consequent as a valid conclusion.

The x stands here for the 'object' of the universe of discourse (anything to which φ is applicable); the role of the function φ is not to predicate a semantic feature or complex of features to the given 'object', but to give, so to say, an instruction for the hearer which tells him how to identify the 'object' in question. Thus, for example, *The man who is standing next to me* could be represented by means of the iota operator as: $(\iota x)\varphi(x)$, where φ stands for the given description which is intended by the speaker as an instruction uniquely identifying a given 'object', and the 'object' thus conceived corresponds to the value of the variable x. If the hearer assumes that an utterance which contains such an index is used appropriately, then he may rightly conclude: *The speaker believes that there is an 'object' such that it is a man who is standing next to him*.

Similarly, an utterance which contains — or is a close paraphrase of one which contains — the definite description:

The one who has married Ann,

independently of whether it is a question

Who is the one who has married Ann?

a negation (2b′), or a statement which expresses doubt

I doubt whether the one who has married Ann is happy,

it implies in any case the proposition:

The speaker believes there is someone who has married Ann.

Such facts additionally support our analysis.

The investigation of utterances which have different modal frames (not only those that express a denial) shows clearly the necessity of differentiating the LS structures of the utterances presented here as examples, which are illustrative for endless other cases. Thus our analysis of (1a) and (1b) is confirmed not only by showing analogous structures in the respective negations (1a′) and (1b′), but also by the possibility of disclosing analogous structures in the corresponding questions, wishes, *etc.* Compare, for instance,

Czy Jan przyjechał? 'Has John arrived?'

with

Czy to Jan przyjechał? 'Is it John who has arrived?'

The same correspondence of structures holds for all the other examples, too.

Let us now give a rule-of-thumb definition of the notion of linguistic index by determining it in terms of those expressions which function as indices on the surface of utterances. The definition only roughly corresponds to linguistic indices in Polish; incidentally it also roughly corresponds to English indices. However, it covers generic descriptions, which should obviously be excepted, and thus it is too wide.

A linguistic index is:

(a) a simple designation (proper name, personal or demonstrative pronoun, *etc.*)
(b) a nominal group preceded by a definite determiner (demonstrative pronoun).
(c) an expression constructed with the aid of linguistic indices according to the following pattern: definite determiner + nominal group + restrictive relative pronoun ...

(where in the place of dots there may occur several — at least one — linguistic indices within the subordinate construction of the restrictive relative clause).

Thus linguistic indices may be, for instance,

Jan 'John', *on* 'he',

ta pani ubrana na czarno 'the lady in black',

ten pan który trzyma tę książkę którą dostałam od Jana 'that man who is holding the book which I got from John',

ten astronauta który pierwszy wylądują na księżycu 'that astronaut who will be the first to land on the moon',

etc.[13]

Clearly not all linguistic indices play the role of a logical subject. We may say, however, that the function of logical subject in sentences of particular reference should be assigned to those linguistic indices that are neither part of another linguistic index nor part of any other nominal phrase, and which together with the predicate make up a proposition. Thus a logical subject corresponds to the notion of argument,[14] and evidently there may be more than one logical subject in case the predicate is not only a one-place predicate. Obviously, we cannot take into consideration only those linguistic indices which occur on the surface, but we must take into account those indices which are implied by the LS structure of a given utterance and in terms of which a

---

[13] The expressions which occur on the surface of utterances may considerably differ from those shown as examples. Linguistic indices may only be signaled on the surface (as in the utterances discussed above), or they may appear on the surface not in their full form. For instance, *dziewczyna* 'girl' does not always function in Polish as a linguistic index, but if such is the case, then the corresponding part of the LS structure representation should be the same as that corresponding to the expression *ta dziewczyna* 'this girl, the girl'.

[14] The term 'argument' seems to be more convenient for this use than the ambiguous term 'logical subject', as it appeared from my further considerations that other types of arguments may also be represented by means of an expression prefixed by a quantifying operator (Bellert, 1969).

hearer understands to what 'object' a given predicate applies. Thus, for instance, in our example (1b'), the index 'that one who has arrived here' does not appear on the surface, but is somehow implied and thus should be accounted for by the LS structure representation.

The proposed semantic interpretation of a logical subject in sentences of particular reference will then be approximately as follows:

'That 'object' of the universe of discourse which the speaker is referring to by means of the given linguistic index in order to ascribe it a predicate, and which the hearer is supposed to identify as one that $\begin{Bmatrix} \text{has been just indicated} \\ \text{is (will be) known to him} \end{Bmatrix}$.

According to this interpretation, a logical subject functions as an instruction which tells the hearer how to identify the object referred to. Such is clearly the intention of the speaker who assumes that the instruction is sufficient for this purpose, for otherwise he would choose a more detailed instruction (for instance, *your cousin John* instead of *John*, if the hearer has a brother whose name is also John). If the hearer cannot identify the intended 'object' correctly, he misunderstands the message. This may be because the instruction is not sufficient or is intentionally misleading, but such considerations are irrelevant to our purposes. For if a speaker wants to mislead his hearer by saying or implying something which is not the case, no semantic analysis can detect such intentional misuses of linguistic terms. After all, what is the object of the analysis of language, if not precisely all linguistic devices, by means of which we can also mislead people, if we want to, and which make human language a powerful tool for both expressing or concealing thought.[15]

Since our investigations should be confined strictly to linguistic considerations, the LS structure representation cannot be dependent on the ontological status of the 'objects' referred to, nor on the question of whether certain utterances are true or not, or whether they are used appropriately to the situation or not. We have to assume, however, that any utterance is used appropriately, that is, in accordance with the speaker's purported belief or the speaker's assumption. If the speaker's purported belief is in disagreement with the actual situation, then obviously — as far as ordinary or scientific discourse is concerned — the content of the utterance (the description of the situation) will be incompatible with the existing situation. But this is not a problem for the linguist, who is not supposed to detect lies or investigate this sort of incompatibilities; the linguist can only detect inconcistencies between utterances in a discourse (where instead of the situation we are concerned with a linguistic context), and between parts of utterances. Besides, linguistic utterances are not always intended to describe any real situations at all, as in the case of fiction. But it would be unreasonable to

---

[15] Compare the well known discussion by logicians (Frege, Russell, Strawson, and others) of the sentence *The present king of France is bald*, in which — from the point of view presented here — the phrase *the present king of France* corresponds to the logical subject of an utterance, which may be misleading, for instance, if uttered nowadays, or may not be so, if used in the context of a historical novel.

assume that the LS structure of an utterance depends on whether it occurs within the context of ordinary conversation, in the context of a novel or a reported dream. What differs here from the semantic point of view is a general frame of reference which distinguishes various types of discourses.

Consider now an utterance in which the noun in the nominative case does not function as a linguistic index:

(3) *(To)jakiś cudzoziemiec teraz przemawia* 'It is a foreigner who is holding a speech now'

where the main stress falls on the noun. The utterance (3) can be paraphrased by

Teraz przemawia jakiś cudzoziemiec

In conformity with what has been said above, the function of logical subject cannot be assigned to the phrase *jakiś cudzoziemiec* 'a foreigner', as it is not a linguistic index. The utterance is, however, a statement with a logical subject. Its LS structure should correspond to its more explicit paraphrase

Ten kto teraz przemawia jest cudzoziemcem 'The one who is holding a speech now is a foreigner'

and the function of logical subject should be assigned to the index *ten kto teraz przemawia* 'the one who is holding a speech now'. A fact which supports our interpretation is that the corresponding negation of (3) can only be:

(3') *Ten kto teraz przemawia nie jest cudzoziemcem* 'The one who is holding a speech now is not a foreigner'

Notice that the utterance

Jakiś cudzoziemiec teraz nie przemawia 'A foreigner is not holding a speech now'

which is hardly interpretable without a very specific context, is obviously not a negation of (3).

In general it is worth noticing that utterances which differ only in the occurrence of a definite or indefinite determiner (*e.g.*, *ten* or *jakiś* in Polish, *the* or *a* in English) have quite different semantic structures, which are only signaled by different types of determiners. Compare, for instance, the utterance

This foreigner (or *the foreigner*) *is holding a speech now*

which differs from (3) only by the determiner, and its negation

This foreigner (or *the foreigner*) *is not holding a speech now.*

We will discuss now the problem of a possible LS structure representation of utterances which contain indefinite descriptions. We shall start, however, with such utterances in which no linguistic index as could be used to form a logical subject is explicitly or implicitly contained. Thus no instruction for the hearer will be contained in the utterance, which would tell him how to identify the 'object' in question with one that is known to him, or has been just indicated in the preceding context. Consider the following utterances:

(4) *Pewnien człowiek ożenił się mając przeszło dziewięćdzeisiąt lat* 'A certain man has got married in his nineties'
(5) *Jakiś astronauta popełnił samobójstwo* 'An astronaut has committed suicide'

We will disregard the difference between the interpretation of indefinite pronouns *pewien* and *jakiś*, as it will not be relevant for the present cases. Suppose now that we try to represent the LS structure of such utterances in terms of the formal devices used in logic. We would probably do it with the aid of an existential operator — which, I claim, is not adequate for this purpose. Roughly, the above utterances would then correspond to the formula

(6) $(\exists x) [\varphi(x) \wedge \psi(x)]$

The question of how to represent the modal frames is taken aside as being not directly relevant to the matters discussed. The interpretation of our utterances according to (6) would then be as follows:

(4) *There is at least one 'object' such that it is a man and that got married at his nineties*
(5) *There is at least one 'object' such that it is an astronaut and that has committed suicide*

Such an interpretation would be wrong in several respects. First, what is really meant here is 'one particular object' rather than 'at least one object', for the speaker would clearly mean so by uttering (4) or (5). Our utterances (4) and (5) certainly would not be used as intended negations of universal statements. For instance, (5) is not a paraphrase of

I deny that there are no 'objects' such that are astronauts who have committed suicide

whereas an existential formula $(\exists x)\varphi(x)$ may be treated as an abbreviation of the formula with a general operator:

$\sim (x) \sim \varphi(x)$

Second, there seems to be a difference in the way we interpret the expressions represented in formula (6) by φ and ψ. The expression represented by ψ has a predicating function which seems to be lacking in that represented by φ. Thus, for instance, one might react to (5) by the utterance:

In fact somebody has committed suicide, but it was not an astronaut.

On the other hand, it would sound rather strange for the receiver to react by the utterance:

In fact somebody was an astronaut, but he has not committed suicide.
except in a jocular reply.

The third argument runs as follows. In the calculus of predicates, if we want to add a new predicate to the same argument x which satisfies the conditions specified in (6) (that is, the argument x such that it is φ and ψ), we have no other way to refer to it, but we repeat the whole expression and add one more predicate to the variable x bound by the same operator:

(7) $(\exists x) [\varphi(x) \wedge \psi(x) \wedge \chi(x)]$

In a natural language, however, we constantly refer to the 'objects' mentioned earlier, and not only to those determined uniquely by proper names or definite descriptions, but also to those which have been described by indefinite descriptions, which obviously are not intended to identify uniquely. Thus in a discourse, such as

(8)   *Jeden młody chłopiec oblał egzamin maturalny. Postanowił on zrezygnować z dalszych studiów.* 'One young boy has flunked his matriculation exam. He decided to give up further studies'

it might seem strange that we employ a pronoun *on* 'he' which is a linguistic index pointing to an 'object' somehow determined in the preceding utterance — although no linguistic index is contained there; it cannot be determined by the indefinite description either, for the use of an indefinite determiner clearly shows that the description is not intended to cover only one specific 'object'.

The answer to this puzzle lies in that the discussed interpretation of such utterances is inadequate. The LS structure of utterances which contain indefinite descriptions cannot be adequately represented with the aid of an existential operator.

Let us introduce into the LS structure description an operator which will be called referential operator, and which would better fit the semantic interpretation of the discussed indefinite descriptions in sentences of particular reference.

By analogy to the expression assumed to represent a linguistic index $(\iota x)\varphi(x)$, which has the category of an argument (not of a statement), we may use the referential operator denoted by Ref in an expression $(Ref\ x)\varphi(x)$ which will also have the category of an argument. Such an expression will, however, be interpreted as: that 'object' which the speaker is referring to at the time of producing the given indefinite description, and which is φ (or: and to which φ applies).

Thus the 'object' indicated by the argument $(Ref\ x)\varphi(x)$ is uniquely determined only implicitly by the intention of the speaker, while the description represented by φ is clearly intended only to determine the class to which such an 'object' belongs.

A necessary condition for the appropriate use of an indefinite description for which a particular reference is assumed, and which may be represented by $(Ref\ x)\varphi(x)$ is the speaker's purported belief or assumption that: (1) there is one and only one 'object' being referred to by him at the given time, and (2) such an 'object' is φ (or: φ is applicable to such an 'object').

Such a belief or assumption of the speaker may be formally expressed by the statement (9) given below, which as a matter of fact could be taken for defining the use of the referential operator (as it corresponds to the condition which has to be satisfied).

(9) $(\exists x) \, [R_t(x) \land \varphi(x)]$

where R_t is an implicit unit function which has an invariant semantic interpretation independent of φ: 'that 'object' which the speaker is referring to at a given time t', and where φ is a function representing the given description.

The description represented here by φ is thus used only to form the argument (*Ref x*) $\varphi(x)$, and has no predicating role, that is, it does not function as a predicate in the proposition expressed by the given utterance.[16] Thus independently of whether φ is a unit function in the expression $(\imath x)\varphi(x)$, or an ordinary function in the expression $(Ref\, x)\varphi(x)$, it represents a description which has no predicating role in the utterance, but an identifying or indicative role. For it is intended to indicate the class to which the given 'object' belongs; in the former case it is a unit class to which a unique element, the 'object' being referred to, is supposed to belong, and in the latter case it is a class to which other, non-referred elements are supposed to belong, too.

It is evident through our examples that there are utterances in which the 'object' being referred to can be uniquely determined only by the intention of the speaker who produces the given indefinite description at some given time. R_t is then a "token-reflexive function" — to use Reichenbach's term (1948) — or a "pure shifter" in Jakobson's sense of the term (1957), which is restricted to the time at which a given description is uttered, or to the place at which it stands in a given written text. The function R_t, which is only implicit in the LS structure, appears to justify the use of linguistic indices in the second utterance of a given discourse, as, for instance, in our example (8). The postulation of such an abstract construct is, however, justified on empirical grounds by our understanding such utterances in which reference is made to an 'object' described explicitly only by an indefinite description, for it constitutes a description of the way we intuitively understand the reference made by an index in the second utterance.

Let us now compare the semantic interpretation of logical subject with the presently suggested interpretation of indefinite descriptions used for particular reference, which as such always coincide with the first mention of an 'object'. Here the 'object' referred to is not supposed to be determined uniquely by the description used, and thus the hearer is given no instruction for identification. In the former case, the interpretation has been:

'that "object" which the speaker is referring to by the given linguistic index φ ..., and which the hearer is supposed to identify as one that is known to him, or has just been mentioned.

---

[16] It has the function of predicate only in the implied proposition *The speaker believes that there is an x which is φ*, but the same holds true of a definite description or a proper name represented as a unit function.

In the latter case, it is:

'that "object" which the speaker is referring to by means of the implicit function R_t, and which is φ', but which the hearer is not supposed to identify with any "object" that is known to him, or has been just mentioned.

Here lies the essential difference between the two. A logical subject, that is, an argument which corresponds to a name or definite description, is supposed to identify uniquely an 'object' from the point of view of both the intention of the speaker AND the interpretation of the hearer, whereas an argument corresponding to an indefinite description is supposed to identify uniquely an 'object' only in the intention of the speaker (the indefinite description serves only to indicate the class which, among other elements, contains that 'object').

By virtue of this essential difference, all utterances that contain no linguistic indices (and thus no logical subject), and in which the argument corresponds to an indefinite description, share a very peculiar characteristic. It appears that the predicate applied to 'objects' determined uniquely only by the intention of the speaker must have some features in common.

Consider first our examples (4) and (5), which represent a specific class of utterances which need not be followed by some further utterances to be interpreted as normal self-sufficient statements. Both our examples say something unusual, not trivial, or so-to-speak make a story by themselves. It is clear that if a speaker applies a predicate to an 'object' being referred to and determined uniquely only by his intention, then the predicate must be such as to characterize that 'object' somehow, to make it worth mentioning at all. Thus we do not encounter utterances of this sort without a further context which adds some other predicates to the same 'object':

(10) *Pewien człowiek był żonaty* 'A certain man was married'
(11) *Pewna dziewczyna jest Eskimoską* 'A certain girl is an Eskimo'

The reason seems to be as follows. If we try to interpret such utterances as suggested above, that is, as utterances with no logical subject, as utterances in which the 'object' indicated by the argument is determined only by the intention of the speaker through the implicit function R_t, they will appear to say too little about such an enigmatic 'object' to be worth communicating at all. Notice that analogous utterances with a definite determiner in place of the indefinite one are normal statements which may be often encountered without a further context:

(12) *Ten człowiek był żonaty* 'This man was married'
(13) *Ta dziewczyna jest Eskimoską* 'This girl is an Eskimo'

Notice also that we do have utterances such as (10) and (11), but they always constitute only part of a discourse in which some other predicates are added with respect to the same 'object':

(14) *Pewien człowiek był żonaty i miał dwoje dzieci. On …* 'A certain man was married and had two children. He …'

(15) *Pewna dziewczyna była Eskimoską i żywiła się tylko rybami. Dziewczyna ta …* 'A certain girl was an Eskimo and ate only fish. The girl …'

We also have stylistic variants of such utterances which are used as initial utterances of a story. For instance

> *Była sobie pewna dziewczyna, Eskimoska. Ona…* 'Once there was a girl who was an Eskimo. She…'

Thus if a predicate applied to an 'object' introduced by a referential operator makes a noninformative statement, which therefore does not constitute a normal message, the hearer can rightly infer that some other utterances will follow. His expectations are a consequence of the assumed interpretation on the grounds of a very general assumption that people normally try to convey messages which are somehow informative for the hearer, that is, to communicate something the hearer may not know. No speaker would therefore sensibly communicate a message, say, that one and only 'object' being referred to by him, but not identified explicitly otherwise than as one belonging to the class of men, was married — without adding something more about such an 'object' by further utterances.

Another characteristic feature of utterances which contain no linguistic indices is that they are never genuine negations, *i.e.*, they are not paraphrases of denials in which the negation occurs in the modal frame

$$\begin{Bmatrix} I\ deny\ that \\ It\ is\ not\ true\ that \end{Bmatrix} S.$$

In other words, they cannot be formally represented as $\sim S$. Except in very specific contexts which would impose an interpretation, we would not use utterances such as (16, 17, 18) even for initiating a discourse, whereas we would use analogous ones with definite determiners.

(16) *Pewna kobieta nie ma dwojga dzieci* 'A certain woman has not got two children'

(17) *Jakiś człowiek nie złamał nogi* 'A man has not broken his leg'

(18) *Jakaś dziewczyna nie ma niebieskich oczu* 'A girl has not got blue eyes'

The 'object' referred to by the speaker and determined only by his intention must be positively ascribed a predicate, whereas a genuine denial does not say anything positively — it only 'cancels' a corresponding statement. Accordingly, whenever we come across an admissible utterance of the type discussed which contains a negation, it appears that the negation does not occur in the modal frame. The utterance is not paraphrasable then as *I deny that S*, but is interpretable as: 'The "object" which I am referring to is such that …'. Such utterances do not correspond then to denials but to statements which assert something positively by the use of a negated predicate; such a predicate indirectly discloses certain features which additionally characterize the given 'object', and thus the statement is informative. Consider the examples:

(19) *Pewna kobieta nie miała dzieci* 'A certain woman had no children'[17]
(20) *Pewien stary człowiek nie miał domu* 'A certain old man had no home'
(21) *Pewna dzieczynka nie słuchała swojej matki* 'A certain little girl did not obey her
    mother'.

In each of these utterances, the negative predicate contributes something to the characteristic of the 'object' referred to. None of them is a genuine negation which corresponds to a cancellation of a corresponding statement ($\sim S$). The intention of the speaker is not to deny anything, but to assign a predicate to the given 'object'. It is rather usual for a woman to have children, for an old man to have a home, and for a little girl to obey her mother; the corresponding negative predicates provide then a more specific characterization of the given 'object' than a corresponding non-negated predicate would do.

So far we have discussed utterances which contain no linguistic indices. It is on the basis of such utterances that the referential operator has been proposed. Obviously not all indefinite descriptions fall under such an interpretation. Indefinite descriptions, when they cooccur with linguistic indices — independently of the fact which position the former or the latter occupy (grammatical subject or objects) — are often used with no particular reference (*cf., John needs a pencil*). Accordingly, in order to represent indefinite descriptions we would need, in addition to the referential operator, another quantifying linguistic operator which would express only the singleness of an 'object' which belongs to *such and such* a class, uniqueness not being assumed, not even implicitly from the point of view of the speaker. Such a quantifying operator would also be needed in the case of indefinite descriptions preceded by numerals, when no particular reference is assumed, the difference consisting only in the indicated number of 'objects', which instead of 'one' may be 'two', 'three', *etc*.

The reference which is made in the subsequent utterance in a given discourse by means of a linguistic index, is determined in terms of the entire preceding utterance and thus also with the aid of a linguistic index if such cooccurs with the indefinite description. Consider, for instance, the discourse

Mary received a new book. It concerned astrophysics.

where *it* is an index which refers back to the indefinite description *a new book*, but is interpreted as 'the new book which Mary received'.

There are other cases of use of indefinite descriptions, such as for instance the generic use (*A dog will not bite its master*), in which obviously neither particular reference nor singleness is assumed. There are also such cases in which indefinite descriptions are not even interpreted as arguments, but as predicates. For instance,

[17] This example has been suggested to me by Manfred Bierwisch; moreover, I am indebted to him for his having read my manuscript and given some comments.

our example (3) shows that the indefinite description corresponds to the predicate. Such is also the case when an indefinite description follows the copula *is* and a logical subject coincides with the grammatical subject (*John is a student, She is a French girl, etc.*). The indefinite article *a* is not used in such utterances as a device with a quantifying function. It has no semantic function at all; the use of *a* in such cases is subject to surface-grammar rules only, for if a predicate is applied to an 'object' which through the use of a linguistic index is interpreted as a unique one, there is no need of using another quantifying linguistic operator which would be redundant in expressing the singleness of that unique 'object'. For it is obvious that we cannot use here any other quantifier incompatible with the assumed singleness (**John is two students, *She is three girls, etc.*).

All the above mentioned cases fall outside the scope of the present paper, but it is evident that they require a thorough analysis. The present considerations are much too narrow in scope to throw enough light on this problem. They have been intended only to give some suggestions concerning a possible LS structure representation of utterances which express an elementary proposition; a representation which would consist of a predicate with its arguments. We discussed here only those arguments which may be used for particular reference.

It seems that in general all arguments should be represented in such a way that what is being referred to — the 'objects' of the universe of discourse — would be uniformly conceived of as values of the variables, no ontological implications being involved. This seems important in view of the fact that such investigations should be extended to utterances for which the arguments would correspond to such queer 'objects' as events, situations, *etc.*, and also abstract entities, such as properties and, generally, relations. The LS structure of such utterances could perhaps be represented with the use of higher order variables, but little can be said at the moment about the language which could be used for such a description. We cannot apply, however, a higher-order functional calculus to the representation of just the surface structures along the lines of Reichenbach's pioneer attempts in this direction, but we should investigate thoroughly the semantic structure of utterances and make our description compatible with, and testable against, the competent speaker's intuitions.

It is not at all clear whether we can proceed by only introducing certain modifications to the language of modern logic, or whether it will prove necessary to set up a different formalized language. I believe, however, that prior to establishing any formalized language, which would be fit for such a description, we have to be aware of what is the semantic interpretation of such or other syntactic relations, and thus know what we want to describe in a formalized language. Accordingly, it seems worthwhile to examine thoroughly the semantic structure of utterances — including their modal frames — in its very complex relationship to the various syntactic devices used on the surface. For we still have very little knowledge about the semantic interpretation of syntactic relations. And this is not amazing in view of the fact that the domain of semantics, forbidden to linguists until very recently, has only now appeared to be an integral part of linguistic description.

REFERENCES

Bach, E.,
        Nouns and Noun Phrases in English (preliminary version, mimeographed, University of Texas).

Bar-Hillel, Y.,
    1967   Review of: J. A. Fodor and J. J. Katz (eds.), *The structure of language: Readings in the philosophy of language* (Englewood Cliffs, N. J.) in: *Language* 43,2.

Bellert, I.,
    1968   "On a Condition of the Coherence of Texts", paper delivered at the International Symposium of Semiotics, Warsaw, August 1968, to appear in the *Proceedings* thereof, and in *Semiotica*.
    1969   "Arguments and Predicates in the Logico-Semantic Structure of Utterances", F. Kiefer (ed.), *Studies in Syntax and Semantics* (= *Foundation of Language Supplementary Series*) (D. Reidel en Co., Dordrecht–Holland).

Chomsky, N.,
    1965   *Aspects of the Theory of Syntax* (Cambridge, Mass., M. I. T. Press).

Jakobson, R.,
    1957   "Shifters, Verbal Categories, and the Russian Verb" (Harvard University)

McCawley, J. D.,
        "Meaning and the Description of Languages" (mimeographed, University of Chicago).

Peirce, Ch. S.,
        Collected Papers of Charles Sanders Peirce, Vol. III (ed., Arthur Burks)

Reichenbach, H.,
    1948   *Elements of Symbolic Logic* (New York, Macmillan)

MANFRED BIERWISCH

ON CLASSIFYING SEMANTIC FEATURES

1. INTRODUCTION

The semantic analysis of natural languages rests crucially on at least the following two assumptions: (i) the meaning of a given sentence can be accounted for on the basis of the words or, more precisely, the dictionary entries of which it consists, and the syntactic relations connecting these items; (ii) the meanings of dictionary entries are not unanalyzable wholes, but can be decomposed into elementary semantic components. These two assumptions are, of course, closely related to each other. The internal organization of the meanings of dictionary entries must be of a form which determines how they enter the composite meaning of more complex constituents according to the syntactic relations within these constituents. The syntactic relations in turn must be specified in such a way that the correct combination of the meanings of related constituents can be determined. A first attempt in this direction has been made by Fodor and Katz (1963) and Katz and Postal (1964). It is based on the assumptions that the syntactic relations in question can be defined in terms of underlying or deep phrase markers as specified in Chomsky (1965), and that the meaning of dictionary entries as well as of more complex constituents is given by strings of basic semantic components. The latter assumption was only a first approximation which turned out to be far too simple. It has been changed rather radically in the meantime.[1] In the present paper I shall concentrate on certain problems deriving from assumption (ii) above, more precisely on some aspects of the nature of basic semantic elements. It follows from the introductory remarks that even a discussion of such problems must keep in mind the important interdependence of assumptions (i) and (ii).

The set of basic semantic elements has been divided by Fodor and Katz (1963) into two types of elements, called semantic markers and distinguishers. Although Katz

---

[1] See Katz (1964a, 1964b, 1966, 1967). For a reinterpretation of several of Katz' proposals, see Bierwisch (1969). We shall discuss some of the changes involved in more detail below. Weinreich (1966) has sharply criticized the original assumption of mere concatenation — or logical conjunction, for that matter — of semantic components. His counterproposal of distinguishing clusters and configurations of components does not work, however, for reasons briefly discussed in Bierwisch (1968).

has defended this distinction recently (Katz, 1967), it seems to me that it is an outcome of a rather early stage in the development of a semantic theory and must be rejected as theoretically unmotivated. I have presented my arguments for this rejection in Bierwisch (1969, section 5) and will not repeat them here. We are left then with only one type of basic semantic elements which might be called semantic features. These primitive terms, from which semantic descriptions of natural languages are constructed, do not, however form an unstructured, amorphous set. Rather they are classified into several subtypes according to certain aspects, thus ultimately constituting a highly structured system of underlying elements. Some of these aspects of classification will be discussed in the present paper.

2. THE FORMAL STATUS OF SEMANTIC FEATURES

Let us first introduce certain basic assumptions concerning the theoretical status of semantic features. It seems to me most natural to consider semantic features essentially as predicate constants in the sense of the predicate calculus as developed in modern logic. This assumption has been stipulated by other authors as well (see *e.g.*, McCawley, 1968). It can be motivated by several considerations. I will briefly discuss two of them here.

Firstly, as already mentioned, it turned out that mere concatenation of features as introduced in Fodor and Katz (1963) is not sufficient to account for the semantic interpretation of words and sentences. Thus additional machinery for the combination of semantic features became necessary. One of the means that has been used in this connection, *e.g.* in Katz (1966, 1967) and Bierwisch (1967), was that of grouping features by simple brackets. Such grouping was meant to express that certain features of a reading are more closely connected than others. It does not specify, however, how differences in grouping are to be interpreted conceptually. In fact, rather different conceptual relations between semantic features have been expressed by identical means in the references quoted.[2] This means that the burden of interpreting the formal relations between semantic elements remains with the conceptual content of particular features. The same formal relation between certain features in a given reading would be interpreted differently depending on the features involved. This is of course quite unsatisfactory. On the one hand, the formal means of semantic representations become rather empty. On the other hand, the problem is postponed, but not solved: the intrinsic interpretation of semantic features would have to provide the formal

---

[2] Thus in Bierwisch (1967) I used groupings such as (Physical Object (3 Space (Vertical) (Maximal) (Secondary))) to indicate that a given reading refers to a three-dimensional physical object with a vertical, a maximal, and a secondary extension. Obviously, the connection between the element 'Physical Object' and the rest of the configuration represents a conceptual relation completely different from that expressed by the connection between '3 Space' and 'Vertical', 'Maximal', and 'Secondary' respectively. We will return to the problem of a more adequate solution below. Similar problems with respect to several examples given in Katz (1967) are discussed in Bierwisch (1969).

means giving substance to the empty grouping relations. This in turn would conflict with the assumption that the semantic features are linguistically primitive terms. Katz has tried to avoid difficulties of this type by using certain informal means such as *of, at, etc.* in combinations such as ((Condition (Possession *of* Y) *of* X *at* t_i) where X and Y are slots to be filled in by feature complexes and t_i is a variable over a time interval. These and similar means, introduced only casually, have no clear theoretical status, however. The most natural way to remedy shortcomings of this kind seems to be to construe semantic features as predicates and to reconstruct the more complicated connections among them by using the formal means of the fully fledged predicate calculus, admitting of course adaptations and controlled modifications if necessary. This appears to be at least a promising program. Some steps in this direction have been made in Bierwisch (1969).

The second point to be noted here concerns the fact that semantic features, if taken as predicates, must be assigned to suitable arguments and that, therefore, these arguments must be part of the semantic representations. They are considered most naturally as variables which are substituted by representations of the referents which are talked about by means of particular occurrences of the expressions to whose readings the variables belong. From this it follows that dictionary entries also must contain appropriate variables which are to be substituted by more specific variables if they occur in particular sentences. In this vein, Weinrich (1962) has pointed out that lexical entries even for single words should have the form of propositional functions, *i.e.* of (complex) predicates with unbounded variables as arguments. The projection rules of Katz and Fodor's theory, which combine the readings of composite constituents according to the relevant syntactic relations, reduce then essentially to the substitution of suitable arguments for the variables occurring in the dictionary entires. This in turn requires that these variables be indexed with respect to the syntactic relations in question. Thus for example transitive verbs such as *love, meet, hit, etc.* must contain variables indexed for the relations Subject-of and Object-of, for which the pertinent variables occurring in the readings of the Subject-NP and the Object-NP respectively are substituted.[3] Notice that all variables appearing in the reading of a given sentence (more precisely of a sentence type) indicate identity or distinctness of reference. They do not represent particular objects referred to. Otherwise a sentence such as *I saw a car* would have indefinitely many readings, differing only in the respective arguments.

It is important that essentially the same indication of identical or distinct reference is required for purely syntactic reasons. The relevant phenomena are primarily pronominalization, reflexivization, deletion of identical NP's. Using subscripts to represent identical or distinct reference, we have examples of the following type:

---

[3] This process is sketched in somewhat more detail in Bierwisch (1969, section 3). — Note incidentally that the slot variables X, Y, *etc.* which Katz has introduced, as mentioned above, in his recent writings serve a rather similar purpose. In fact, the revised projection rules based on these variables amount roughly to a substitution of argument expressions, if the semantic markers are reformulated as (complex) predicates.

(1)(a) *James$_1$ phoned James$_2$* vs. **James$_1$ phoned himself$_2$*

   (b) **James$_1$ phoned James$_1$* vs. *James$_1$ phoned himself$_1$*

(2)(a) *Lotte Lenya$_1$ sang a song$_2$ and then Satchmo$_3$ sang one$_4$*

   (b) *Lotte Lenya$_1$ sang a song$_2$ and then Satchmo$_3$ sang it$_2$*

   (c) **Lotte Lenya$_1$ sang a song$_2$ and then Satchmo$_3$ sang one$_2$*

   (d) **Lotte Lenya$_1$ sang a song$_2$ and then Satchmo$_3$ sang it$_4$*

(3)(a) *John$_1$ expected him$_2$ to pass the examination*

   (b) **John$_1$ expected* $\begin{Bmatrix} him_1 \\ himself_1 \end{Bmatrix}$ *to pass the examination*

   (c) *John$_1$ expected to pass the examination*

I cannot comment on the details of these phenomena.[4] For the aims of the present paper it is sufficient to realize that certain aspects of reference are crucial for any attempt to account for the facts displayed by (1-3). Chomsky (1965:145) first proposed in this connection to mark certain lexical items as 'referential' and to assign to them integers representing identical or different reference [for a fairly elaborate application of this idea, see Isenberg (1968)]. But since reference is actually not a property of lexical categories, it seems more appropriate to assign reference indexes to NP's. Though even that is an oversimplification which ignores certain complications in the analysis of NP's, it will do for the present purpose.

We may assume now that for every NP$_i$ there is a variable X$_i$ functioning as an argument in the semantic representation of the expression of which the NP$_i$ is a part. This argument does not only occur in the reading of the NP$_i$ in question, but is also substituted, by the procedure mentioned above, for variables in the readings of other constituents to which the NP$_i$ bears the relevant syntactic relations.

This provisional sketch of the status of semantic features immediately leads to a first aspect of classification. Semantic features fall into different classes according to the number of arguments required. They may be one-place predicates representing properties, two-place predicates representing two-place relations, *etc.* We will see below that they must be classified not only with respect to the number, but also with respect to different types of arguments.

In the following discussion I will slightly deviate from the usual predicate calculus notation (4a) for a k-place predicate assigned to its k arguments. Instead of (4a) I will use (4b):

(4)(a) $P(x_1 x_2 \ldots x_k)$

   (b) $[P] X_1 X_2 \ldots X_k$

It must be noted that the X$_i$ in (4b) are variables over sets of individuals, including sets of one element as a particular case. Thus [P] X is to be understood as 'the ele-

---

[4]   They are in fact rather complicated and involve several transformational processes and principles governing them. A careful investigation of some of them will be found in Postal (in preparation).

ments contained in X have the property represented by P'. This modification of the predicate calculus, which is by no means a marginal one, is to account for the parallelism between sentences such as (5a) and (5b):

(5)(a) *My friend came soon*
   (b) *My friends came soon*

I cannot discuss here the details involved in this modification. Some of its motivations, however, will become obvious below. For some additional motivation of the notation (4b), see Bierwisch (1969).

3. DELIMITATION AND PREDICATION

On the basis of the previous convention we are led to a distinction of two rather different types of semantic elements applying to the reference variables X_i. The first type delimits the set substitutable for the variable X_i, the second type represents the properties and relations predicated of the elements of this set. Before turning to problems of the latter elements, I will make some remarks concerning the former. These are essentially the elements which constitute the readings of articles, quantifiers, and similar syntactic formatives. And though many attempts to arrive at a syntactic account of the interrelated phenomena of reference and delimitation have been made (with no conclusive result so far), very little is known with respect to the question how the semantic problems involved are to be dealt with.

Notice first of all that delimiting features have a status completely different from that of predicating features. While these specify the conditions to be met by the objects of the set referred to, delimiting features do not apply to these objects as such, but to the set as a whole, specifying its size — relative or absolute —, its role in the discourse, etc. In order to make this distinction somewhat more precise we may compare the delimiting features with certain operators introduced in modern logic. We will do this by means of some examples.

Consider first the feature DEFINITE. This feature, characteristically realized by the definite article in languages displaying articles, indicates that the set forming the reference instance is already given and uniquely identifiable by means of the respective predicative features. DEFINITE thus corresponds in a sense to the iota-operator which forms definite descriptions. But whereas the iota-operator is bound to unique individuals, the feature DEFINITE applies to uniquely specified sets — those containing one element being a special case. Thus DEFINITE comprises in a sense also the lambda-operator which forms the class of precisely those elements exhibiting the property represented by a given predicate. But whereas the iota- and the lambda-operator yield expressions of different types — *viz.* individuals and classes respectively —, an expression formed by means of the feature DEFINITE is always of the same type, irrespective of the number of elements in the set X_i to which DEFINITE applies. This is a direct consequence of the digression from the quantification theory stipulated in the previous section.

The correspondence between the feature DEFINITE and the iota-operator has its counterpart in the correspondence between the feature — DEFINITE or INDEFINITE and the eta-operator, which forms indefinite descriptions (for indefinite descriptions, see *e.g.*, Reichenbach, 1966: 265). The term 'indefinite' is extremely misleading, however, as in a sentence like *A boy came* no vagueness or indefiniteness is involved. Rather a particular set of (one or more) elements is introduced and might be taken up later on by means of the feature DEFINITE. I will therefore use the term 'specifying' which should be understood as selecting a particular fraction of the universe which has not been referred to previously.[5] The feature INDEFINITE on the other hand might be more appropriate for the treatment of the following by now well known phenomenon:

(6)   *James asked me for* [*a newspaper*]$_{NP_1}$

(7)(a) *and I will send* [*it*]$_{NP_1}$ *to him*
   (b) *and I will send* [*one*]$_{NP_2}$ *to him*

(6) is ambiguous with respect to the status of the NP_1 *a newspaper*: if continued by (7a), the set X_1 is introduced by the feature SPECIFYING which constitutes a fixed object also for future reference, taken up by the NP_1 *it* in (7a). In this case James was asking for a particular newspaper, say the Pravda from May 1, 1967. If (6) is continued by (7b), then NP_1 remains unspecified; it does not constitute a fixed object. Therefore the corresponding NP in (7b) cannot refer to the same set. In this case X_1 in the reading of (6) is bound by the feature INDEFINITE. Notice that the indefinite article represents the feature INDEFINITE in the sense illustrated here only if it appears within the scope of intentional verbs like *ask for*, *want*, *look for*, *will*, etc., or of the negation.[6]

---

[5]   The proposed element SPECIFYING corresponds closely to the referential operator introduced in Bellert (1970), the main difference being the fact that Bellert's operator applies to individuals, whereas SPECIFYING introduces sets of individuals. — It goes without saying that DEFINITE and SPECIFYING are not negations of each other, as the notation [± DEFINITE] would suggest by its parallelism to such features as [± Human], *etc.* In fact, the element DEFINITE is not subject to negation at all.

[6]   The phenomena connected with (6) have been discussed recently by several writers. The latest treatment known to me is that of Karttunen (1968). The distinction between the two readings of (6) is explained there by assuming an individual constant for the continuation (7a) and an individual variable bound by an existential quantifier for the continuation (7b). There are several objections, however, even if we ignore the fact that sets instead of individuals are required for reference. Firstly, sentence types, which are the only object of linguistic analysis, cannot contain individual constants, but only variables to be replaced by constants if the sentence is used in a particular discourse. Secondly, a constant would be required also in the case of definiteness. Thus the distinction between the definite and indefinite article would be obscured. And thirdly, the claim of existence expressed by the existential quantifier is not justified. In a sentence like *John was looking for a tack, but he didn't find one* nothing is presupposed or asserted with respect to the existence of a tack. The only claim is that John presumed the possible existence of a tack in that spatial area where his looking for was to take place. Notice that this has nothing to do with ontological problems. The same consideration applies with respect to fictitious objects: *The witch was looking for a unicorn, but she couldn't see one.*

After this extremely provisional illustration of delimiting features like DEFINITE, SPECIFYING, INDEFINITE, *etc.*, we may ask how they are to be incorporated into semantic representations. I have no definite answer to this question, but I will briefly present two alternatives indicating the lines along which, in my opinion, a solution might be constructed. Let Q be a variable over the features in question. Every feature of this type applies to precisely one argument X_i. We will write now $(Q X_i)$ for the application of Q to X_i thereby forming an operator which specifies X_i in the way represented by Q. This operator may now be introduced into semantic representations in one of two ways: (i) we prefix it to the reading of the whole sentence, or at least to that constituent of which the corresponding NP_i is a constituent. In this case the status of $(Q X_i)$ is analogous to that of the existential (and universal) quantifier of logical systems. (ii) we prefix it to the reading of the NP_i itself. In this case the status of $(Q X_i)$ is parallel to that of the iota- and eta-operator of logical systems. It forms terms which function as arguments for other predicative features. The operations combining readings of syntactically related constituents and the form of the resulting readings are different in both cases. In the case of (i) only the argument X_i of an NP_i is to be substituted for the variables of the related constituents, while the operator $(Q X_i)$ is prefixed to the whole resulting reading. In the case of (ii) the whole reading of the NP_i, beginning with the operator $(Q X_i)$, is to be substituted for the pertinent variables. Thus the reading of *The boys saw the girls* would be (8) according to (i) and (9) according to (ii), if we represent the readings of *boy*, *see*, and *girl* by B, S, and G, respectively. We use brackets to indicate the scope of the $(Q X_i)$:

(8) $(\text{Def } X_1) ([B] X_1 . (\text{Def } X_2) ([G] X_2 . [S] X_1 X_2))$

(9) $[S] (\text{Def } X_1) ([B] X_1) (\text{Def } X_2) ([G] X_2)$

The alternative (ii) and the corresponding representation (9) is similar to Katz' recent proposal according to which the readings of the whole Subject-NP and Object-NP are substituted for corresponding variables within the reading of the verb. However, the operator $(Q X_i)$ that we have introduced gives a clear representation of the fact that the argument of a given NP but not its complete reading is an argument of the semantic features of the verb. The latter interpretation would lead to a completely wrong higher level predication.[7]

The choice between (i) and (ii), if these are reasonable alternatives at all, depends on unsolved problems of both syntactic and semantic structure. The former are mainly those of the internal structure of NP's, in particular of the deep structure status of

---

[7] Notice that the alternatives (i) and (ii) correspond somehow to the *definiens* and the *definiendum* of the definition by which the iota-operator is usually introduced: the formula

$$G(\iota x) F(x) \equiv (\exists x) [F(x) . G(x)]$$

where F is a unique function and $G(x)$ an arbitrary propositional function would be parallel to the equivalence

$$[G] (Q X_i)([F] X_i) \equiv (Q' X_i)([F] X_i . [G] X_i)$$

where Q and Q' are the delimiting features according to interpretation (ii) and (i) respectively.

restrictive relative clauses. There are serious doubts whether relative clauses can be an internal subconstituent of the NP which they restrict, since this solution, which has been accepted until recently, leads to certain absurdities. The most crucial difficulty, which has been noticed by several authors, originates with relative clauses that contain each other. An example is

(10) $[A$ boy $[$who bought $[a$ book $[$that pleased $[him]_{NP_1}]_{S'}]_{NP_2}]_{S''}]_{NP_1}$ finally got rid of $[it]_{NP_2}$

where the NP's underlying the pronouns *him* and *it* would contain an infinite alternating self-embedding of S' and S'', if relative clauses are part of them. The solution of this and similar problems is obviously relevant to the treatment of the $(Q\,X_i)$. The alternative (ii) seems to be unnatural or even inapplicable if restrictive relative clauses must in general be removed from the NP's they modify.

The semantic problems on which the choice between (i) and (ii) depends comprise among other things the behavior of $(Q\,X_i)$ with respect to negation. Consider the following paradigm:

(11)(a) *It is not true that the girl trusted him*
   (b) *The girl didn't trust him*

(12)(a) *It is not true that a girl trusted him*
   (b) *A girl didn't trust him*
   (c) *No girl trusted him*

(11a) and (11b) are synonymous in the sense that identical truth conditions are associated with them. The situation is more complicated with the sentences under (12). In its normal interpretation, (12a) is synonymous with (12c), but not with (12b).
A plausible account for this difference seems to be the assignment of INDEFINITE to *a girl* in (12a) and SPECIFYING to *a girl* in (12b). Thus (12b) is the negation of *A girl trusted him* with a specifying article *a*, whereas (12c) (and (12a)) is the negation of the nonexisting homophonous sentence with indefinite *a*.[8] This means that, given a negated sentence, $(\text{Indef } X_i)$ is always within the scope of negation, whereas $(\text{Spec } X_i)$

---

[8] It is worth noting that (12b) and (12c) are in a sense analogous to the two possible scopes of negation in indefinite descriptions (see *e.g.*, Reichenbach, 1966: 262ff): given the formula (a), then its negation (b) can be interpreted either as (c) or (d), if no convention for the scope of negation is stated. (c) and (d) are not equivalent, however, as can be seen from their reformulation as (e) and (f) respectively:

(a)	$G(\eta x)\,F(x)$	(b)	$\sim G(\eta x)\,F(x)$
(c)	$(\sim G)(\eta x)\,F(x)$	(d)	$\sim (G(\eta x)\,F(x))$
(e)	$(\exists x)\,F(x).\sim G(x)$	(f)	$(\forall x)\,F(x) \supset\, \sim G(x)$

With respect to $(\text{Indef } X_i)$, the scope interpretation would then be analogous to (d) and its equivalent (f), as can be seen from (12a) and (12c). The problem of ambiguous scope arises with respect to the iota-operator, if F is not a unique function, *i.e.*, in the case of improper definite descriptions. Since this possibility is excluded by definition with respect to DEFINITE and SPECIFYING, whose argument X_i is always uniquely given, there is only one possible effect of negation. This is expressed by sentences of the type (11b) and (12b) respectively.

never is. In other words, there is a certain trading relation between (Indef X_i) and (Spec X_i) with respect to negation. No such trading exists with respect to (Def X_i). Hence the lack of (11c). Any revealing account of this different behavior of the features discussed clearly bears on the choice between (i) and (ii) above. We may face even the possibility that both alternatives are required, some operators being treated according to (i), others according to (ii).

A further set of rather complicated problems arises from the fact that quantifications also have the function of delimiting the X_i. They do this, however, in a way different from that of the specifying features discussed so far. Quantifications comprise first of all the cardinal numbers, but also indefinite quantifications like *many, few, some.* Let us briefly consider first the status of numbers. Since we have claimed above that the X_i represent sets, not individuals, and that the delimiting features apply to these sets as a whole, not to the elements contained in it, we get a natural representation of the fact that numbers are properties of sets, irrespective of other properties of their elements, and not properties of individuals. But whereas numbers are usually treated in the predicate calculus as second level predicates, which are predicated only of the predicates ascribed to the primary arguments, we will apply them to the arguments directly, as these are sets, not individuals. This consideration brings out the difference between predicative and delimitative features more clearly: specifying the properties of the elements and the scope of reference respectively, they represent, so to speak, two aspects of abstraction simultaneously.

Numbers may now be combined with the features DEFINITE, SPECIFYING, and INDEFINITE, as illustrated in the following examples:

(13)(a) *He was looking for the two dollars and he found them*
   (b) *He was looking for two dollars and he found them*
   (c) *He was looking for two dollars and he found two*

There is, moreover, overwhelming evidence that in general the so-called indefinite article in English and several other languages is nothing but the unstressed realization of the numeral 'one'. For details, see Perlmutter (1970). In other words, the features SPECIFYING and INDEFINITE are not assigned to a separate phonemic matrix, whereas in most cases DEFINITE is overtly realized . The formal representation of the combination of numbers with the features discussed above is a difficult problem, depending again in part on the behavior with respect to negation. I cannot go into these details here. For the present discussion we simply assume that the Q in the operators (Q X_i) is a variable not only over DEF, INDEF, and SPEC, but also over combinations of these with numerals, the precise nature of this combination being left open.

Indefinite quantifications like *many, few, some* are similar to numerals in many respects, the main difference being that they provide no absolute quantification, but one which is relative to a certain norm.

Notice that features representing absolute or relative quantification can to a certain extent be combined with true predicative features in a way characteristic for such predicative elements. Thus we have *very many books* alongside with *very good books*. Other cases are *more than fifty books, at most fifty books, etc.* This still further complicates the internal semantic structure of the (Q X_i).

A particular combination of quantifying features and those specifying reference instances appears in the readings of *all, every, each, any,* and the determiner constituents of the different types of generic NP's. What they have in common seems to be the fact that they may or must relate the set X_i to the complete class characterized by the pertinent predicative features, a relation which is not involved in absolute and relative quantification. This is accomplished however in completely different ways resulting in similarly different consequences. Consider, *e.g.,* the following sentences:

(14)(a) [*Every logician*]$_{NP_1}$ *would infer that*

    (b) [*All logicians*]$_{NP_1}$ *would infer that*

    (c) [*Logicians*]$_{NP_1}$ *would infer that*

    (d) [*A logician*]$_{NP_1}$ *would infer that*

    (e) [*The logician*]$_{NP_1}$ *would infer that*

One might perhaps argue that these sentences are synonymous in one reading in the sense that identical truth conditions are associated with this reading. I have some doubts in this respect, however. In any case, the truth conditions are arrived at by means of completely different operations. The X_1 of (14a) *e.g.,* is a set consisting of one element, and the delimiting features of *every* represent an instruction which might be paraphrased as 'substitute for this element the representation of each single object such that the conditions expressed by *logician* are met.' The X_1 of (14b) on the other hand consists of a representation of the class of logicians and the delimiting features of *all* represent an instruction to the effect that predicates assigned to X_1 apply to all elements of this class. That these loosely indicated operations may have different results is brought out quite clearly by the following examples:

(15)(a) [*Every student of our college*]$_{NP_1}$ *likes baseball*

    (b) [*All students of our college*]$_{NP_1}$ *like baseball*

(16)(a) [*Every student of our college*]$_{NP_1}$ *performs a play*

    (b) [*All students of our college*]$_{NP_1}$ *perform a play*

Whereas (15a) and (15b) are synonymous, (16a) and (16b) are not, (16a) requiring as many one-man-performances as there are students. I will not pursue the problems of universal and generic sentences any further, as they constitute a large topic on their own. Let me add only that the operators involved behave differently again with respect to negation: the sentences (14b) and (14c) are at least similar in meaning in a way in which (17a) and (17b) are not, these being synonymous with (18a) and (18b) respectively:

(17)(a) *It is not true that all logicians would infer that*

    (b) *It is not true that logicians would infer that*

(18)(a) *Not all logicians would infer that*
   (b) *Logicians would not infer that*

Let me summarize briefly the lengthy and inconclusive discussion of delimitations. We first assumed that the reference indices i correspond to variables X_i functioning as arguments of the predicative features. These variables range over sets of possible objects which must meet the conditions represented by the predicative features. We then faced the necessity of elements delimiting the sets to be substituted for the X_i. These delimiting elements have a status completely different from that of the predicative elements. The delimiting features form operators of the form $(Q\ X_i)$ where the Q is a variable over (complexes of) those features. For each NP_i of the deep structure there is precisely one $(Q\ X_i)$ prefixed either to the reading of that NP_i or of a constituent containing that NP_i.[9] The delimiting features in turn subdivide into quantifying and specifying elements. The former represent absolute, relative, and universal characteristics of the extension or scope of the set to be substituted for the X_i. The latter represent instructions to pick up the set referred to in one or the other way. Specify ng and quantifying features are combined in a still unexplored way to form the operators $(Q\ X_i)$. The quantifying features may also be modified by certain predicative features, this modification being governed by the principles pertinent to the combination of predicative features in general.

It is worth noting that our interpretation of the arguments X_i and the pertinent delimitations, which is based so far on observations concerning countable objects, accounts at the same time in a very plausible way for mass objects:

(19)(a) *[The wine you gave me]*$_{NP_1}$ *was excellent*
   (b) *[Water]*$_{NP_1}$ *is still missing*
   (c) *Would you like [some coffee]*$_{NP_1}$
   (d) *[All iron]*$_{NP_1}$ *rusts*

The X_1 of these examples are to be substituted simply by representations of improper sets, as it were, which cannot be individualized at all, since they are not conceived as consisting of individuals. From this it follows immediately that certain quantifications do not apply. (This restriction must be derived from the inherent semantic and/or syntactic features of the respective nouns in a way not to be discussed here.) All other decisions however remain unchanged; the predicative features apply to the elements of the set X_1 referred to, *i.e.*, in this case to a single improper object. Quantifying features concern the set as a whole. And the selection of the appropriate referent represented by the specifying features is as usual. Thus the features DEF, SPEC, and INDEF account for (19a), (19b), and (19c), respectively. And the operation represented by *all* works for (19d) in the same way as for (14b), (15b), and (16b).

---

[9] An exception to this statement are predicative NP's in sentences like *John is a doctor* which do not identify but describe the referent of the Subject-NP. Such predicate nouns do not provide a new reference instance. They differ from all other NP's in other respects as well and must be treated separately in any case.

4. PROBLEMS OF RELATIONAL FEATURES

Having settled provisionally the problem of arguments and their delimitation, we return to the predicative features. We already mentioned that these are to be classified in part according to the number of their arguments. This then raises questions of the following type: is there an upper limit for the number k of k-place predicates to be included in the inventory of basic semantic elements? Is there a fixed number of arguments for each predicate or are there those with a varying number of arguments? We will see furthermore that predicative features may differ not only with respect to the number, but also to the type of arguments. Let us consider these problems by means of some examples.

It is obvious from the foregoing discussion that the number of arguments of a predicative feature must be somehow connected to the number of NP's required by the lexical entry whose reading contains that feature. Thus the verbs *hit* and *give*, for example, are often considered as expressing two- and three-place relations, respectively, *buy* and *sell* on the other hand as expressing relations with two, or three, or even four arguments:

(20) $[John]_{NP_1}$ *hit* $[Bill]_{NP_2}$

(21) $[John]_{NP_1}$ *gave* $[Bill]_{NP_2}$ $[a \ book]_{NP_3}$

(22) $[John]_{NP_1}$ *sold* $([Bill]_{NP_2})$ $[a \ book]_{NP_3}$ $(for \ [three \ florins]_{NP_4})$

However, the fact that *give* requires three NP's to form a non-elliptic sentence, does not imply that its reading contains a three-place predicate. In fact, it has been shown by Bendix (1966) that the meaning of *give* should be analyzed into two two-place relations in the following way:

(23) C *causes* (A *has* B)

where C represents the referent of the Subject-NP, B that of the direct object, and A that of the indirect object. If we assume that X_S, X_D, and X_I represent variables of a dictionary reading to be substituted by the X_i of the subject, direct object, and indirect object respectively, then (23) can be replaced by (24):

(24) $[CAUS] \ X_S \ ([HAVE] \ X_I \ X_D)$

Such a combination of features, where the second argument of the predicate CAUSATION is not a variable over a set of individuals but a proposition, raises several problems that will be discussed below.

With respect to *buy* and *sell*, Katz (1967) has proposed an analysis that reduces the apparent four-place relation essentially to a combination of several two-place features of the form *X possesses Y* with varying arguments and different time specifications, thus characterizing the process of exchange of goods and money between the subject and the indirect object referent of *buy* and *sell*. There are several possibilities to represent the necessary time specifications. One of them is the introduction of an abstract relation [R] t (P) where t is a variable over time intervals and P a proposition representing a process or a state occurring at time t. With this convention we can represent Katz' analysis of *sell* in the following way, using X_F as the variable to be substituted by the X_i of the prepositional phrase with *for*:

(25) [R] t ([Poss] X_S X_D . [Poss] X_I X_F) . [R] t' ([Poss] X_S X_F . [Poss] X_I X_D)

The time interval t' immediately follows t.[10]

What I have tried to show by means of these examples, which could easily be extended, is that many — if not all — lexical entries requiring or admitting three or more NP_i are to be analyzed into appropriate combinations of two-place features. Thus the number *k* of possible arguments for elementary predicative features can certainly be strongly restricted. In fact, one might hypothesize that in general only one- and two-place relations are required.[11]

It seems reasonable, furthermore, to assume that each particular feature always has the same number of arguments. The varying number of NP's permitted in sentences such as (22) does not imply that there are features with a varying number of arguments, but merely that some of these arguments are not specified by additional lexical items and thus do not appear in the surface structure in the form of separate constituents. (Whether a lexically unspecified argument must leave at least an indefinite pronoun as its trace, or whether it can be dropped altogether, or left unspecified even in the deep structure representation is part of the syntactic characterization of particular lexical items.)

We must now consider somewhat more detailed features like CAUS which take propositions as one of their arguments. First of all, the existence of such features leads to a further classification of features, which must then be specified not only with respect to the number but also to the type of their arguments. Though CAUS and HAVE are both two-place relations, they obviously belong to different types of fea-

---

[10] This analysis is oversimplified in many respects not relevant for the present discussion. Thus I ignore here and throughout this paper the problem of selection restrictions or presuppositions. In fact, the lexical reading of 'sell' must contain at least the following selectional features: [Human] X_S . [Human] X_I . [Money] X_F . [Physical Object v Artifact] X_D. Furthermore, I doubt that Katz' analysis is correct, insofar as it is based on the assumption that *buy* and *sell* are in a sense inverse relations. See Katz (1967) and Bierwisch (1969) for further discussion. Notice incidentally that *give* also must contain a time specification. Thus (24) should be rendered into [R] t ([Caus] X_S ([Have] X_I X_D)).

[11] An apparent counterexample to this speculation is the preposition *between* and its equivalents in other languages:

(i) *John₁ was seated between Bill₂, Paul₃, Sam₄,..., and Peterₙ*

Sentences like

(ii) *John₁ was seated between them₇*

suggest, however, that NP_2 through NP_n in (i) must be analyzed as dominated by a single NP, whose reference index is a set-theoretical union of 2, 3, ..., n. The corresponding variable would then be the second argument of the feature characterizing *between*, just as X_7 is its second argument in (ii). If this assumption is right, *between* would contain a two-place predicate which requires its second argument variable to be a set of more than one object.

tures. However, this classification must be specified still further. Consider the following sentences:

(26) $[John]_{NP_1}$ regrets $[that\ [Paul\ was\ waiting]_S]_{NP_2}$

(27) $[John]_{NP_1}$ believes $[that\ [Paul\ was\ waiting]_S]_{NP_2}$

The reading of *regret* and *believe* must contain, among other things, relational features representing a certain attitude of their first argument — the X_1 provided by the NP_1 *John* in (26) and (27) — towards their second argument, provided by the complement *that Paul was waiting*. These features, which we may abbreviate by BELIEVE and REGRET for the sake of simplicity, are similar to CAUS in that they take a proposition as their second argument. But whereas BELIEVE represents indeed an attitude towards a proposition, *viz.* that the individuals represented by the first argument are inclined to take it as a true proposition, REGRET represents an attitude not towards a proposition, but towards a fact represented by the proposition in question. In this respect, CAUS must be classed with REGRET, as it is the fact described by its argument proposition, not that proposition itself, which is brought about by the first argument of CAUS. Thus *John gave Mary some wine* does not mean that John causes the proposition expressed by *Mary has some wine*, but the fact represented by that proposition. Let us call features of the CAUS and REGRET type 'fact-features' — or for short 'F-features' — and those of the BELIEVE type 'proposition-features' or 'P-features'. It seems to me that the difference between F-features and P-features is closely connected to the problem which Reichenbach (1966:268-74) tries to explicate by means of so-called fact variables. For every proposition, Reichenbach claims, there may be a fact such that the proposition describes that fact.[12] This suggests that P-features take a proposition as their second argument, whereas F-features take the name of a fact.[13] The difference between these two types of arguments must be explicitly represented for both syntactic and semantic reasons. For syntactic consequences I refer to Kiparsky and Kiparsky (1970). The revealing distinction between Factive and Non-Factive predicates proposed there has at least one of its most important sources in the distinc-

---

[12]   Reichenbach introduces the following notation: $p \equiv (\exists v)\,p^*(v)$. In other words: p is true if and only if there is a fact v such that v is described by p. The asterisk on p transforms the proposition p in a predicate assigned to a fact variable. Since this p uniquely specifies a particular fact, the name of that fact can always be given by means of a definite description: $(\imath v)\,p^*(v)$, meaning 'the fact that p'.

[13]   Actually the distinction between fact arguments and proposition arguments, discussed here with respect to relational features, need not be restricted to these. There may be one-place predicates taking propositions and fact names respectively as their only arguments. Adjectives like *important*, *odd*, *tragic*, etc., in one of their readings contain one-place F-features, *true*, *possible*, etc. corresponding P-features. The same holds for verbs like *count* and *seem* respectively. I am somewhat cautious with respect to one-place F- and P-features, because it is not *a priori* clear whether most of the relevant items do not contain an implicit second argument representing the speaker of the utterance. This means that it might turn out that *That he comes, is true* must be analyzed as something like 'The proposition expressed by *he comes* is true for me'. Notice, incidentally, that F-features and P-features need not necessarily be disjoint sets. There may be features alternatively taking propositions and fact names as arguments.

tion of F-features and P-features. (It would be premature to claim that both distinctions are identical, though one might at least look for arguments in this direction.) Among the semantic reasons for the necessity of an explicit distinction between factive and propositional arguments are at least the problems of negation and of opaque contexts. As to the first problem, there are several of the P-features where the negation of that feature and of its argument are synonymous, whereas no such possibility exists for F-features. A rough illustration is given by the negations of (26) and (27):

(28)(a) *John does not believe that Paul was waiting*
　 (b) *John believes that Paul was not waiting*

(29)(a) *John does not regret that Paul was waiting*
　 (b) *John regrets that Paul was not waiting*

Whereas the sentences under (28) are synonymous, those under (29) are obviously not. I cannot go into the details of the problems involved, *e.g.* a characterization of those P-features which have the property in question and those which have not, *etc.*

　The problem of opaque contexts can be stated — with many oversimplifications — as follows. Given two propositions P_1 and P_2 which are logically equivalent, but not synonymous. (We might say that in a sense P_1 and P_2 describe the same fact but in different ways.) Then a context is opaque if P_1 cannot be substituted for P_2 *salva veritate*.[14]

　Assume, for example, that, given a certain setting, *Paul was waiting* is true if and only if *Paul was wasting his time* is true. Then both sentences describe the same fact. In this case, (31) is true if and only if (27) is true, whereas (30) might be false, even though (26) is true, and *vice versa*:

(30) *John believes that Paul was wasting his time*

(31) *John regrets that Paul was wasting his time*

Hence (26) is an opaque context, while (27) is not. The relevant fact is, that P-features can constitute opaque contexts, while F-features cannot.

　It follows from these remarks that a formal explication of the distinction in question and a suitable notation to represent it depend on several problems of semantic representations. Most of these problems are scarcely understood, to say nothing about their solution.

　So far we have discussed problems of relational features occurring in the readings of verbs. These considerations apply directly to adjectives governing objects, *e.g.*, *free, due, etc.*, or complements, such as *eager, able, etc.* I will now touch briefly on relational features occurring in readings of relational nouns such as *father, friend, side, roof, etc.* Nouns of this type express social roles, the part-whole relation, *etc.* Semantically the representation of such relations is straightforward, by means of such two-

---

[14]　The problem of opacity has been discussed mainly in connection with Believe-sentences. See, *e.g.*, Carnap (1964) and references quoted therein.

place predicates as PARENT, PART, *etc.* The problem here is the syntactic index required for the variables in the lexical reading. Notice first of all that every noun must contain in its lexical reading a variable which is to be replaced by X_i, if the noun in question functions as the head noun of an NP_i. This variable will be indexed for the relation Subject-of, since it is precisely this variable which is to be substituted by the argument expression provided by the subject NP, if a noun is used in the predicate NP of a copula sentence. The question then is: what is the syntactic index of the second-argument occurring in relational nouns? This question is directly related to the problem of the structure underlying such NP's as *John's father, the left side of a chair, etc.* It has been assumed, at least implicitly, by many writers that possessive genitives should be derived from underlying relative clauses with *have.* This seems to me unnatural, however, in the case of inherent relations pertinent to relational nouns of the type discussed here. It seems more reasonable to assume that relational nouns 'govern' an object NP in much the same way as verbs and adjectives do. Thus the structure underlying *John's father* should be something like

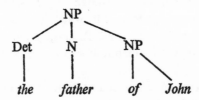

A similar proposal has recently been made by Fillmore (1968).[15]

If we abbreviate the syntactic function of an attributive NP of the type in question by the index G, the reading of *father* can be given as:

(33) [MALE] X_S . [PARENT] $X_S X_G$

From this lexical reading, (35) can be derived as the semantic interpretation of (34):

(34) $[[John's]_{NP_1} father]_{NP_2}$

(35) (DEF X_2) ([MALE] X_2 . [PARENT] X_2 (DEF X_1) ([J] X_1))

An example of unalienable possession would be *hand,* whose lexical reading is given in

(36) with HAND as an abbreviation for a rather complex set of semantic features:

(36) [HAND] X_S . [HUMAN] X_G . [PART] $X_S X_G$

[15] Fillmore discusses several details of the particular syntactic behavior of NP's in the case of unalienable possession, which is an instance of inherent relation of the type discussed here. Even if one does not agree with all the details of the 'Case-Grammar' proposed by Fillmore, his observations give clear evidence for the assumption that relational nouns admit (or require) a governed NP.

5. PARASITIC ARGUMENTS

So far, we have discussed predicative features whose arguments are provided essentially by NP's bearing the relevant syntactic relation to the constituent containing the features in question. I will now consider some phenomena which seem to require a different sort of argument, thereby inducing a further classification of semantic features. The need for such subsidiary arguments can be illustrated by means of the so-called relative adjectives such as *heavy, old, loud, big, long, high*, and their antonyms.

Relative adjectives specify a certain parameter and indicate that the object(s) referred to exceed (or fall short of) a certain point within that parameter. This point can be indicated explicitly in comparative constructions such as (37), it is understood implicitly in cases like (38) and hence must also be part of their readings .

(37) *John has a bigger house than Bill (has)*

(38) *John has a big house*

Analyzing a set of German adjectives describing spatial dimensions, which are a proper subset of relative adjectives, I tried to account for the facts just mentioned by means of simple markers such as (Vertical), (Maximal), (Secondary), *etc.*, specifying the relevant parameters, and the pair of markers (+ Pol) and (− Pol) to indicate the extension with respect to the specified parameter (for details, see Bierwisch, 1967). This analysis is unsatisfactory for at least two reasons. Firstly, it does not represent correctly the connections between the different features occurring in one reading (*cf.* footnote 2). Secondly, it cannot capture certain important empirical facts. Consider the following examples:

(39)(a) *Towers are high*
   (b) *Towers are high for buildings*
   (c) *Towers are higher than average buildings*

(40)(a) *These towers are high*
   (b) *These towers are high for towers*
   (c) *These towers are higher than average towers*

The sentences in (39), and again in (40), certainly are close paraphrases. This shows that even the positive form of relational adjectives must have a reading similar to that of the comparative, the term for comparison being provided by the average elements of a certain class. This class is that of the subject NP if it is not generic; it is the next larger class, *i.e.*, the *genus proximum*, if the NP is generic.[16] What is important here

---

[16] This differentiation between generic and non-generic sentences with respect to the class used for comparison is obviously necessary, and raises a problem that cannot be dealt with by means of the relative semantic marker proposed by Katz (1967) in this connection. According to Katz' analysis the comparison is always made with respect to the lowest category in the subject's reading, *i.e.*, its *genus proximum*. But the differentiation introduced above is still an oversimplification in several respects. Thus the sentence

is that we need a relational feature representing the comparison involved in relative adjectives. Thus we will replace the elements $(+\text{Pol})$ and $(-\text{Pol})$ by the relation Greater-than and its converse, represented as $[\text{GR}]\ Y\ Z$ and $[\text{GR}^{-1}]\ Y\ Z$, respectively. But what is represented by the arguments Y and Z? Obviously, Y refers to the extent to which an object X_i occupies a certain parameter which is specified by the rest of the adjective's reading. In other words, Y represents, in the present example, a certain spatial extension of the objects referred to by X_i. The second argument of GR, then, indicates the corresponding extension of the compared objects. Thus the arguments of GR are of a rather different type than the X_i considered so far. In fact, they represent not objects, but properties of objects where these properties are treated as a kind of parasitic or subsidiary argument. They must be established by a further type of relational features extracting extensions (or other parameters) from the primary arguments. For example, $[\text{VERT}]\ X_i\ Y$ with the interpretation 'Y is the vertical extension of X' and $[\text{MAX}]\ X_i\ Y$ with the interpretation 'Y is the maximal extension of X_i' may specify the relevant parameters of *high* and *long*, respectively.[17] The argument Y in these examples represents stretches. In other cases, *e.g.*, in one reading of *big*, we need global extensions, *i.e.*, something like the product of all relevant extensions. These might be introduced by a feature $[\text{VOL}]\ X_i\ Y$.

Since the extensions introduced so far are constituted by the corresponding dimensionality of the primary objects, they must occur not only in the adjectives which assign to them a certain value (*e.g.*, greater than a certain average), but also in the reading of nouns which specify the dimensionality of the objects referred to. Thus the fact that *line*, *square*, and *house* designate conceptually one, two, and three dimensional objects, respectively, might be expressed by the features $[1\ \text{EXT}]\ X_i\ Y_i$, $[2\ \text{EXT}]\ X_i\ Y_1\ Y_2$, and $[3\ \text{EXT}]\ X_i\ Y_1\ Y_2\ Y_3$.[18] Features of this type are part of the explication of

---

(i) *The high towers of the town will be reconstructed* is ambiguous, according to the restrictive or non-restrictive interpretation of the adjective *high*:

(ii) *The towers of the town which are high will be reconstructed*

(iii) *The towers of the town, which are high, will be reconstructed*

These imply different norms for comparison, as can be seen from these paraphrases:

(iv) *The towers of the town which are higher than the average towers of the town will be reconstructed*

(v) *The towers of the town, which are higher than average towers, will be reconstructed*

In other words: restrictive modifiers behave like non-generic sentences, nonrestrictive modifiers like generic ones with respect to the choice of the class for comparison. These and several other problems connected with the correct determination of the class to which the subject is compared deserve a careful analysis of both syntactic and semantic conditions which go far beyond the present aims. In the following discussion, I will simply presume that the class is somehow determined.

[17] This is, of course, an oversimplification. Certain additional qualifications are required. The situation is still more complicated in other cases, such as *wide*, *broad*, *deep*, etc. My present purpose, however, is not a detailed analysis of the adjectives in question, but a discussion of certain formal aspects of their readings. For the details ignored here, see Bierwisch (1967) and Teller (1969).

[18] We thus have a set of features of the general form $[n\ \text{EXT}]\ X_i\ Y_1\ldots Y_n$ which would replace the element (n Space) used in Bierwisch (1967). Notice that n EXT would be an exception to the above speculation that at most two-place features are necessary to account for the semantic structure of natural languages. This would force us to restrict the tentative claim to primary arguments. Another possibility would be to split up the $n+1$-place predicate n EXT into n two-place features

the hitherto used global marker (Physical Object). They provide the arguments which must be substituted for the corresponding variables within the readings of the relative adjectives.

Given the conventions discussed so far, the reading of *high* can be given provisionally as (41).

(41) $[\text{VERT}]\ X_S\ Y_i\ .\ [\text{GR}]\ Y_i\ Z$

Z is still used as an unexplicated abbreviation for the vertical extension of the compared average object. (In comparative constructions it must be substituted by the representation of the concerned extension of the compared NP.) Y_i is a variable that is to be substituted by an extension of the reading of the subject-NP that does not contradict the condition VERT. We thus get (42) as the reading of *The table$_1$ is high*, if we abbreviate all the features of *table* not relevant here by TABLE.

(42) $(\text{DEF}\ X_1)\ ([\text{TABLE}]\ X_1\ .\ [3\ \text{EXT}]\ X_1\ Y_1\ Y_2\ Y_3\ .\ [\text{VERT}]\ X_1\ Y_2\ .\ [\text{GR}]\ Y_1\ Z)$

Notice that the parasitic arguments that we have introduced represent sets of extensions (or other parameters), just as the primary arguments represent sets of objects: a sentence as *These tables are high* says something about the set of vertical extensions of the set of objects involved.[19]

We must still go one step further in specifying the subsidiary arguments. According to our previous assumptions, the 'normal height' Z in the reading of *high* must be replaced by the vertical extension of NP_2 in a sentence like (43):

(43) $[\textit{This table}]_{NP_1}\ \textit{is higher than}\ [\textit{that one}]_{NP_2}$

Hence the reading of (43) would contain a component $[\text{GR}]\ Y_1\ Y_1$. But this is obviously wrong. What we need is an indexing of the subsidiary arguments with respect to the primary arguments whose parameters they represent. Instead of the Y_i we must have something like $Y_{X_S}^i$ where the subscripts must be substituted by the same X_i which replaces the primary argument variable X_S. This then would yield the correct component $[\text{GR}]\ Y^1_{X_1}\ Y^1_{X_2}$ instead of the rejected $[\text{GR}]\ Y_1\ Y_1$ in the reading of (43).

A moment's reflection shows that this double indexing is in a sense redundant, since

---

[1 Ext] $X_i\ Y_1$, ..., [n Ext] $X_i\ Y_n$ where the direction of Y_j is orthogonal to Y_{j-1} for $1 \leqslant j < n$. 1 EXT in turn might be replaced by VERT, in cases where the noun in question has a designated vertical axis. Similarly for MAX, etc. In this case *j* EXT would be the indication of an extension without any further specification. All these are details of an adequate axiomatization of the conceptual structure according to which spatial objects are organized by human perception. I am not concerned here with substantive questions of this kind.

[19] This can be seen more clearly in nominalizations such as *the height of these tables* where the parasitic arguments are turned into primary ones in a way not to be discussed here. *The height* in this case clearly refers to a set of extensions, not to a single one, as can be seen from examples like *The height of the tables is different*. In spite of the fact that a set containing more than one object is referred to, it is treated morphologically as singular.

it simply repeats information already expressed by the relational features VERT, MAX, *etc.*, which specify extensions of particular objects, not arbitrary ones. Our notation thus somehow obscures the relevant facts. We may remedy this deficiency by adapting another notion developed in modern logic, *viz.* that of relational descriptions.

Given a two-place predicate $R(x,y)$ whose first argument is always uniquely specified if the second argument is given, an individual can be identified as the one which bears R to a given y. A relational description of this type is usually written as $R'y$. The element R' introduced here can be understood as a function mapping every y on a particular x, roughly speaking. Hence the following equivalence holds:

(44) $R(x,y) \equiv R'y = x$

$R'y$ is an individual of the same type as x, more precisely, it is a name of x. Notice now, that the features VERT, MAX and several others have precisely the property discussed here, except that it is the second argument which uniquely depends on the first, not *vice versa*. But this is only a notational arbitrariness. Based on the feature VERT we may thus introduce a corresponding function by the following definition:

(45) $Y = [\text{VERT}]' X =_{\text{def}} [\text{VERT}] X Y$

Similar functions can be derived from MAX, VOL, *etc.* From (45) it follows that an expression of the form $[\text{VERT}]' X_i$ is the name of the same set of extensions formerly represented as a variable with double index. Hence $[\text{VERT}]' X_i$ has the status of an argument and must enter readings in precisely this role. If we assume that X_N represents the above mentioned average object with respect to which the modified noun is compared, the reading of *high* can now be given as follows:

(46) $[\text{GR}] [\text{VERT}]' X_S [\text{VERT}]' X_N$

Functions of the type discussed can also be derived from combinations of relational features. Thus $[\text{VERT} . \text{MAX}] X_i Y$ would say that Y is an extension of X_i which is both vertical and maximal. Hence $[\text{VERT} . \text{MAX}]' X_i$ designates this extension. Combinations of this type are required for several adjectives. I cannot go into these details here.

What has been said with respect to relative adjectives, in particular to those referring to spatial extensions, applies to other parameters as well. A case of particular interest is time. The relation 'R' that was introduced provisionally to express the time-placement of a fact described by a proposition relates a fact to a time interval just as VERT relates an object to its vertical extension. The variables representing time intervals are thus subsidiary arguments of the same kind as the variables over space intervals. Time designations such as *morning, hout, year, etc.* are then nouns where these subsidiary variables are turned into primary ones — just as in nominalized adjectives like *length, height, width, etc.* Problems of this type, however, are topics of separate investigations.

6. CONCLUSIONS

Presupposing the general framework of transformational generative grammar, we have discussed some formal aspects of semantic representations. These are considered as complex structures that are built up from basic primitive terms and assigned to syntactic surface representations by the syntactic rules of the grammar of a given language. We assumed that an uninterpreted grouping of the basic semantic elements, proposed previously, *e.g.*, in Katz (1966, 1967), or Bierwisch (1967), is not sufficient. We claimed that an adaptation of certain means developed in modern logic might be at least a promising program. Pursuing this proposal along certain fairly different lines, we arrived at the following provisional conclusions:

Semantic representations presuppose at least the following basic requirements (or their equivalents in certain other notations):

(1) A set of variables representing sets of objects to which linguistic expressions can refer. Variables occurring in readings of sentences are indexed with respect to sameness or difference of reference.

(2) A set of semantic features which are classified according to several aspects into at least the following subsets: (2.1) Predicative features representing properties and relations ascribed to the elements of the sets represented by the variables in (1). Predicative features are further subclassified according to the number of their arguments into one-place predicates, two-place predicates, *etc.* The possibility was suggested that the number of arguments might be restricted to two. Another subclassification of predicative features might be induced by the type of arguments they take: those representing true objects, facts, propositions, parasitic objects, or parameters of objects.[20] Predicates may also take predicates as arguments, thus leading to higher level predication. This possibility obviously bears on the classification of semantic features. It has not been dealt with in the present paper. For some discussion, see Bierwisch (1969). (2.2) Delimiting features characterizing the sets of objects referred to with respect to quantity and to the operations that constitute these sets. Delimiting features fall into two classes: Features specifying reference instances and features indicating absolute and relative quantity.

The predicative semantic features (2.1) correspond to predicate constants, the

---

[20] To what extent the classification according to types of arguments is a purely formal aspect of semantic features, is a dubious question, since it presupposes a subclassification of arguments. But whether, *e.g.*, primary arguments and parasitic arguments can be distinguished on purely formal grounds, *i.e.*, without dragging ontological questions into the semantic theory, is not at all obvious. Since I know, for the time being, of no empirical consequences, the question will be left open here. Notice, however, that one has to be careful to avoid arbitrary subdivisions of the argument variables. Assume, for example, we were to introduce a set of primary variables and a set of variables ranging only over parasitic objects, *i.e.*, properties or parameters. We might then subdivide the former into those ranging over abstract entities and those ranging over concrete, physical objects, the latter being subdivided into variables over animate and inanimate objects, *etc.* This would either duplicate the information expressed by the semantic features or even transfer it from the semantic features to the argument variables. But it is the set of semantic features that should formally reconstruct the substantive content of meaning.

delimiting features (2.2) to quantifiers and certain other operators of modern logic. Whereas the variables in (1) have no substantial content and serve only the purpose of representing identical and different reference, the semantic features in (2) must have a constant interpretation in terms of cognitive and perceptual conditions inherent in human organisms and governing their interaction with the physical and social environment.

(3) The elements listed under (1) and (2) are combined according to a set of rules or conventions to form semantic representations. These rules are clearly connected to the different classes of semantic features discussed above. We have touched on them only marginally in the present paper.

The requirements (1), (2), and (3) specify an infinite set of semantic representations, where the rules postulated in (3) may be considered as the syntax of such representations. These requirements then indicate, at least partially, what semantic representations look like. They are, of course, by no means a full semantic theory of natural languages. An empirically motivated formal classification of the basic elements of a semantic theory is, however, a necessary part of such a theory.

The formal classification of semantic features discussed here is not the only type of structure organizing the set of primitive semantic terms. A fairly complex system of mutual inclusion, exclusion, hierarchical subordination, *etc.*, must be assumed to govern this basic inventory. The nature of this structure, which reflects the substantive content of semantic features, is as yet poorly understood. Some of its aspects may be expressed by redundancy rules, which are similar in certain respects to the meaning postulates of modern logic.

According to our basic assumption, semantic representations must be connected to syntactic surface representations. Let us assume that for this purpose it is sufficient to specify the connection between syntactic deep structures and semantic representations, the former being mapped by transformational rules on the appropriate surface structures. The connection between syntactic deep structures, which specify a set of basic syntactic relations, and semantic representations is provided by the lexicon, which associates semantic representations with basic syntactic formatives, and general conventions specifying the semantic effect of the basic syntactic relations.

Semantic representations of lexical entries are of the same character as those of syntactically complex expressions, with one exception: Lexical entries do not contain referentially indexed variables, since lexical entries do not refer to particular sets of individuals.[21] Instead they contain variables that are categorized with respect to the syntactic relations defined by the syntactic deep structure. The general conventions specifying the semantic effect of syntactic relations are based on precisely these cate-

---

[21]   They do not even refer to the whole class of individuals specified by the concept in question. A word like *father* can be used in generic sentences to refer to the class of all fathers, but it does not refer to it as a dictionary entry. The fact that unique terms like *the sun*, *New York*, *etc.* always refer to a particular object, is in this respect a fact of encyclopedic knowledge, not of the lexicon of a given language.

gorized variables. We have touched upon two alternative principles according to which these conventions might operate.

Throughout this paper I have ignored the fact that lexical readings are generally subdivided into two parts: the proper semantic content and the selection restriction — or more generally: the presuppositions for its appropriate use. This topic involves a number of different problems. It has no bearing, however, on the classification of features. Every semantic primitive that can be part of the proper conceptual content of a lexical reading can also be part of a selection restriction, and *vice versa*.[22]

I have made only very vague claims about the precise content of the syntactic deep structure and the relations defined by it. A more precise formulation of the classification of semantic features than that given here must obviously be related to certain specific assumptions with respect to the syntactic representations. This concerns, *e.g.*, the syntactic status of quantifiers, determiners, negation, and even of noun phrases. Thus the specification of the form of semantic representations depends to a fairly large extent on the presupposed syntactic analysis. But it is equally obvious, on the other hand, that the syntactic behavior of particular lexical entries can be predicted to a large extent on the basis of its semantic structure, if this is made explicit in an appropriate way.

REFERENCES

Bach, Emmon and Robert T. Harms
   1968   *Universals in Linguistic Theory* (New York, Holt, Rinehart and Winston Inc.).
Bellert, Irena
   1970   "On the Problem of a Semantic Interpretation of Subject-Predicate in Relations Sentences of Particular Reference", in: Bierwisch and Heidolph (1970).
Bendix, Edward Herman
   1966   *Componential Analysis of General Vocabulary* (Bloomington, Indiana University).
Bierwisch, Manfred
   1967   "Some Semantic Universals of German Adjectivals", in: *Foundations of Language* Vol. 3: 1-36.
   1968   Review of Weinreich, "Explorations in Semantic Theory", in *Current Anthropology* Vol. 9: 160-1.
   1969   "On Certain Problems of Semantic Representations", in: *Foundations of Language* Vol. 5: 153-84.
Bierwisch, Manfred, and Karl Erich Heidolph, eds.
   1970   *Progress in Linguistics* (The Hague, Mouton).
Carnap, Rudolf
   1964   "On Belief-Sentences", reprinted in: Rudolf Carnap, *Meaning and Necessity* (The University of Chicago Press).
Chomsky, Noam
   1965   *Aspects of the Theory of Syntax* (Cambridge, Mass., The M.I.T.-Press).
Fillmore, Charles J.
   1968   "The Case for Case", in: Bach and Harms (1968: 1-88).

[22] Katz (1967) has made a different claim, *viz.*, that only semantic markers can appear in selectional restrictions, whereas distinguishers cannot. I have argued in Bierwisch (1967) that this claim, together with the whole notion of distinguisher, should be given up.

Isenberg, Horst
  1968   *Das direkte Objekt im Spanischen* (= *Studia Grammatica IX*) (Berlin).
Karttunen, Lauri
  1968   "What do Referential Indices Refer to?" (mimeographed, The RAND Corporation).
Katz, Jerrold J.
  1964a "Analyticity and Contradiction in Natural Language", in: Fodor and Katz, eds. *The Structure of Language* (Prentice Hall, Inc.), 519-43.
  1964b "Semantic Theory and the Meaning of 'Good'", in: *The Journal of Philosophy*, 61: 739-66.
  1966   *The Philosophy of Language* (Harper and Row, New York).
  1967   "Recent Issues in Semantic Theory", in: *Foundations of Language* Vol. 3: 124-94.
Katz, Jerrold J. and Jerry A. Fodor
  1963   "The Structure of a Semantic Theory" in: *Language* Vol. 39, 170-210.
Katz, Jerrold J. and Paul M. Postal
  1964   *An Integrated Theory of Linguistic Descriptions* (Cambridge, Mass., M.I.T.).
Kiparsky, Paul, and Carol Kiparsky
  1970   "Fact", in: Bierwisch and Heidolph (1970).
McCawley, James D.
  1968   "The Role of Semantics in a Grammar", in: Bach and Harms (1968), 125-69.
Perlmutter, David M.
  1970   "On the Article in English", in: Bierwisch and Heidolph (1970).
Postal, Paul M.
        Cross-Over Phenomena (in preparation).
Reichenbach, Hans
  1966   *Elements of Symbolic Logic* (reprinted by The Free Press, New York).
Teller, Paul
  1969   "Some Discussion and Extension of Manfred Bierwisch's Work on German Adjectivals", in: *Foundations of Language* Vol. 5, No. 2.
Weinreich, Uriel
  1962   "Lexicographic Definition in Descriptive Semantics" in: Householder and Saporta (eds.) *Problems in Lexicography* (Bloomington).
  1966   "Explorations in Semantic Theory" in: Sebeok, ed. *Current Trends in Linguistics* Vol. 3, 395-477, Mouton, The Hague.

PAUL G. CHAPIN

ON AFFIXATION IN ENGLISH*

Among the regularities of language which interest linguists are the relationships between words and their derivatives. These relationships are generally referred to collectively as the derivational morphology of a language. This paper is an investigation into a part of the derivational morphology of English from the point of view of a generative grammar, *i.e.*, a set of explicit rules which characterize a language fully and precisely.

The rules governing the formation of derivatives from stems lie at the crossroads of a grammar. Both morphological and syntactic information are often relevant in determining the applicability of a rule. The complexity of interaction between morphology and syntax is such that a theory of language which postulates a grammar divided sharply into a generative syntax and an interpretive phonology[1] encounters serious difficulties at this point. A decision to place rules of derivation in either the syntactic or the phonological component, in this theory, leads to the undesirable result that some generalizations will be unstatable. Various somewhat speculative proposals have been made as to ways to alleviate the situation. They include the postulation of a 'derivational component' and a greatly enriched theory of the structure of the lexicon.

The proper characterization must of course be determined empirically, by examining the facts of derivation as they relate to other known facts about language. The focus of this paper will be on one factual area, the ordering of some derivational rules of English. A great deal of evidence has been accumulated, independently of any questions of derivation, as to the ordering of the phonological and syntactic rules of English.[2] Thus if the facts of derivation ordering are known, a test is available as to the compatibility of the derivational rules with the other rule systems. In case of failure of compatibility with any system, a new theory which includes derivation must take the facts of ordering into account.

* The research reported on in this paper was carried out in part at the Massachusetts Institute of Technology and in part at the MITRE Corporation. I am grateful to Noam Chomsky, G. H. Matthews, and Donald E. Walker for their helpful suggestions and encouragement.
[1] Such a theory is outlined, for example, in Katz and Postal (1964).
[2] For the phonological evidence, see Chomsky and Halle (1968); for the syntactic evidence, see any large-scale grammatical sketch of English, *e.g.*, Lees (1960).

Some points must be clarified at the outset. The word *rule* is used rather loosely when it refers to the "typically sporadic and only quasi-productive" processes of derivation (Chomsky, 1965:184). Its use here will be systematically loose in this way; it is not intended to imply anything about degree of productivity or regularity of output.

Secondly, it is necessary to differentiate two sorts of ordering. It often happens in systems of formalized grammatical rules that the applicability of some rule Y is logically dependent on the prior application of some rule X. This happens, for instance, when rule X is the first rule to introduce some element on which rule Y operates. A familiar example is a phrase-structure grammar which contains the rules $S \rightarrow NP + VP$, $VP \rightarrow V + NP$, $NP \rightarrow DET + N$, $DET \rightarrow ART + S$. Obviously the rule which expands DET can have no effect until DET has been introduced by the rule which expands NP. Thus DET expansion must follow NP expansion. This kind of ordering is called INTRINSIC ORDERING, and is of little interest.

The significant kind of rule ordering characteristic of linguistic systems is EXTRINSIC ORDERING. This is the ordering imposed on rules when they can logically appear in any order, but can in fact be stated most simply if given in one particular order. An illustration of this phenomenon is to be found in English syntax. There is a well-attested rule of English which converts active structures into passive structures, thus

(1) *Gene is cleaning the beans*
(2) *The beans are being cleaned by Gene*

In both sentences the auxiliary *be* agrees in number with the subject. A simple and highly general agreement rule can be stated for English which applies to both actives and passives. This rule must follow the application of the rule of passivization, since passivization may change the number of the subject, as it does in the derivation of (2) from (1). If this ordering is not imposed, the grammar must be complicated in some fashion to avoid generating the non-sentence

(3) **The beans is being cleaned by Gene*

It is well known that in English suffixes may be attached to suffixed words, to a depth of several layers, and that the order of attachment is in general fixed. Thus the word *intentionally* is formed from the stem verb *intend* by adding the suffixes *-tion, -al, -ly* in that order (with a slight phonological adjustment in the case of *-tion*). No other order of suffixation is possible: **intendal, *intendly, *intentionly* are not English words. But consider the particular suffixes involved. *-tion* nominalizes verbs; *-al* forms adjectives from nouns; and *-ly* applies to adjectives to yield adverbs. Thus the order in which the suffixes are attached is an automatic consequence of the formulation of the rules which attach them; that is, it is an intrinsic ordering. I shall argue that an EXTRINSIC ordering must be imposed on the rules of affixal derivation in English, and shall adduce evidence of the sort just discussed regarding the passive and number agreement rules of English, namely, that the statement of some derivational rules is simplified by ordering them before (or after) some other rules.

Consider first derivative adjectives in *-ful*. On the most superficial level, *-ful* derivatives appear to be formed from one- and two-syllable noun and verb stems, including a great many which function as both noun and verb. Thus *peaceful, pleasureful, suspenseful, mournful, forgetful, hopeful, worshipful, disdainful*. A few stems have three syllables: *disrespectful, disregardful*. Out of the multitude of stems in English which meet this description, however, fewer than 150 can actually take the *-ful* suffix in my dialect. The linguistic problem is to specify as fully and economically as possible the constraints which characterize this class of stems.

The most extensive study of this class was made by A. F. Brown (1958) within the theoretical framework of Zellig Harris' "Co-occurrence and Transformation in Linguistic Structure" (1957). Brown argues first of all that only nouns, or more precisely only phonological alternants of nominals, may serve as *-ful* stems. His reasoning is as follows: of the unambiguous stems, the vast majority are nouns. Some have no obvious verbal alternant, *e.g., peaceful, gleeful*, but many are morphologically closely related to a cognate verb, e.g. *deceitful, prayerful, thoughtful, useful*. Since there is no phonological reason to exclude **prayful, *thinkful* (compare *playful, thankful*), this indicates a syntactic constraint to the effect that among noun-verb pairs, *-ful* attaches to the noun.

There are some apparent counterexamples, however: *forgetful, resentful, mournful, inventful, thankful*. *Thankful* can be explained as belonging to a class of derivatives of nouns whose normal free form is plural but which lose the plural morpheme when they serve as stems of derivatives. Other such nouns are *scissors, guts*. Consider their derivatives in *-less*: *scissorless, gutless*. Similarly *thankless* is derived from *thanks* (there is no question about the nominal status of *-less* stems). The derivation *thanks-thankful* is therefore quite plausible. No such argument may be made for the other derivatives. Brown proposes that their stems are nonetheless phonological alternants of the underlying nominals *forgetting, resentment, mourning* (and on the same argument *invention*, though *inventful* is not among Brown's data). On this assumption he is able to give a (Harris-type) transformational analysis of all *-ful* forms.

The obvious difficulty confronting this analysis is why *forgetting, mourning, resentment*, and *invention* should be excluded as *-ful* stems in their free forms while *thought, truth, pleasure, deceit, etc.*, are not. Brown attempts to explain this by positing a characteristic stress pattern to which nouns must conform in order to serve as *-ful* stems. He symbolizes this pattern as

$$[(\overset{\backprime}{-})\,\overset{\cdot}{-}]\,\overset{\acute{}}{-}\,[\overset{\cdot}{-}]$$

The symbolism is as follows. The horizontal lines represent syllables. The grave accent represents secondary stress, the acute accent primary stress, and the raised point zero stress. The parentheses indicate optionality of what they enclose, and the brackets a kind of Sheffer stroke relation between the bracketed elements: either may appear, or neither, but not both. The expansion of the schema is interpreted as follows: possible stem nouns for -*ful* derivatives are (a) stressed monosyllables; (b) bisyllabic words with primary stress on one syllable and zero stress on the other (this would exclude, *e.g., blackboard*); (c) trisyllabic words with secondary stress on the first syllable, zero stress on the second syllable, and primary stress on the third syllable. This last group is quite small, apparently including only *disrespect, disregard, disbelief,* and *disarray.* In particular, it omits *forgetting, resentment,* and *invention.*

This explanation is initially implausible, on external grounds. Stress in English is in general irrelevant to the operation of syntactic and derivational rules. Brown adduces no other case in which it is crucial.[3]

Moreover, even in its own terms the stress test is inadequate to explain the restriction on -*ful* derivation. Many nouns which pass the stress test as well as Brown's other restrictions (ability to appear without an article, cooccurrence) are still not possible -*ful* stems. Some may be explained by restrictions which Brown did not notice; for example, there is apparently a phonological constraint that nouns ending in /f/ or /v/ are excluded, thus **loveful, *griefful.* For many excluded forms, however, there is no such explanation; Brown must regard their exclusion as accidental. A few examples are **firmnessful, *judgmentful, *tensionful, *wisdomful, *weaknessful, *movementful, *actionful, *dotingful, *daringful,* and **mourningful.* The last example is particularly glaring since Brown considers it specifically. His comment is

The loss of -*ing* in the alternant *mourn-* of *mourning* and the retention of -*ing* in *meaning* before -*ful* both result in forms that fit the stress pattern of the bases. (Brown, 1958: 8).

The *meaning* case is interesting. There is independent evidence that *meaning* is quite different from participial nominals like *mourning.* For example, it can pluralize — *several meanings,* but **several mournings* — and it can be superordinate to a genitive construction — *The meaning of the poem,* but **The mourning of Alice.* If the derivation of *meaning* is different from that of *mourning,* one might expect an explanation for the possibility of *meaningful* and the impossibility of **mourningful* which takes that difference into account. But on Brown's argument, the fact that one form exists and the other does not is purely fortuitous; it might just as well have been the other way around. In particular, there is no explanation based on the stress pattern why *mourning* is excluded as a stem for -*ful* since it fits the pattern just as well as *mourn-*.

Brown's generalization that only nominals can be -*ful* stems is an attractive and plausible one, which it would be nice to maintain. A better explanation for the apparent counterexamples and the classes of excluded nominals would strengthen the generalization.

A likely candidate for such an explanation is an extrinsic ordering of the rules of suffixation. As the examples of impossible -*ful* forms have indicated, excluded stems

---

[3] Recent work by Chomsky and Halle (1968), in fact, indicates that stress in English is assigned by a complex series of rules which operate interpretively on surface syntactic structures. If this is the case, the rules which generate those structures are logically prior to the stress rules, and information about stress is not available to the generative rules.

fall into classes. No noun ending in the suffixes *-ness*, *-ment*, *-ing* (except *meaning*' whose *-ing* is different), *-ity*, or *-tion* can be a *-ful* stem. On the other hand, nominalizations which involve radical changes rather than suffixation — *use, thought*, etc. — are permitted, as is *meaning*. Ordering the *-ful* rule after the formation of these and before the suffixational rules would explain this difference. It might be claimed that *truth, youth, mirth, sloth*, which are all possible stems, are suffixationally nominalized adjectives; if this is the case, it indicates that the *-ful* rule is ordered after the *-th* rule.

The next evidence for extrinsic ordering of suffixational rules has to do with the suffixes *-ment*, *-tion*, and *-less*. Joseph Emonds (1966) has demonstrated that the choice between the nominalizing suffixes *-ment* and *-tion* is determined phonologically, by the systematic phonemic (*i.e.*, underlying) representation of the stem verb. Briefly and without some refinements, the rules he gives are as follows: verbs with the prefixes *eN-* and *be-* take *-ment* (*bedevilment, bereavement, embezzlement, encouragement*); verbs ending in oral or nasal stops (*invite, defame*), verbs ending in /v/ or /s/, preceded by an optional liquid, nasal, or peripheral stop, preceded by a lax vowel (*starve, sense, fix*), verbs ending in /v/ or /z/, preceded by a high or low tense vowel (*accuse, derive, cause*), and verbs ending in a liquid preceded by a vowel (*console, explore*) all take *-(A)tion*; all other verbs take *-ment*. These rules are disjunctively ordered as given; a number of verbs with the prefix *eN-* otherwise meet the specifications for *-tion* assignment (*enthrone, enfranchise, entail*). Homogeneity of rules can be maintained, however, as Emonds does, by the expedient of marking verbs in *be-* and *eN-* as exceptions to the rule for *-tion* assignment and then assigning *-ment* to all verbs to which *-tion* is not assigned.

Emonds' rules are not without their exceptions, which he conscientiously lists (some examples are *commandment, containment, assessment, involvement, amusement, requirement, condolement, encapsulation, continuation*). The generalizations he has achieved, however, are much more striking than any which appear to be possible on the basis of syntactic or semantic constraints. It may be concluded that the only systematic difference between nominalizations in *-ment* and those in *-tion* is phonological. Two things emerge from Emonds' work which are of interest here.

In the first place, it is significant that Emonds is able to make his rules more general by his assumption of extrinsic ordering of rules of suffixation. That is, he excludes from consideration all verbs which do not take either *-ment* or *-tion*, but some other nominalization, *e.g.*, *occur-occurrence, arrive-arrival, erase-erasure, advise-advice, neglect-neglect, respond-response*, on the assumption that these nominalizations have already been assigned at the point in the grammar at which his rules apply (Emonds, 1966:3). If this were not assumed, his rules as formulated would apply to every verb in English. Whether a reformulation of the rules which avoided this assumption would be possible at all is highly questionable; it would certainly be considerably more complex.

Secondly, the interaction of nominalizations formed by these two suffixes with the adjectivalizing suffix *-less* is very interesting. *-less* takes as stems lexical and derivative nouns with no apparent semantic restrictions. Some random examples are *cloudless*, *treeless*, *heedless*, *mindless*, *truthless*, *distanceless*, *moistureless*, *leaderless*, *teacherless*, *weightless*, *sexless*. Among the derivative nouns which can serve as *-less* stems are many in *-tion*: *occupationless*, *foundationless*, *vibrationless*, *actionless*, *directionless*, *oppositionless*. But what is striking is that *-ment* nominalizations cannot be *-less* stems. Thus *contentmentless*, *appointmentless*, *developmentless*, *adornmentless*, *involve-mentless*, *agreementless*, etc., are impossible forms. The only possible counter-example listed in the *Reverse English Word List* (Brown, 1963) is *decrementless*, which could be taken as derivative from *decrease*, although not by Emond's rules. This form, together with the clearly lexical-stem derivatives *raimentless*, *sentimentless*, *garment-less*, *monumentless*, *filamentless*, indicate that the constraint which prohibits *-ment* before *-less* is *not* phonological. But if the only systematic difference between nominal-izations in *-tion* and nominalizations in *-ment* is phonological, and there is no phono-logical reason to exclude the latter from *-less* stem position, there can be no principled reason for doing so at all except extrinsic ordering, with the rule attaching *-less* inter-posed between the *-tion* and *-ment* rules.

   Other restrictions on the productivity of *-less* are interesting in this regard. Nomi-nalizations in *-ness* and *-ity*, as well as those in *-ment*, are excluded. *Happinessless*, *consciousnessless*, *painfulnessless*, *legalityless*, *stabilityless*, *generosityless* are some examples of semantically plausible but nonetheless impossible forms. The valid words *witnessless* and *universityless* show that these constraints are not phonological. Extrinsic ordering is suggested once again as the simplest explanation. Here there is another consideration to take into account, however. *-ness* and *-ity*, unlike *-ment*, apply to adjectives. *-less* forms adjectives. If the nominalization rules are ordered after the adjectivalization rule, one would expect them to apply to the derivative adjectives it forms. In the case of *-ness* this is no problem. Any *-less* adjective can take the suffix *-ness*, e.g. *witlessness*, *truthlessness*, *expressionlessness*. The same is not true for *-ity*; no word ends in *-lessity*. This might appear to be a problem, since neither order produces valid results. Similarly, it was argued that the *-ful* rule was ordered before *-ity* formation; but *-fulity* is not a possible ending. Some other observa-tions offer a resolution to the problem. The first has to do with *-ity*. The one over-whelming regularity in *-ity* derivation, which has been noticed by every student of the subject (*e.g.*, Sweet, 1960: 489; Jespersen, 1961: 448-450; Marchand, 250-253), is that it is limited to stems of Romance origin. Among the few counterexamples mentioned by Jespersen and Marchand, only *oddity* has any currency today. Another possible counterexample, not mentioned by Jespersen or Marchand, is *jollity*, from *jolly*, whose etymology, however, is uncertain (Skeat, 1953:316). Second, it is in general the case in English that when a free morpheme serves as a derivational suffix, it imposes its own characteristics on the derivatives it forms with respect to its susceptibility to further derivation. Thus for example derivatives in *-able* (with exceptions to be discussed below) nominalize to *-ability*, regardless of whether the stem verb was of Romance origin or not. If it is assumed that *-ful* and *-less* are the suffixal forms of *full*

and *less*, then the observation that these morphemes are of Germanic origin is sufficient to explain the impossibility of *-ity* nominalization of adjectives in *-ful* and *-less*.

A large class of derivative adjectives is formed by suffixation of *-able* to a verb
(*breakable, believable, commendable*). There are also adjectives which end in *-able*
which do not have a stem verb. One class of these has non-free stems (*probable,
potable, amicable, sociable*). Another class has noun stems:

peaceable	actionable	sensible
marriageable	objectionable	comfortable
knowledgeable	reasonable	sizable
salable	treasonable	charitable
fashionable	seasonable	forcible
companionable	personable	profitable
impressionable	pleasurable	contemptible

Possible other candidates for membership in this class are *honorable, miserable,* and
memorable, with phonological changes in the stems of the last two corresponding to
that in the stem of *charitable.*

It is remarkable that among all adjectives ending in *-able* it is just the members of
this class, except *marriageable, knowledgeable,* and *salable,* which do not nominalize
in *-ity.* Most of them nominalize in *-ness,* although it could be said that the stems of
sensible and *comfortable* are their nominalizations.

Clearly there can be no phonological restriction against *-ity* nominalization of these
forms. Not enough is known about *-ity* derivation to exclude the possibility of an
independently motivated syntactic or semantic constraint which rules them out as
stems. If a way can be found to handle the exceptions, however, extrinsic ordering
again provides a simple answer. That is, the *-ity* rule applies after the rule attaching
-able to verbs but before the rule which forms these noun-stem derivatives in *-able.*

So far we have dealt exclusively with suffixation. We shall now consider some evidence that prefixational rules must be extrinsically ordered among the suffixational
rules.

There are at least two different prefixes in English with the shape *un-*. One, call it
*un-*1, attaches to verb stems with the characteristic result that the meaning of the
derivative is an action which reverses the action designated by the stem (*unlock, untie,
undress*). These verbs contain no syntactically observable negative element according
to Klima's tests (Klima, 1964). They do not change the indefinite prearticle from *some*
to *any*:

(4) *He locked some doors*

(5) *He didn't lock any doors*

(6) **He unlocked any doors*

Tag questions behave as for affirmative sentences:

(7) *He locked the door, didn't he?*

(8) *He didn't lock the door, did he?*
(9) **He didn't lock the door, didn't he?*
(10) *He unlocked the door, didn't he?*

Another *un-* (*un-*2) attaches to adjective stems with the semantic effect of simple negation: *unhappy, unwise, unfaithful.* Among the possible stems for *un-*2 are derivatives in
-able. Thus *unbelievable, unwashable, unstartable, unreadable.* Some possible stems
for *-able* derivation are the verbs *lock, tie, dress.* Since verbs prefixed by *un-*1 have no
negative element, and there is no reason to suppose there to be any other syntactic
difference between these verbs and their stems, there is no apparent reason to exclude
them from any position appropriate to their stems. In particular, there is no reason to
exclude them as stems for *-able* derivation, any more than verbs prefixed by *re-* are
excluded (*relockable*). Therefore one would predict that the derivatives *unlockable,
untiable, undressable* are systematically structurally ambiguous between the bracket-
ings (*unlock*)*able* (*un-*1) and *un*(*lockable*) (*un-*2). This ambiguity does not occur, however; only the *un-*2 reading is possible. Also one would predict that *un-*2 could apply
to *-able* derivatives with stems in *un-*1, but the forms **ununlockable, *ununtiable,
unundressable are impossible. Therefore it must be concluded that *un-*1 forms are
excluded from *-able* derivation. The only principled way that this can be done is by
extrinsically ordering the *un-*1 rule after the *-able* rule.[4]

The arguments for extrinsic ordering of the derivational rules discussed are based
on constraints on the applicability of particular rules which would otherwise be completely *ad hoc*, and which would complicate the rules if stated therein. Thus the rule
for formation of *-less* derivatives would have to specify that it applied to nouns and to
nominalizations in *-er* (agentive nominals) and *-tion*, but not to nominalizations in *-ity*
and *-ness*, unless the rules were ordered in such a way that these constraints were automatic. The examples offered in evidence, however, have been somewhat isolated, argu-
ing in each case for the relative ordering of just a few rules. Thus from the characteristics of *-ful* attachment, we know that it must happen fairly early among the derivations;
-less attachment is somewhere in the middle; and *-ness* is attached toward the end of the
derivational rules, since derivatives in *-ness* can receive no further suffix. But there are
many other affixes in English. It is reasonable to assume that if some derivational
rules are extrinsically ordered, all are. The question then becomes, can the derivational
rules of English be put in some order which does not exclude any permissible derivation? The simplest kind of ordering is in a straight linear sequence, so this is the first
kind to try. It turns out that a linear ordering of the rules is not possible. There are
two three-member groups of suffixational rules which cannot be formulated if linear
ordering is imposed on them.

---

[4] I have recently been surprised to learn that there is dialectal variation on this. The facts reported
are from my dialect. Several people have told me that their intuitions are exactly the opposite: that
the *un-*1 reading of these derivatives is far more natural for them. Halle has shown that a variety of
dialects of Russian differ phonologically only in the ordering of their phonological rules. The facts
reported here would appear to indicate the usefulness of a similar approach to syntactic dialectology.

The first group consists of the suffixes *-tion, -al,* and *-ize.* The nominalizing suffix *-tion* we have already discussed. The *-al* under consideration is not the verbal nominalizer of *refusal, arrival,* but the adjectivalizing suffix which applies to nominal stems, as in *verbal, autumnal, national.* It applies not only to lexical nouns, but also derivatives in *-tion: educational, processional, formational, directional.*

-ize is the most productive verb-forming suffix in English. It applies to lexical nouns (*unionize, carbonize, vaporize*), lexical adjectives (*modernize, standardize, immunize*), and to derivative adjectives (*theatricize, americanize*) including in particular derivative adjectives in *-al* and its variant *-ar* (*centralize, industrialize, brutalize, polarize, circularize*). It applies to those derivative adjectives ending *-tional* as well (*directionalize, coeducationalize, sensationalize*).

But the nominalizing suffix for all *-ize* derivatives is *-(A)tion:*

unionization	americanization	standardization
carbonization	centralization	immunization
vaporization	industrialization	circularization
modernization	brutalization	polarization
directionalization	coeducationalization	theatricization
		sensationalization

Thus the *-tion* rule must apply to *-ize* derivatives, the *-ize* rule to *-al* derivatives, and the *-al* to *-tion* derivatives, an untenable situation under linear ordering.

The second group of suffixes to be considered includes *-ist, -ic,* and *-al.* The situation here is less clear than before because of the semantic complexities of the suffixes. *-ist* is a nominalizing suffix which attaches to lexical and derivative adjectives and nouns (*purist, urbanist, nudist, instrumentalist, geneticist, motorist, stylist, columnist, zionist, segregationist*) and sometimes alternates with *-y* or *-ism* (*biologist, philanthropist, theist, communist*). Nominalizations in *-ist* always refer to human agents, but the relationship between the human agent and the stem can be quite varied, as the above examples show. A *theist, communist,* or *zionist* believes in a certain body of doctrine; a *philanthropist* practices *philanthropy;* a *segregationist* is characterized by both beliefs and practices. *Urbanists, biologists,* and *geneticists* are students of fields; *stylists* and *columnists* are employed in certain ways; *motorists* and *instrumentalists* are operators.

-ic derivatives are adjectives formed from nouns, also with varied semantic relationships. *Metallic* means 'made of or resembling metal'; *cyclic* means 'occurring in cycles'; *angelic* means 'having the qualities of an angel'; *atomic* means 'of or pertaining to atoms'. Derived nouns are not in general possible *-ic* stems, although many stems are polymorphemic, e.g., *microscopic, telegraphic, photoelectromagnetic.* A great many *-ic* forms, however, end in *-istic: realistic, Hellenistic, pianistic, atheistic, atomistic, Platonistic, futuristic, modernistic, journalistic.* In every case these forms have no human element in their semantics; they are apparently unrelated, except by common, stems, to the *-ist* nominalizations which appear to be proper parts of them.[5] Some of

[5]   It is remarkable that none of the great students of English derivation seem to have noticed this fact.

the -*istic* forms are adjective alternates of -*ism* forms (*atheistic, realistic*), others designate qualities appropriate to the field of endeavor surrounding their stem nouns (*pianistic, journalistic*), and some appear to be infixational derivatives of -*ic* forms, referring to qualities which imitate in some way the qualities designated by the source -*ic* form (*Hellenistic, Platonistic*).

It is an open question whether the -*al* suffix which interacts with this group is the same as the one in the former group. Both form derivative adjectives, and the derivatives differ in no systematic way that I have observed. However, the extensive group of -*ic* derivatives are the only adjectives which can serve as -*al* stems, with the exception of a few forms in -*atory* (*dedicatorial, piscatorial, investigatorial*), and a number of forms in -*oid* (*spheroidal, androidal*) which are probably to be taken as nouns. It may be, therefore, that the -*al* which appears after -*ic* derivatives is unique to that position.[6]

In many cases the -*al* after -*ic* is optional, as with *idiotic(al), mystic(al), microscopic(al), orthographic(al), periodic(al)*. When this is the case, it sounds rather redundant, and it is generally omitted for stylistic reasons. In some cases, however, the -*al* is required: *typical, mythical, farcical, paradoxical, psychological*, and in general all derivatives of words in -*ology*; in other cases it is impossible: *basic, alcoholic, athletic, patriotic*. In a few cases -*al* introduces a semantic difference, as in *economic/economical, historic/historical, politic/political, fantastic/fantastical, psychic/psychical*.

Following this discussion, it may be that we are dealing not with the suffixes -*ist*, -*ic*, and -*al*, but simply with -*ic* and two of its alternants, -*istic* and -*ical*. Whatever the truth is on this matter, there is a cyclic pattern here also: -*istical*, -*alistic*, and -*icalist* are all occurring word-final sequences (*egotistical, nationalistic*, and *periodicalist* are among the examples attested in the *Reverse English Word List* (Brown, 1963)).

With cyclic patterns such as these, one might expect the possibility of recursion. This expectation is born out in both cases. Cases in point are derivative sequences like *organize, organization, organizational, organizationalize, organizationalization, etc.*; *physical, physicalist, physicalistic, physicalistical, physicalisticalist, etc.* Each new derivative receives an increasingly preceise semantic interpretation. By the end of the second cycle, the derivative is so narrowly precise as to be totally useless, and so internally complex as to be difficult to understand. This does not make it an impossible form, however, any more than a sentence with multiple self-embeddings, which would never be used in an actual utterance, is thereby ungrammatical.

English is not the only language with cyclic derivational patterns. German has an adjectivalizing suffix -*lich* and a nominalizing -*keit*, each of which can apply to derivatives formed by the other. Thus we observe the sequence *Schade* 'shame', *schädlich* 'shameful', *Schädlichkeit* 'shamefulness', *schädlichkeitlich* 'shamefulnessful', *schädlichkeitlichkeit, etc.*

It was mentioned at the beginning of this paper that a considerable amount of evidence is now available as to the ordering of phonological and syntactic rules of

---

[6]   See Marchand: 182-188 for discussion.

English. One important hypothesis which has emerged from the study of this evidence is that large blocks of these rules are cyclically ordered. All of the rules in a cyclically ordered block apply over a domain restricted to a specified subpart of a linguistic structure. After the last rule has applied, the domain is expanded and the sequence of rules is applied again from the beginning (see Chomsky and Halle, 1968; Ross, 1967). Such a cyclic process might seem to offer a solution to the problem of cyclic derivational patterns. However, the derivational rules as a whole cannot be cyclically ordered. The arguments for ordering these rules at all are vitiated if the rules are cyclically ordered, since derivatives formed on one cycle of application would be available as stems for derivation on subsequent cycles unless *ad hoc* restrictions were imposed to avoid it. Thus for example a nominalization in *-ment* would be formed after the derivation of adjectives in *-less* on one cycle, and on that cycle could therefore not take *-less* as a suffix. On the next cycle, however, nothing would prevent *-less* from applying to the *-ment* derivative. It must therefore be concluded that the rules are not cyclically ordered.

In summary then, the problem is the following. The derivational rules of English as a whole cannot be cyclically ordered. Some subgroups of them, however, must be cyclically ordered. Therefore the derivational rules cannot be linearly ordered as a whole, in spite of the considerable evidence that many individual rules are extrinsically ordered with respect to each other. How are these contrary bodies of evidence to be mutually accommodated? That is, what is the strongest statement that can be made about the ordering of derivations?

The available evidence, which is admittedly scanty, indicates that it may be possible to order the rules in such a way that rules which must be cyclically ordered can always be ordered adjacent to each other; that is, that no rule which does not participate in a given cycle need be ordered (extrinsically or intrinsically) between any two rules which do. This can be made clearer by a diagram.

$$A \text{ --- } B \text{ --- } C \text{ --- } D \text{ --- } E \text{ --- } F \text{ --- } G$$

Assume that A, B, *etc.* are derivational rules and the '---' are ordering relations, extrinsic or intrinsic (typically not every pair of rules in a sequence will be ordered). Then the proposal under dicussion is that cyclical ordering is possible only among groups of alphabetically adjacent rules. Possible cyclical groups would be B-C, F-G, C-D-E, A-B-C-D, and so on; C-D-F, A-E, and so on would not be possible cyclical groups. Thus in terms of the examples just discussed, the hypothesis holds that the rules for attachment of *-tion*, *-al*, and *-ize* may be ordered immediately adjacent to each other, with no necessity for the interposition between two of them of some other rule, say the rule of *-less* attachment, which does not enter into the cyclic pattern. We may call this the EPICYCLE HYPOTHESIS.

The importance of the epicycle hypothesis is that if it is true, the theory of grammar can be made stronger than if any random set of derivational rules can participate in a cycle. In the latter case, a 'pointer' must accompany every rule to indicate the next rule or rules which can apply to its output, and the generalizations that are achieved by extrinsically imposed sequential ordering are lost. If the epicycle hypothesis holds, however, individual notation on each rule is not needed; order is sequential, and a special notational device brackets groups of rules which form an epicycle.

Some possible counterevidence to the epicycle hypothesis from English has to do with the suffix *-ment*. A number of words which end in *-ment* can take the suffix *-al*. Many are lexical nouns, not derived by suffixation (*sentiment, detriment, segment, department*). In two cases, however, possible recipients of *-al* are apparently *-ment* nominalizations of verbs: *government, development*. If these two words are only formed by the *-ment* rule discussed earlier, the epicycle hypothesis is untenable. One of the arguments for extrinsic ordering presented above indicated that *-ment* attachment must follow *-tion* attachment, with *-less* attachment intervening. But if *-al* attaches to *-ment* derivatives, part of the ordering of derivations must be

$$\textit{-tion} \text{ --- } \textit{-less} \text{ --- } \textit{-ment} \text{ --- } \textit{-al} \text{ --- } \textit{-ize}$$

This order violates the epicycle hypothesis, since two suffixes intervene between two members of the cyclical group *-tion, -al, -ize*. To account for the possibility of *-tion* nominalization of verbs in *-ize* under this ordering, it would be necessary to place a pointer from *-ize* attachment back to *-tion*.

To avoid this consequence, it would be necessary to show that *government* and *development*, at least in the sense in which they appear as stems for *-al* derivation, are not derived by the general rule of *-ment* nominalization. These is some evidence that this is the case. One piece of evidence is the strength of the pattern to which they are apparent exceptions. For every clear case of *-ment* nominalization, *-al* suffixation is impossible: **embarrassmental, *improvemental, *amusemental, *confinemental*. On the other hand are the many lexical nouns ending in *-ment* which can take *-al*, exemplified above. If this were not the problem we were trying to explain, this evidence would be taken as nearly conclusive that *government* and *development* are lexical nouns. Another more tenuous piece of evidence is the fact that both *govern* and *develop* violate Emonds' rules (Emonds, 1966) for the phonology of *-ment* stems; by those rules they should nominalize with *-tion*. Finally in the case of *government* it can be argued that semantically it does not have only the characteristics of a nominalized verb, referring to an action or its result, as in

(11) *The government of these territories is a burden*

but also may be used as sort of a collective noun, as in

(12) *Spain has not elected a new government for some years*

This is particularly clear in British English, where *government* is plural when used in the latter sense:

(13) *The government are studying the problem now*
(14) **The government of these territories are a burden* [In the sense of (11)]

I know of no analogous argument for *development*. It may be the crucial counter-example to the epicycle hypothesis. The matter deserves further study, bearing in mind, of course, that the history of science teaches us caution in dealing with epicycles.

REFERENCES

Brown, A. F.,
  1958 *The Derivation of English Adjectives Ending -ful* (Unpublished doctoral dissertation, Philadelphia, University of Pennsylvania).
  1963 *Normal and Reverse English Word List*, 8 volumes (Philadelphia, University of Pennsylvania).
Chomsky, N.,
  1965 *Aspects of the Theory of Syntax* (Cambridge, Mass., M.I.T.-Press).
Chomsky, N. and M. Halle,
  1968 *The Sound Pattern of English* (New York, Harper & Row).
Emonds, J.,
  1966 "A study of Some Very Confusing Suffixes; or, Phonetic Regularities in Some Words Derived from Romance Tongues" (Unpublished paper. Mimeograph, Cambridge, Mass., M.I.T.).
Harris, Z.,
  1957 "Co-occurrence and Transformation in Linguistic Structure". *Language*, 33: 283-340. Reprinted in: Fodor and Katz, eds. (1964), *The Structure of Language* (Englewood Cliffs, N.J.: Prentice-Hall) 155-210.
Jespersen, O.,
  1954; 1958; 1961 *A Modern English Grammar on Historical Principles*, 7 volumes (London, George Allen & Unwin). First published complete in 1949.
Katz, J., and P. Postal,
  1964 *An Integrated Theory of Linguistic Descriptions* (Cambridge, Mass., M.I.T.-Press).
Klima, E.,
  1964 "Negation in English" In: Fodor and Katz, eds., (1964) *The Structure of Language*, (Englewood Cliffs, N.J.: Prentice-Hall) 246-323.
Lees, R.,
  1960 *The Grammar of English Nominalizations* (The Hague, Mouton & Co).
Marchand, H.,
  The Categories and Types of Present-Day English Word-Formation. No date given; Library of Congress Catalog Card No. is 66-26622 (Alabama, The University of Alabama Press).
Ross, J.,
  1968 "On the Cyclic Nature of English Pronominalization" In: *To Honor Roman Jakobson*, II (The Hague, Mouton & Co.), 1669-1682.
Skeat, W.,
  1953 *An Etymological Dictionary of the English Language*. (London, Oxford University Press). Revised Edition first published 1909.
Sweet, H.,
  1960 *A New English Grammar, Logical and Historical*. 2 parts. (London, Oxford University Press). Part I first published 1891; Part II first published 1898.

MORRIS HALLE

ON METER AND PROSODY

INTRODUCTION

The utterances that make up a piece of metrical verse exhibit regularities in the sequential arrangement of their phonetic, morphological or syntactic components which are not found consistently in normal everyday language. In composing a poem in a particular meter, the author may, therefore, be said to select from among the utterances of the language those that conform to the meter which he has chosen for his poem. By characterizing in this manner the poet's activity — or rather one aspect of this activity — I intend to bring out the distinction between the METER of a poem, which is a sequential pattern of abstract entities, and the MAPPING OR ACTUALIZATION of this meter by concrete sequences of words, syllables, or sounds that make up the lines of the poem. This distinction is absolutely fundamental to an understanding of metrics and should constantly be kept in mind. In what follows I shall consider each of the two aspects in turn.

MAPPING RULES

Perhaps the simplest sequential pattern of the type that interests us here is one in which the pattern is constituted by entities of a single type and only their number is subjected to some constraint. Examples of such patterns are

(1)   xxx   xxxx   xxxxxx
             xxx   xxxx   xxxxxx
             xxx   xxxx   xxxxxx

It is obvious that there is an infinity of arrangements of physical objects that can be said to exhibit these patterns: flowers in a flower bed, desks in a classroom, windows on the side of a house, *etc*.

The examples just cited are all of spatial arrangement objects, but it is equally easy to visualize the same patterns implemented in temporal sequences: a series of drum beats; a rudimentary dance consisting of four steps followed by a pause; a series of light flashes; and finally, lines of verse each with an identical number of syllables; as for example the lines in Verlaine's well known

(2a)   O bruit doux de la pluie
                            Par terre et sur les toits!
                            Pour un coeur qui s'ennuie
                            O le chant de la pluie!

all of which are six syllables long. Thus, we may say that the metrical scheme underlying this poem is

$$xxxxxx$$

by virtue of a mapping rule that establishes a one:one correspondence between syllables of the lines and the x's of the metrical pattern.

This, however, is only a first approximation of the correct rule mapping the abstract pattern onto the actual line of verse. One sees this readily if one compares the stanza cited with the one that precedes it in the poem:

(2b)   Il pleure dans mon coeur
                            Comme il pleut sur la ville,
                            Quelle est cette langeur
                            Qui pénètre mon coeur?

If we count the syllables in the first line we notice that there are only five, and the same is true of the third and fourth line of the poem. We note, however, that lines 1 and 4 would be regular if the reduced vowel — the e-*muet* — were to count as a syllable. Unfortunately if we count the e-*muet*, then lines 2 and 3 of the above stanza are irregular: the second line would have eight syllables, and the third line seven. This irregularity, however, is only apparent, not real, for in French verse a reduced vowel is not counted if it immediately precedes another vowel, or if it is the last vowel in the line. It is clear from the preceding, which incidentally does not exhaust all the complications of the subject, that the mapping rule must establish a one:one correspondence NOT between the x's of the meters and the syllables of the line, but rather between the x's of the meters and CERTAIN syllables of the lines. The mapping rule for the main type of French verse would, therefore, read:

(3) Each element of the meter (each x) must correspond either to an e-*muet* followed by consonant or to a vowel other than e-*muet* regardless of context.

Since metrical patterns are separate from the rules that map these patterns onto actual lines of verse, we must expect to find cases where by virtue of totally different mapping rules a given metrical pattern is implemented by totally different verbal material. Compare from this point of view the lines from Hugo's "Le pas d'armes du roi Jean" given in (4a) and the English nursery rimes (4b):

(4a)   M*a* vieille *a*rme
                              E*n*rageait
                              C*ar* m*a* l*a*me
                              Qu*e* r*o*ngea*i*t
                              C*ette* rou*i*lle
                              Qu*i* l*a* sou*i*lle
                              E*n* qu*e*nou*i*lle
                              S*e* ch*a*ngea*i*t

(4b)   A sw*a*rm of b*ee*s in M*a*y
                              is w*o*rth a l*oa*d of h*a*y;
                              A sw*a*rm of b*ee*s in J*u*ne
                              is w*o*rth a s*i*lver sp*oo*n;
                              A sw*a*rm of b*ee*s in Jul*y*
                              *i*s not w*o*rth a fl*y*

In the French example the mapping rule is that of (3). In the English example the mapping rule is

(5) Each element of the meter must correspond to a fully stressed vowel which is neither preceded nor followed directly by a fully stressed vowel that has greater stress.

We see readily that the rime in (4b), has three stressed vowels per line and, therefore, satisfies the same metrical pattern as the Hugo poem, but in a totally different way, by virtue of a totally different mapping rule.

In the nursery rime (4b) that we have just examined, each fully stressed vowel is flanked by unstressed vowels and/or the verse boundary. It would, therefore, seem that the special qualification in (5) concerning the absence of an adjacent vowel with greater stress is not necessary. We see the need for this constraint when we examine the examples (6a) and (6b):

(6a)   R*ai*n, r*ai*n, g*o* aw*a*y
                              C*o*me ag*ai*n an*o*ther d*a*y
                              L*i*ttle J*o*hnny w*a*nts to pl*a*y

(6b)   R*i*de a cock-h*o*rse to B*a*nbury Cr*o*ss
                              To s*ee* a fine l*a*dy up*o*n a white h*o*rse
                              R*i*ngs on her f*i*ngers, b*e*lls on her t*oe*s
                              Sh*e* shall have m*u*sic wher*e*ver she g*oe*s

As the line

                              R*i*ngs on her f*i*ngers, b*e*lls on her t*oe*s

clearly shows, (6b) is a poem consisting of four-unit lines. There are, however, additional stressed vowels in other lines; *e.g.*

                              To s*ee* a f*i*ne l*a*dy up*o*n a wh*i*te horse

where we find six fully stressed vowels. We note, however, that *fine* is subordinate in stress to *lady*, and *white* is subordinate in stress to *horse* by the normal rules of English stress. Hence in line with the qualification in (5) no metrical entity (no x) corresponds to *fine* or to *white*. The line, therefore, has four metrically relevant stresses and can be regarded as being an instance of the pattern $xxxx$.

The situation is somewhat different in (6a). Here in the first line we have three fully stressed monosyllables in a row, but since these are two vocatives followed by an imperative, they all have main stress, as the rules for stress subordination do not operate across major syntactic boundaries. As a result each of the vowels in the first three words is metrically significant and the line is a regular actualization of the pattern $xxxx$.

The meters of English nursery rimes commonly allow one optional x; thus, in addition to the patterns in (6) we have also patterns such as (7) where one of the x's is optional.[1]

(7a) $(x)xx$ Three wise men of Gotham
                      Went to sea in a bowl
                      If the bowl had been stronger
                      My song had been longer

(7b) $(x)xxx$ Thirty days hath September,
                      April, June and November;
                      February has twenty eight alone,
                      All the rest have thirty one,
                      Excepting leap year, that's the time
                      When February's day's are twenty nine.

The mapping rules examined thus far have operated on metrical patterns that are constituted by entities of a single type. There are numerous metrical patterns, however, that are made up of entities of two distinct types, and, as one would expect, the associated mapping rules differ accordingly. The following metrical patterns (to which we return below) illustrate this.

(8)(a) w w s w w w w s   Serbo-Croatian epic decasyllable
   (b) s w s w s w s w s w s s   Classical hexameter
   (c) w s w s w s w s w s   Iambic pentameter

The first meter is that underlying the Serbo-Croation epic decasyllable [2] This poetry, which is still a live form of folk art, has been studied in great detail by R. Jakobson (1932), among others. Jakobson established that the constraints of the so-called epic decasyllable are: the obligatory occurrence of a word boundary after the fourth and the tenth syllable, and the obligatory absence of a word boundary (*zeugma*) after the third and the ninth syllable. This is tantamount to requiring that the third and fourth, and the ninth and tenth syllables in the line be occupied by the last two syllables of a

---

[1] For a discussion of the meter of the Old English alliterating verse which provides instructive parallels to the above, see S. J. Keyser (1968) and Halle and Keyser (1970).
[2] The formulation (8a) was suggested to me by S. Anderson.

word. More formally we may state that the mapping rule for the Serbo-Croatian epic decasyllable is:

(9)(a) the *w*'s of the meter must correspond one:one to the syllables in the line of verse
   (b) the *s*'s of the meter must correspond to a sequence of two syllables which terminate a word.

The mapping rule (9) applies also in other languages. It appears to be operative in the Lithuanian decasyllabic *dainas* (Jakobson, 1952:65). In a slightly modified form it appears to apply in the Russian epic verse, the *byliny* (Jakobson, 1952) and a rule quite similar to (9) applies in the so-called 'trochaic' folk songs of Latvian (of which more, directly below). In the Latvian folk song, moreover, the metrical pattern is not (8a), but rather (10)

(10)   wws wws

This meter, however, is also found in other Slavic languages; *e.g.*, in the Serbo-Croatian laments (*tùžbalice*) (Jakobson, 1935). Finally, in an unpublished study, S. Anderson has noted that the meter of the Icelandic Skalds must be assumed to have the form wwwws and a mapping rule that is quite reminiscent of (9). To what extent these parallels are due to a common source appears at present to be an open question. While the similarities are quite striking and thus would argue in favor of a common source, it must not be overlooked that the similarities concern extremely rudimentary properties of words (mapping rules) and of sequential arrangements of abstract entities (meters). In view of their rudimentary character it is not *a priori* implausible that the parallels are the accidental result of identical inventions made independently in a number of places and periods.

As noted above the mapping rule of the Latvian 'trochaic' folksong is related to (9), but not identical with it. This meter was studied by Zeps (1963), whose discussion is briefly summarized below. If rule (9) had applied to the metrical pattern (10) each well formed line of these songs would have been eight syllables long. Even a very cursory examination of Latvian folksongs reveals numerous lines that are shorter than the required eight syllables [*cf.* (10)]. Modern Latvian (see Halle and Zeps, 1966) is subject to a synchronic phonological rule that truncates a vowel in word final position (and in certain other contexts). As a result a significant proportion of Latvian morphemes appear in a shorter form in word final position than elsewhere. For example, the infinitive suffix is /ti/ and it appears in this form in the middle voice *mazgā+ti+es* 'wash' (*es* is the middle voice marker), whereas in the active voice the vowel of the infinitive suffix is lacking; *e.g.*, *mazgā+t*. The word final reflex of the infinitive suffix /ti/ is derived with the help of the truncation rule (as well as other relevant phonological rules). Zeps (1963) has shown that in the Latvian folk song, many lines that appear to lack syllables would be regular if the words are spelled in their abstract representations; *i.e.*, with the truncated vowels of all morphemes written out:

Forms having a smaller number of syllables after the application of the truncation rule than they had before the application of the truncation rule, are counted as having the larger number if they occur at the end of a colon (half-line —MH); otherwise they may be considered as having either the larger or the smaller number of syllables... (p. 125).

Thus *Rīga dimd* is a correct half-line as it derives from the abstract /Rīgaa dimda/ as is *redzēt Rīgu* 'to see Rīga' from the abstract /reʒēti rīgua/; but *Rīgu redzēt* 'to see Riga' from an abstract /rīgua reʒēti/ is an incorrect half-line as the truncated /i/ at the end of the half-line must be counted, thus yielding one syllable too many. The Latvian folk song meter requires therefore a somewhat more complicated mapping rule than (9):

(11)(a) The *w*'s of the meter must correspond one:one to the syllables of the line of verse either in their surface or in their underlying representation, provided that no more than one syllable be truncated by the truncation rule.

(b) The *s*'s of the meter must correspond to a word final sequence of two syllables in the underlying representation.[3]

The metrical pattern (8b) is that of the classical (Greek) hexameter. It is customary to say that Greek verse is quantitative in that it distinguishes between long and short syllables. It must, however, be noted that 'length' here is not a simple phonetic property. Thus, for instance, the last syllable of a word such as πετρός is metrically long when followed by a word that begins with a consonant, but is metrically short otherwise. There is, of course, no claim intended about the phonetic length of the syllable, which remains the same in all contexts. The mapping rule of the classical hexameter requires therefore a special definition:

(12)(a) *Definition*: A syllable containing a lax vowel separated from the following vowel or from the verse boundary by no more than a single consonant or liquid (but not glide) is METRICALLY SHORT; all other syllables in the line are METRICALLY LONG.

(b) *Mapping rule*: The syllables in the line must correspond to the *s* and *w* of the metrical pattern (8b) in such a way that to each *w* there corresponds either one metrically long syllable or two consecutive metrically short syllables, and a long syllable corresponds to each *s*.

(c) The last syllable of the line may be metrically either short or long.[4]

---

[3] In a recent study of the meter of the Kalevala, Paul Kiparsky (1968) has discussed an even more elaborate example of mapping rules that require reference not to the surface (phonetic) representation of the words, but rather to their abstract (phonological) representation. At the present time I do not know of similar examples from other parts of the world, but it is hardly likely that mapping rules referring to abstract representations quite remote from the surface phonetics should be restricted to a few languages spoken in the Baltic area. As the rest of this paper will hopefully make clear, metrical conventions are of an extremely abstract nature and it is, therefore, to be expected that they may require reference to quite abstract representations of the linguistic material.

[4] As we are not interested here in a detailed examination of the hexameter, I have omitted certain further complications such as the obligatory appearance of a sequence of two metrically short syllables (rather than a single metrically long syllable) in the fifth *w* of the line.

In (13) below I scan two Homeric lines. I have utilized the traditional symbols, the *makron* for metrically long syllables, and the *breve* for metrically short syllables:

(13) *elθe d'epi psūxē mētros kata teθnēuyēs* (λ 84)

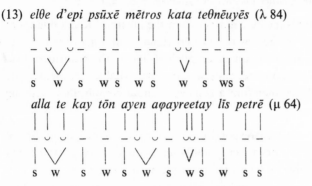

alla te kay tōn ayen aφayreetay līs petrē (μ 64)

The third metrical pattern illustrated in (8) is that of the iambic pentameter, the favorite meter of English poets from Chaucer to the beginning of the twentieth century. The discussion here is quite summary as a more detailed discussion of the problems of this meter has been given by Halle and Keyser (1966), Keyser (1968) and Halle and Keyser (1970). Perhaps the most widely held view concerning the mapping rule of this meter is that:

(14a) Each *s* and *w* of the metrical pattern corresponds to a single syllable of the verse line.

(14b) The stress on a syllable corresponding to a given *s* must be greater than the stress on the syllables corresponding to the *w* that precedes and follows the *s* in question.

It takes little familiarity with the canon of English iambic pentameter verse to discover that the proposed mapping rules are inadequate. As they are somewhat more obvious I shall first examine violations of (14b) and only then turn to violations of (14a). Consider to this end (15)

(15)   The beauty *of* the morning: silent, bare,
              Ships, towers, *domes*, theatres, and temples lie
              Open unto the fields, and *to* the sky,...

Above in the three lines from Wordsworth's sonnet we find six violations of the rule (14b). In the first line an unstressed syllable corresponds to the second *s*; in the second line, the stressed syllables *Ships* and *domes* correspond to the first and second *w* of the meter; and in the third line the first *w* corresponds to a stressed syllable, the first and the fourth *s* correspond to unstressed syllables. These violations of (14b) in a poem by one of the best poets of the language show that (14b) does not correctly characterize the English iambic pentameter; it must be replaced by (16):

(16) *w* may not correspond to a stress maximum *i.e.*, to a syllable that by the normal English rules of stress subordination carries more stress than the two vowels adjacent to it.

The mapping rule (16) does not require that a stress minimum correspond to a w; it only prohibits a stress maximum from corresponding to a w. Hence the unstressed fourth syllable in the first line of (15) is not a violation. The second line of (15) is a list of nouns. Hence the rules of stress subordination do not apply here, and the four first words have all the same stress. Since none is a stress maximum the line does not violate the mapping rule (16). Note, moreover, that the first syllable in a line can never be a stress maximum as it is not adjacent to two syllables. This fact is important in the third line where the stress on the first syllable is greater than that on the second. Since the first syllable is not a stress maximum however, the line does not violate the mapping rule (16).

The concept of the stress maximum makes it possible, thus, to account for the fact that a considerable variety of stress configurations in lines of verse are lawful instances of the iambic pentameter. In more traditional treatments of metrics these facts are accounted for differently. Lines satisfying (14b) are regarded as basic; stress configurations that are not covered by (14b) yet are found in metrically regular iambic pentameter lines are treated by being included in a list of 'allowable deviations'. The disadvantage of listing such phenomena as 'allowable deviations' in this way is that it provides no general characterization of the set of 'allowable deviation'; *i.e.*, it fails to provide criteria for deciding whether or not a given deviation will be 'allowable'. That the formulation (16) provides the criteria for making this decision has been illustrated by the discussion of the lines from Wordsworth quoted in (15), and this is a point in favor of the proposed formulation.

The formulation (16) fails, however, to draw another distinction that plays an important role in metrics; it does not differentiate between a rudimentary and a complex, highly unusual actualization of a given metrical pattern. *E.g.*, if we compare the two lines (17a) and (17b):

(17a)　　　　　　　　　　the curfew tolls the knell of dying day

(17b)　　　　　　　　　　of man's first disobedience and the fruit

It is obvious that (17b) is a much more complex, a much more marked line than (17a), yet looked upon from the point of view of the mapping rule (16) both are lawful actualizations of the iambic pentameter and nothing more.

These differences in complexity can be brought out if (16) is restated so as to spell out its positive consequences:

(18) w may not correspond to a stress maximum; it may, therefore, be occupied by a $\begin{Bmatrix} \text{unstressed} \\ \text{stressed} \end{Bmatrix}$ syllable

　　(a) in verse medial position which has $\begin{Bmatrix} \text{lower stress than} \\ \text{the same stress as} \end{Bmatrix} \begin{Bmatrix} \text{both} \\ \text{one} \end{Bmatrix}$ of the syllables adjacent to it.

(b) in verse terminal (*i.e.*, absolute initial or final) position which has

$$\begin{bmatrix} \text{lower stress than} \\ \text{the same stress as} \\ \text{greater stress than} \end{bmatrix} \text{ the syllable adjacent to it}$$

The phrases enclosed in braces represent different alternatives. The formulation (18a) describes, therefore, eight separate regular actualizations of *w* in verse medial position, and the formulation (18b) describes six regular actualizations of *w* in verse terminal position. At first sight (18) may appear to be superior to a list of 'allowable deviations' only in that it includes in its preamble an abstract characterization of the set of 'allowable deviations'. But this overlooks the fact that (18) contains a formal means for judging the complexity of different actualizations, for the alternatives in the braces have been arranged so that later alternatives are more complex than earlier ones. The eight alternatives contained in (18a) are:

(19)   (i)   *w* is occupied by an unstressed syllable that has lower stress than both of the syllables adjacent to it: *e.g.*,

Enfolding *sunny spots* of greenery   (Coleridge, "Kubla Khan")

(ii)   *w* is occupied by an unstressed syllable that has lower stress than one of the syllables adjacent to it; *e.g.*,

Not charioted by *Bacchus and his pards*
(Keats, "Ode to a Nightingale")

COMMENT 1: Since any line satisfying (19i) will also satisfy (19ii), it will be assumed that the different alternatives are disjunctively ordered, so that in evaluating a given part of a line of verse the statements in (19) are applied in the order given and the first applicable statement is taken as the proper characterization of the part of the line under consideration. *Cf.* Comment 2 below.

(iii)   *w* is occupied by an unstressed syllable that has the same stress as both syllables adjacent to it; *e.g.*,[5]

Young Lyci*das, and hath* not left his peer   (Milton, "Lycidas")

(iv)   *w* is occupied by an unstressed syllable that has the same stress as one of the syllables adjacent to it,

COMMENT 2: Since in case (iv) *w* is occupied by an unstressed syllable, a syllable that has the same stress will also be unstressed, hence (iv) will always be a special instance of either (ii) or (iii). In view of the principle of disjunctive ordering (*cf.* Comment 1 above) the situation in which (iv) is applied can never arise.

---

[5]   We shall assume that in evaluating stress differences for purposes of the mapping rules the non-main stresses on full words as well as on monosyllabic auxiliary verbs, pronouns, prepositions, and conjunctions are treated on a par with totally stressless syllables.

(v) *w* is occupied by a stressed syllable that has lower stress than both of the syllables adjacent to it; *e.g.,*

> (Driving sweet *buds like flocks* to feed in air)
> (Shelley, "Ode to the West Wind")

(vi) *w* is occupied by a stressed syllable that has lower stress than one of the syllables adjacent to it; *e.g.,*[6]

> The course of *true love ne*ver did run smooth
> (Shakespeare, "A Midsummer Night's Dream", I, 1.)

> Ere half my days in *this dark world* and wide
> (Milton, "On his Blindness")

(vii) *w* is occupied by a stressed syllable that has the same stress as both of the syllables adjacent to it; *e.g.,*

> Rocks, *caves, lakes, fens,* bogs, dens, and shades of death
> (Milton, "Paradise Lost", ii, 621)

(viii) *w* is occupied by a stressed syllable that has the same stress as one of the syllables adjacent to it; *e.g.,*

> O, *wild West Wind,* thou breath of Autumn's being
> (Shelley, "Ode to the West Wind)

COMMENT 3: In view of the principle of disjunctive ordering (see comment 1) the only instances covered by (viii) will be lines where the equally stressed syllables adjoin a syllable that has lower stress, since all instances where they adjoin a syllable that has greater stress are covered by (vi).

Since it is perfectly self-evident I shall not expand (18b). It must, however, be remarked that because of the principle of disjunctive ordering only five of the six possible cases will ever be applicable.

As noted above later alternatives among the statements in (19) describe more complex actualizations. As a first approximation one might propose that (19i) be assigned a complexity of zero, (19ii) a complexity of one, *etc.,* and that a parallel scale be associated with (18b). Given such a scale the complexity of a line of verse can readily be computed. To illustrate such a computation consider the lines in (17). In (17a) all verse medial *w*'s are occupied by unstressed syllables that have less stress than the two syllables adjacent to them. The complexity of these *w*'s is therefore equal to zero. The verse initial *w* is occupied by an unstressed syllable that has lower stress than the syllable following. It has, therefore, also a complexity of zero. The line (17a) is, therefore, a totally unmarked line, a line that is metrically as 'simple' as possible.

The situation is somewhat different in (17b). The verse initial *w* is occupied by the word *of* which has lower stress than the immediately following *man's*. The complexity of this *w* is, therefore, zero. The second *w* in the line is occupied by *first* which is stressed, but its stress is lower than that on the following syllable *dis*, but metrically

---

[6] We assume here that adjective+noun collocations are not subject to stress subordination; *i.e.,* have "level stress"; see Halle and Keyser (1966).

equal to that of the preceding *man's*; it is, therefore, an instance of (19vi) and its complexity is 5. The third *w*, which corresponds to the *o* in *disobedience*, is an instance of (19ii). Since it has less stress than the following but not the preceding syllable its complexity is one. The fourth *w*, corresponding to the syllable *ience* in *disobedience* is again an instance of (19ii) and has, therefore, a complexity of one. Finally, the fifth *w* of the line *the* must again be assigned a complexity of one, as it has less stress than the following *fruit* but not less stress than the preceding *and*. The complexity of (17b) is, therefore, equal to eight, whereas that of (17a) was zero. The numbers in this case correctly reflect the different complexities of the two lines. It is, however, still an open question whether as the proposal is applied to a larger body of data the complexity assignments will properly reflect the intuitive judgments of complexity made by qualified readers of poetry.

Violations of (14a); *i.e.*, of the convention that there be a one:one correspondence between the syllables of the line of verse and the *w* and *s* of the metrical pattern can readily be found in the standard iambic pentameter verse.

(20a)   All other loving *being* estranged or dead
                                        (W. B. Yeats "After long silence")

(20b)   Yet dearl*y I* love *you a*nd would be lovèd fain
                                        (J. Donne, Holy Sonnet XIV).

(20c)   His temple right against the temp*le of* God
                                        (J. Milton, "Paradise Lost", I, 402)

To account for these examples it is necessary to modify (14a) to:

(21) each *s* and *w* of the metrical pattern corresponds to a single syllable of the verse
      line except that they may correspond to two consecutive syllables if the syllabic

      phonemes of these syllables are $\begin{cases} \text{directly adjacent to} \\ \text{separated by a sonorant from} \end{cases}$ each other

Hence (20b) is scanned as follows:

$$\text{yet dearly I love you and would be lovèd fain}$$
$$| \quad |\diagdown\diagup \quad | \quad \diagdown\diagup \quad \quad | \quad | \; | \; | \quad |$$
$$\text{w} \quad \text{s} \;\; \text{w} \quad \text{s} \quad \text{w} \quad \quad \text{s} \quad \text{w} \;\text{s}\; \text{w} \quad \text{s}$$

It should be noted that only if the syllables of the verse are placed in correspondence with the *s* and *w* of the metrical pattern in the above manner can it be shown that the condition on stress distribution (16) is satisfied. In addition, there is the possibility of letting the first *w* in the line be unactualized thereby creating the so-called HEADLESS LINE:

(22)   twenty bokes clad in blak or redd   (Chaucer, CT, A. Prol, 294)
              while their hearts were jocund and sublime
                                        (J. Milton, "Samson Agonistes", 1669)

Finally, extrametrical syllables are freely admitted at the end of the line and, very infrequently, before major syntactic breaks within the line.

(23)   of rebel angels, by whose aid aspir*ing*   (J. Milton, "Par. Lost", I, 38)

farewell thou art too dear for my possess*ing*

(Shakespeare, Sonnett 87)

and as I past I wor*shipt*: if those you seek   (Milton, "Comus", 302)

from mine own know*ledge*. As nearly as I may

(Shakespeare, "Anthony and Cleopatra", II, 2.)

These facts can be readily accounted for by appropriate extensions of the mapping rule, but as they appear to have only little general theoretical interest we shall not do so here.[7]

ABSTRACT METRICAL PATTERNS

In the construction of the metrical patterns a number of quite obvious constraints are at work. First, the length of the verse line is limited; it can probably be safely restricted to a maximum of twenty or thirty sequential entities of which patterns in excess of twelve or fifteen are quite rare. Moreover, metrical patterns are composed of entities of one, two, or, at most, three types. Patterns composed of entities of a single type were illustrated above in our discussion of the meters of standard French poetry and of English pure stress verse. Patterns composed of entities of two types were illustrated in (8) above and the discussion following. Patterns composed of entities of three distinct types are exceedingly rare; the only meters of this kind known to me are certain of the meters of pre-Islamic Arabic poetry (*i.e.*, the meters of the so-called fourth cycle; *cf*. M. Halle (1966)).

Meters composed of entities of a single type can restrict only the number of entities per line. Meters composed of entities of two types exhibit additional regularities. One may first distinguish meters that are PERIODIC from those that are APERIODIC. Periodic meters consist of repetitions of relatively simple subsequences, traditionally called FEET. Periodic meters are familiar from much of Western poetry; *e.g.*, the favorite meters of English and Russian poetry are periodic, as are those of classical antiquity.

Since the number of entities in a foot is restricted — apparently this number must not exceed four (hyper-dactyls, *etc*.) — the variety of feet, and hence, also of periodic meters, is severely restricted. Moreover, we usually find that if a given poetic tradition utilizes periodic meters it will utilize all possible feet that can be generated by cyclical permutation from the basic type of foot. This fact was explicitly recognized over a thousand years ago by the founder of Arabic prosody, Al Xalil, who represented the sixteen traditional meters of pre-Islamic Arabic poetry with the help of five circles such as the one shown in (24).

To obtain an actual meter one can start at any point along the circumference of the circle and copy the entities in the order given. Thus to generate the meter termed *hazaǰ* one must begin with an *s* and follow the procedure just outlined. The mapping

---

[7]   Since this was written in 1967 we have had occasion to go over much of the above material again. This review has led us to modify some of the theoretical formulations. The new results will be found in Halle and Keyser (1970).

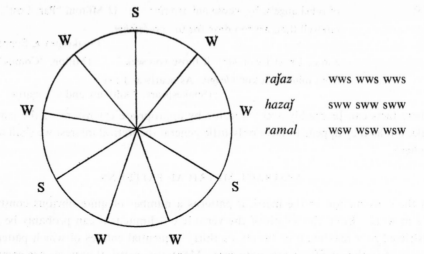

rules for this type of verse are quite different from those discussed above, and hence the phonetic configurations that one finds in Arabic verse lines are quite different from those found in Western verse. Nonetheless the underlying metrical pattern of the *hazaǰ* is the same as that of the dactylic trimeter.

While periodic meters are composed of identical subsequences, the component parts of aperiodic meters are different one from another. Thus, the meter of the Serbo-Croatian epic verse exemplified above in (8a) and repeated here as

(25)   WWS WWWWWS

consists of the two parts separated above by a space. These two parts are identical in their terminations but differ in the number of *w* that precede the terminal *s*.

The Vedic meters, *jagatī* and *triṣṭubh*, are aperiodic meters of a different type. They differ from one another in that the former is twelve, whereas the latter is eleven syllables long. While the quantity of the first seven syllables of the line is free, the quantity of the remaining syllables 8, 9, 10, 11, (12), presents the alternation '*short, long, short, long, (short)* where length and shortness of syllables is defined as in (12a) and the quantity of the last syllable is free as noted in (12c). Assuming the mapping rule (26)

(26)   *s* must correspond to a metrically long syllable, *w* must correspond to a metri-
       cally short syllable

       x must correspond to a single syllable without limitation as to its quantity;

the metrical pattern of the Vedic meters is

(27)   x x x x x x x w s w s (w)

i.e., a metrical pattern consisting of two parts, one in which only the number of syllables is regulated and the second, in which both the number of syllables and their quantity is subject to rule.

A somewhat higher degree of organization is to be found in the Greek Alcaic and

Sapphic meters, which according to Meillet (1923) are genetically related to the two Vedic metres just discussed. The Alcaic and Sapphic are subject to mapping rules that are practically identical to (26). The lines of the verse are eleven syllables long and reflect the metrical patterns

(28) *Alcaic*   w s w s w w s w s w s

     Sapphic   s w s w s w w s w s w

The first observation to be made about these two meters is that the latter can be derived from the former by moving the initial *w* to the end of the line (cyclical permutation). As pointed out to me by J. R. Ross, the two metrical patterns are mirror images of each other; both are structured around the verse central *w*. This *w* is flanked on both sides by subsequences of five units which are made up of alternations of *w* and *s*. In the Alcaic the alternation begins with a *w* in the initial subsequence and with *s* in the subsequence following the verse central *w*. In the Sapphic, on the other hand, the alternations begin with *s* to the left of the verse central *w*, and with *w* to the right of it. The Vedic meters show the same type of alternation of *w* and *s*, except that there the alternation began with the eighth position in the verse [*cf.* (27)]. The Vedic meter is thus less highly structured than the Alcaic and the Sapphic, since in the latter the quantity of all syllables in the verse is regulated, whereas in the former the quantity of the first seven syllables is free.

The most complicated of the aperiodic meters known to me is that of the Regulated Verse of Chinese poetry of the Tang dynasty. Before examining the metrical pattern it is necessary to sketch briefly the mapping rule of this meter. This language of the Tang poets had four tones, of which two were level (*pyng*) and two, deflected (*tsê*). I assume that in the operation of the mapping rules a feature was associated with each syllable which classed it as either [+ level] or [− level]. The question as to the phonetic nature of this feature must remain open for the present, since there is yet very little understanding of the nature of the framework of the prosodic features. We shall, however, adopt here the convention standard in phonological descriptions of representing the coefficients of features by variables, utilizing to this end the lower case Greek letters. The variables can assume the two values, '+' or '−', and can be negated in the standard fashion so that if '$\alpha = -$', then '$-\alpha = +$', and if '$\alpha = +$' then '$-\alpha = -$'.

Unlike the verse that has been examined to this point the lines of a Tang poem are not composed of a single meter. However, although the metrical patterns differ in different lines, all the lines are constructed in accordance with the same rule (29):[8]

(29) In every line let the second position be occupied by a syllable with tonal value [α level], and the fifth position by a syllable with tonal value [β level]. The first position must then be occupied by a syllable with tonal value [α level], and the

---

[8] These comments are restricted to five syllable verses. Longer verse types are constructed in accordance with the same principles.

fourth position by a syllable with tonal value $[-\alpha$ level], whereas the third position must be occupied by a syllable with tonal value $[-\beta$ level].

The values of α and β, moreover, are free only in the second line of the poem. If '$\alpha = \gamma$' in the second line, then '$\alpha = \gamma$' also in lines 3, 6, and 7; and '$\alpha = -\gamma$' in lines 1, 4, 5, and 8. If '$\beta = \delta$' in the second line, then '$\beta = \delta$' in all even numbered lines (since these must rime), and '$\beta = -\delta$' in all odd numbered lines except for the first line where β may also equal δ.

Utilizing these rules one can generate eight distinct metrical patterns for a poem, of which (30) illustrates one:

(30)

$$
\begin{array}{ccccc}
+ & + & - & - & + \\
- & - & + & + & - \\
- & - & - & + & + \\
+ & + & + & - & - \\
+ & + & - & - & + \\
- & - & + & + & - \\
- & - & - & + & - \\
+ & + & + & - & + \\
\end{array}
$$

CONCLUSION

In the preceding we have illustrated a number of metrical patterns from a variety of languages and poetic traditions, and we also have examined several different kinds of mapping rules; *i.e.*, rules that relate the abstract metrical patterns to concrete lines of verse. Perhaps the main conclusion to be drawn from the study of metrical patterns is that these are of an extreme simplicity and that as a consequence there appear to be few important restrictions other than those limiting the length of the line and/or the foot as well as the number of different kinds of entity that constitute the pattern. I was struck by the similarity between the metrical patterns and the patterns used in threading looms or those encountered in certain very rudimentary types of ornament. Because of the utter simplicity of these patterns it is hardly surprising that they are found in the most diverse languages and in widely separated areas. A consequence of this observation is that extreme caution must be exercised in postulating genetic relationships between meters in even genetically related languages.

Unlike the metrical patterns, the mapping rules which relate the patterns to concrete instances of verse are of considerable variety. Nonetheless some important regularities may be observed here. Metrical entities are apparently mapped into syllables, morae, or sequences of syllables or of morae. In the simplest cases there is a one:one relationship between the entities of the meter and the syllables of the line of verse. In more complicated cases additional conditions are imposed; *e.g.*, the syllable must possess some phonetic property such as a particular stress, pitch or length; or the metrical entity must be mapped into more than one syllable; or the syllable must occupy a particular position in the word; or it must begin with a particular consonant (alliteration). *etc*, It is surely no accident that the so-called prosodic features of stress, pitch or length invariably play a primary role in the mapping rules, and it is obvious that one must try to find reasons for these observations.

As every reader of poetry knows not all actualizations of a given meter are equal. Donne's and Milton's pentameters are considerably more elaborate, less simple than those of Pope or Gray. Accordingly, I have attempted to advance some suggestions as to how the mapping rules might be formulated so as to distinguish not only metrical from unmetrical lines but also less complex from more complex mappings of a given metrical pattern. These suggestions are obviously in need of much further study. In particular, these phenomena must now be explored in languages other than English, for without such information it will be impossible to gain insights into the general properties of metrical 'markedness' or complexity.

Beyond this there remain questions of general interest such as the relation between the mapping rules favored by a particular language and the phonetic properties of the language, or the limitations that the human perceptual mechanism imposes on the variety and complexity of the metrical patterns and of the mapping. Even our present, rudimentary knowledge of these facts makes it appear that the relatively simple answers that have been given to these questions in the past are inadequate. There is, for instance, no direct relationship between the phonetic features that function to distinguish minimal pairs in a language and the phonetic features that play a role in the mapping rules of that language. However, it is clearly no accident that in French, *e.g.*, stress plays no role either in the mapping rules or in the rules that determine the phonetic constitution of words. At present not much is known about the reasons for these and similar facts. There is, however, little doubt that the attempt to find these reasons will lead to new and fruitful insights.

This work was supported in part by the National Institutes of Mental Health (Grant MH-13390).

REFERENCES

Halle, M.,
1966 "On the metrics of pre Islamic Arabic poetry", MIT–RLE, *QPR* 83: 113-6.
Halle, M. and S. J. Keyser,
1966 "Chaucer and the study of prosody", *College English*, 28: 187-219.
Halle, M. and S. J. Keyser,
1970 *English Stress: Its Form, Growth and Utilization in Verse*
Halle, M. and V. J. Zeps,
1966 "A Survey of Latvian Morphophonemics", MIT – RLE, *QPR* 83: 105-13.
Jakobson, R.,
1952 "Studies in Comparative Slavic Metrics", *Selected Writings* IV: 414:465.
Jakobson, R.,
1932 "Über den Versbau der serbokroatischen Volksepen", *Selected Writings* IV: 51-60.

Keyser, S. J.,
    1968   "The Linguistic basis of English Prosody", in: S. Schane and D. Reibel, eds., *Modern Studies in English*.

Kiparsky, P.,
    1968   "Metrics and Morphophonemics in the Kalevala", *Studies Presented to Professor Roman Jakobson by His Students*.

Meillet, A.,
    1923   *Les origines indo-européennes des mètres grecs* (Paris).

Zeps, V. J.,
    1963   "The meter of the so-called trochaic Latvian folksongs", *Journal of Slavic Linguistics and Poetics*, 7: 123-8.

DAVID G. HAYS*

LINGUISTIC PROBLEMS OF DENOTATION

My topic is knowledge. I propose a form for the representation of what a person knows, demanding of this form that it permit convenient characterization of four classes of processes: SPEAKING, UNDERSTANDING speech, THINKING, and OBSERVING, *i.e.*, the perception of all that is not speech. Two of these processes are linguistic, two psychological.

My position is psycholinguistic, not philosophical. A philosopher can be satisfied with the detection of fallacies; psychology and linguistics must account for their human possibility. A philosopher can study DENOTATION as a relation between words and things; if we are not to confound linguistics and psychology, we must give each its

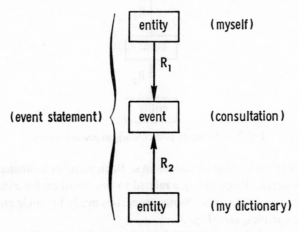

Fig. 1 — An event statement

* Any views expressed in this Paper are those of the author. They should not be interpreted as reflecting the views of The RAND Corporation or the official opinion or policy of any of its governmental or private research sponsors.

This Paper was prepared for presentation at the Xth International Congress of Linguists, Bucharest, August 28-September 2, 1967, and will appear (without illustrations) in the *Proceedings* of the Congress.

share of the denotation problem. A suitable form for the representation of knowledge would help us do so by isolating linguistic from psychological processes.

Part of a person's knowledge is knowledge of individual things. Perhaps it will help to make this discussion comprehensible if we imagine a person's knowledge as a network in which some of the nodes represent things. One node in my own network represents my desk, another my wife, another my unabridged English dictionary. Call these nodes ENTITIES (see Fig. 1).

One kind of knowledge that a person has about things is that they have participated in certain events. I know that my wife bought new shoes for our children yesterday because she told me so; I know that I looked for a word in my dictionary yesterday, and found a remarkable definition, because I participated in that event. Some of the nodes in the network represent actions; call them EVENTS. An EVENT STATEMENT consists of an event and one or more entities. Typically, because things endure, a single entity participates in many statements, whereas an event is related to only a few entities (see Fig. 2).

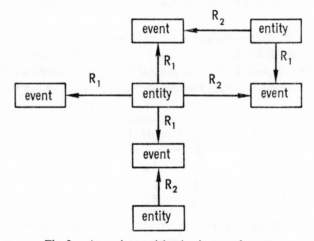

Fig. 2 — An entity participating in several events

Another class of nodes is that of PROPERTIES. Each member is labeled with the name of a different property. Properties are related to one another, for example, by IMPLICATION or by MUTUAL EXCLUSION. Some properties apply to single entities or events, others to couples, triples, *etc*. (Fig. 3).

Entities, events, and properties can have names (Fig. 4). (To suppose that their names are ordinary words of the speaker's natural language would be to forget the intervening linguistic process.) Entities, therefore, differ from one another in three ways. (i) The properties applied to them can differ. (ii) They can have different names. (iii) They can participate in different event statements. These entities, be it remembered, are the things that exist for a certain person. In an imaginary world there are presumably some individuals for whom Clark Kent and Superman are one entity, and

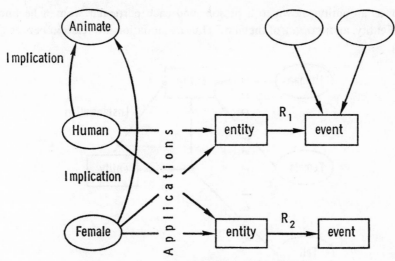

Fig. 3 — Relations among properties and entities

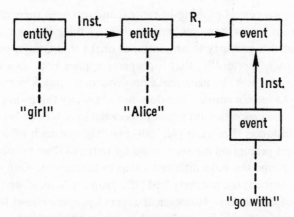

Fig. 4 — Naming

others for whom they are two. Whatever the proper treatment of this problem may be in philosophy, a linguistic model of human performance must allow speakers to disagree with each other about what entities exist.

Because entities are in the mind of the individual, they can be fictitious or real with respect to the external universe. A person not only knows certain facts, he knows how he knows them. One way to account for second-order knowledge is to include such properties as 'being real', 'being fictitious', etc. However, a person often knows that a certain fact was told him in a particular conversation; statements can be participants in statements.

A man may know many women, including his wife, as individuals. He also knows that certain properties apply to women in general. I propose to regard 'woman in general' as an entity known to a person, and each particular woman he knows as another entity, an INSTANCE of the first. Thus instantiation is a relation between nodes (Fig. 5).

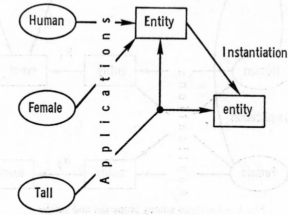

Fig. 5. — Instantiation

With respect to properties of thing-in-general and instance, there are several possibilities. (i) A person knows that a property applies to a thing-in-general; he can deduce the application of this property to any instance of the thing, or he can fail to do so. (ii) A person knows, specifically, that a property applies both to a thing-in-general and to one of its instances; he need make no deduction. (iii) A person knows that a property applies to certain entities, but does not know any things-in-general to which it applies. (iv) Some properties are relations between instances or between a thing-in-general and an instance. For example, 'tall' and 'big' are such RELATIVE properties.

Objects of direct perception are recognized by virtue of their properties. That is to say, entities and properties have different status in perception. One sees not redness but a red-haired woman; the property 'red', the property 'female' and others are used to identify the object one sees. However, the form I propose allows for knowledge of entities that are not perceptible. Seeing a horse is one thing, seeing a mother's love for her child is another. The use of such a term as *love* depends upon operations with stored knowledge, and not directly on perception.

Events are related to one another, *e.g.* by 'causality' and 'sequence', although sequencing alone is not enough to account for a person's time sense; a representation of the time line is needed.

The first stage in understanding an utterance is linguistic processing; the result is a network comparable to the one already stored in the hearer's mind. The next stage is identification of known entities, either directly by virtue of a proper name, or indirectly by way of event statements. One says *the girl I went to the movies with last night*..., and if the hearer already knows of that event the identification is made, unless he believes that two girls were involved. If an entity is new, the listener must decide whether it is a thing-in-general or an instance. Languages provide clues, but there can be ambiguity: *A leaf is born in the Spring and dies in the Fall*. Is this the 'leaf'-in-general, or a particular 'leaf' about which the author plans to tell us more? In any case, the new entity must be added to the listener's knowledge, at least temporarily and perhaps permanently.

The next stage is testing compatibility of the content of the new utterance with prior knowledge. If one hears the property 'green' applied to the entity 'idea', he can make several tests. If 'green' is not a known property of 'idea'-in-general, or of a thing-in-general with properties implied by the properties of 'idea' (or instances of such an entity), the hearer can reject what he has heard.

A *colorful ball* is accepted by the same procedure, since 'ball' is an instance of a thing-in-general with the property 'solid' or 'physical object', and many instances of 'physical object' have color properties.

Compatibility testing can also use event statements. Generalizations are event statements in which the entities are things-in-general. If a person understands *alligator shoes* and *horse shoes* differently, it is because he knows that 'horses wear shoes' (*i.e.*, 'horse'-in-general), that 'some shoes are made of alligator hide', and so on.

The properties an individual uses in thinking about his world are related to one another and applied to entities. That part of a person's knowledge comprising properties, entities, events, and their names, but no relationships among entities and events, can be called a DICTIONARY. Processes of thought that use these elements and the linkages among them can be called INTENSIONAL; an utterance is analytic for the hearer if he can verify it within this part of his knowledge. Instantial entities, the application of properties to them, and event statements in which they participate, refer in basic cases to the world outside the knower. How a person relates perception to knowledge is the psychological problem of DENOTATION. Generalizations, which have the same form as referential statements and property applications, must aid perception of situations in which new instances of known kinds of objects appear. All knowledge outside the dictionary is ENCYCLOPEDIC.

The uniformity of human culture and language argues that the form in which knowledge is stored is innate, but most of the content is learned and no person knows all about his world or his own language. Some few PROPERTIES must be available to almost every human creature, but others are available only in one culture or one art. What is analytic to most adults may be a mere fact to every child. Learning includes the addition of event statements, instantial and general; formation of generalizations; and establishment of new properties. How learning takes place is a psychological problem; linguistics can help solve it by contributing to knowledge about knowledge.

I believe that the form I propose here, which separates dictionary and encyclopedia conceptually but links them substantively, deserves further consideration. I believe yet more strongly that discovery of a suitable form for representation of knowledge is crucial for the future of linguistics: to clarify its role *viz-a-viz* psychology, to escape some philosophical dilemmas, and to guide theorization about the processes of speaking and understanding.

KARL ERICH HEIDOLPH

ZUR BEDEUTUNG NEGATIVER SÄTZE

(1) Die linguistische Entwicklung der letzten Jahre gibt die Möglichkeit, einige der Fragen genauer zu formulieren und versuchsweise zu beantworten, die mit der semantischen Struktur negativer Sätze verbunden sind.[1] In diesem Beitrag geht es um die folgenden Teilfragen:

(a) Gibt es zu jedem positiven Satz genau einen negativen und umgekehrt?
(b) Haben die negativen Sätze in demselben Sinn eine Bedeutung wie die positiven Sätze?
(c) Können die semantischen Momente des Verständnisses negativer Sätze von den pragmatischen isoliert werden?
(d) Welchen semantischen und pragmatischen Status hat das Negationselement selbst?

SEMANTISCHE UND SYNTAKTISCHE VORAUSSETZUNGEN

(2) Die Satzbedeutungen können nicht als bloße Mengen von semantischen Merkmalen betrachtet werden, die nur durch die mit ihnen verbundenen syntaktischen Strukturen gegliedert und organisiert werden.[2] Sie haben ihre eigene Struktur, die von der syntaktischen Struktur unabhängig ist und durch die folgenden Faktoren bestimmt ist:

(a) Beim Verständnis des Satzes wird die Satzbedeutung auf Objekte oder Klassen von Objekten bezogen. Die Merkmale, die zur Satzbedeutung gehören, werden von den Objekten prädiziert. Die Objekte spielen die Rolle von Argumenten.[3]

---

[1] Speziell die Arbeiten von Katz und Fodor (1963), Katz (1966), und Bierwisch (1967) zur Theorie der Semantik und die Arbeiten von Klima (1964), Katz und Postal (1964), Kraak (1966), Lakoff (1965), die teils speziell die Syntax und Semantik negativer Sätze betreffen, teils die Probleme der negativen Sätze berühren, außerdem die Arbeit von Wierzbicka (1967), die semantische und pragmatische Gesichtspunkte einbezieht.

[2] Vergleiche die Diskussion über komplexe semantische Marker bei Bierwisch (1967:1-10); für das folgende, siehe Bierwisch (1967:26-27).

[3] Vergleiche die Tiefenstruktur, die Bach den Nominalphrasen zuschreibt. Die Nomina sind Bach zufolge Prädikative zu Konstituenten, die mit Bezeichnungen für Individuen besetzt sind. In der Oberflächenstruktur erscheinen nur die Nomina.

Die semantischen Strukturen haben Leerstellen für solche Argumente.[4]
(b) Die semantischen Merkmale sind bezüglich der Objekte, die als Argumente fungieren, Prädikate erster, zweiter usw. Stufe.[5]
(c) Die semantischen Merkmale bilden, entsprechend der Anzahl ihrer Argumente, verschiedene Klassen (Bierwisch, 1967: 26).
(d) Zwischen den semantischen Merkmalen gibt es Beziehungen der gegenseitigen Toleranz, der Implikation, der Äquivalenz und des gegenseitigen Ausschlusses.[6]

Die unter (a-d) genannten Faktoren haben zur Folge, daß Satzbedeutungen Komplexe von Merkmalen mit selbständiger Struktur sind.

(3) Die unter (d) genannten Eigenschaften der semantischen Merkmale liegen mit den in (b) und (c) genannten Eigenschaften nicht in einer Linie. Wenn nämlich zwei Merkmale M und N in einer Satzbedeutung als Prädikate verschiedener Stufe auftreten, so daß M ein modifizierendes Prädikat von N ist, während N unmittelbar von einem Objekt a prädiziert wird, dann drückt sich diese Beziehung unmittelbar in der Struktur der Satzbedeutung aus. Strukturen wie $M(a)$ sind ausgeschlossen, Verstöße sind nicht interpretierbar (*Peter ist sehr).

Die unter (d) genannten Beziehungen zwischen den semantischen Merkmalen wirken sich auf die Wohlgeformtheit der Satzbedeutungen aus, sind aber nicht konstitutiv für die Hierarchie innerhalb der Satzbedeutung. Wenn die Geltung eines Merkmals M von einem Objekt a impliziert, daß auch $N(a)$ gilt, so sind doch die beiden Merkmale innerhalb der Satzbedeutung nur konjunktiv miteinander verknüpft. Die unter (d) genannten Beziehungen zwischen den Merkmalen legen die Kookkurrenzmöglichkeiten der Merkmale innerhalb der Satzbedeutungen fest. Sie werden für die Struktur der Satzbedeutungen von negativen Sätzen relevant, weil sie Einfluß auf die Abgrenzung zwischen affirmativer Basis und Domäne der Negation haben.[7]
(4) Wenn zwei Merkmale P und Q miteinander äquivalent sind, dann enthält eine Satzbedeutung S, in der P von einem Objekt a prädiziert wird, auch eine Prädikation $Q(a)$ und umgekehrt. Wenn $P(a)$ fehlt, muß auch $Q(a)$ fehlen und umgekehrt. Die beiden Merkmale FUNDIEREN SICH GEGENSEITIG. Die semantischen Marker wie z.B. physisches Objekt, Lebewesen, Mensch usw. dürften u.a. jeweils Komplexe von Merk-

---

[4] Der Bezug auf unterschiedliche Objekte allein konstituiert natürlich nicht verschiedene Satzbedeutungen. Sonst müßte der Satz Der Junge muß sich erst noch die Hände waschen verschiedene Bedeutungen haben, je nach dem, ob der Junge auf Thomas oder auf Klaus referiert. Die Besetzung der Leerstellen mit Objekts-Indices spielt u.a. bei der Reflexivierung und bei unterschiedlichen Arten der Pronominalisierung eine Rolle. Es wird hier davon abgesehen, daß die Argumente, die in die Satzbedeutungen eingehen eigentlich nicht einzelne Objekte sondern jeweils Objektsmengen sind: Peter, Klaus und Thomas ziehen sich zurück.
[5] In dem Satz Die Kinder singen zu tief enthalten Kinder und singen Merkmale, die sich als Prädikate erster Stufe auf bestimmte Objekte beziehen. Tief enthält Merkmale, die sich nicht auf diese Objekte, sondern auf die in singen enthaltenen Merkmale beziehen.
[6] Vergleiche Katz (1966:229-236), wo die Rolle der Implikatonsbeziehungen für die Redundanzregeln behandelt wird. Zu den semantischen Markern, siehe § 4.
[7] Siehe unten § 12.

malen enthalten, die sich gegenseitig fundieren (Bierwisch, 1967:1-2). Die Merkmale, die einem Objekt Ausdehnung und Gewicht zuschreiben und das Objekt als Körper charakterisieren, scheinen nur zusammen aufzutreten. Merkmale, die von demselben anderen Merkmal fundiert werden, bilden ein Paradigma. Zwischen zwei Merkmalen P und Q, die zu einem Paradigma gehören, kann gegenseitige EXKLUSION bestehen. Besteht ein solches Verhältnis, dann kann in einer Satzbedeutung S nur entweder P ODER Q von einem Objekt a prädiziert werden. Merkmale P und Q, die sich gegenseitig ausschließen, müssen entweder direkt von einem Merkmal R fundiert sein, oder sie müssen fundiert sein von Merkmalen P' bzw. Q', die ihrerseits untereinander exklusiv sind und von einem Merkmal R fundiert werden.[8]

Zwei Merkmale, die sich gegenseitig ausschließen, können nur dann innerhalb einer Satzbedeutung S von demselben Objekt a prädiziert werden, wenn eine der beiden Prädikationen negiert ist. Sind P und Q zwei solche Merkmale, dann kann die Satzbedeutung S entweder $P(a)$ allein oder $Q(a)$ allein oder $\sim P(a) \wedge Q(a)$ oder $P(a) \wedge \sim Q(a)$ enthalten, nicht aber $P(a) \wedge Q(a)$. Es ist aber nicht notwendig, daß jede Prädikation $P(a)$ verbunden wäre mit $\sim Q(a)$, wenn zwischen beiden Exklusionsbeziehungen bestehen.[9] Ebenso ist nicht anzunehmen, daß alle Merkmale, die von demselben Merkmal fundiert werden, untereinander exklusiv sein müßten. Diejenigen Merkmale, die Objekte als konkrete oder abstrakte Entitäten charakterisieren, sind einigen Auffassungen zufolge exklusiv.[10] Nichtexklusiv sind die Merkmale, die Objekten auf der Basis anderer Merkmale einen der beiden Sexus zuschreiben, obwohl dies vielfach angenommen wird.[11]

Zwischen zwei Merkmalen P und Q kann schließlich gegenseitige TOLERANZ bestehen. Diesen Fall haben wir z.B. angenommen für Merkmale, die zwar von demselben Merkmal fundiert werden, sich aber nicht gegenseitig ausschließen. Gegenseitige Toleranz kann aber auch zwischen Merkmalen bestehen, die nicht zu demselben Paradigma gehören. Zwei Merkmale, die sich gegenseitig tolerieren, können in der-

[8]   Das fundierende Merkmal "eröffnet eine Domäne" (Bierwisch, 1967:15). Man braucht nicht anzunehmen, daß wechselseitig exklusive Merkmale P, Q usw. dem entsprechenden fundierenden Merkmal R innerhalb der semantischen Strukturen hierarchisch untergeordnet sind. Die Fundierungsbeziehungen wie auch die Exklusionsbeziehungen gehören zur Struktur des Inventars. Anders Bierwisch (1967:10-19).

[9]   Wenn das Paradigma nur die beiden exklusiven Merkmale P und Q umfaßt, dann ist der Interpretationsbereich des ganzen Paradigmas komplementär zwischen den beiden sich ausschließenden Merkmalen aufgeteilt. Das heißt aber nicht, daß das Merkmal P die Interpretation 'Komplement von Q' hätte oder Q die Interpretation 'Komplement von P' hätte. Die Interpretation 'Komplement von Q' gehört zu $\sim P(\ )$. Die Gleichsetzung von $Q(a)$ mit $\sim P(a)$ ergibt sich erst sekundär aus den Beziehungen zwischen den beiden Merkmalen.

[10]   Siehe zum Beispiel Drange (1966:24; Fn. 7; 33).

[11]   Die gegenseitige Exklusion der beiden Sexus gilt keineswegs für alle Lebewesen. Es muß also semantische Strukturen geben, in denen demselben Objekt beide Merkmale zugeschrieben werden. Daneben gibt es Strukturen, in denen ein Objekt als männlich und als nichtweiblich bzw. als weiblich und nichtmännlich charakterisiert wird. Diesen Strukturen entsprechen bestimmte Lexikoneinheiten, die höhere Tiere bezeichnen und in Bezug auf das Geschlecht antonym sind. Vergleiche solche Wörter wie *Hahn* und *Henne*.

selben Satzbedeutung demselben Objekt zugeordnet sein, ohne daß aber eins die Anwesenheit des anderen voraussetzt.

(5) Die im § 2 unter (a-d) genannten Eigenschaften der semantischen Merkmale und Strukturen haben zur Folge, daß Satzbedeutungen als Verbindungen von ELEMEN-TAREN PROPOSITIONEN dargestellt werden können, worin jede Proposition ein semantisches Merkmal als ein- oder mehrstelliges Prädikat von bestimmter Stufe und Prädikate niedrigerer Stufe oder Objekte als Argumente enthält.[12]

Das Lexikon besteht aus Einheiten, von denen jede einen Komplex von semantischen Merkmalen — die Wortbedeutung — sowie eine syntaktisch-morphologische und eine phonologische Charakteristik enthält. Ein Wort, dessen Bedeutung einem Teilkomplex aus einer Satzbedeutung entspricht, kann zusammen mit anderen Wörtern, die dieselben Bedingungen erfüllen, eine Folge von LEXIKALISCHEN PROPOSI-TIONEN bilden, die zusammen eine neue Repräsentation des Satzes sind. Das Prädikat einer solchen lexikalischen Proposition ist ein Wort, dessen Bedeutung die semantischen Merkmale einer Teilfolge von Elementarpropositionen umfaßt. Als Argumente fungieren alle Argumente, die in den Elementarpropositionen der erwähnten Teilfolge auftreten. Schematisch:

(1) (i) *Teilfolge von Elementarpropositionen*:

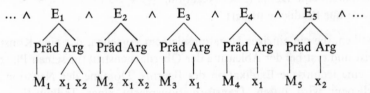

(ii) Im Lexikon existiert eine Einheit J mit den Merkmalen $M_1, ..., M_5$ als Wortbedeutung. J gehört zur syntaktischen Wortklasse K.

(iii) *Lexikalische Propositionen*:

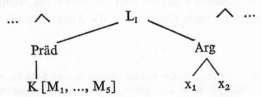

Die Verbalisierung der Satzbedeutung dürfte mit der Auswahl eines Verbs beginnen, das dann eine entsprechende lexikalische Proposition konstituiert. Für andere Teilfolgen von Elementarpropositionen müssen passende nominale Lexikoneinheiten gefunden werden. Teilfolgen, die nur durch mehrere Wortbedeutungen erfaßbar sind, können die Basis für subordinierte Sätze sein.

[12] Zu den Bedingungen für die Wohlgeformtheit von Satzbedeutungen, die im § 4 genannt sind, kommen noch andere, die hier nicht betrachtet werden können.

Teilfolgen von Elementarpropositionen, die von verschiedenen Wortbedeutungen erfaßt werden, können sich überschneiden. In den Bedeutungen von *Kind* und von *lächeln* tritt z.B. derselbe Merkmalskomplex "belebt" auf. Auf diesen Überschneidungen zwischen den verschiedenen lexikalischen Propositionen und auf den Fundierungsverhältnissen beruhen die Selektionsbeziehungen zwischen den Wörtern innerhalb des Satzes.

In den syntaktischen Strukturen entsprechen den Argumenten der verbalen lexikalischen Propositionen die nominalen Satzglieder. Ihre Satzglied-Rolle ergibt sich im einzelnen sowohl aus ihrer semantischen Charakterisierung wie aus den syntaktischen Merkmalen des jeweiligen Verbs. Damit wird zugleich die Konstituenten-Struktur des entsprechenden Satzes bestimmt. Die nominalen lexikalischen Propositionen werden an den Argumentsstellen — den *NP* der syntaktischen Struktur — eingebettet.[13][14]

DIE STELLUNG DER NEGATION IN DER SEMANTISCHEN UND IN DER SYNTAKTISCHEN STRUKTUR

(6) Bei der Behandlung der Negation werden häufig die beiden folgenden Annahmen zugrunde gelegt:

(a) Die Negation betrifft nur Teile des Satzes, nicht den ganzen Satz; es gibt innerhalb des Satzes eine Domäne der Negation.

(b) Es werden nur Prädikate negiert.[15]

Grammatiken, die ein einziges Negationselement vorsehen, das eine Konstituente des Satzes ist und erst bei der Ableitung der Oberflächenstruktur seinen Platz erhält liefern nur eine technische Explikation des Begriffs 'Domäne der Negation'.[16] Das Negationselement wird durch Transformationsregeln einer Teilkonstituente des Satzes zugeordnet, die dann als die Domäne der Negation erscheint. Die semantische Relevanz solcher Adjunktionen wird nicht klar. Sowohl (a) als auch (b) wird verfehlt.

Als Alternative ist denkbar, daß die von der Negation betroffenen Teile des Satzes Prädikat eines übergeordneten Satzes sind, während die nicht betroffenen Teile spezielle Substrukturen ergeben. Dann wären die Annahmen (a) und (b) syntaktisch expliziert:

---

[13]   Dies scheint der Platz für Fillmores Kasusmechanismus zu sein. Subjekts- und Objektsplätze sind semantisch nur relativ bestimmt. Wenn das Verb keine besonderen Festlegungen enthält, nimmt ein belebter Aktant gegenüber einem unbelebten die Subjektsrolle an, sind beide belebt, wird der Urheber des Vorgangs Subjekt. Die übrigen Aktanten können als Adverbialbestimmungen Rollen annehmen, die ihrem semantischen Charakter entsprechen. Die als Subjekt markierten *NP* werden beim Aufbau der Konstituentenstruktur direkt *S* untergeordnet, Objekte gehen in *VP* ein, Adverbialbestimmungen in *S* oder *VP*.

[14]   Hier sind alle Probleme umgangen, die mit der temporalen Struktur des Satzes oder mit seiner Aufteilung in Thema und Rhema (*Topic* und *Comment*) verbunden sind.

[15]   Nicht so Wierzbicka (1967:18-21).

[16]   In einem gewissen Sinn gilt dies auch für die Arbeit von Klima (1964), obwohl dort das *Neg*-Element an verschiedenen Stellen der Basisstruktur eingeführt wird.

(2) *Er liest keinen Brief = Es ist kein Brief, was er liest*

Zudem ergibt sich die Möglichkeit, bestimmte Ambiguitäten zu erklären:

(3) *Er liest den Brief nicht in seinem Zimmer =*
  (i) *Es ist nicht Lesen, was er mit dem Brief in seinem Zimmer tut*
  (ii) *Es ist nicht in seinem Zimmer, wo er den Brief liest*[17]

Lakoff nimmt für Sätze wie *I don't beat my wife enthusiastically* eine Tiefenstruktur an, in der das Adverb das Hauptverb des Satzes, der Satz *I beat my wife* ein Objektssatz ist. Negiert ist die Relation *enthusiastically* (Lakoff, 1965: F-14ff.):[18]

(4)

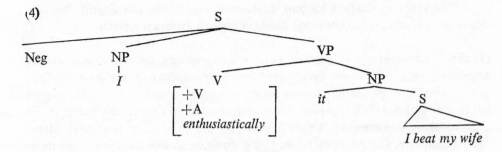

Cleft-Sätze und normale Sätze unterscheiden sich nur in der Oberflächenstruktur:[19]

(5)

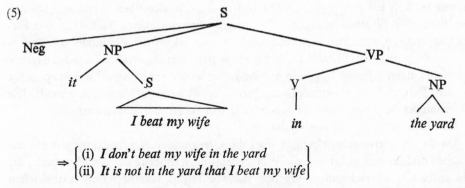

$\Rightarrow$ $\begin{cases} \text{(i) } \textit{I don't beat my wife in the yard} \\ \text{(ii) } \textit{It is not in the yard that I beat my wife} \end{cases}$

Wir fassen die Beziehungen zwischen den Cleft-Sätzen und ihren normalen Parallelen anders auf. Für negierte Sätze mit Objekten läßt sich überdies zeigen, daß es Bedeutungsunterschiede zwischen beiden Konstruktionen gibt.[20] Schließlich gibt es Unter-

---

[17] Von der möglichen Bedeutung, in der jede Beziehung zwischen den im Satz genannten Objekten bestritten ist, ist bei (2) und (3) — wie auch im folgenden — abgesehen. Zur Grammatikalität von Cleft-Konstruktionen im Deutschen, siehe Motsch (1966, 4).

[18] Bei anderen (lokalen, kausalen, instrumentalen usw.) Adverbialbestimmungen tritt der Kern des Satzes als Subjektsatz auf; vergl. (5).

[19] Lakoff (1965: F-17f.); die genannte Auffassung von den Beziehungen zwischen Cleft-Konstruktionen und normalen Sätzen wird Seite F-40ff. revidiert.

[20] Siehe unten §12; es gibt Berührungen mit Lakoffs zweiter Auffassung, siehe Fn. 19.

schiede in der Abgrenzung des Negationsbereiches, die sich nicht durch unterschiedliche Cleft-Konstruktionen ausdrücken lassen. So kann

(6)	*Er hat sein Motorrad nicht im Haus abgestellt*

einmal besagen, daß das Haus nicht der Platz ist, an dem das Motorrad abgestellt wird, (6) kann aber auch besagen, daß das Haus zwar als Lokalisierung dient, aber nicht in der Weise, die der semantischen Chakteristik der Präposition *in* entspricht. In der ersten Bedeutung könnte (6) fortgesetzt werden mit ... *sondern im Schuppen*, in der zweiten mit ... *sondern vorm Haus*.[21] Man darf nicht voraussetzen, daß ein semantisches auch als syntaktisches Prädikat erscheinen müsse, noch, daß der Bereich einer Prädikation syntaktisch als Satz manifestiert sein müsse. Der Begriff 'Domäne der Negation' sollte semantisch und nicht syntaktisch expliziert werden.

(7) Eine Satzbedeutung ist negativ, wenn mindestens eins der Merkmale, die ihr angehören, negiert ist; in der Folge von Elementarpropositionen, die ihr entspricht, muß es eine Teilfolge aus mindestens einer Elementarproposition geben, die negiert ist. Ist ein Merkmal (Prädikat einer Elementarproposition) negiert, das andere in der Satzbedeutung enthaltene Merkmale fundiert, so müssen auch die fundierten Merkmale negiert sein. Die Negation reicht also mindestens so weit wie die Fundierungsbeziehungen.

Die Repräsentation der Satzbedeutung durch eine Folge von lexikalischen Propositionen verläuft bei den negativen Satzbedeutungen in derselben Weise wie bei den positiven. Die Wortbedeutungen erfassen sich überschneidende Teilfolgen von Elementarpropositionen. Die entsprechenden Wörter bilden die Prädikate von lexikalischen Propositionen. Enthält die von einer Wortbedeutung erfaßte Teilfolge negierte Elemente, dann geht die Negation auf die ganze lexikalische Proposition über, außer in dem Fall, daß die Wortbedeutung bereits selbst negierte Merkmale enthält. Die Domäne der Negation kann also auch Teile von Wortbedeutungen enthalten.

Dies ist eine Quelle für Ambiguitäten.

Da die Fundierungsbeziehungen über die Grenzen der Wortbedeutungen hinausreichen und da sich außerdem die Wortbedeutungen inbezug auf die Merkmale, die sie enthalten, überschneiden, ergeben sich Teilfolgen von negierten lexikalischen Propositionen. In den syntaktischen Repräsentationen werden die Negationen jedoch teilweise wieder getilgt, woraus sich ebenfalls Ambiguitäten ergeben können.[22] Die Auffassung, daß einem positiven Satz genau ein negativer entspreche und umgekehrt, ist also aufzugeben. Jeder Bedeutung eines positiven Satzes können mehrere syntaktisch gleich manifestierte negative Satzbedeutungen entsprechen.

[21]	Die Begrenzung des Negationsbereichs wird durch die *sondern*-Sätze nicht GESCHAFFEN, sie wird lediglich EXPLIZIT GEMACHT. Dasselbe gilt für die Akzentuierung: *im Schúppen / ím Schuppen*.
[22]	Die Tilgung geht in den einzelnen Sprachen unterschiedlich weit; das moderne Deutsche hat z.B. einfache Negation, wo das Mittelhochdeutsche 'doppelte' Negation hat:
	Es weiß niemand, wer er ist
	jâ enweiz nieman wer er ist.

MEHRDEUTIGKEIT NEGATIVER SÄTZE

(8) Mit entsprechend starker Vereinfachung kann man in der Bedeutung des Verbs *malen* zwei Merkmalskomplexe P und Q unterscheiden: P charakterisiert den Vorgang als die Schaffung eines neuen Objekts y durch die Person x, Q bezieht sich auf die Besonderheiten des Malens gegenüber anderen künstlerischen Techniken, wie z.B. Zeichnen oder Fotografieren. Q ist von P fundiert.[23]

Unter diesen Voraussetzungen ergibt sich eine Erklärung für die Mehrdeutigkeit von (7):

(7) *Mein Bruder hat das Bild nicht gemalt*[24]

Satz (7) kann mindestens zwei Bedeutungen haben:

(7)(a) *Mein Bruder ist nicht der Autor dieses Bildes*
  (b) *Mein Bruder ist der Autor, das Bild ist aber kein Gemälde*

Im Falle von (7a) ist sowohl P als Q negiert:

(8) $\sim P(a,b) \land \sim Q(a,b) \land P(x,b)$

Dabei steht a für 'mein Bruder', b für 'das Bild'; beides sind Konstanten. Wegen der Fundierungsbeziehungen zieht die Negation von $P(a,b)$ die von $Q(a,b)$ nach sich. Weil b als Bild, d.h. als Artefakt charakterisiert ist, muß es einen Autor x von b geben. Daher gehört $P(x,b)$ zur semantischen Struktur. Die Proposition braucht aber im folgenden nicht beachtet zu werden.

In (7b) ist nur die Herstellungstechnik negiert:

(9) $P(a,b) \land \sim Q(a,b)$

Eine von Q verschiedene Herstellungstechnik Q' ist durch (9) zwar impliziert, in der entsprechenden Satzbedeutung aber nicht ausgesagt.

Während in (7a) und (7b), resp. (8) und (9) die Domäne der Negation nur die Verbmerkmale einschließt, gibt es von (10) zweifellos auch legitime Bedeutungen, in denen auch die semantischen Merkmale des Objektsnomens in den Negationsbereich einbezogen sind:[25]

(10) *Mein Bruder hat kein Bild gemalt*

---

[23] P faßt zusammen: (a) Merkmale, die den Vorgang als willkürliche Handlung beschreiben, (b) Merkmale, die dem dinglichen Relat eine Zustandsveränderung zuschreiben, (c) Merkmale, die dieses Relat als Artefakt bestimmen.
Tatsächlich fundieren (a) und (b) zusammen (c). Davon kann aber im folgenden abgesehen werden, weil der Artefaktcharakter des Objekts außerhalb der Domäne der Negation bleibt. Q hängt tatsächlich nur von (a) und (b) ab.
[24] Für (7) ist angenommen, daß die Relate von *malen* bereits in einem vorangehenden Satz genannt sind. Der Hauptakzent des Satzes liegt dann auf dem Verb, der zweitstärkste auf dem ersten Satzglied. Satz (7) ist in keiner Weise kontrastiv oder emphatisch. Vergleiche Heidolph (1966:275-278).
[25] Etwa: *Mein Bruder hat etwas hergestellt, aber nicht durch Malen, und der hergestellte Gegenstand war kein Bild.*

Die Domäne der Negation braucht also keineswegs mit syntaktischen Konstituenten kongruent zu sein. Eine syntaktische Struktur, die das Negationselement enthält, ist normalerweise mehrdeutig.

BEDEUTUNG NEGATIVER SÄTZE UND VERSTÄNDNIS NEGATIVER SÄTZE

(9) Jede Satzbedeutung charakterisiert eine Klasse von Sachverhalten: Wenn die Satzbedeutung durch bestimmte n-Tupel von Objekten interpretiert wird, so daß sie auf diese Objekte referiert, charakterisiert sie einen Sachverhalt.[26] Bei der Besetzung der Argumentsstellen bleiben die Fundierungs- und Exklusionsbeziehungen gewahrt: Es dürfen beispielsweise nicht Merkmale, die einander ausschließen, als Prädikate desselben Arguments auftreten.

Auch die Bedeutungen der negativen Sätze beziehen sich auf Klassen von Sachverhalten. Aber sowohl die Bildung dieser Klassen wie auch das Verständnis der negativen Sätze (die Erkennung der Bedeutung und der Gebrauch, der von der Bedeutung gemacht wird) vollziehen sich anders als bei den positiven Sätzen.

Ein positiver Satz mit der Bedeutung S charakterisiert eine Klasse V von Sachverhalten. S kann in mindestens einer Weise in zwei Teilkomplexe von Merkmalen M und N zerlegt werden, so daß M keine Merkmale enthält, die von Merkmalen in N fundiert werden. M charakterisiert dann eine Klasse W von Sachverhalten, die die Klasse V echt enthält. Durch die Merkmale von N wird W auf V eingeschränkt.

In der Bedeutung S' eines parallelen negativen Satzes ist M ebenfalls enthalten. Die in N enthaltenen Merkmale treten aber negiert auf in einem Komplex N'. M ist dann im Verhältnis zu S' die AFFIRMATIVE BASIS, N' ist die DOMÄNE DER NEGATION von S'. So wie es für S mehrere alternative Zerlegungen in verschiedene M_i und N_i geben kann, kann es auch mehrere S'_i geben, die sich durch verschiedene Abgrenzungen zwischen affirmativer Basis und Domäne der Negation unterscheiden. Das ist z.B. der Fall bei (7a) und (7b).

Durch das jeweilige M wird durch S' eine Klasse von Sachverhalten — nämlich W — direkt und positiv charakterisiert. W wird jedoch durch die Domäne der Negation, das heißt durch den negierten Merkmalskomplex N', auf eine Klasse V' eingeschränkt. V' ist die Komplementärklasse von V auf der Basis der Klasse W. V' ist nur indirekt charakterisiert: die Komplementsklasse V' kann erst durch den Umweg über die in N und in N' faktisch enthaltene Charakteristik von V konstituiert werden. Dieser Umweg kompliziert das Verständnis negativer Sätze auch dann, wenn die Ambiguität hinsichtlich der Abgrenzung zwischen affirmativer Basis M und Domäne der Negation N' bereits aufgelöst ist.

(10) Die in § 9 beschriebenen Beziehungen zwischen affirmativer Basis und Domäne der Negation treffen nur für einen Teil der negativen Sätze zu. In einer anderen Klasse

---

[26] Siehe Fn. 4; die Probleme der generellen Sätze können hier nicht behandelt werden.

von Sätzen werden demselben Objekt Merkmale zugeschrieben, die sich gegenseitig ausschließen. In solchen Sätzen muß dann jeweils eins der gegenseitig exklusiven Merkmale zur Domäne der Negation gehören, das andere zur affirmativen Basis. Das ist z.B. der Fall bei den Negationen von sogenannten *Type crossings*.[27] In dem Satz *Peter ist eine Flüssigkeit* sind mit *Peter* und *Flüssigkeit* demselben Objekt einander ausschließende Merkmale zugeschrieben. Eine wohlgeformte Satzbedeutung ergibt sich nur, wenn einer der entsprechenden Merkmalskomplexe negiert ist: *Peter ist keine Flüssigkeit*.[28] Dranges Diskussion der *Type crossings* deckt bestimmte Schwierigkeiten beim Verständnis ihrer Negationen auf. Diese Schwierigkeiten lassen sich auflösen, wenn man annimmt, daß die Abgrenzung zwischen Negationsdomäne und affirmativer Basis nicht mit den Wortgrenzen zusammenfällt.

In dem Satz

(11) *Die Relativitätstheorie ist blau*

werden mit *Relativitätstheorie* einem Objekt Merkmale zugeschrieben, die durch das Merkmal 'abstrakt' fundiert sind. Mit *blau* werden ihm Merkmale zugeschrieben, die durch das Merkmal 'konkret' fundiert sind. Die beiden fundierenden Merkmale sind gegenseitig exklusiv. Damit ist (11) logisch falsch und sinnlos.[29]
Der parallele negative Satz

(12) *Die Relativitätstheorie ist nicht blau*

wird von einigen für sinnlos gehalten, von anderen für sinnvoll und wahr (Drange, 1966:19ff.). Der einen Ansicht zufolge ist (12) sinnlos, weil der Satz in normaler Redeweise besage, daß die Relativitätstheorie irgendeine andere, von Blau verschiedene Farbe habe. Nach der anderen Ansicht besagt (12), daß die Relativitätstheorie gar keine Farbe hat. Die Annahme, (12) beschreibe eine abstrakte Entität als Farbträger, sei nicht in der Struktur der Sprache begründet, sondern entspreche lediglich einer unkontrollierten Denkweise (Drange, 1966:22).

Wenn (12) besagt, daß die Relativitätstheorie irgendeine von Blau verschiedene Farbe habe, dann ist (12) sinnlos und falsch. Wenn (12) besagt, daß die Theorie überhaupt kein Farbträger ist, dann ist der Satz sinnvoll und wahr.

Wir nehmen an, daß zu dem Merkmalskomplex, der ein Objekt als physisches Objekt charakterisiert, auch ein Merkmal gehört, daß das Objekt als Farbträger beschreibt. Dieses Merkmal fundiert andere, die dem Objekt spezielle einzelne Farben, z.B. Blau, zuschreiben. Der Markmalskomplex, zu dem 'Farbträger sein' gehört,

---

[27] Vergl. Drange (1966). Von Drange ist die Bezeichnung *Type crossing* übernommen.

[28] Es ist nicht klar, wie überhapt abweichende Strukturen von der Art der *Type crossings* zustande kommen können. Von der Kompetenz sind sie ausgeschlossen, praktisch aber möglich. Type crossings könnten sich z.B. als Schlüsse aus Prämissen ergeben, deren Widersprüchlichkeit noch nicht durchschaut ist.

[29] So Drange (1966:35); die Sinnlosigkeit (*meaninglessness*) solcher Sätze und ihre notwendige Falschheit werden auf die Undenkbarkeit der ihnen zugrundeliegenden Propositionen zurückgeführt (p. 180).

schließt aber die Merkmale aus, die für *Relativitätstheorie* fundamental sind. Wird nun das Merkmal 'Farbträger sein' negiert, dann fällt das von ihm fundierte Merkmal der blauen Farbe automatisch mit in die Domäne der Negation [siehe § (7)]. Dann wird von dem als Theorie charakterisierten Objekt nichts behauptet, was andere Eigenschaften physischer Objekte zur Folge hätte. Die Merkmale, die sich gegenseitig ausschließen sind auf Affirmationsbasis und Domäne der Negation verteilt. Mit dieser Bedeutung ist (12) ein wahrer und sinvoller Satz.

Ist dagegen nur das spezielle Merkmal der blauen Farbe negiert, dann gehört das Merkmal 'Farbträger sein' samt den entsprechenden anderen Merkmalen, die für physische Objekte gelten, zur affirmativen Basis. Diese enthält aber auch alle die Merkmale, die das fragliche Objekt als etwas abstraktes charakterisieren. Damit enthält die affirmative Basis auch Merkmale, die einander ausschließen. Die *Type-crossing*-Eigenschaften von (11) bestehen also trotz der Negation in der affirmativen Basis von (12) fort. Der Satz (12) ist in dieser Bedeutung falsch und sinnlos; seiner syntaktischen Struktur nach scheint er die Negation eines Type crossings zu sein, semantisch gesehen ist er selbst ein *Type crossing*. In der zuerst beschriebenen Bedeutung ist er hingegen auch semantisch die Negation eines *Type crossing*.

(11) Bei Sätzen wie (7), *Mein Bruder hat das Bild nicht gemalt*, ergibt sich die Abgrenzung zwischen affirmativer Basis und Domäne der Negation nicht wie bei (12) aus Wohlgeformtheitsbedingungen. Es gibt mehrere gleichermaßen sinnvolle Abgrenzungen. Die Entscheidung verlangt zusätzliche Informationen. Solche Informationen können sich aus der Situation, aus dem vorangehenden Text oder aus sonst vorhandenen Kenntnissen ergeben. Zugleich liefern die verschiedenen Bedeutungen der negativen Sätze auch verschiedene Konklusionen, die, in den Bedeutungen selbst nicht enthalten sind. Zwischen den Informationen, die, vorgegeben, zu einer bestimmten Abgrenzung führen, und denjenigen, die nach vollzogener Abgrenzung aus der Satzbedeutung folgen, besteht kein prinzipieller Unterschied.

Ist im Fall von Satz (7) z.B. explizit als zusätzliche Information gegeben, daß $P(a,b)$ gilt (das heißt, daß der Bruder des Sprechers Autor des Bildes IST), dann kommt nur noch die Bedeutung (7b) in Frage, dann kann nur noch die Proposition $Q(a,b)$ negiert sein. Das x in der Proposition $P(x,b)$, die der Charakterisierung des Bildes b als Artefakt entspricht, muß also — folglich — mit der Person a identisch sein. Das Bild b selbst kann kein Gemälde sein. Zugleich ist impliziert, daß $Q'(a,b)$ gelten muß, d.h. daß b eine Zeichnung, eine Fotografie oder dergleichen sein muß.

Ist dagegen $\sim P(a,b)$ explizit vorgegeben, dann ist $Q(a,b)$ ebenfalls negativ. Es kommt nur Bedeutung (7a) in Betracht. Das x in $P(x,b)$ muß folglich von a verschieden sein. Es bleibt aber offen, ob das Bild b ein Gemälde ist oder nicht. Das kann — ebenso wie die Frage ob die Person a überhaupt als Hersteller von Bildern in Frage kommt — nur durch andere zusätzliche Informationen entschieden werden.

Die Mehrdeutigkeit von Sätzen wie (7) kann jedoch auch auf Grund von indirekten zusätzlichen Informationen aufgelöst werden, die sich in Propositionen ausdrücken, die selbst nicht zu einer der Bedeutungen von (7) gehören. So kann z.B. gegeben sein, daß $P(c,b)$ gilt und daß $c \neq a$. Dann folgt $\sim P(a,b)$ und damit Bedeutung (7a). Dasselbe würde aus einer Vorgabe $Q(c,b)$ folgen müssen. Auch die Information, daß a überhaupt keine Bilder herstellt, würde (7b) ausschließen. Ist das Bild b als Gemälde bekannt, so ist (7b) als Bedeutung von (7) ausgeschlossen, denn (7b) behauptet einerseits die Autorschaft von a, leugnet aber $Q(a,b)$. Die Information, daß b kein Gemälde ist, reicht aber nicht aus, um zwischen (7a) und (7b) zu entscheiden.

Viele Informationen, die den Bedeutungen negativer Sätze zugeschrieben werden, sind nicht selbst in den Bedeutungen vorhanden, sondern folgen nur aus ihnen. Daher werden Sätze mit komplexer Struktur, in deren Bedeutungen diese Folgerungen bereits explizit enthalten sind, leicht als Paraphrasen für eine oder andere Bedeutungsvariante eines negativen Satzes mit einfacherer Struktur in Anspruch genommen.

(12) Der Satz (7) hat Stellungs- und Pronominalisierungsvarianten, die sämtlich dieselbe Art von Mehrdeutigkeit aufweisen wie (7) selbst. Zum Beispiel:

(13) *Er hat es nicht gemalt*

(14) *Das Bìld hat mein Bruder nicht gemált*
Das hàt er nicht gemált

Daneben gibt es Sätze, die eine der Bedeutungen von (7), bzw. (13) und (14) zu paraphrasieren und explizit zu machen scheinen:

(15) (i) *Das Bìld hat nicht mein Brúder gemalt*
(ii) *Nicht mein Brúder hat das Bild gemàlt*
(iii) *Es ist nicht mein Brúder, der das gemàlt hat*

Parallele Stellungs-, Betonungs- und Strukturunterschiede gibt es auch bei positiven Sätzen. So steht neben (16) (17):

(16) *Das Bìld hat mein Bruder gemált*
Das hàt er gemált

(17) (i) *Das Bild hat mein Brúder gemált*
(ii) *Mein Brúder hat das gemàlt*
(iii) *Es ist mein Brúder, der das gemàlt hat*

Die Sätze von (16) kann man wie folgt analysieren:

(18) (i) b *ist ein Bild*
(ii) a *hat* b *gemalt*
(iii) a *ist mein Bruder*

Die in *malen* enthaltenen Prädikate werden unmittelbar dem Paar (a,b) zugeschrieben, a ist eine Konstante.

Die Sätze von (17) müssen anders analysiert werden:

(19) (i) b *ist ein Bild*
  (ii) x *hat* b *gemalt*
  (iii) a *ist mein Bruder*
  (iv) x *ist mit* a *identisch*

Die in *malen* enthaltenen Prädikate werden x und b zugeschrieben: x ist eine Variable. In (iv) wird dieses x eigens mit a identifiziert. Die Variable x ergibt sich aus der Zweistelligkeit von *malen*, ihre Ersetzung durch die Konstante a ist das eigentliche kommunikative Motiv der Sätze von (17). (17i) ist reduziert aus

(20) *Das Bild hat jemand gemalt, der mein Bruder ist*

(17ii) ist eine reduzierte Form von (17iii). In den letztgenannten Sätzen ist die Identifizierung von x und a Thema des Satzes, in (17i) und (20) nicht.

Die Sätze von (17) haben eine komplexere Struktur als die von (16). Sie spielen beim Erwerb und bei der Überarbeitung von Kenntnissen eine andere Rolle als die von (16), dem logischen Gehalt nach besteht kein wesentlicher Unterschied: Aus den Sätzen beider Gruppen lassen sich dieselben Folgerungen ableiten. Bei den negierten Sätzen ergeben sich allerdings Unterschiede.

Der Satz (15i) kann als eine Stellungsvariante, der Satz (15ii) als eine reduzierte Form von (15iii) betrachtet werden. (15iii) enthält folgen Propositionen:

(21) (i) b *ist ein Bild*
  (ii) x *hat* b *gemalt*
  (iii) a *ist mein Bruder*
  (iv) x *ist nicht identisch mit* a

Negiert ist nur (iv), die Identifizierung von x und a. Die Ähnlichkeit zwischen (7a) und (15iii) besteht darin, daß a weder als Maler noch überhaupt als Hersteller in Frage kommt. Die Nichtidentität von x and a, die aus (7a) nur folgt, ist aber in (15iii) explizit behauptet. Ein weiterer Unterschied besteht darin, daß (7a) offen läßt, ob b ein Gemälde ist, was in (15iii) explizit behauptet ist. Wegen dieser zusätzlichen Festlegungen sind die Sätze von (15) keine genauen Paraphrasen von (7a). Logisch besteht eine gewisse Ähnlichkeit, hinsichtlich der kommunikativen Rolle bestehen große Unterschiede. Es ist somit nicht berechtigt, (7) in der Bedeutung (a) die syntaktische Struktur von (15iii) zuzuschreiben.

Bei den sogenannten Satzgliednegationen (*nicht ihr, nicht Peter, nicht dieses Bild*), wo das Negationselement Teil einer definiten NP der Oberflächenstruktur ist, liegt die Domäne der Negation innerhalb der Konstituentensätze. Sie blockiert die Identifizierung einer im Matrixsatz auftretenden Variablen mit einer Konstanten.

(13) Bedeutungen von negativen Sätzen charakterisieren Komplementärklassen von Sachverhalten. Die Basis der Komplementsbildung wird durch die affirmative Basis

bestimmt. Interpretiert durch bestimmte Objekte referieren die negativen Satzbedeutungen auf Sachverhalte, an denen diese Objekte beteiligt sind und die Elemente dieser Komplementärklasse sind. Die Rekonstruktion einer positiven, direkten Charakteristik dieser Sachverhalte ist weder in allen Fällen möglich, noch gehört sie zur eigentlichen pragmatischen Funktion der jeweiligen negativen Sätze.[30]

Die pragmatische Funktion der negativen Sätze ist erkennbar beim Vergleich bestimmter partikulärer positiver Sätze mit ihren negativen Gegenstücken. Positive Sätze wie z. B. die von (22)

(22) *Es kommt jemand*
      Dieses Bild hat mein Bruder gemalt
      Das Radio von nebenan ist zu laut

können unter anderem dazu dienen, Beobachtetes zu beschreiben und in den Kenntnisbestand zu überführen: Der Hörer soll veranlaßt werden, die dargestellten Sachverhalte in dieser Darstellung in seine Kenntnis aufzunehmen. Andere Sätze, unter anderem die generellen, entsprechen nicht der Verarbeitung von Beobachtungen und der Aufnahme neuer Kenntnisse. Sie entsprechen vielmehr Operationen auf bereits vorhandenen Kenntnissen, die verallgemeinert werden sollen oder in Prädiktionen eingehen. Es ist zu zeigen, daß die negierten Gegenstücke von Sätzen wie (22) NICHT Sätze sind, die Beobachtungen verarbeiten und in den Kenntnisbestand überführen, sondern Sätze der zuletzt genannten Kategorie.

Äußerungen wie z. B. *Ich sehe niemand* oder *Es kommt niemand* mag in der Situation beispielsweise der Anblick der leeren Straße entsprechen. Was sich nicht auf dieser Straße befindet, kann nicht beobachtet werden.[31] Die Bedeutung von *Ich sehe niemand* betrifft einen Sachverhalt in der Komplementärklasse von *Ich sehe jemand*, die alle von 'Sehen' verschiedenen Relationen enthält, so weit der Sprecher des Satzes als eins der Relate auftritt. Zu dem, was tatsächlich beobachtet werden kann, verhält sich *Ich sehe niemand* im Prinzip nicht anders als *Es kommt kein Einhorn*. Beide negative Sätze beschreiben die Beobachtungen nicht. Sie sind mit ihnen nur — gleich gut und gleich schlecht — verträglich.

Trotzdem dürfte in der angenommenen Situation *Ich sehe niemand* bevorzugt werden, denn auf der Straße erwartet man eher Leute als ein Einhorn, so daß die Mitteilung, daß die Straße leer von Menschen ist, in der Kommunikation einen größeren Wert hat. Eine Erwartung der genannten Art tritt auf, wenn auf der Basis vorhandener Kenntnisse ein bestimmter Sachverhalt erschlossen wird, das heißt, wenn für bestimmte zeitliche und örtliche Umstände eine bestimmte Instanz einer bestimmten Relation behauptet wird. Der erschlossene Sachverhalt wird in einer

---

[30] Für *Peter hat diesen silbernen Löffel nicht gekauft* ist die Rekonstruktion einer direkten Charakteristik leicht, weil es eine reiche affirmative Basis gibt, die nur wenige Alternativen offen läßt. Ganz anders ist das z.B. bei *Es kommt niemand*, wo eine direkte Charakteristik nicht aufgebaut werden kann, weil die affirmative Basis extrem arm ist und keinerlei Anhaltspunkte bietet.

[31] "'I see nobody on the road,' said Alice. 'I only wish I had such eyes,' the King remarked in a fretful tone. 'To be able to see Nobody! And at that distance too...'" Carroll, 286.

referentiell interpretierten Satzbedeutung beschrieben. Diese Satzbedeutung ist positiv. Wenn die Beobachtungen den erschlossenen Sachverhalt nicht decken, dann wird die entsprechende Satzbedeutung negiert. Die negierten Sätze beziehen sich also nicht auf Beobachtetes, sondern auf Erschlossenes und seine Relation zu den Beobachtungen. Die negierten Sätze blockieren Prädiktionen aus Bekanntem. Die Folge einer solchen Blockierung können zum Beispiel Teilrevisionen im Kenntnisbestand oder Überprüfung von Beobachtungen sein.[32]

(14) Auf der Basis vorhandener Kenntnisse wird ein Sachverhalt postuliert. Das geschieht durch den Aufbau einer Satzbedeutung, die eine ganze Klasse von Sachverhalten beschreibt, und durch die referentielle Interpretation der Satzbedeutung. Die damit geschaffene Prädiktion wird durch die Negation des Satzes blockiert. Negiert gibt der Satz eine indirekte Beschreibung des Sachverhaltes als Element einer Komplementärklasse. Diese indirekte Charakteristik ist mit den Beobachtungen nur verträglich.

Die zu blockierende Folgerung aus den Kenntnissen ist in einer positiven Satzbedeutung repräsentiert. Es könnte scheinen, als spielten die unterschiedlichen Bedeutungen, die der negierte Satz haben kann, für die pragmatische Funktion des negativen Satzes gar keine Rolle, weil eben die eine in der positiven Satzbedeutung repräsentierte Folgerung zu blockieren ist. Wenn die Unterschiede in den Bedeutungen beim vollen Verständnis der negativen Sätze gar keinen Effekt haben, dann ist es überflüssig, den negativen Sätzen überhaupt Bedeutungen zuzuschreiben.

Das träfe zu, wenn die von der Negation betroffene Bedeutung nichts außer der zu blockierenden Folgerung enthielte. In der jeweiligen affirmativen Basis enthält sie aber einen Teil der Kenntnisse, auf denen die zu negierende Folgerung beruht. Diese ist in dem Teil der Satzbedeutung repräsentiert, der die Domäne der Negation bildet. Zwei verschiedene Bedeutungen eines negativen Satzes entsprechen zwei verschiedenen Beziehungen zwischen Kenntnis und Folgerungen aus der Kenntnis.

Die syntaktische Struktur des negierten Satzes entspricht einer negierten Konjunktion $\sim (P \wedge Q)$. Die Auflösung der Ambiguität ist die Auswahl zwischen den in der entsprechenden Disjunktion $\sim P \vee \sim Q$ enthaltenen Möglichkeiten. Diese Möglichkeiten sind durch die Fundierungsbeziehungen eingeschränkt. Bei gegenseitiger Toleranz von P und Q ist nur $P \wedge Q$ ausgeschlossen; $\sim P \wedge \sim Q$, $\sim P \wedge Q$, $P \wedge \sim Q$ sind möglich. Ist Q von P fundiert, dann scheidet auch $\sim P \wedge Q$ aus. Der Auswahl aus diesen Möglichkeiten entspricht die Entscheidung für eine bestimmte Abgrenzung zwischen Affirmationsbasis und Domäne der Negation. Sie hängt ab von den direkt im Satz oder indirekt vorgegebenen Kenntnissen.

Wenn das Verhältnis von in der Satzbedeutung explizit enthaltener Information

[32] In dieser Auffassung der pragmatischen Funktion der Negation stimme ich überein mit A. Wierzbicka (siehe Wierzbicka, 1967:20). Ich nehme jedoch an, daß die Negation tatsächlich stets Prädikaten zukommt, wenn auch nicht immer syntaktischen Prädikaten. Die pragmatische Funktion eines negativen Satzes basiert auf der Negation bestimmter in der Satzbedeutung enthaltener Prädikate (das heißt: bestimmter Merkmale und Merkmalskomplexe). Siehe dazu §14.

und aus der Satzbedeutung nur erschlossener Information verkannt wird, werden Mehrdeutigkeiten entweder übersehen oder als Folge unterschiedlicher syntaktischer Strukturen betrachtet.

Wenn die pragmatische Einbettung des negativen Satzes übersehen wird, dann scheint die pragmatische Funktion der in der syntaktischen Struktur gegebenen negierten Konjunktion anzuhaften, und die Bedeutungen des negierten Satzes erscheinen als irrelevant. Die pragmatische Funktion der negativen Sätze realisiert sich erst über ihre Bedeutungen. Das Negationselement selbst hat jedoch keine Bedeutung, wenigstens nicht in demselben Sinne wie Wörter oder Sätze. Es entspricht einer Blockierungsoperation bei der Bearbeitung bereits vorhandener Kenntnisse.

BIBLIOGRAPHIE

Bach, Emmon,
"Nouns and Nounphrases" in: E. Bach and R. J. Harms (eds.) *Universals in Linguistic Theory* (New York 1968), 91-122.
Bierwisch, Manfred,
1967 "On Certain Problems of Semantic Features" (Berlin, unveröffentlicht), jetzt: *Foundations of Language* 5 (1969), 153-184.
Carroll, Lewis,
"Through the Looking Glass", in: Lewis Carroll, *Alice's Adventures in Wonderland and Through the Looking Glass* (London, Penguin Books, Puffin Book 169).
Drange, Theodor,
1966 *Type Crossings. Sentential Meaninglessness in the Border Area of Linguistics and Philosophy* (= *Janua Linguarum, Series minor*, XLIV) (The Hague, Mouton).
Fillmore, Charles J.,
1966 "Toward a Modern Theory of Case", in: *POLA Report*, 13:1-24 (Ohio State University).
Heidolph, Karl Erich,
1966 "Kontextbeziehungen zwischen Sätzen in einer generativen Grammatik", *Kybernetika*, 3/2:274-281.
Katz, Jerrold J.,
1966 *The Philosophy of Language. Studies in Language* (New York).
Katz, Jerrold J. and J. A. Fodor,
1963 "The Structure of a Semantic Theory", *Language*, 39:170-210.
Katz, Jerrold J. and Paul M. Postal,
1964 *An Integrated Theory of Linguistic Descriptions* (= *M.I.T. Research Monograph*, 26) (Cambridge, Mass.).
Klima, E. S.,
1964 "Negation in English", in: J. A. Fodor and Jerrold J. Katz (eds.), *The Structure of Language. Readings in the Philosophy of Language* (Englewood Cliffs, N.J.), 246-323.
Kraak, A.,
1966 *Negatieve Zinnen. Een methodologische en grammatische Analyse* (Hilversum).
Lakoff, George,
1965 *On the Nature of Syntactic Irregularity* (= *Report* No. NSF-16, *Mathematical Linguistics and Automatic Translation to the National Science Foundation*) (Cambridge, Mass., The Computational Laboratory, Harvard University).
Motsch, Wolfgang,
1966 "Ein Typ von Emphasesätzen im Deutschen" (unveröffentlicht).
Wierzbicka, A.,
1967 "Negation — A Study in Deep Grammar" (M.I.T., March, unveröffentlicht).

С. Д. КАЦНЕЛЬСОН

ПОРОЖДАЮЩАЯ ГРАММАТИКА И ПРОЦЕСС СИНТАКСИЧЕСКОЙ ДЕРИВАЦИИ

Хотя порождающая грамматика и не ставит перед собой задачу моделирования реальных процессов порождения и восприятия речи, как они протекают в голове говорящего и слушателя, и является 'порождающей' лишь в особом, логико-математическом смысле, тем не менее в ряде существенных пунктов она приближает нас к пониманию действенности языковых механизмов и совершающегося в акте речевого общения перехода от системы языка к речи-мысли. В зародыше идея порождения речи была заложена уже в традиционном синтаксисе, как учении о соединении слов в предложения. Порождающая грамматика вдохнула новую жизнь в старое учение о предложении, указав на динамическую роль синтаксических структур и синтаксической деривации в формировании предложений. Именно в этом состоит, как нам представляется, общелингвистический смысл новой грамматической теории, независимый от целей логической формализации.

Согласно порождающей грамматике, процесс образования предложения не сводится к простой сцепке слов и их линейной арранжировке. Соответственно, и структура предложения не является результатом сцепления слов, как это кажется порой задним числом, при анализе готового предложения. Структура предложения динамична; в известном смысле она, можно сказать, предшествует предложению, направляя процесс его формирования. Для того, чтобы язык мог порождать речь, в арсенале его средств должны наличествовать не только слова и морфологические элементы, но также синтаксические структуры как схемы-прообразы порождаемых предложений.

Выделив роль синтаксических структур в процессе формирования высказываний, порождающая грамматика выявила деривационные связи, существующие между синтаксическими структурами, и здесь обнаружилось различие основных (или 'базальных') и производных образований. За вычетом простейших случаев, структура 'готового', т.е. засвидетельствованного в тексте, предложения оказалась производной, т.е. полученной из базальной структуры в результате последовательных преобразований. Синтаксические структуры и их преобразования стали, таким образом, стержневыми понятиями порождающей грамматики.

Единичные типы преобразования синтаксических структур были известны и традиционной грамматике — такие, например, как обращение активного оборота в пассивный или утвердительного предложения в вопросительное. Теперь же процессы преобразования были обособлены и положены в основу теории фразообразования. Исследование 'деривационной истории' предложений стало синонимом теоретической реконструкции порождающего процесса.

Новый подход к синтаксису как своеобразному 'порождающему устройству' имеет принципиальное значение для всей теории языка. Система языка это — не только инвентарь разнотипных строевых элементов, но и действующий механизм порождения речи. То, что Соссюр именовал 'исполнением' или 'реализацией' языка, предстало теперь как сложный и противоречивый процесс, требующий специального изучения. Теоретическое воссоздание этого процесса открывает перед языкознанием реальную перспективу глубокого функционального осмысления структуры языка и его строевых элементов.

Порождающий процесс непосредственно не доступен наблюдению, как не доступна наблюдению и система языка. Непосредственно даны только тексты, анализ структуры которых поставляет материал для суждений о системе языка и — через посредство системы языка — о природе порождающего процесса. Чтобы строить догадки о формировании речевых текстов, необходимо располагать знаниями об инвентаре языка и его речевых механизмах. Но если инвентарь языка, основной фонд его строевых элементов — слов, морфем и фонем — относительно легко извлекается из текстов путем их последовательного анализа, то механизмы речи и процессы ее порождения требуют гораздо более сложной методики исследования. Методы анализа и классификации, применявшиеся в описательном языкознании, здесь явно недостаточны. Требуется более абстрактный уровень исследования и навыки обращения с теоретическими понятиями, такими как "взаимоотношение формы и содержания в языке и речи", "логическая природа порождающего процесса" и некоторые другие. Неслучайно поэтому порождающая грамматика чуть ли не с первых своих шагов натолкнулась на ряд серьезных теоретических трудностей и противоречий.

Начнем с рассмотрения синтаксической деривации.

Понятие деривации пришло в синтаксис в конечном счете из области словообразования, где деривационные связи длительное время смешивались с этимологическими и получали однобокое историко-генетическое освещение. Лишь относительно недавно была распознана принципиальная грань между омертвелыми этимологическими связями, характеризующими лексику в генетическом плане, и живыми функциональными связями, характеризующими словопроизводство в синхронической системе. Когда в результате ряда последующих исследований обнаружилось наличие функциональной деривации и в других областях языкового строя — формообразовании, фонематике и семасиологии[1] — стало ясно общее значение деривации как принципа организации 'языковой памяти' и упорядочения хранящихся в ней инвентарных единиц.

Открытие синтаксической деривации укрепило вывод об универсальной значимости принципа функциональной деривации в системе языка. Вместе с тем перед теорией языка встал ряд новых и сложных вопросов. Если в других областях языковой структуры деривация это способ сведе́ния элементов инвентаря в парадигматические ряды, то в синтаксисе она выступает как синтагматический механизм, как средство развертывания языковых элементов в синтагматические ряды. Другими словами, синтаксическая деривация это не статическое понятие, определяющее место той или иной 'единицы хранения' в системе языка, а динамическая структура, отражающая специфическую особенность процесса перевода элементов языка в речевой текст.

Инвентарь языка складывается из 'готовых' строевых элементов, накопленных историей языка и организованных в единую систему. Деривационные связи между элементами инвентаря это связи между 'готовыми' элементами. Производное слово, в отличие от новообразования, это — закрепленная в языке словарная единица, которая по мере надобности извлекается в готовом виде из 'запасника' языка. Деривация в этом случае определяет способ хранения слова, отмечая его 'место' в парадигматическом ряду. Другое дело синтаксическая деривация, порождающая всякий раз новые предложения.

Трудности начинаются здесь уже при попытке определения базальных синтаксических структур.

В работах Хомского можно найти двоякое решение этого вопроса. В качестве базальных структур у него выступают то структуры ядерных предложений, то так наз. 'глубинные структуры'. Ядерные предложения это, по определению Хомского, простейшие активные утвердительные предложения, своего рода "элементарные строительные блоки", из которых, с помощью разных операций, строятся производные предложения.[2] Что же касается глубинных структур, то в их состав входят не только ядерные предложения, необходимые для образования порождаемого предложения, но и перечень всех преобразований, которым должны подвергнуться эти ядерные предложения до их выхода на поверхность речевых текстов. Легко заметить, что эти понятия неравнозначны. Одно из них предполагает, что в системе языка заданы лишь элементарные синтаксические структуры и что система языка не предусматривает заранее, каким операциям и в какой последовательности подвергнется такая элементарная структура в ходе порождающего процесса. С этой точки зрения поверхно-

---

[1]   J. Kuryłowicz, "Dérivation lexicale et dérivation syntaxique", *B.S.L.*, XXXVII (1936), p. 79-92; R. Jakobson, *Kindersprache, Aphasie und allgemeine Lautgesetze* (Uppsala, 1941); J. J. Katz and J. A. Fodor, "The Structure of a Semantic Theory", *Language*, 39 (1963), p. 170-210.
[2]   N. Chomsky, *Syntactic Structures* (*Janua Linguarum*, IV, The Hague, 1957), p. 46; N. Chomsky, "Logical Structures in Language", *American Documentation*, 8,4 (1957), p. 286.

стные предложения, за исключением простейших случаев, прямых прототипов в системе языка не имеют. Другое решение, напротив, исходит из существования подобных моделей-прототипов, и фактически предполагает, что в 'глубинной сфере' представлены модели для всех реально засвидетельствованных и мыслимых поверхностных предложений.

В сущности, речь идет о соотношении исходной структуры и ее последующих преобразований. В одном случае предполагается, что между ними нет жесткой связи и что исходная структура может в принципе подвергнуться различным трансформациям. В другом случае предполагается, что между ними существуют взаимооднозначные отношения. Собственно говоря, только первое решение ставит перед исследованием задачу реконструкции базальных структур, тогда как второе — сводится к простому проецированию поверхностной структуры в глубинную сферу. Предлагаемые Хомским решения не только различны, они — диаметрально противоположны.

Логическая противоречивость предложенных Хомским решений обозначится еще резче, как только мы обратимся к содержательной стороне порождающего процесса. Порождающая грамматика утверждает, что содержание поверхностного предложения зависит только от его базальной структуры и что преобразования ничего нового в исходное содержание не вносят. С такой точки зрения глубинная структура обладает всей полнотой информации, требуемой для ее 'семантической интерпретации', т.е. насыщения конкретными значениями. Оставляя в стороне само понятие 'семантической интерпретации', подразумевающее, что синтаксическая структура возникает как 'чистая' структура, лишенная семантических характеристик и что ее семантическое насыщение происходит позднее (точка зрения, которая уже подверглась критике в литературе по порождающей грамматике),[3] отметим лишь то, что в таком изображении все преобразования оказываются функционально бессодержательными.

Но, с другой стороны, в порождающей грамматике встречаются утверждения, которые приводят к противоположным заключениям. Согласно Хомскому, глубинные структуры образуют 'универсальный компонент' языковой системы, ту сетку мыслительных категорий, которая является основой единства всех языков. В этой связи Хомский даже вспоминает о 'понятийных категориях' Есперсена.[4] Что же касается поверхностных структур, то в них, по Хомскому, универсальные категории отражаются не в чистом виде, а завуалированно, под покровом 'характерологических', или 'идиосинкратических' категорий — таких как падеж, грамматическое число или вид — в сумме придающих каждому языку его неповторимый и своеобычный характер. Напрашивается вывод, что при переходе от глубинных структур к поверхностным имеет место преобразование универсальных категорий в идиосинкратические и что, следовательно,

---

[3] U. Weinreich, "Explorations in Semantic Theory", *Current Trends in Linguistics*, III (The Hague, 1966), p. 395-477.
[4] N. Chomsky, *Aspects of the Theory of Syntax* (Cambridge, Massachusetts, 1965), p. 6, 28.

процессы преобразования отнюдь не нейтральны по отношению к содержанию преобразуемых структур.

Снова перед нами два логически противоречивых и несовместимых подхода. Преобразования синтаксических структур предстают перед нами то как чисто формальные, лишенные содержательной функции операции, то как операции, вносящие дополнительную информацию в порождающий процесс. При первом подходе вопрос о функциональном содержании той или иной трансформации не возникает. Второй из них ставит этот вопрос с настоятельной необходимостью.

Теоретические трудности, связанные с трактовкой содержания порождающего процесса, сказываются и при определении логической природы порождающего процесса.

Порождающая грамматика стремится к логической формализации процесса порождения предложения, представляя его в виде исчисления, в котором конечный результат однозначно предрешен исходной структурой. Синтаксис в таком понимании это устройство, механически преобразующее входные (т.е. глубинные) сообщения в выходные (т.е. поверхностные). При этом предполагается, что между глубинными и поверхностными сообщениями существует изоморфизм. Нетрудно заметить, что механическая концепция порождающего процесса основывается на допущении, что в исходной структуре задана вся необходимая для порождения поверхностной структуры информация и что преобразования нейтральны по отношению к содержанию порождаемых предложений. Но, как отмечалось выше, в самой порождающей грамматике имеются предпосылки для иной постановки вопроса.

Если исходить из тезиса, что глубинные структуры — универсальны по своему категориальному содержанию, а поверхностные структуры — идиосинкратичны, и что порождающий процесс протекает в направлении от универсальных структур к идиосинкратичным, то придется признать, что лежащие в глубинной сфере базальные структуры еще не заключают в себе всей полноты информации, необходимой для появления поверхностных структур, и что такую добавочную информацию несут с собой последующие преобразования. Иначе говоря, можно думать, что содержание поверхностного предложения зависит не только от входного сообщения, но также от свойств идиосинкратического преобразователя (т.е. индивидуальной структуры языка, во многом предопределяющей строение порождаемого сообщения) и от структуры акта коммуникации (т.е. характера участников речевого общения, уровня их общей и языковой подготовки, общей ситуации общения и т.д.).

Конечно, если задана синтаксическая структура и определился способ ее преобразования, то результат преобразования предрешен. Иначе говоря, между преобразуемой и преобразованной структурой существует жесткая, однозначная связь, если задан опосредствующий их способ преобразования. Но из этого не следует, что в целом порождающий процесс характеризуется такой жесткой закономерностью. Напротив того, каждый способ преобразования, до того как он определился, является одним из нескольких или многих способов преобразования, возможных в данной ситуации, и отбор одного из них является вероятностным процессом, исключающим автоматическое исчисление.

Прослеживая порождающий процесс в обратном направлении, от поверхностных структур к глубинным, мы выделяем последовательные фазы этого процесса и смены способов преобразования. При этом легко впасть в ошибку, полагая, что способы преобразования неразрывно связаны с сообщением. Такая ошибка тем более естественна, что в поверхностном предложении преобразования уже осуществлены. Но из этого вовсе не следует, как полагает Хомский, что способы преобразования заданы в исходной структуре. Процесс восприятия речи тем отличается от процесса порождения, что задача выбора того или иного способа преобразования перед ним не возникает. Слушатель имеет дело с результатом порождения, в котором выбор уже определился. Его ум движется по готовым каналам от поверхностной структуры к глубинной и в этом отношении процесс восприятия менее активен, чем процесс порождения. Когда порождающая грамматика рассматривает порождение предложения как жесткий процесс, все фазы которого предусмотрены в исходной структуре, она, в сущности, становится на точку зрения слушателя, имеющего дело с готовой поверхностной структурой. Порождающий процесс типологически более сложен. Наряду с 'жесткими' фазами, он содержит в себе вероятностные, селекционные фазы.

Попытаемся теперь в общих чертах охарактеризовать процесс порождения речи, как он представляется нам на основе высказанных выше соображений.

Порождающий процесс это процесс формирования целостных сообщений, а не обособленных предложений. Структура предложения в определенной степени зависит от целостной коммуникации и места данного предложения в ней. Предложение представляет непосредственную цель порождающего процесса только в случае, когда им исчерпывается все сообщение.

Исходной структурой порождающего процесса является, как можно думать, пропозиция, понимаемая в духе логики отношений. Восходящее к Лейбницу[5] понятие пропозиции отличается от элементарного высказывания тем, что оно выражает определенное 'положение дел', или точнее говоря, событие или состояние, как отношение между логически равноправными объектами. Предложения

> *Я вернул брату книгу*
> *Брат получил от меня книгу обратно*
> *Книга возвращена мной брату*

в сущности, выражают одно и то же событие, участниками которого являются 'я', 'мой брат' и 'книга'. Приведенные предложения различаются порядком слов, грамматическим оформлением членов предложения, отчасти лексическим

---

[5]   G. W. Leibnitz, "Hauptschriften", Philosophische Bibliothek, Bd. 107/108, S. 185

составом и т.д. Но мыслительное содержание в них одинаково. Именно это единое мыслительное содержание и называется пропозицией. Как объект науки пропозиция представляется некоторой идеализацией равнозначных элементарных (т.е. состоящих только из предиката и подразумеваемых им 'дополнений') предложений. В процессе порождения речи она, как можно думать, необходимо предваряет весь процесс.

В составе пропозиции вычленяются носители отношения, выраженного предикатом пропозиции (в нашем примере — 'я', 'мой брат' и 'книга') и связывающий их реляционный предикат (в нашем примере отражающий перемещение объекта обладания в обратном направлении, от временного обладателя к прежнему). Каждый из членов пропозиции сам по себе, не является ни подлежащим, ни прямым дополнением, ни косвенным, а в составе возникших на базе пропозиции предложений может оказаться в любой из таких синтаксических функций. В этом отношении пропозиция напоминает образ или картину. Как на картине, и здесь событие отображено глобально, каждый из участников события схватывается взором в непосредственной связи с целостной картиной.

Реляционный предикат определяется числом предполагаемых им аргументов. Так например, предикат "вернуть–получить обратно–быть возвращенным" является трехаргументным или, иначе, трехместным. Чтобы превратить реляционный предикат в пропозицию, необходимо придать его 'местам' конкретные значения, т.е. актуализировать его аргументы. До его актуализации реляционный предикат это только 'пропозициональная функция', абстрактная возможность пропозиции.

Чтобы охарактеризовать пропозициональную функцию недостаточно знать, сколько при ней аргументов или мест. Необходимо еще специфицировать категориальную значимость каждого 'места'. Так, пропозициональная функция, обозначающая перемену субъекта владения, как "дать–взять–быть отданным" имеет при себе три места, одно — для обозначения субъекта обладания, другое — для обозначения лица, вступающего в эту роль, а третье — для обозначения объекта обладания. К данному типу валентности относятся многие пропозициональные функции, например, такие еще как "продать–купить–быть проданным", или "подарить–получить в дар–быть подаренным", "быть обокраденным–украсть–быть украденным" и т.д. Принадлежность пропозициональных функций к одному типу обусловлена их логической валентностью, т.е. способностью придать значениям, заступающим то или иное 'место', определенную категориальную значимость. Внутри данного типа валентности отдельные пропозициональные функции отличаются одна от другой всякими дополнительными характеристиками, указывающими на способ осуществления перемены владения, осуществлена ли она по доброй воле или насильно, по долгу или в знак внимания, в порядке обмена ценностями или безвозмездно и т.д.

Пропозициональные функции являются умственными образованиями особого рода: они совмещают в себе семантические и синтаксические функции. Как семантические единицы они предполагают возможность их лексического выражения, как элементарные синтаксические единицы они являются структурными прототипами пропозиций, моделями их развертывания. В процессе актуализации хранящихся в сознании знаний о мире пропозициональные функции выполняют роль механизмов, обусловливающих квантование знаний на дискретные единицы. Вместе с тем они несут с собой возможность синтаксической категориализации понятий, которые заполняют места в пропозициональной функции, превращая ее в пропозицию.

Активизация пропозициональной функции и образование пропозиции не является механическим актом. Одни и те же сообщения могут быть развернуты по-разному, с большей или меньшей полнотой. Уже на этой исходной ступени порождения возникает необходимость выбора между разными возможностями, осуществляемого в зависимости от многих объективных и субъективных предпосылок акта коммуникации.

Выраженное пропозициями сообщение составляет первую фазу процесса порождения речи. В целом процесс порождения речи-мысли можно разделить на два основных этапа — этап 'внутренней речи' или 'речи-для-себя' и этап 'внешней речи' или 'речи-для-других'. На первом этапе формируется содержание сообщения, на втором — это содержание эксплицируется и осложняется добавочной информацией в ориентации на предметные и языковые знания слушателя.[6]

На этапе внутренней речи мысль не нуждается в особых грамматических уточнениях. Картинность пропозициональной функции и конкретность восполняющих ее актуализированных понятий делает излишней такую внешнюю детализацию. Внутренняя речь отличается от внешней не только 'обеззвученностью', но и всем своим строем.[7] Синтаксис внутренней речи предельно сжат. Все, что представляется заведомо ясным и самоочевидным, в ней отсутствует. Переходы от одной пропозиции к другой остаются немотивированными. Обрывочный характер и недостаточная оформленность речи-мысли на этом этапе хорошо объясняется семантическими свойствами ее элементов.

Переход от внутренней речи к внешней сопровождается рядом преобразований, обусловленных как содержанием пропозиций, так и условиями ее экспликации.

Из содержания пропозиции непосредственно вытекает тип порождаемого предложения, будет ли оно вопросительным или утвердительным. Если одно из мест при пропозициональном предикате остается незаполненным либо пропозиция в целом представляется недостоверной и есть надежда, что слуша-

---

[6] Л. С. Выготский, *Мышление и речь* (Москва-Ленинград, 1934), стр. 292-294. См. также: С. Л. Рубинштейн, *Принципы и пути развития психологии* (Москва, 1959), стр. 112; Н. И. Жинкин, *Механизмы речи* (Москва, 1958), стр. 360.

[7] Л. С. Выготский, *Мышление и речь*, стр. 293.

тель может разрешить возникшее недоумение, то возникают условия для вопросительного предложения. В прагматической ситуации, позволяющей надеяться, что слушатель может выполнить определенное задание в порядке просьбы, побуждения или повеления, возникает повелительное предложение.

Другой тип преобразования — синтаксическая конверсия — обусловлен особенностями словесного предиката сравнительно с пропозициональным. Содержание предиката многоместной пропозиции, т.е. пропозиции с двумя и более местами, не передается однозначно словесным предикатом. Выше в этих целях мы пользовались комбинированными обозначениями, вроде "продать–купить–быть проданным". Каждому многоместному пропозициональному предикату соответствует не один, а несколько словесных предикатов, различающихся своей синтаксической направленностью, интенциональностью. Словесный предикат отображает действие со стороны одного из участников действия, выступающего в качестве отправного пункта высказывания. Поскольку в многоместной пропозиции таких участников несколько и каждый из них может в принципе стать отправным пунктом высказывания, то и словесных предикатов, призванных заменить предикат пропозиции, может быть несколько.

Необходимость конверсии диктуется переходом от свойственных пропозиции многочленных отношений к двучленным. Словесное высказывание строится по правилам бинарного развертывания, требующим расчленения содержания пропозиции на две части, 'тему' и 'рему', с последующим расчленением каждой из этих частей снова на две части и т.д., пока все содержание не окажется исчерпанным. Возведение одного из членов пропозиции в ранг темы высказывания отбрасывает остальные ее члены вместе с предикатом в группу ремы.

Выбор темы зависит от соотношения 'известного' и 'неизвестного', 'старого' и 'нового' в содержании высказывания и от связей данного высказывания с предшествующим изложением. Предложение развертывается в последовательности от 'известного' к 'неизвестному', т.е. в порядке возрастания того, что пражцы называют 'коммуникативным динамизмом' членов предложения.[8] Говоря об 'известном' и 'неизвестном', необходимо помнить, что речь идет не о том, что известно или неизвестно говорящему, а о том, что по мнению говорящего уже известно и еще неизвестно его слушателю. В порядке развертывания предложения отражается таким образом 'равнение' на слушателя, учет степени его осведомленности. Темой высказывания становится член пропозиции, который, по догадке говорящего, наиболее известен слушателю и может поэтому послужить трамплином для скачка к неизвестному, к реме. Выбор темы данного предложения часто зависит еще от темы предшествующего изложения. В последнем случае тема предложения является средством сохранения тематического единства коммуникации.

В функции темы чаще всего выступает 'подлежащее' (грамматический

8   J. Firbas, "Non-Thematic Subjects in Contemporary English", *Travaux linguistique de Prague*, 2 (1966), p. 240.

субъект), т.е. выделенная формой падежа или места в предложении морфологическая категория, специализированная для этой цели. Но в роли темы могут выступать и другие формы, как в случае безличных предложений (ср.: *мне везет, меня тошнит, у меня нет денег*), так и в других случаях (ср.: *у меня болит голова, у меня есть деньги* и т.д.).

Тип конверсивного преобразования пропозиционального предиката определяется темой (ее логической природой и грамматической формой) и имеющимися в языке средствами конверсии. Так, в русском языке целям конверсии служат: (а) лексические средства, ср.: *дать–взять, дарить–получить в дар, дать взаймы–занять, сдать в наем–снять, доставить удовольствие–получить удовольствие, наказать–подвергнуться наказанию* и т.п.; (б) пассив: *убить–быть убитым, отдать–быть отданным* и т.д. Средством конверсии является также инверсивный порядок слов, ср.: *эту книгу я писал в течение долгих лет,* где выдвижение 'книги' на первое место выделяет ее как тему высказывания.

В ходе конверсии накапливается информация, необходимая, но еще недостаточная для воплощения содержания пропозиции в языковые формы. Результат конверсии еще непроизносим, он намечает лишь синтаксический каркас порождаемого предложения, но не содержит в себе полной информации для грамматического оформления его членов. Очередной шаг в порождении внешней речи призван оснастить этот каркас формами актуализации.

Внутренняя речь, пока она остается 'речью–для-себя', не нуждается в актуализации, так как она оперирует конкретными знаниями и конкретными понятиями. Но совершаемая в интересах слушателя экспликация внутренней речи не может не прибегнуть к формам актуализации, так как без них члены предложения предстанут перед слушателем в абстрактном и расплывчатом виде. В обязательный минимум актуализации входит использование относящихся сюда морфологических категорий, таких как грамматическое число и, там где он наличен, артикль у имен существительных, видо-временные формы — у глагола. К ним примыкают слова-кванторы типа *один, все, некоторые, многие,* а также выражения, указывающие на меру осуществления действия, его частоту и т.п. К факультативным средствам акутализации относятся атрибутивные характеристики всякого рода, в том числе и обстоятельственные определения предиката.

Уточненное в лексическом и грамматическом отношении предложение в принципе уже готово для фонологического его 'исполнения' и отчуждения во-вне. Но в зависимости от внешней ситуации речи и контекста, т.е. внутренних условий речевого текста и места предложения в тексте, возникают возможности дальнейшего его преобразования. В предложение могут быть включены элементы, указывающие на его связь с предшествующим изложением (пространственные, временные, логические и т.д.), например, анафорические местоимения типа *тот, там, тогда, потом, поэтому* и т.д. Кроме того может появиться потребность в опущении компонентов, оказавшихся избыточными **в** силу контекстуальных или ситуативных условий. Опущение самоочевидных и повторных компонентов превращает предложение в 'неполное'. Наконец, возможны и так называемые операции обобщения, в результате которых несколько предложений сливаются в одно — слитное или сложное — предложение.

Из перечисленных выше типов преобразования основными являются преобразования, связанные с конверсией и грамматической актуализацией. Без них невозможен переход от внутренней речи к внешней и от свойственных внутренней речи универсальных смысловых категорий к грамматическим категориям индивидуального языка. Менее обязательны операции по атрибутивной актуализации и ситуативно-контекстуальному преобразованию предложений. Но и в основных операциях есть элемент свободы и выбора, препятствующий рассматривать их как однозначно предсказуемые. Момент вероятности, заключенный в таких операциях, в действительности еще более значителен, так как к грамматическим преобразованиям на данной фазе подключаются и селекционные операции по отбору лексического материала из числа имеющихся в языке синонимов и возможных парафраз. Но вероятностные закономерности в процессе порождения речи не исключают, как сказано выше, наличия в нем и элементов жесткой причинной связи. Если дан исходный материал для преобразования и отобран тип преобразования, то результат преобразования определяется однозначно.

Порождающий процесс, с характерным для него переплетением вероятностных и жестких закономерностей, является ключевым для понимания речевой деятельности в целом. Процесс восприятия речи, в котором селекционные моменты не играют существенной роли, в этом отношении менее показателен. Конечно, общая теория речевой деятельности вправе отвлечься от обоих процессов и сосредоточить свои усилия на выяснении их общих теоретических предпосылок. Но такой абстрактный подход будет оправдан только при условии, если тем самым будет опосредован переход к речевой деятельности в ее конкретных проявлениях. Исследованию, которое продолжает витать в абстрактных сферах, принципиально отвергая необходимость такого перехода, всегда будет угрожать опасность подмены процесса порождения речи относительно менее активным и менее сложным процессом ее восприятия.

Порождающий процесс, т.е. процесс формирования речи вплоть до ее озвучения и отчуждения вовне, нередко называют синтезом речи. В этом термине явно сквозит дескриптивистическое понимание фразообразования, как постепенного построения единиц речи из разноформатных единиц языка. Морфемы, с такой точки зрения, складываются из фонем, словоформы из морфем, синтаксические группы из словоформ, предложение из синтаксических групп. Это явно упрощенный взгляд на вещи, основанный на иллюзии, будто целое по правилам механической сборки составляется из своих частей. Порождающая грамматика возвысилась над такой точкой зрения, показав, что поверхностные структуры вырастают из структур других уровней и что в конечном счете они восходят к глубинным структурам, непосредственно совпадающим с универсальными мыслительными структурами.

Рассматриваемый со стороны мысли, порождающий процесс является скорее последовательностью ряда актов анализа содержания мысли, вычленения отдельных сторон и воссоздания мысли с помощью средств языка. Но и взятый со стороны языка, этот процесс менее всего походит на сборку конструкции из деталей по заданному чертежу. Принцип деривации, пронизывающий весь процесс, по самой своей сути предполагает последовательное сочетание актов анализа и синтеза. Сначала подвергается анализу пропозиция, и ее содержание синтезируется в первичном предложении с помощью основных членов предложения — сказуемого и его 'дополнений'. На первых порах это еще не конкретные словоформы, а некие их идеальные прообразы, лишенные внешних форм актуализации. Затем подвергается анализу содержание каждого из членов первичного предложения, и это содержание эксплицируется с помощью средств актуализации. И так далее, вплоть до момента, когда общие звуковые схемы словоформ расчленяются на отдельные фонемы и акцентуационные типы, из сочетания которых воспроизводится звуковой облик фразы. Что процесс порождения речи не может быть сведен к механическому сцеплению морфем, видно также из того, что в этом процессе, как показано выше, существенную роль играет не только содержание пропозиций, но также учет конкретной ситуации речи, степени осведомленности слушателя, общих целей коммуникации, места данного предложения в составе коммуникации и т.д.

Соответственно и процесс слушания — понимания не может быть односторонне охарактеризован как процесс анализа воспринимаемой речи. И здесь анализ необходимо сочетается с синтезом в деривационных актах, протекающих в обратном направлении. Вычленение отдельных фонем приводит здесь к синтезу двухсторонних знаков, и этот процесс продолжается в восходящем порядке, перерастая, по выражению Л. В. Щербы, в операции "сложения смыслов, дающих не сумму смыслов, а новые смыслы" и ведущих в конечном счете к преобразованию предложений в пропозиции и глобальные элементы сознания.

MARTIN KAY

FROM SEMANTICS TO SYNTAX*

Language is an instrument of communication. Speakers of a common language exchange tokens and thereby influence what goes on in one another's minds in more or less predictable ways. Two people speak the same language if they not only agree on what counts as an acceptable token, but if they are also able to predict fairly accurately what effect each token will have on the other. It seems, therefore, that a linguistic theory — a model of human language — must provide for two kinds of objects corresponding to the tokens and their predictable effects respectively. These can conveniently be labeled SENTENCES and MEANINGS. It must also provide a characterization of the way sentences are paired with meanings.

As Lyons (1963) points out, this is not the only possible view of language. It is true that a token must be meaningful to be linguistic, but this does not entail that there is necessarily something which is its meaning. The so-called structural semanticists view meanings not as entities apart from sentences but as relations among sentences. To say that one sentence is true if and only if another is true, or that one entails another, or that one is incompatible with another, is to state, at least in part, the meanings of these sentences; it is not to state facts which are true by virtue of relations among some distinct set of entities, the true meanings.

This view is appealing because it avoids one of the traditional philosophical difficulties in discussions of meaning. The meaning of a sentence cannot be separated from its linguistic embodiment; it can be stated only in the terms of some linguistic system, which is to say, in effect, as a sentence. No principle is readily available for choosing one of a set of paraphrases and claiming that it IS the meaning of the others. More reasonable seems to be to say that their meaning IS the equivalence relation that unites them, and the relations of entailment that sets them off from other such sets.

But, while this view may have some short-term philosophical appeal, it is almost totally barren from the standpoint of scientific linguistics. It leaves unexplained the fact that meanings, as well as relating sentences, do affect people. More important,

* I am indebted to David G. Hays of The RAND Corporation and Meyer Wolf of Michigan State University for many fruitful discussions of these ideas, but the foolishnesses are mine.

it fails to explain how people can correctly tell the meanings of new sentences. The number of sentences in a language is usually supposed to be infinite and the number of expressable meanings is presumable not smaller. The fact that all the members of a speech community identify essentially the same set of pairs therefore demands explanation.

It is true that meanings can never be exhibited in a pure form, but only as represented by sentences, but this is not to say that every sentence is semantically as perspicuous as every other. The sentence *The person who lived in the house at the side of theirs bought the car* means substantially the same as *The automobile was sold to their next-door neighbor* but the two sentences have almost no words in common and their grammatical structures are clearly distinct. A semantically perspicuous notation would express similar meanings in similar ways. It would be such that if one sentence entailed another, then the second could be derived from the first by applying certain very general rules.[1] There are no general rules that will derive *One of my parents had an accident today* directly from *My father fell downstairs and hurt himself badly this morning*. For a perspicuous notation, the rules could be written.

As I said at the outset, it is part of the work of linguistics to characterize the set of sentence-meaning pairs that make up a language. Since the number of such pairs is infinite, linguistic theory must enumerate them recursively; it will therefore be what is called a GENERATIVE theory.

Many generative theories are, in principle, possible. Chomsky's theory of transformational grammar has a BASE COMPONENT which characterizes a set of BASE P-MARKERS each of which is translated into a SEMANTIC INTERPRETATION by a SEMANTIC COMPONENT and into a sentence by TRANSFORMATIONAL and PHONOLOGICAL COMPONENTS. A base P-marker therefore corresponds to zero or more sentence-meaning pairs, and the total set generable in this way constitutes the language characterized.

An alternative plan is to make the base, or productive, component semantic. The base P-markers would then be semantic interpretations, and the transformational and phonological components would translate them into sentences.

There are several objections that can be made to both of these formulations of generative grammar (see Hays and Kay, forthcoming). Most important is the objection that they provide the worst possible basis for an attack on the problems of what Chomsky calls PERFORMANCE. A language is a set of sentence-meaning pairs, but it is also an instrument of communication. It is therefore of the essence that a speaker of a language should not only know the proper set of sentence-meaning pairs, but that he should be able effectively to translate sentences into meanings and meanings into sentences. He must be able to use his linguistic competence in performance and the linguist must, sooner or later, explain how he does this.

---

[1] This should not be taken as meaning that the particular set of rules required to derive one from the other should itself be discoverable algorithmically. We must expect the semantic formalism to be such that equivalence and entailment relations will be formally undecidable.

A linguistic theory which provides a realistic basis for the study of performance must characterize a transducer capable of translating meanings into sentences and *vice versa*. Chomsky's theory certainly does not do this and there is every reason to suppose that it will not be possible, in general, to construct a transducer of the required kind from the rules of a transformational grammar.

Henceforeward, I shall use the term TRANSDUCTIVE to refer to a linguistic theory which defines a semantic and a phonetic notation, a TRANSDUCTION RULE form, an UPWARD TRANSDUCER or algorithm which translates phonetic expressions into semantic expressions and a DOWNWARD TRANSDUCER which translates semantic into phonetic expressions. A particular language will be characterized by a set of transduction rules which specify the operation of both transducers.

The grammar of a language must distinguish a set of well-formed phonetic expressions, or SENTENCES, and a set of well-formed semantic expressions, or MEANINGS. The question of whether the set of meanings is a linguistic universal is important, but it would be premature to try to solve it now. Another important question, which must be answered at least provisionally before any further progress can be made, concerns the ranges and domains of the transducers and the way in which sets of well-formed expressions are to be defined. The simplest solution is to require that the transducers produce at least one well-formed expression as output in response to every well-formed input and that they produce no output in response to an ill-formed input.

A second possibility is to require that the transducers produce well-formed output in response to every input. In such a system, the well-formedness of an expression could be decided by translating it into one or more expressions of the other type with one transducer and translating each of these into one or more expressions of the original type with the other transducer. The expression is well formed if, and only if, it is found among the expressions resulting from the second transduction.

This plan is attractive because it offers the possibility of explaining how ungrammatical sentences are understood and how grammatical sentences can be only partially coherent, or cognitively anomalous.

A host of other possibilities suggest themselves. We can imagine a system which mapped a sentence onto meanings and non-meanings according to the various natural and anomalous interpretations it had and which mapped non-meanings sometimes onto sentences and sometimes onto non-sentences. In this case, however, the transducers themselves make no distinction between well- and ill-formed expressions and the grammar would therefore have to contain at least one extra component with a function similar to that of Chomsky's base component. But if this were found necessary in a satisfactory theory, it would weaken the claims that could be made for the transductive theory because these rest heavily on the proposition that a base component cannot be satisfactorily motivated. At this stage, it is altogether unclear which approach will be most fruitful.

The theory to be sketched shortly takes the simplest approach. Well-formed ex-

pressions are carried onto well-formed expressions and ill-formed expressions give
no output.

In what follows, I shall describe a form of rules which translate semantic expressions
in a notation akin to that of the predicate calculus into P-markers. The same rules,
interpreted by a slightly different transducer will translate P-markers into semantic
expressions. I have chosen to concentrate on the downward transduction process
partly because the operation of the upward transducer is simpler, and partly to stress
the difference between the view of language advocated here and the more fashionable
one in which semantics is regarded as purely interpretive.

To say that we propose to write semantic expressions in a notation akin to that of
the predicate calculus is, on the face of it, to say very little because the notation is
rich enough to talk about objects of any kind and to describe any kind of relational
structure over them. There is no limit to the number of ways in which even so simple
a sentence as *The man ran* could be translated. The following are some possible
candidates:

(1)   ran(man)
(2)   run(man) past(run)
(3)   run(human) male(human) past(run)
(4)   def(human) male(human) run(human) past(run)

In a sentence consisting of a subject and an intransitive verb, we are used to thinking
of the verb as specifying properties predicated of the subject. Example (1) therefore
seems to be a natural translation. We know however that, for many purposes, the
feature of tense needs to be separated out, and this is done in (2). Here *run* must be
thought of as implying no particular temporal reference. The past tense is represented
by conjoining a second elementary proposition in which 'past' is predicated of 'run'.
There is reason to believe that it will be profitable to separate out the feature of sex
as is done in (3). The content of the English word *man* is now represented by a pair
of primitives, namely 'human' and 'male'. Example (4) is an attempt to accommodate
the definite article.

It is by no means clear at what point the process of factoring notions into simpler
notions should stop. Outside logic itself it is difficult to find a notion so elementary
that it cannot, with a little thought, be expressed as a combination of others. But
this is not to say that the entire enterprise is misbegotten. It is indeed possible to
state properties that semantic expressions with any real explanatory value must have
and to develop a theory of the lexical structure of a language by considering examples
and counter-examples and the semantic expressions that can be associated with them
by a set of formal rules.

As I have said, semantic expressions must be perspicuous. If two sentences are
judged to be exact paraphrases of one another, then their semantic representations
must be equivalent. If one sentence logically entails another, then the semantic
representation of the second should be derivable by formal rules from that of the

first. This is a reasonable requirement of a semantic theory because a notion of entailment is, in fact, often crucial to deciding whether a text is well formed. Consider a fairy story which begins as follows:

Once upon a time a lion and a unicorn decided to go hunting together. But one of the animals was afraid of the other because of what he might do when they got into the forest. It was the lion that was afraid of the unicorn.

If the second sentence is left out, the result is no longer acceptable as the beginning of a well-behaved fairy story. The sentence *It was the lion that was afraid of the unicorn* can be introduced only when it has been established that a lion and a unicorn are involved in the story, and that someone is afraid of someone else. Notice however that the following is entirely acceptable:

"Once upon a time a lion and a unicorn decided to go hunting together. The lion was afraid of the unicorn."

The sentence *The lion was afraid of the unicorn* is true if and only if the sentence *It was the lion that was afraid of the unicorn* is true. But the latter is unacceptable in at least some contexts where the former sounds entirely natural. But for the latter to be acceptable there must be some previous sentence in the text which implies that somebody is afraid of somebody. A semantic theory must therefore provide some formal mechanism for deducing *somebody is afraid of somebody* from *but one of the animals was afraid of the other*.

Another story might begin as follows:

John Doe was a school master who, at the age of seventy, fell in love with an airline hostess. The girl decided to give up her job and marry him.

If not in the best literary style, this is at least more acceptable than the following:

John Doe was a school master who, at the age of seventy, fell in love with an airline hostess. The boy decided to give up her job and marry him.

The second example sounds strange for several reasons, one of which is that no boy has been introduced into the story. There is no parallel difficulty in the first example because airline hostesses are, in general, girls. It is presumably up to the semantic component of the grammar to record this fact and to infer that one of the characters in the story is a girl because one of them is an airline hostess. The sentense *John Doe was a school master who, at the age of seventy, fell in love with an airline hostess* presumably differs in its semantic representation from *John Doe was a school master who, at the age of seventy, fell in love with a girl* in containing a few extra predicates — those necessary to make the meaning of *girl* more specific so that it becomes the meaning of *airline hostess*.

It is not the purpose of this paper to provide even the most tentative set of semantic primitives. I am concerned only with providing the formal system which will relate expressions involving semantic primitives with sentences in a real language. This is, of course, a much simpler task, but it must precede any serious work on the primitives themselves, because, in the absence of rigorous method of associating sentences with semantic representations, there is no sure means of judging the effect of introducing or deleting this or that primitive, and the discussion rapidly loses all contact with reality. However we cannot proceed to set up the formalism without taking notice of some more substantive issues and the most important of these concerns the relationship between the expressions we shall write and expressions in a genuine logic such as the first-order predicate calculus.

The humanist is quite right to claim that language is not logical if, by that, he means that the language of semantic representations cannot itself be a logic. Expressions in natural language can be logically equivalent without being linguistically equivalent. The sentence *It was the lion that was afraid of the unicorn* is true if and only if the sentence *The lion was afraid of the unicorn* is true. But, as we have seen, the latter can be used in places where the former is anomalous. It is, of course, possible to claim that pairs of sentences such as these should be regarded as having the same meaning and that the differences between them should be accounted for on some other basis. The grammar might, for example, contain a kind of super-syntactic component describing the way in which sentences are collected to form discourses. Or there might be a stylistic or rhetorical component, concerned with such matters as emphasis, in which these sentences would be distinguished. But, for reasons I shall present shortly, I prefer to regard these sentences as having different meanings even though they are logically equivalent.

The second reason why the language of semantic representations cannot itself be a logic is that it must be capable of expressing certain notions which must be regarded as meaningless in any logic. There must, for example, be no restriction on the ways in which predicates can be applied to other predicates and, in particular, there must be no restriction against a predicate being applied to itself. Allowing this is, of course, exactly what leads to Russell's famous paradox for, if of any one place predicate p the proposition $p(p)$ is meaningful, then we can construct the predicate q such that $q(p)$ is true if and only if $p(p)$ is false. But, substituting q for p, we have the logical fact that $q(q)$ is true if and only if $q(q)$ is false.

This paradox has led logicians to reject any system in which predicates can be applied indiscriminately to other predicates and to deny the meaningfulness of such notions as self-predicability. But self-predicability is not meaningless. The word *short* is itself short and is therefore self-predicable; the word *long* is not long and is therefore not self-predicable.

It is probably true to say that Russell's paradox came to light precisely because natural languages are capable of expressing ideas which logic cannot accommodate. If such terms as 'self-predicable' and 'the set of all sets' did not sound beguilingly natural, they would never have caused any difficulty. And if they were not meaningful then it is difficult to see how they could have been so closely analyzed as to show their underlying illogicality. The point is this: Logic must be purged of contradictions if it is to be useful for its intended purpose, namely to construct arguments that can be faulted only by faulting the premises on which they are based. Such a system is just as necessary for constructing arguments about language as anywhere else. But our concern here is not with constructing a metalanguage for linguistics, but with constructing a language capable of expressing the things that people express in normal speech. It is true that we have said that the possibility of making inferences in this language by means of formal rules will be one of its crucial properties. But these inferences will have their basis in the culture and the structure of the language, and not in axioms and theorems. The examples (1)–(4) are not therefore to be rejected simply because the same word appears now as a predicate and now as an argument. But they are unsatisfactory from at least one other point of view, namely that they fail to make a necessary distinction between intension and extension. Translating the sentence *The boy saw the man* in a similar way, we might have something like:

$$\text{see(human, human). male(human). male(human). young(human). past(see)}$$

assuming, perhaps unrealistically, that the representation of 'boy' differs from that of 'man' only by the additional predicate 'young'.

This is clearly unsatisfactory because each instance of the term 'human' refers to one of two different people and there is no way of telling them apart. Another possibility is the following:

$$\text{human}(x). \text{human}(y). \text{male}(x). \text{male}(y). \text{young}(x). \text{see}(x,y). \text{past(see)}$$

Here the variables, x and y, correspond to referents. Reference is another notion that needs to be interpreted more broadly in a linguistic than a logical or philosophical context. It is clearly not profitable to think of referents as objects in the real world because it is highly unlikely that the sentence *The boy saw the man* in which *the boy* and *the man* may refer to real people is interpreted in a different way from *The unicorn saw the lion* in which the unicorn is presumably fictional. In fact, from a linguistic point of view, there is reason to suppose that the sentence like *The boy saw the man* involves more than two referents because there are also sentences like *The boy saw the man and when he did he ran away.* The word *did* in this sentence clearly refers to the same event as the word *saw.* In the sentence *The boy saw the man and so did the girl* on the other hand, the word *did* refers to a different event, though one which can have the same name.

The rules for developing P-markers will usually contain two parts, one referring to conditions that must hold in the semantic representation if the rule is applied and the other referring to conditions that must hold in the P-marker, as so far developed, and specifying additions to be made to the P-marker. The second part of a rule will look essentially like a sequence of one or more context-free phrase-structure rules of the familiar type. Let us assume for the moment that the representation of the sentence *The boy saw the man* is as follows:

$$\text{human}(x). \text{human}(y). \text{male}(x). \text{male}(y). \text{young}(x). \text{see}(z). \text{past}(z). z(x,y)$$

Some of the rules that might be used in producing the P-marker from this expression are as follows:

(i) $a(b,c)$ $\Big|$ $S \rightarrow NP_b\ VP$
$\qquad\qquad\ \Big|\ VP \rightarrow\ V_a\ NP_c$

(ii) $see(a).past(a)$ $\Big|$ $V_a \rightarrow saw$

(iii) $human(a).male(a).young(a)$ $\big|$ $N_a \rightarrow boy$

The two parts of each rule are separated by an upright bar. Variables $(a,\ b,\ c...)$ appearing in the first part of a rule can match any variables $(x,\ y,\ z...)$ in the semantic expression. Rule (i) is interpreted as follows: If the semantic expression contains one variable predicated of two others and if the symbol S appears at some node in the P-marker which does not, so far, have any descendents, then the symbols NP and VP can be written against two new nodes dominated by the S. Two more new nodes are to be introduced beneath VP, labelled V and NP respectively.

The subscripts appended to certain symbols in the second half of a rule allow nodes in the P-marker to be associated with variables in the semantic expression. Thus, in rule (i), the NP node introduced below S is to be associated with the first argument of the predicate translated by this rule. Similarly, the newly introduced node V is to be associated with the predicate itself and the second NP is to be associated with the second argument of the Predicate. Rule (ii) is to be interpreted as follows: If *see* and *past* are predicated of the same variable in the expression and the P-marker contains a node labelled V which has been associated with that variable, and if, furthermore, that node in the P-marker has no descendent, then a node labelled *saw* may be introduced beneath it. Interpretation of rule (iii) is similar. The *boy* can be introduced into the P-marker beneath a node labelled N provided that this has been associated by some previous rule with a variable in the semantic expression of which 'human', 'male' and 'young' are all predicated.

A fourth rule might be as follows:

(iv) $human(a).male(a)$ $\big|$ $N_a \rightarrow man$

We are assuming, perhaps unrealistically, that the representation of *boy* differs from that of *man* only by the addition of the predicate 'young'. It apparently follows that wherever rule (iii) applies rule (iv) will apply also. In principle it would be possible to avoid conflicts of this sort so that whenever the semantic properties specified by one rule included those specified by another, then the more inclusive rule would always be applied first. But this solution will not work. In the first place, since one of the main aims is to construct a model which will account for paraphrase, it must be possible to derive several different P-markers from the same semantic expression. This can only be achieved if rules are in general optional and there is little to be gained by ordering optional rules. In the present case nothing important is lost because if our assumptions about the semantic representations of *boy* and *man* were correct, then it would presumably be at least in part because we were prepared to accept any sentence containing the phrase *young man* as a paraphrase of the same sentence with this phrase replaced by *boy*. The following would presumably be included in the set of rules:

(v) young(a) | ADJ$_a$ → *young*

Using this rule we can produce the sentence *The young man hit the man* from the same original semantic expression.

As the rules are refined to represent more and more semantic facts about the language, the expressions that will have to be written to represent even very simple sentences are likely to become long and involved. Furthermore, since the rules are optional and since some may be applicable at many places the same expression, the process of producing a P-marker may often block, *i.e.*, reach a place where it cannot continue owing to lack of applicable rules, but where some parts of the expression have still not been translated. We can imagine the strategy which continues to explore different sequences of rules until it finds one which yields a translation of the expression or demonstrates that no such sequence can be found. But this is both tedious and unrealistic. If a grammar contains the rule (i) suggested above, then any two-place predicate could be used as the starting point for a P-marker. The same would presumably also have to be said of one-place predicates. Hence they will be the normal representatives of intransitive verbs. The production of a sentence could therefore begin almost anywhere.

However, expressions that adequately represent the meanings of sentences will almost certainly have to contain RHETORICAL predicates, that is, predicates that do not influence the truth value of the sentences in which they occur but which relate the information in a given sentence to a whole discourse — in other words, which present the thread of the argument.

The sentence *It was the lion that was afraid of the unicorn* differs from *It was the unicorn the lion was afraid of* in the information that must be assumed for its understanding and the information it purports to offer as new. In the first sentence, it is taken as given that someone was afraid of the unicorn; the question answered by the sentence is *Who?*. In the second sentence it is given that the lion was afraid of someone, but whom was he afraid of? The distinction comes out particularly clearly when the sentences are embedded in certain kinds of other sentences. Compare, for example, *I do not believe that it was the lion that was afraid of the unicorn* with *I do not believe it was the unicorn the lion was afraid of*. What I disbelieve is very different in the two cases. In the first case, I positively do believe that the unicorn was feared, but not necessarily by the lion; in the second, I believe that the lion was afraid, but not necessarily of the unicorn.

Consider now the sentence *I do not believe that the lion was afraid of the unicorn*. Here, what I disbelieve is either that the lion was not afraid or that the unicorn was not feared, or both. In other words, this sentence is ambiguous; it can have the meanings of either or both of the other two.

In the light of this, let us introduce the two-place rhetorical predicate 'new' and represent *It was the boy that saw the man* somewhat as follows:

$$\text{human}(x).\text{human}(y).\text{male}(x).\text{male}(y).\text{young}(x).\text{see}(z).z(x,y).\text{past}(z).\text{new}(x,z)$$

'new(a,b)' means that the predication '$b(...,a,...)$', which must appear in the same conjunct, gives new information. The first rule used to generate the sentence *The boy saw the man* could now be

$$a(b,c).\text{new}(b,a) \left| \begin{array}{l} S \rightarrow NP_b \ VP \\ VP \rightarrow V_a \ NP_c \end{array} \right.$$

However, since no transformations are to be included in the grammar so that the output of this transducer will have the same status as surface structure in transformational grammar, the *VP* node created by this rule has no obvious function outside phonology. But for phonology, the rule could be written

$$a(b,c).\text{new}(b,a) \left| \ S \rightarrow NP_b \ V_a \ NP_c \right.$$

The cleft sentence *It was the boy that saw the man* is also generable from the expression (5). In this case, the initial rule must be something like

(5) $a(b,c).\text{new}(b,a) \left| \ S \rightarrow \textit{it} \ BE_a \ NP_b \ \textit{that} \ V_a \ NP_c \right.$

If the extra nodes are needed for the phonology, the rule would have to be something like

$$a(b,c).\text{new}(b,a) \left| \begin{array}{l} S \rightarrow NP \ VP \\ NP \rightarrow N \\ N \rightarrow \textit{it} \\ VP \rightarrow V \ NP \\ V \rightarrow BE_a \\ NP \rightarrow NP_b S \\ S \rightarrow NP \ VP \\ NP \rightarrow N \\ N \rightarrow \textit{that} \\ VP \rightarrow V_a \ NP_c \end{array} \right.$$

A slight variation of the formalism would allow

$$a(b,c).\text{new}(b,a) \left| \ S \rightarrow NP(N(\textit{it})) \ VP(V(BE_a) \ NP(NP_b \ S(NP(N(\textit{that})) \right.$$
$$VP(V_a \ NP_c))))$$

In what follows, I shall ignore phonology and assume that the simpler form of rule can be used. These can always be expanded into the more complex form if necessary.

The sentence *It was the man the boy saw* is derived from a semantic expression including '$a(b,c).\text{new}(c,a)$' and the initial rule is

(6) $a(b,c).\text{new}(c,a) \left| \ S \rightarrow \textit{it} \ BE_a \ NP_c \ (\textit{that}) \ NP_b \ V_a \right.$

The similarity between (5) and (6) can be captured if they are both replaced by

$$a(b,c).new(d,a) \mid S \rightarrow it\ BE_a\ NP_d\ that\ C_a$$
$$a(b,c).new(b,a) \mid C_a \rightarrow V_a\ NP_c$$
$$a(b,c).new(c,a) \mid C_a \rightarrow NP_b\ V_a$$

The symbol *BE* will be replaced in a subsequent rule by an appropriate part of the verb 'to be'. The subscript will allow the proper tense to be chosen.

A distinction between given and new, topic and comment, theme and rheme has been discovered and rediscovered from time to time throughout the history of linguistics. In many languages, like Chinese and Japanese, it is reflected in the gross syntactic structure of sentences and it must therefore by explained to beginning students. It has been a major center of attention for the Prague school because, while there is relatively free order among the major constituents of sentences in the slavic languages, the diverse possible orders have different rhetorical effects. It is doubtful whether only one rhetorical predicate, the one I have called 'new' underlies all these distinctions. Certainly, there are others and the kind of linguistic theory advocated here would provide a very apt framework in which to study them.

The principal motivation provided so far for the predicate 'new' in this discussion, namely of marking possible starting points for the transducer, is, in a sense, a very old idea. Every semantic expression that underlies a declarative sentence must have at least one occurrence of the predicate 'new'. But this is only to recall one of the most ancient definitions of what a sentence is, namely that it introduces a new thought.

I have already remarked that, in sentences like

(7) *I believe it was Brutus that killed Caesar*
and
(8) *I believe it was Caesar that Brutus killed*

the embedded sentences are, by the usual criteria, logically equivalent but that what I am claiming to believe is different. Using the notions of given and new, (7) and (8) can be paraphrased somewhat as follows:

(9) *I believe (given that Caesar was killed, Brutus was responsible)*
and
(10) *I believe (given that Brutus killed someone, Caesar was the victim)*

Now, notice that what is given can be removed from the parentheses without change of meaning, whereas what is new cannot. (11) and (12) are not semantically distinguishable from (9) and (10).

(11) *Given that Caesar was killed, I believe (Brutus was responsible)*
(12) *Given that Brutus killed someone, I believe (Caesar was the victim)*

This suggests linking rhetorical predicates with what Ross and others call PERFORMA-

TIVES and what the philosopher Austin calls ILLOCUTIONARY ACTS. Ross suggests that declarative sentences come from an underlying structure in which the highest-level sentence is something like 'I assert that S'. Austin points out that, as well as enshrining facts about the world, sentences can also change those facts. This is particularly true of sentences containing words like *promise, undertake,* and *assert.*

If we say that every sentence involves at least one performative in its semantic structure, or that every sentence is an illocutionary act, we can represent (13) and (14) as (15) and (16).

(13) *It was Brutus that killed Caesar*
(14) *It was Caesar that Brutus killed*
(15) *Brutus*(b). *Caesar*(c). *killed*(x,c). b = x
(16) *Brutus*(b). *Caesar*(c). *killed*(b,x). c = x

Clauses like $b = x$ now take the place of the 'new' predicate. The representation of sentences like (7) and (8) becomes something like (17) and (18).

(17) *Brutus*(b). *Caesar*(c). *I*(i). *killed*(x,c). *believe*(i, b = x)
(18) *Brutus*(b). *Caesar*(c). *I*(i). *killed*(b,x). *believe*(i, c = x)

Rhetorical predicates, or devices like the '=' in the above examples are crucial to the study of semantics in natural languages and serve to set those languages off against most artificial languages. Just how many of them there are is, of course, not known — probably very few. The 'new' predicate is certainly responsible for the distinction between restrictive and non-restrictive relatives, the latter being precisely those that involve new information, or, more precisely, information that purports to be new. It may also underlie the distinction between *The house is near the store* and *the store is near the house.* It almost certainly does not account for the difference between *the glass is half full* and *the glass is half empty,* or between *who am I?* and *which is me?.*

Informally, the function of a rhetorical predicate is fairly clear. When I talk to you, I normally have a construct in my mind and I want to erect a copy of it in yours. I must build the picture piece by piece, telling you where each new piece is to be placed relative to what has already been built, and checking from time to time that the contruction is proceeding as I intend. Each piece comes in a sentence which also contains the necessary information about where it is to be put. It must, therefore contain old and new information to be effective — probably more old than new. What is new does not always have to be marked explicitly because it will be clear from what has been done already and the course that the construction is taking. A sentence like *It was Brutus that killed Caesar* marks what is to be taken as new very clearly, whereas the simpler sentence *Brutus killed Caesar* is relatively ambiguous.

But it would be absurd, at this stage, to make any psychological claims for the model of language sketched here. Far too many details have been left out. But, though the specific proposal made here may turn out wrong in almost every detail, and though there is no reason to claim any psychological reality for it, there is never-theless very great importance in having models in linguistics which actually work — models of performance or, at least, performance-oriented competence. A model which claims to account for paraphrase must produce paraphrases even if some of the procedures it uses are of no eventual theoretical interest. The trouble with a purely interpretive theory of semantics is that, though one may argue about it endlessly, it is very difficult to see what it would be like to demonstrate that a grammar written according to it was wrong. In the interest of intellectual hygiene alone, it is important to study a subject as difficult as semantics with models that actually work and which therefore lay themselves open to specific attack.

REFERENCES

Hays, David G. and Martin Kay,
    "The Failure of Chomskian Theory in Linguistics" (The RAND Corporation, forthcoming).
Lyons, John,
  1963 *Structural Semantics. An Analysis of Part of the Vocabulary of Plato* (Oxford, Blackwell).

FERENC KIEFER

ON THE PROBLEM OF WORD ORDER

(1) Early works on transformational grammar (*e.g.*, Chomsky, 1957) considered word order changes as straightforward effects of optional transformational rules. In later works (*e.g.*, Chomsky, 1965), too, word order was looked upon as a mere stylistic matter and, as a consequence, the question was raised as to whether word order changes should be accounted for in grammar at all. In other words, Chomsky and others were inclined to relegate the problem of word order *in toto* to performance rather than to consider it as a matter of competence. To show that this contention is not quite justified is one of the aims of the present paper. We shall put forth, though tentatively, the general principles of handling the problem of word order. Our present considerations are based on my earlier study of word order in Hungarian (Kiefer, 1967). Here, however, I will treat several points differently. Recent developments in the theory of grammar (Bierwisch, 1969; Fillmore, 1968a and b; McCawley, 1967; a.o.) make several improvements on my earlier treatment possible. Furthermore, so far I have focussed my attention on the role of emphasis in determining word order. Yet it is clear that apart from emphasis the topic-comment relation constitutes another important factor in word order changes (Daneš, 1958; Firbas, 1964; Heidolph, 1966; Novak, 1966; and most recently Sgall, 1967; with respect to Hungarian, *cf.* also Elekfi, forthcoming; Dezső, 1965 and 1968; Dezső-Szépe, 1967). Finally, here I will not restrict myself to Hungarian though Hungarian seems to be particularly appropriate for a study of word order.

(2) Emphasis is not only a syntactic problem because it can be predicted by syntactic rules as claimed by Lu (1965), but also, and more importantly, because several syntactic rules are triggered by a syntactic feature which might be referred to as Emph. The question of how this Emph gets into syntax will be one of our main concern. Before going into this problem let me adduce some of the syntactic constructions that are determined by Emph.

(a) In English the two best-known examples are
    (i) the cleft-sentences like

It is Mary that I want to marry
It is the big book that I have read

(ii) and the emphatic *do*

I do hope that she will come

(b) In French the constructions with *c'est ... qui* and *c'est ... que* cannot be explained without Emph. The same holds with respect to the repetition of personal pronouns like in

Moi, je ne comprends rien

(c) In German, apart from some word order changes, there are several (transformational) rules that make use of Emph. *E.g.*,

nicht ein ⇒ *kein*

is obligatory except in case of emphasis, because then we may have either

nicht ein ... (sondern zwei)
nicht ein Buch ... (sondern ein Heft)

or

kein Buch ... (sondern ein Heft)

(d) The ambiguity of the Russian sentence

мать видела дочь

can be explained only by means of Emph. The two possibilities are

мать видела дочь
мать *видела дочь*

On the other hand,

мать видел сын

is only grammatical if 'мать' is emphatic.

(e) In Hungarian if the verb 'van' ('to be') is used existentially, it must be emphatic. In this case, some word order changes are obligatory. Consider, for example,

Peter van az osztályban
Peter is   the class-in
(There is somebody called Peter in the class)

versus

Péter az osztályban van
Peter is in the classroom

On the other hand,

Levelet olvas János
letter   reads John

is only possible if "levelet" (or, possibly, "olvas") is emphasized:

Levelet olvas János
It is a letter that John is reading

These examples will suffice to show that emphasis is an important syntactic problem.

Undoubtedly, there are several types of emphasis. In the case of emotional emphasis everything can receive emphasis (any morpheme or even any phoneme). Therefore, no rules govern this kind of emphasis. Consequently, it falls outside the scope of a competence model. In contrast to emotional emphasis, logical emphasis reveals a well-defined syntactic structure that can be rendered roughly by the following diagram

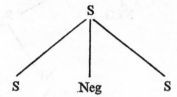

where the two lower S's are almost identical; they differ in one lexical item only. This fact has already been observed by Lu who propounds the following deep structure for the sentence "*John* bought a book" (Lu, 1965:41):

(1)

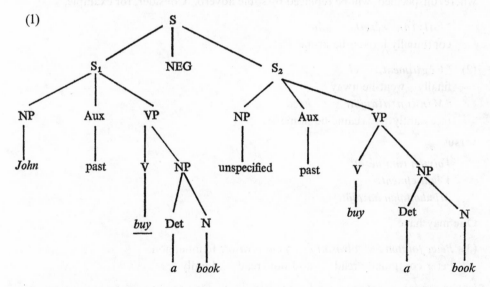

In order to get the surface structure "*John* bought a book" one has simply to apply some transformational rules to (1):

T1: Delete the whole S_2.
T2: Delete NEG
T3: Add stress to the word in S_1 whose counterpart in S_2 is unspecified.

This proposal leaves, however, several important questions unanswered. First of all, in which way can structures like (1) be generated? Secondly, the aforementioned deletion transformations seem to contradict the well-known conditions of deletability (*cf.*, Chomsky 1965:182).

As to the first problem, notice that in Hungarian there are many adverbials that can occur in structures like (1) but cannot receive emphasis. What I mean by that is that one may also have

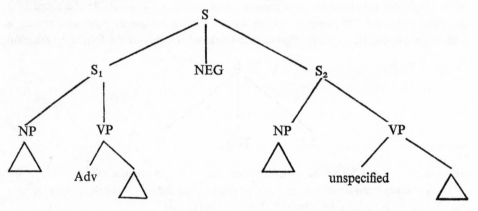

where 'unspecified' will be replaced by some adverb. Consider, for example,

> *Folyton nézett   rám*
> continually looked-he at-me

(2) *Végül ment   el*
finally   went-he away
Minduntalan jött   haza
incessantly   came-he home

versus

> *Folyton rám nézett*
> *Végül elment*
> *Minduntalan hazajött*[1]

One may have

(3) *Péter folyton   olvasott és   nem olvasott fennhangon*
Peter continually read   and not read   loudly

This fact indicates that structures like (1) can be interpreted as a deep structure of an emphatic sentence only if the lexical items do not prove the contrary. Before proceeding, however, another remark is necessary. Instead of (3) we may also have

(4) *Péter folyton olvasott és nem fennhangon olvasott*

---

[1] Notice, incidentally, that in emphatic sentences the particle always comes after the verb.

where the adverb *folyton* is emphatic. This is, however, not logical emphasis but rather a metalinguistic emphasis that does not affect meaning.[2]

One can quite easily adduce a great number of further examples where emphasis is not possible. For instance, in many languages articles cannot take emphasis. In Hungarian, one may have

Az ember ment el otthonról és nem egy ember

Here emphasis has a metalinguistic character and when we assert that no emphasis is possible then this is to be taken in the sense that logical emphasis is out of the question. The same holds for emphasis in the following examples

Der Mann ging weg und nicht die Mann
Der Mann ging weg und nicht ein Mann

It is interesting to note that whenever the indefinite article is emphasized it becomes the numeral *one*.[3]

I do not want to dwell on this problem any further.[4]

It seems to be beyond any doubt that emphasis is not only a purely syntactic but also a lexical problem. If so, then either structures like (1) are not the most appropriate way to handle it, or it must be supplemented by some conditions as to the lexical items.

In fact, one might think of other possibilities for generating emphatic sentences. This is apparently supported by some further syntactic properties of emphasis, the most important being the fact that no simple sentence can have more than one emphatic constituent. Here 'simple' means that the deep structure of the sentence contains only one *S*. This suggests the following rule for the introduction of emphasis as a syntactic feature:

(5) S → (Emph) ... NP VP

Then one wants Emph, optionally introduced in (5), to be attached to the right nodes in the base P-markers. Otherwise one would need extra filtering transformations, *i.e.*, transformations that do not perform other tasks except for filtering out the wrong deep structures, a solution which seems to me quite counterintuitive. One simply does not like rules in a grammar that exhibit only a filtering function. Of course, simplicity, too, is violated by this solution. In order to avoid this one may stipulate other solutions. As far as I can see, two possibilities present themselves. One could

[2] This kind of emphasis can be conceived either as a correction of mispronunciation or of the inappropriate use of a word. In (4) one has the latter case. This means that (4) involves somehow that one should not say "loudly" with respect to his reading. From a semantic point of view, *folyton* cannot be contrasted with other adverbs. In other words, one is unable to grasp the meaning of *folyton* if it is emphatic and not used metalinguistically. It is, so to speak, void of meaning.

[3] Lu observes that the indefinite article in English, if emphasized, should be interpreted as 'one' or 'a single'. Does not this indicate that indefinite articles cannot take emphasis? (*Cf.* Lu, 1965:40.)

[4] For further details, see Kiefer, 1967:4-53.

introduce transformational rules into the base that attach Emph just to the right node. The effect of these transformational rules would be something like this:

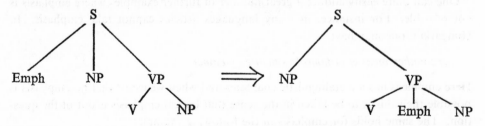

These transformations, called attachment transformations (*cf.* Kuroda, 1965), can perform the task desired. They are, however, against the principle that no transformational rules should work in the base. If we allow transformational rules to operate in the base, then I see no way of drawing a line between deep and surface structure, between the base of a grammar and its transformational component.[5]

In view of the above, one should make use of transformational rules in the base only if no other possibility is available. As far as I know an argument to this effect could not be found up to now.

A further possibility would be to generate the correct structures for emphatic sentences by means of categorial (phrase-structure) rules. This can be done if we increase the number of rules, for example, in the following way

$$
\begin{aligned}
(6)\quad S &\rightarrow NP'\ VP' \\
NP' &\rightarrow Det\ (Emph)\ N \\
VP' &\rightarrow V\ NP\ PrepP \\
PrepP &\rightarrow Prep\ NP'' \\
S &\rightarrow NP''\ VP'' \\
NP'' &\rightarrow Det\ N \\
VP'' &\rightarrow \begin{cases} (Emph)\ V\ NP''\ PrepP \\ V\ NP'\ PrepP \\ V\ NP''\ PrepP' \end{cases} \\
PrepP' &\rightarrow \begin{cases} (Emph)\ Prep\ NP'' \\ Prep\ NP' \end{cases}
\end{aligned}
$$

It is clear that it is not a system of rules like (6) that we want. In the case of more constituents the number of rules grows still more rapidly. Therefore, at least for the time being, one must drop the claim that Emph should be introduced by categorial rules. It would seem that (1) is still the best way of handling emphasis.[6]

[5] One cannot argue here that transformational rules are needed anyway in the base if one accepts the more plausible alternative of the organization of the base propounded in Chomsky (1965). The lexical insertion rules are, in fact, transformational rules, but transformational rules of a special kind. They do not alter the syntactic structure of the sentence structures generated by the base.

[6] It is conceivable that a generative semantic approach will offer us new possibilities. At present it would, however, be too early to put forward some proposals to this effect. The scattered remarks and

The lexical items that cannot take emphasis will be marked so in their lexical characterization. Thus we must add to (1) the following condition:

Condition 1: Emphasis must not be derived from structures like (1) if this contains in S_1 in the position corresponding to the node labelled "unspecified" a lexical item that is negatively specified with respect to emphasis.

Compare the following types of emphatic sentences with each other:

(7) *Your handbag is light and not heavy*
    This problem is difficult and not easy
    The boy is fat and not meagre

(8) *John is at home and not Paul*
    The mail arrived and not the newspaper
    He read the book and not the newspaper

(9) *The book is mine and not yours*
    He is going to do the job and not me
    I will read this book and not that one

n (7) the adjectives form antonymous pairs, the assertion of one of them implies the negation of the other and conversely, the negation of one of them implies the assertion of the other. S_2 can here be deleted because the lexical entry referred to as "unspecified" can be inferred on the basis of S_1. In (9) the scope of the contrast is well-defined but not the particular instance. In the first sentence of (9) "mine" may also contrast with "his, her, ours, yours, theirs". In other words, the deletion of S_2 is only justified under the presupposition that not only the scope but also the instance of the item "unspecified" is known. Similar conclusions can be drawn with respect to (8), though there the scope of emphasis is less clear. Now we are able to formulate the condition of deletability for (1).

Condition 2: In (1), S_2 can be deleted only if either (a) the item "unspecified" can uniquely be inferred from the corresponding term in S_1, or (b) the presuppositions arising from the situational context of (1) allow this inference.

I cannot go into the question of presuppositions in more detail here (*cf.* Fillmore, 1968b), but it is plain that presuppositions play an essential role in the case of deletion.[7]

The structure (1) together with *Condition 1* must be considered what Perlmutter calls output conditions of the base (*cf.* Perlmutter, 1968). Such conditions are necessary for various independent reasons.

---

ideas about a generative semantics have not been developed to a full-fledged theory as yet (*cf.*, for example, Bierwisch, 1970 and McCawley, 1967).

[7] It should be made clear that presuppositions are also necessary for the general interpretation of emphatic sentences. Notice, that no emphatic sentence can initiate a discourse. Each emphatic sentence presupposes a certain kind of discourse (*cf.* Kiefer 1967: 122-155). So far as I can see, the theory of sentence presuppositions is a very promising step towards a new theory of discourse.

In most cases, emphasis requires special word order in free-word order languages. Hence *Condition 2* cannot be lumped together with *Condition 1*. (1) and *Condition 2* form an output condition on the transformational component of grammar.

To sum up, a structure like (1) and *Conditions 1* and *2* will account for the syntactic description of emphasis except for the word order changes that will be described in a subsequent section.[8]

(3) While the syntactic description of emphasis is relatively novel, the topic-comment relation has been investigated for some time, especially by the Prague linguists (Mathesius, Daneš, Dokulil, Firbas, Novak, Sgall — to mention only some of them). The topic-comment relation, called functional sentence perspective in the Prague school, was also used as an argument to set up a stratificational model of language (*cf.*, for example, Sgall, 1967). The functional sentence perspective was separated from the syntactic description of sentences on the ground that it does not tell us anything about the syntactic structure but about the ways in which a given syntactic structure is used in the process of communication. Thus, word order is conceived as belonging to the pragmatic level of linguistic description rather than to the syntactic structure proper. In the process of communication each communicational unit (which is not necessarily a sentence) is supposed to convey new information. Moreover, if language is aptly used, each communicational unit adds new information to something that is already known. Hence communicational units can be split up into two types of information: the novel information is conveyed by the comment(s), the already known information is the topic of the communicational unit. This distinction is indicated in language by stress (hence intonation), word order, *etc.*[8a] We may now ask how the topic-comment relation can be accounted for in a generative description of language. There have already been some attempts to account for this relation in the framework of generative grammar (Staal, 1967; Dezső-Szépe, 1967). I shall comment upon these later on. First let me point out that the topic-comment relation is in several points akin to emphasis. At the same time it essentially differs from the latter:

(1) First of all, there is no way to describe the topic-comment relation by means of a structure like (1) because (a) to be a comment does not involve negation; (b) it does not involve a parallel structure.

Notice, for instance, that the topic of a sentence[9] is by no means determined by its position in the sentence. Consider, for example,

(10) (i) *I saw Sally reading a book*
   (ii) *She read an interesting book*

---

[8] This is not all that can be said about emphasis, of course. Here I had to content myself with a brief summary of my earlier and present thoughts about this topic. A more detailed discussion would go beyond the scope of the present paper.

[8a] It should be made clear that this is only *one* interpretation of "topic-comment". Several other aspects may enter into play.

[9] For simplicity's sake we shall identify the communicational unit with *sentence*.

In (10i) under the presuppositions that we do not initiate a discourse by it and that *I saw Sally* is already known, we may say that *reading a book* is the comment. In (10ii), however, only *interesting* is the comment.

(2) In languages with free word order the impact of the topic-comment relation is in general different from that of emphasis. In Hungarian, for example, in emphatic sentences the emphatic constituent must always precede the verb and in the case of verbs with particle the particle must come after the verb (except for the case when the verb itself receives emphasis). Thus, one has

> *A postára   János vitte   el   a   levelet*
> the post-office to John   carried-he away the letter
> (It was John who took the letter to the post-office)

versus

> *János a postára elvitte a levelet*
> *János elvitte a postára a levelet, etc.*

where the comment can be *a postára, elvitte a levelet, a levelet, etc.* In other words, comment is much less determined by word order than emphasis. The stress pattern is more significant from the point of view of topic-comment than word order, though the latter can also be decisive (see below).

(3) It is clear that in emphatic sentences the emphatic constituent is supposed to convey the novel information. Therefore, the emphatic constituent must be considered the comment of the sentence. Thus, every emphatic constituent is the comment of a sentence but not every comment is emphatic.

(4) Emphasis affects meaning, not so the topic-comment relation. If we follow Fillmore's distinction between meaning and presupposition (*cf.*, Fillmore, 1968b) then we may say that negation (and also question, command, *etc.*) affects the meaning of sentences but not their presuppositions. But we have (at least) two kinds of presuppositions, one concerns the presuppositions originating in the lexical items of the sentence, the other comes from the sentence structure. Fillmore's distinction holds for the former type of presuppositions but not for the latter. Take, for instance, Fillmore's example

(11) (i) *Open the door!*
    (ii) *Don't open the door!*

The presuppositions concerning *open* and *door* and *you* are the same for (11i) and (ii). At the same time, the meanings of (i) and (ii) are different. On the other hand, however, if I say

(12) (i) *I will open the door.*
    (ii) *I will not open the door.*

here there will be a difference in presuppositions as well, the sentence (12ii) being

an answer to a question or command, *i.e.*, it cannot, normally, initiate a discourse while
(12i) can. In this sense some meaning changing operations will also change the presuppositions. Since the topic-comment relation will affect only the stress pattern, or
word order, *etc.*, of sentences, only the presuppositions with respect to the possible
positions in the communication process of the given sentence will change but not
their meaning. In the case of emphasis, however, besides some changes in the presuppositions also the meaning of the sentence will change.

I cannot but agree with Sgall who says that

"the functional sentence perspective, as well as the means of its realization, has a systematic
character and a full description of a language system as a system of 'forms' and 'function'
is not possible without respecting it." (Sgall, 1967: 206.)

In other words, the topic-comment relation must be accounted for in a competence
model of language. Let us say that the topic of a sentence is the unmarked category
and the comment is the marked category. Furthermore, let us denote comment by
Com. The question is now how Com is to be assigned to a sentence or its parts.

To begin with, we must seek an answer to the following questions:
(a) What can be Com?
(b) How many Com's can occur in a sentence?

As to (a), it is easy to see that a sentence that initiates a discourse is a Com. Hence
Com can be assigned to whole sentences. On the other hand, it has been observed
that there is a close connection between questions and Com's (*cf.*, for example,
Hatcher, 1961). Moreover, it has been stated that Com can be assigned only to constituents that can be questioned (Staal, 1967). It is a well-known fact that one questions
mostly noun phrases.[10] It seems to me, however, that not only must Com be assigned
to sentences, but in some cases also to verb phrases. In fact, one can ask a question
about the whole verb phrase or about the activity, state, *etc.* expressed by the verb.
Take, for instance, the sentences

(13) *What are you doing? I am walking*
      What are you doing? I am writing a letter
      What are you doing? I am feeding my dog with bread and butter

versus

(14) *What are you writing?*
      I am writing a letter
      What are you feeding your dog with?
      I am feeding my dog with bread and butter
      Who are you feeding with bread and butter?
      I am feeding my dog with bread and butter

In (13) we are questioning the verb phrase, hence in the answers the verb phrases

---

[10] Katz and Postal even argue that one can question noun phrases only. *Cf.* Katz Postal (1964:
79-120).

are to be considered as Com's. In (14) we are asking about some parts of the verb phrase.

We deliberately leave open the problem of how questions are treated in the base. It might very well be that grammatical categories that appear at the surface as nouns, verbs, adjectives, *etc.*, are considered as a single category in the base component. It is clear, however, that (13) and (14) must be handled differently.

As to (b) we must disagree with Staal who claims that every sentence has only one topic. Even if we restrict ourselves to simple sentences, this is not true. This is simply a consequence of the symmetrical behavior of topic and comment. That more than one Com can occur in a simple sentence is without any doubt because of questions like

> *Who is going to kill whom?*
> *Who sends what to whom?*

Let us now take a sentence S_1 with three Com's and one topic. This should be followed in the discourse by S_2 that repeats the three Com's of S_1 and replaces the topic of S_1 by something else. Thus, S_2 will have three topics and one Com. If we agree, however, that topic is the unmarked category, we do not have to bother about it. It is enough if we can manage somehow to indicate the possible or necessary Com's for a given sentence.

Several authors have pointed out that Com determines the place of break (or breaks) and the stress pattern in a sentence. Thus, Com plays an essential role in determining the phonological structure of sentences (Daneš, 1964; Pala, 1966; Dezső-Szépe, 1967; Elekfi, forthcoming; a.o.). This means that the assignment of Com must come before the phonological component is put to work. A rule like

(15) $S \rightarrow (Com) \ldots NP \; VP$

would obscure the issue because Com does not affect the meaning proper of sentences. Furthermore, in many languages Com can possibly be accounted for by means of presuppositions only. Therefore, (15) does not tell us anything about what is really going on. Here it is quite impossible to set up a structure like

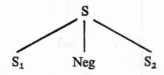

as in the case of emphasis, because on the basis of Com the syntactic structure of the preceding sentence in the discourse cannot be inferred (as it can in the case of emphasis). On the basis of Com we can only state what information has already been previously mentioned.

As far as I can see, in view of the structure of grammar as presently conceived, Com should be assigned to sentences or their parts after the word order rules have

already done their work. Com can then be attached to P-markers by means of transformational rules. These rules can be either obligatory or optional. They are obligatory in case of emphasis or in case of some word order. If you say in German

Den Abendstern sah er

then one has either

Den Abendstern sah er und nicht den Mond

i.e., with emphasis on *Abendstern* or

Er sah einen Stern am Himmel. Den Abendstern sah er

where *Abendstern* is to be assigned Com but not Emph.

The assignment of Com entails different presuppositions. These must be accounted
for by a theory of presuppositions that will tell us how sentences with various presuppositions should be interpreted. Is this to mean that also surface structures must
be interpreted semantically? This is quite possible. It would seem that our problem
is closely related to that of presuppositions in general.[11]

In order to illustrate what I am after let me take the sentence

(16) *Den Abendstern sah er*

again. Let us now leave aside emphasis. The (surface) structure of (16) is approximately

(17)

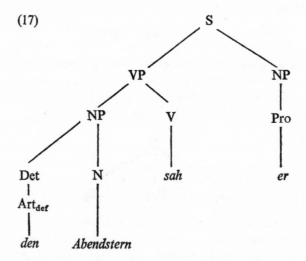

---

[11] It may be that a new component will be needed, that will take care of these phenomena. It is also
possible that a 'revised' stratificational approach will suit our purpose better. At present, however, all
this cannot be more than mere speculation.

Here the transformational rule

(18) Art_{def} N V NP $\Rightarrow$ 1 Com 2 3 4
                          1   2 3 4

obligatorily applies. We obtain the structure

(19)

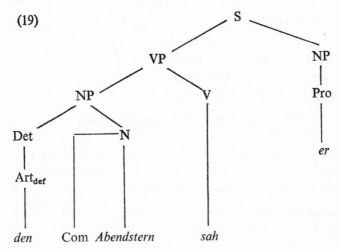

On interpreting (19) one must assign to (19) the presupposition that whenever it is uttered everything except for *Abendstern* is taken as already being known (from a previous sentence or by some other means). What we want to communicate is the fact that we are talking about something called *Abendstern*. Everything else in the sentence is not important; it is important to the extent only that it is necessary in order to express ourselves in some linguistically acceptable way.

In languages with much freer word order than German (Hungarian, Russian, *etc.*) the rule (18) would not apply obligatorily but the interpretation of a structure like (19) would be the same.

(4) What has been said so far has an important bearing on word order. I have already pointed out that in Hungarian 'emphatic' word order reveals two important features:

(i) the emphatic constituent must always precede the verb (except, of course, if the verb itself is emphatic); as a consequence a sentence where the verb stands in initial position can be emphatic only if the verb receives emphasis.

(ii) in case of verbs with particle the particle must come after the verb (once again, with the exception of emphatic verbs).[12]

[12] This is, by the way, a good proof for emphasis. It even enables us to differentiate between con-trastive and emphatic stress. Take, for example, the sentence

Peter is working in Vienna and John in Paris.

where *Peter–John* and *Vienna–Paris* receive so-called contrastive stress. In Hungarian if we take a verb with particle the order is Part V in case of contrastive stress, but V Part in case of emphasis.

It is not possible here to discuss in detail the word order regularities of emphatic sentences in Hungarian.[13] It should be made clear, however, that some word order rules must apply obligatorily; others are optional like the rules that will account for the following changes

(20) *Tegnap   Péterrel találkoztam az utcán*
     'yesterday Peter-with met-I   the street-on'
     (*Yesterday I met Peter in the street*)

     Péterrel találkoztam tegnap az utcán
     Az utcán tegnap Péterrel találkoztam
     Tegnap az utcán Péterrel találkoztam, etc.

The changes in (20) seem to be mere stylistic variants, their semantic interpretation remains apparently unchanged.

A similar situation seems to hold with respect to Com. In general the observation has been made that if the direct object is moved from the postverbial to a preverbial position it must be either emphatic or it is a Com:

(21) *Az autódat láttam az utcán*
     the car-yours saw-I   the street-in

     Péter levelet írt   anyjának
     Peter letter   wrote-he mother-his-to

(16), too, is a pertinent example.

Here, too, some changes can be considered with good reason to be mere stylistic ones.

     Péter anyjának levelet írt
     Anyjának levelet írt Péter

The obligatory changes in case of Com are, however, less clear than with emphatic sentences.

It seems safe to conclude that any work on word order must take into account both Emph and Com and that some of the word order rules will be obligatory and others will be optional. Before concluding our remarks on word order we must take up the following problem. In languages with free word order is there any distinguished word order that can be considered to be basic? For basic word order we may stipulate the following definition. *A word order is referred to as basic if it can stand without any presupposition as to what should be considered as being already known.* Thus, the word order represented by either (20) or (21) cannot be considered to be basic. For (20) and (21) one would, quite intuitively, set up the following basic orders:

(22) *Tegnap találkoztam Péterrel az utcán*
     Láttam az autódat az utcán[14]

---

[13]   This has been done at some length in Kiefer (1967).
[14]   I have left out the third sentence deliberately. Intuitively, *Péter levelet írt anyjának* seems to be

Alongside (22), however, one may also have

(23) *Tegnap találkoztam az utcán Péterrel*
      Találkoztam az utcán Péterrel tegnap
      Láttam az utcán az autódat, etc.

This may be due partly to the free positional status of some of the adverbials (in the first place those of time and place). It can easily be shown that as soon as some other categories are involved in these changes, presuppositions about the linguistic context will emerge. The sentence

(24) *Az autódat láttam az utcán*

will be felt to be incomplete (without Emph or Com). We would ask *And what?* — *és?* and a possible answer would be:

> *ole nem hittem, hogy rám vársz*
> but I did not think you were waiting for me

Some changes will be felt to be ungrammatical:

> *Olvas levelet János*
> read letter John
> (John is reading a letter)
> *Az autódat az utcán láttam*

Thus, except for some of the adverbials, it seems to be possible to establish a unique basic order which will be generated by the base component of grammar. All changes will be carried out by transformational rules in the transformational component according to the principles put forward in the preceding discussion.

We may conclude this extremely sketchy discussion, that hardly touches upon all important questions of word order and leaves even many of the discussed problems open, that even in languages with so-called free word order, word order is far from being free. This is a fact that can be brought to fore only by means of a more subtle analysis than has been undertaken so far.[15]

REFERENCES

Bierwisch, M.,
   1970   "On Classifying Semantic Features", in: Manfred Bierwisch and Karl Erich Heidolph (eds.),
          Progress in Linguistics (The Hague, Mouton).
Chomsky, N.,
   1957   *Syntactic Structures* (The Hague, Mouton).

the basic order but here Com (or Emph) is obligatory. There are, at least in Hungarian, many sentence structures that trigger off Com or Emph. This indicate, that the definition for basic order must be modified in some way in order to cover these cases as well.

[15] I will discuss the relation between topic-comment and presuppositions in a separate paper (*cf.*, Kiefer, forthcoming).

142   FERENC KIEFER

  1965   *Aspects of the Theory of Syntax* (Cambridge, Mass., The M.I.T.-Press).
Daneš, Fr.,
  1958   "K otázce pořádku slov v slovanských jazycích", *SaS*, 20:1-10.
  1964   "A Three-Level Approach to Syntax", TLP, 1: 225-240.
Dezső, L.,
  1965   "Notes on the Word Order of Hungarian Simple Sentences", *Computational Linguistics*,
      4: 3-59.
  1968   "Typologische Besonderheiten der ungarischen Wortfolge", *Acta Linguistica Hungarica*,
      18:125-59.
Dezső, L. and Gy. Szépe,
  1967   "Adalékok a topic-comment problémához", *Nyelvtudományi Közlemények*, LXIX: 365-388.
Dokulil, M. and Fr. Daneš,
  1958   "K tzv. významové a mluvnické stavbě věty, in: *O vědeckém poznání soudobých jazyků*,
      231-246.
Elekfi, L.,
      "Kriterien der aktuellen Satzgliederung in ungarischen Kernsätzen" (forthcoming).
Fillmore, Ch.,
  1968a   "The Case for Case", in: *Universals in Linguistic Theory* (New York, Holt, Rinehart and
      Winston, 1-88.
  1968b   "Types of Lexical Information", in: *Studies in Syntax and Semantics*, F. Kiefer, ed.
      (Dordrecht, D. Reidel), 109-137.
Firbas, J.,
  1962   "Notes on the Function of the Sentence in the Act of Communication", in: *Sborník prací
      filos. fak. brněnské university*, XI, A10:133-148.
  1964   "On Defining the Theme in Functional Sentence Analysis", TLP, 1: 267-280.
Hatcher, A. G.,
  1961   "Theme and Underlying Question" (= Supplement to *Word*, 12).
Heidolph, K. E.,
  1966   "Kontextbeziehungen zwischen Sätzen in einer generativen Grammatik", *Kybernetika*, 3:
      274-281.
Katz, J. J. and P. Postal,
  1964   *An Integrated Theory of Linguistic Descriptions* (Cambridge, Mass., The M.I.T.-Press).
Kiefer, F.,
  1967   "On Emphasis and Word Order in Hungarian", Indiana University, Uralic and Altaic
      Series, Vol. 76.
      "Topic-comment and Presuppositions" (forthcoming).
Kuroda, S.-Y.,
  1965   "Attachment Transformations" (M.I.T., mimeographed).
Lu, J. H. T.,
  1965   *Contrastive Stress and Emphatic Stress* (= The Ohio State University, *Project Report*,
      No. 10).
Mathesius, V.,
  1929   "Zur Satzperspektive im modernen Englisch", *Archiv für das Studium der neueren Sprachen
      und Literaturen*, 155: 202-210.
McCawley, J.,
  1967   "The Role of Semantics in a Grammar", in: *Universals in Linguistic Theory* (New York,
      Holt, Rinehart and Winston), 125-169.
Novak, P.,
  1966   "On the Three-Level Approach to Syntax", *TLP*, 2: 219-223.
Pala, K.,
  1966   "O nekotorych problemach aktualnogo členenija", *PSML*, 1: 81-92.
Perlmutter, D.,
  1968   "Deep and Surface Structure Constraints" (M.I.T. Dissertation, mimeographed).
Sgall, P.
  1967   "Functional Sentence Perspective", *PSML*, 2: 203-225.
Staal, J. F.,
  1967   "Some Semantic Relations between Sentoids", *FL*, 3: 66-88.

PAUL KIPARSKY AND CAROL KIPARSKY

FACT*

The object of this paper is to explore the interrelationship of syntax and semantics in the English complement system. Our thesis is that the choice of complement type is in large measure predictable from a number of basic semantic factors. Among these we single out for special attention PRESUPPOSITION by the speaker that the complement of the sentence expresses a true proposition. It will be shown that whether the speaker presupposes the truth of a complement contributes in several important ways to determining the syntactic form in which the complement can appear in the surface structure. A possible explanation for these observations will be suggested.

1. TWO SYNTACTIC PARADIGMS

The following two lists both contain predicates which take sentences as their subjects. For reasons that will become apparent in a moment, we term them FACTIVE and NON-FACTIVE.

FACTIVE	NON-FACTIVE
significant	likely
odd	sure
tragic	possible
exciting	true
relevant	false
matters	seems
counts	appears
makes sense	happens
suffices	chances
amuses	turns out
bothers	

* This work was supported in part by the U.S. Air Force (ESD Contract AF19(628)-2487) and the National Institutes of Health (Grant MH-13390-01).

This paper developed through several revisions out of a paper read in 1967 at Bucharest. These revisions were largely prompted by helpful discussions with many colleagues, among whom we would especially like to thank John Kimball, George Lakoff, Robin Lakoff, Haj Ross, and Timothy Shopen.

We shall be concerned with the differences in structure between sentences constructed with factive and non-factive predicates, *e.g.*:

Factive: *It is significant that he has been found guilty*
Non-factive: *It is likely that he has been found guilty*

On the surface, the two seem to be identically constructed. But as soon as we replace the *that*-clauses by other kinds of expressions, a series of systematic differences between the factive and non-factive predicates begins to appear.

(1) Only factive predicates allow the noun *fact* with a sentential complement consisting of a *that*-clause or a gerund to replace the simple *that*-clause. For example,

The fact that the dog barked during the night
The fact of the dog's barking during the night

can be continued by the factive predicates *is significant*, *bothers me*, but not by the non-factive predicates *is likely*, *seems to me*.

(2) Only factive predicates allow the full range of gerundial constructions, and adjectival nominalizations in *-ness*, to stand in place of the *that*-clause. For example, the expressions

His being found guilty
John's having died of cancer last week
Their suddenly insisting on very detailed reports
The whiteness of the whale

can be subjects of factive predicates such as *is tragic*, *makes sense*, *suffices*, but not of non-factive predicates such as is *sure*, *seems*, *turns out*.

(3) On the other hand, there are constructions which are permissible only with non-factive predicates. One such construction is obtained by turning the initial noun phrase of the subordinate clause into the subject of the main clause, and converting the remainder of the subordinate clause into an infinitive phrase. This operation converts structures of the form

It is likely that he will accomplish even more
It seems that there has been a snowstorm

into structures of the form

He is likely to accomplish even more
There seems to have been a snowstorm

We can do this with many non-factive predicates, although some, like *possible*, are exceptions:

It is possible that he will accomplish even more
*He is possible to accomplish even more

However, none of the factive predicates can ever be used so:

> *He is relevant to accomplish even more
> *There is tragic to have been a snowstorm

(4) For the verbs in the factive group, extraposition[1] is optional, whereas it is obligatory for the verbs in the non-factive group. For example, the following two sentences are optional variants:

> That there are porcupines in our basement makes sense to me
> It makes sense to me that there are porcupines in our basement

But in the corresponding non-factive case the sentence with the initial *that*-clause is ungrammatical:

> *That there are porcupines in our basement seems to me
> It seems to me that there are porcupines in our basement

In the much more complex domain of object clauses, these syntactic criteria, and many additional ones, effect a similar division into factive and non-factive predicates. The following lists contain predicates of these two types.

FACTIVE	NON-FACTIVE
regret	suppose
be aware (of)	assert
grasp	allege
comprehend	assume
take into consideration	claim
take into account	charge
bear in mind	maintain
ignore	believe
make clear	conclude
mind	conjecture
forget (about)	intimate
deplore	deem
resent	fancy
care (about)	figure

(1) Only factive predicates can have as their objects the noun *fact* with a gerund or *that*-clause:

Factive: *I want to make clear the fact that I don't intend to participate*
               You have to keep in mind the fact of his having proposed several alternatives

---

[1] Extraposition is a term introduced by Jespersen for the placement of a complement at the end of a sentence. For recent transformational discussion of the complexities of this rule, see Ross (1967).

Non-factive: *I assert the fact that I don't intend to participate*
              We may conclude the fact of his having proposed several alternatives

(2) Gerunds can be objects of factive predicates, but not freely of non-factive predicates:

Factive: *Everyone ignored Joan's being completely drunk*
              I regret having agreed to the proposal
              I don't mind your saying so

Non-factive: **Everyone supposed Joan's being completely drunk*
              **I believe having agreed to the proposal*
              **I maintain your saying so*

The gerunds relevant here are what Lees (1960) has termed 'factive nominals'. They occur freely both in the present tense and in the past tense (*having -En*). They take direct accusative objects, and all kinds of adverbs and they occur without any identity restriction on their subject.[2] Other, non-factive, types of gerunds are subject to one or more of these restrictions. One type refers to actions or events:

He avoided getting caught
**He avoided having got caught*
**He avoided John's getting caught*

Gerunds also serve as substitutes for infinitives after prepositions:

I plan to enter the primary
I plan on entering the primary
**I plan on having entered the primary last week*

Such gerunds are not at all restricted to factive predicates.

(3) Only non-factive predicates allow the accusative and infinitive construction.

Non-factive: *I believe Mary to have been the one who did it*
              He fancies himself to be an expert in pottery
              I supposed there to have been a mistake somewhere

Factive: **I resent Mary to have been the one who did it*
              **He comprehends himself to be an expert in pottery*
              **I took into consideration there to have been a mistake somewhere*

As we earlier found in the case of subject complements, the infinitive construction is

---

[2] There is, however, one limitation on subjects of factive gerunds:

                    **It's surprising me that he succeeded dismayed John*
                    **There's being a nut loose disguntles me*

The restriction is that clauses cannot be subjects of gerunds, and that the gerund formation rule precedes extraposition and *there*-insertion.

excluded, for no apparent reason, even with some non-factive predicates, *e.g.*, *charge*. There is, furthermore, considerable variation from one speaker to another as to which predicates permit the accusative and infinitive construction, a fact which may be connected with its fairly bookish flavor. What is significant, however, is that the accusative and infinitive is not used with factive predicates.

2. PRESUPPOSITION

These syntactic differences are correlated with a semantic difference. The force of the *that*-clause is not the same in the two sentences

> *It is odd that it is raining* (factive)
> *It is likely that it is raining* (non-factive)

or in the two sentences

> *I regret that it is raining* (factive)
> *I suppose that it is raining* (non-factive)

The first sentence in each pair (the factive sentence) carries with it the presupposition 'it is raining'. The speaker presupposes that the embedded clause expresses a true proposition, and makes some assertion about that proposition. All predicates which behave syntactically as factives have this semantic property, and almost none of those which behave syntactically as non-factives have it.[3] This, we propose, is the basic difference between the two types of predicates. It is important that the following things should be clearly distinguished:

(1) Propositions the speaker asserts, directly or indirectly, to be true
(2) Propositions the speaker presupposes to be true

Factivity depends on presupposition and not on assertion. For instance, when someone says

> *It is true that John is ill*
> *John turns out to be ill*

he is ASSERTING that the proposition 'John is ill' is a true proposition, but he is not

---

[3] There are some exceptions to this second half of our generalization. Verbs like *know, realize*, though semantically factive, are syntactically non-factive, so that we cannot say **I know the fact that John is here*, **I know John's being here*, whereas the propositional constructions are acceptable: *I know him to be here*. There are speakers for whom many of the syntactic and semantic distinctions we bring up do not exist at all. Professor Archibald Hill has kindly informed us that for him factive and non-factive predicates behave in most respects alike and that even the word *fact* in his speech has lost its literal meaning and can head clauses for which no presupposition of truth is made. We have chosen to describe a rather restrictive type of speech (that of C.K.) because it yields more insight into the syntactic-semantic problems with which we are concerned.

PRESUPPOSING that it is a true proposition. Hence these sentences do not follow the factive paradigm:

*John's being ill is true
*John's being ill turns out
*The fact of John's being ill is true
*The fact of John's being ill turns out

The following sentences, on the other hand, are true instances of presupposition:

It is odd that the door is closed
I regret that the door is closed

The speaker of these sentences presupposes 'the door is closed' and furthermore asserts something else about that presupposed fact. It is this semantically more complex structure involving presupposition that has the syntactic properties we are dealing with here.

When factive predicates have first person subjects it can happen that the top sentence denies what the complement presupposes. Then the expected semantic anomaly results. Except in special situations where two egos are involved, as in the case of an actor describing his part, the following sentences are anomalous:

*I don't realize that he has gone away
*I have no inkling that a surprise is in store for me[4]

Factivity is only one instance of this very basic and consequential distinction. In formulating the semantic structure of sentences, or, what concerns us more directly here, the lexical entries for predicates, we must posit a special status for presuppositions, as opposed to what we are calling assertions. The speaker is said to 'assert' a sentence plus all those propositions which follow from it by virtue of its meaning,

---

[4] In some cases what at first sight looks like a strange meaning shift accompanies negation with first person subjects. The following sentences can be given a non-factive interpretation which prevents the above kind of anomaly in them:

I'm not aware that he has gone away
I don't know that this isn't our car

It will not do to view these non-factive that-clauses as indirect questions:

*I don't know that he has gone away or not

We advance the hypothesis that they are deliberative clauses, representing the same construction as clauses introduced but that:

I don't know but that this is our car

This accords well with their meaning, and especially with the fact that deliberative but that-clauses (in the dialects that permit them at all) are similarly restricted to negative sentences with first person subjects:

*I know but that this is our car
*John doesn't know but that this is our car

not, *e.g.*, through laws of mathematics or physics.[5] Presumably in a semantic theory assertions will be represented as the central or 'core' meaning of a sentence — typically a complex proposition involving semantic components like 'S_1 *cause* S_2', 'S *become*', 'N *want* S' — plus the propositions that follow from it by redundancy rules involving those components. The formulation of a simple example should help clarify the concepts of assertion and presupposition.

Mary cleaned the room

The dictionary contains a mapping between the following structures:

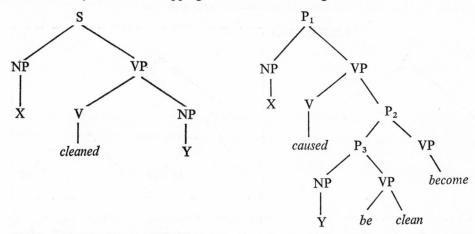

where S refers to the syntactic object 'Sentence' and P to the semantic object 'Proposition'.

A redundancy rule states that the object of *cause* is itself asserted:

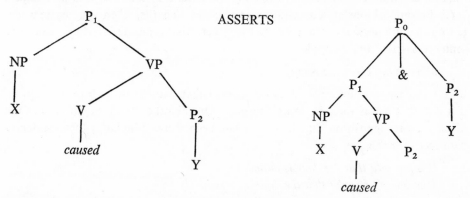

---

[5] We prefer 'assert' to 'imply' because the latter suggests consequences beyond those based on knowledge of the language. This is not at all to say that linguistic knowledge is disjoint from other knowledge. We are trying to draw a distinction between two statuses a defining proposition can be said to have in the definition of a predicate, or meaning of a sentence, and to describe some consequences of this distinction. This is a question of the semantic structure of words and can be discussed independently of the question of the relationship between the encyclopedia and the dictionary.

This rule yields the following set of assertions:

X caused[6] Y to become clean
Y became clean

[Why the conjunction of P_1 and P_2 is subordinated to P_0 will become clear below, especially in (3) and (5)]

Furthermore, there is a presupposition to the effect that the room was dirty before the event described in the sentence. This follows from *become*, which presupposes that its complement has, up to the time of the change referred to by *become*, not been true. This may be expressed as a redundancy rule:

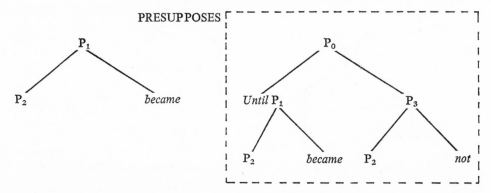

(Presuppositions will be enclosed in dotted lines. Within the context of a tree diagram representing the semantic structure of a sentence, presuppositions which follow from a specific semantic component will be connected to it by a dotted line).

That this, like the factive component in *regret* or *admit*, is a presupposition rather than an assertion can be seen by applying the criteria in the following paragraphs.

(1) Presuppositions are constant under negation. That is, when you negate a sentence you don't negate its presuppositions; rather, what is negated is what the positive sentence asserts. For example:

Mary didn't clean the room

unlike its positive counterpart does not assert either that the room became clean or, if it did, that it was through Mary's agency. On the other hand, negation does not affect the presupposition that it was or has been dirty. Similarly, these sentences with factive predicates

It is not odd that the door is closed
John doesn't regret that the door is closed

presuppose, exactly as do their positive counterparts, that the door is closed.

---

[6]　Though we cannot go into the question here, it is clear that the tense of a sentence conveys information about the time of its presuppositions as well as of its assertions, direct and indirect. Thus tense (and likewise mood, cf. footnote 8) is not an 'operator' in the sense that negation and other topics discussed in this section are.

In fact, if you want to deny a presupposition, you must do it explicitly:

Mary didn't clean the room; *it wasn't dirty*
Legree didn't force them to work; *they were willing to*
Abe didn't regret that he had forgotten; *he had remembered*

The second clause casts the negative of the first into a different level; it's not the straightforward denial of an event or situation, but rather the denial of the appropriateness of the word in question (spaced out above). Such negations sound best with the inappropriate word stressed.

(2) Questioning, considered as an operation on a proposition P indicates 'I do not know whether P'. When I ask

Are you dismayed that our money is gone?

I do not convey that I don't know whether it is gone but rather take that for granted and ask about your reaction.

(Note that to see the relation between factivity and questioning only yes-no questions are revealing. A question like:

Who is aware that Ram eats meat

already by virtue of questioning an argument of *aware*, rather than the proposition itself, presupposes a corresponding statement:

Someone is aware that Ram eats meat

Thus, since the presupposition is transitive, the *who*-question presupposes all that the *someone*-statement does.)

Other presuppositions are likewise constantly under questioning. For instance, a verb might convey someone's evaluation of its complement as a presupposition. To say *they deprived him of a visit to his parents* presupposes that he wanted the visit (*vs. spare him a visit...*). The presupposition remains in *Have they deprived him of a...?* What the question indicates is 'I don't know whether they have kept him from...'

(3) It must be emphasized that it is the SET of assertions that is operated on by question and negation. To see this, compare —

Mary didn't kiss John
Mary didn't clean the house

They have certain ambiguities which, as has often been noted, are systematic under negation. The first may be equivalent to any of the following more precise sentences:

Someone may have kissed John, but not Mary
Mary may have kissed someone, but not John
Mary may have done something, but not kiss John
Mary may have done something to John, but not kiss him

And the second:

> *Someone may have cleaned the house, but not Mary*
> *Mary may have cleaned something, but not the house*
> *Mary may have done something, but not clean the house*
> *Mary may have done something to the house, but not clean it*

All of these readings can be predicted on the basis of the constituent structure:

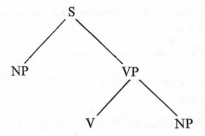

Roughly, each major constituent may be negated.

But the second sentence has still another reading:

> *Mary may have been cleaning the house, but it didn't get clean*

That extra reading has no counterpart in the other sentence. *Clean* is semantically more complex than *kiss* in that whereas *kiss* has only one assertion (press the lips against), *clean* has two, as we have seen above. How this affects the meaning of the negative sentence can be seen through a derivation:

(i)

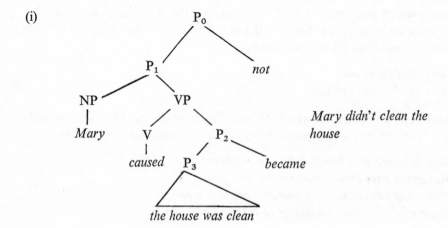

(ii) Application of redundancy rule on 'cause':

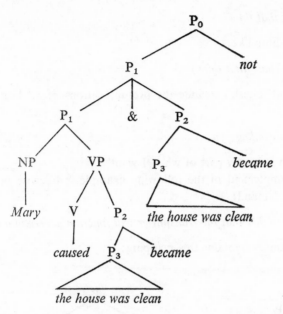

It's not the case that both Mary cleaned the house and the house is clean.

(iii) DeMorgan's Law yields

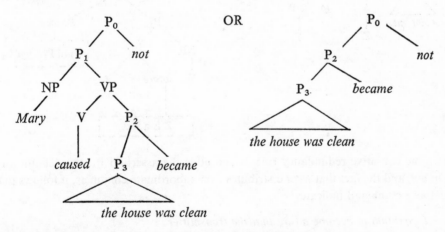

Either 'Mary didn't clean the house' or 'the house didn't get clean'.

Thus to say *Mary didn't clean the house* is to make either of the two negative assertions in (iii). The remaining readings arise from distribution of *not* over the constituents of the lexicalized sentence.

Presumably the same factors account for the corresponding ambiguity of *Did Mary clean the house?*

(4) If we take an imperative sentence like:

(You) chase that thief!

to indicate something like:

I want (you chase that thief)

then what 'I want' doesn't include the presuppositions of S. For example, S presupposes that

That thief is evading you

but that situation is hardly part of what 'I want'.

The factive complement in the following example is likewise presupposed independently of the demand:

Point it out to 006 that the transmitter will function poorly in a cave

Assume the dictionary contains this mapping:

$$
\begin{array}{l}
S \\
\quad NP \;(X) \qquad VP \;(V=point\ out,\ NP=Z,\ NP=to\ NP=Y) \\[4pt]
\longleftrightarrow \\[4pt]
P_0 \\
\quad NP\;(X) \qquad VP\;(cause,\ P_1) \\
\qquad P_1 \to P_2\;(NP=Y,\ VP=aware\ Z\ [\,Z\ is\ a\ fact\,]),\ became\ [\,Until\ P_1\ \underline{not}\ P_2\,]
\end{array}
$$

From the causative redundancy rule, which adds the assertion P_1, the definition of *point out*, and the fact that *want* distributes over subordinate conjuncts, it follows that the above command indicates:

I want 006 to become aware that the transmitter...

However it doesn't in any way convey

I want the transmitter to function poorly in a cave

nor, of course, that

I want 006 not to have been aware...

(5) We have been treating negation, questioning, and imperative as operations on

propositions like implicit 'higher sentences'. Not surprisingly explicit 'higher sentences' also tend to leave presuppositions constant while operating on assertions. Our general claim is that the assertions of a proposition (P_k) are made relative to that proposition within its context of dominating propositions. Presuppositions, on the other hand, are relative to the speaker. This is shown in Figures 1 and 2. Fig. 1 shows that the presuppositions of P_k are also presupposed by the whole proposition P_o. In Fig. 2 we see that whatever P_o asserts about P_k it also asserts about the SET (see (3) above) of propositions that P_k asserts.

Figure 1:   Figure 2:

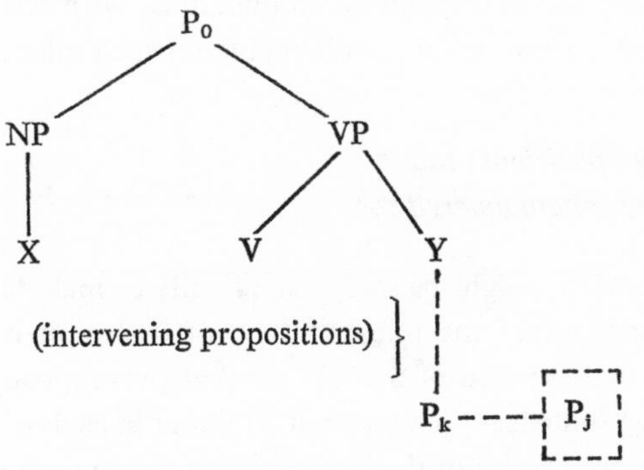

Redundancy rule: Redundancy rule:

P_k presupposes $\boxed{P_j}$ P_k asserts $\{P_a, P_b, ..., P_m\}$

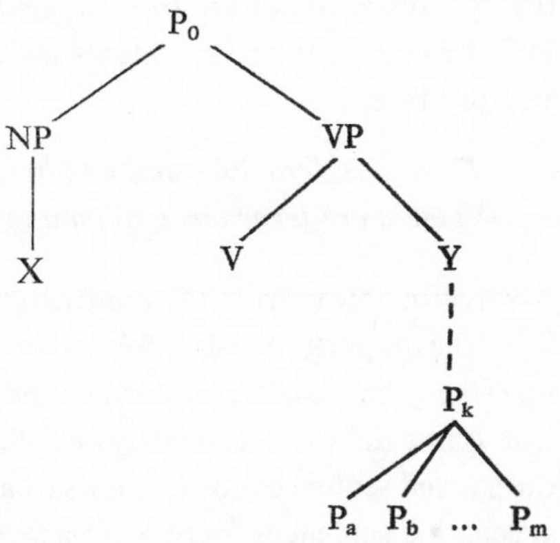

Let us further exemplify this general claim:

John appears to regret evicting his grandmother

Since *appear* is not factive this sentence neither asserts nor presupposes

John regrets evicting her

However it does presuppose the complement of the embedded factive verb *regret*, as well as the presupposition of *evict* to the effect that he was her landlord.

It does not matter how deeply the factive complement (spaced out) is imbedded:

Abe thinks it is possible that Ben is becoming ready to encourage Carl to acknowledge that he had behaved churlishly

This claim holds for presuppositions other than factivity. We are not obliged to conclude from

John refuses to remain a bachelor all his life

that he plans to undergo demasculating surgery, since *bachelor* asserts *unmarried*, but only presupposes *male* and *adult*. Thus it yields:

John refuses to remain unmarried all his life

but not

John refuses to remain male (adult) all his life

(6) A conjunction of the form S_1 *and* S_2 *too* serves to contrast an item in S_1 with one in S_2 by placing them in contexts which are in some sense not distinct from each other. For instance,

Tigers are ferocious and panthers are (ferocious) too
*Tigers are ferocious and panthers are mildmannered too

Abstracting away from the contrasting items, S_1 might be said semantically to include S_2. The important thing for us to notice is that the relevant type of inclusion is *assertion*. Essentially, S_2 corresponds to an assertion of S_1. To see that presupposition is not sufficient, consider the following sentences. The second conjunct in each of the starred sentences corresponds to a presupposition of the first conjunct, while in the acceptable sentences there is an assertion relationship.

John deprived the mice of food and the frogs didn't get any either
*John deprived the mice of food and the frogs didn't want any either
John forced the rat to run a maze and the lizard did it too
*John forced the rat to run a maze and the lizard didn't want to either
Mary's refusal flabbergasted Ron, and he was surprised at Betty's refusal too
*Mary's refusal flabbergasted Ron and Betty refused too

3. A HYPOTHESIS

So far, we have presented a set of syntactic-semantic correlations without considering how they might be accounted for. We shall continue by analyzing these facts and others to be pointed out in the course of the discussion, in terms of a tentative explanatory hypothesis, by which the semantic difference between the factive and non-factive complement paradigms can be related to their syntactic differences, and most of the syntactic characteristics of each paradigm can be explained. The hypothesis which we should like to introduce is that presupposition of complements is reflected in their syntactic deep structure. Specifically, we shall explore the possibility that factive and non-factive complements at a deeper level of representation differ as follows:[7]

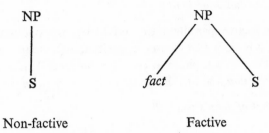

Non-factive   Factive

[7] It is not quite as simple as this. Consider, for one thing, the sentences:

John's eating them would amaze me
I would like John's doing so

These sentences do not at all presuppose that the proposition in the complement is true. This indicates a further complexity of the FACT postulated in the deep structure of factive complements. Like verbs, or predicates in general, it appears to take various tenses or moods. Note that these correspond to the above sentences:

If he were to eat them it would amaze me
I would like it if John were to do so

These can also be constructed as

If it were a fact that he ate them it would amaze me

A second over-simplification may be our assumption that sentences are embedded in their deep structure form. A case can be made for rejecting this customary approach in favor of one where different verbs take complements at different levels of representation. Consider direct quotation, which appears not to have been treated in generative grammar. The fundamental fact is that what one quotes are surface structures and not deep structures. That is, if John's words were 'Mary saw Bill', then we can correctly report

John said: 'Mary saw Bill'

but we shall have misquoted him if we say

John said: 'Bill was seen by Mary'

If we set up the deep structure of both sentences simply as

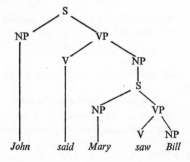

then we have not taken account of this fact. We should be forced to add to this deep structure the

If this interpretation is correct, then closest to the factive deep structure are sentences of the type

> *I regret the fact that John is ill*

The forms in the factive paradigm are derived by two optional transformations: formation of gerunds from *that*-clauses in position after nouns, and deletion of the head noun *fact*. (We do not pause to consider the general rules which take care of the details involving *that* and *of*.) By gerund-formation alone we get

> *I regret the fact of John's being ill*

---

specification that the complement either must or cannot undergo the passive, depending on which of the sentences we are quoting. Since sentences of any complexity can be quoted, to whose deep structures the passive and other optional transformations may be applicable an indefinite number of times, it is not enough simply to mark the embedded deep structure of the quoted sentence as a whole for applicability of transformations. What has to be indicated according to this solution is the whole transformational history of the quoted sentence.

A more natural alternative is to let the surface structure itself of the quoted sentence be embedded. This would be the case in general for verbs taking direct quotes. Other classes of verbs would take their complements in different form. We then notice that the initial form of a complement can in general be selected at a linguistically functional level of representation in such a way that the truth value of the whole sentence will not be altered by any rules which are applicable to the complement. Assuming a generative semantics, the complements of verbs of knowing and believing are then semantic representations. From

> *John thinks that the McCavitys are a quarrelsome bunch of people*

it follows that

> *John thinks that the McCavitys like to pick a fight*

That is, one believes propositions and not sentences. Believing a proposition in fact commits one to believing what it implies: if you believe that Mary cleaned the room you must believe that the room was cleaned. (Verbs like *regret*, although their objects are also propositions, differ in this respect. If you regret that Mary cleaned the room you do not necessarily regret that the room was cleaned).

At the other extreme would be cases of phonological complementation, illustrated by the context

> *John went '..........'*

The object here must be some actual noise or a conventional rendering thereof such as *ouch* or *plop*.

A good many verbs can take complements at several levels. A verb like *scream*, which basically takes phonological complements, can be promoted to take direct quotes. *Say* seems to take both of these and propositions as well.

Are there verbs which require their complement sentences to be inserted in deep structure form (in the sense of Chomsky)? Such a verb X would have the property that

> *John Xed that Bill entered the house*

would imply that

> *John Xed that the house was entered by Bill*

but would not imply that

> *John Xed that Bill went into the house.*

That is, the truth value of the sentence would be preserved if the object clause underwent a different set of optional transformations, but not if it was replaced by a paraphrase with another deep structure source. It is an interesting question whether such verbs exist. We have not been able to find any. Unless further search turns up verbs of this kind, we shall have to conclude that, if the general idea proposed here is valid, the levels of semantics, surface structure, and phonology, but not the level of deep structure, can function as the initial representation of complements.

Fact-deletion can apply to this derived structure, giving

> *I regret John's being ill*

If *fact*-deletion applies directly to the basic form, then the simple *that*-clause is formed:

> *I regret that John is ill*

Although this last factive sentence has the same superficial form as the non-factive

> *I believe that John is ill*

according to our analysis it differs radically from it in syntactic form, and the two sentences have different deep structures as diagrammed above. Simple *that*-clauses are ambiguous and constitute the point of overlap (neutralization) of the factive and non-factive paradigms.

If factive clauses have the deep structures proposed by us, these various surface forms in which factive clauses can appear become very easy to derive. That is one piece of support for our hypothesis. The remaining evidence can be grouped under three general headings:

(1) syntactic insulation of factive clauses (Section 4)
(2) indifferent and ambiguous predicates (Section 5)
(3) pronominalization (Section 6)

4. SYNTACTIC INSULATION OF FACTIVE CLAUSES

Let us first return in somewhat more detail to infinitive constructions, examining first the derivation of infinitives in general and then of the class of infinitive constructions which we mentioned as being characteristic of non-factive predicates. Basic to our treatment of infinitives is the assumption that non-finite verb forms in all languages are the basic, unmarked forms. Finite verbs, then, are always the result of person and number agreement between subject and verb, and non-finite verbs, in particular

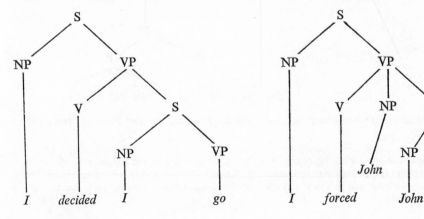

infinitives, come about when agreement does not apply. Infinitives arise regularly when the subject of an embedded sentence is removed by a transformation, or else placed into an oblique case, so that in either case agreement between subject and verb cannot take place. There are several ways in which the subject of an embedded sentence can be removed by a transformation. It can be deleted under identity with a noun phrase in the containing sentence, as in sentences like *I decided to go* and *I forced John to go* (cf., Rosenbaum, 1967).

After prepositions, infinitives are automatically converted to gerunds, *e.g., I decided to go* vs. *I decided on going*; or *I forced John to do it* vs. *I forced John into doing it*. These infinitival gerunds should not be confused with the factive gerunds, with which they have in common nothing but their surface form.

A second way in which the subject of an embedded sentence can be removed by a transformation to yield infinitives is through raising of the subject of the embedded sentence into the containing sentence. The remaining verb phrase of the embedded sentence is then automatically left in infinitive form. This subject-raising transformation applies only to non-factive complements, and yields the accusative and infinitive, and nominative and infinitive constructions:

> *He believes Bacon to be the real author*
> *This seems to be Hoyle's best book*

The operation of the subject-raising rule in object clauses can be diagrammed as follows:

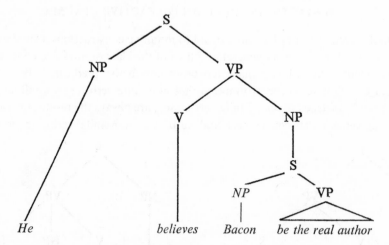

The italicized noun phrase is raised into the upper sentence and becomes the surface object of its verb.[8]

---

[8]   This subject-raising rule has figured in recent work under at least three names: pronoun replacement (Rosenbaum 1967); expletive replacement (Langendoen 1966); and *it*-replacement (Ross 1967). Unfortunately we have had to invent still another, for none of the current names fit the rule as we have reformulated it.

We reject, then, as unsuccessful the traditional efforts to derive the uses of the infinitive from its being 'partly a noun, partly a verb', or, perhaps, from some 'basic meaning' supposedly shared by all occurrences of infinitives. We reject, also, the assumption of recent transformational work (*cf.*, Rosenbaum, 1967) that all infinitives are "*for-to*" constructions, and that they arise from a "complementizer placement" rule which inserts *for* and *to* before clauses on the basis of an arbitrary marking on their verbs. Instead, we claim that what infinitives share is only the single, relatively low-level syntactic property of having no surface subject.

Assuming that the subject-raising rule is the source of one particular type of infinitive complements, we return to the fact, mentioned earlier, that factive complements never yield these infinitive complements. We now press for an explanation. Why can one not say

> **He regrets Bacon to be the real author*
> **This makes sense to be Hoyle's best book*

although the corresponding *that*-clauses are perfectly acceptable? It is highly unlikely that this could be explained directly by the SEMANTIC fact that these sentences are constructed with factive predicates. However, the deep structure which we have posited for factive complements makes a syntactic explanation possible.

Ross (1967) has found that transformations are subject to a general constraint, termed by him the Complex Noun Phrase Constraint, which blocks them from taking constituents out of a sentence *S* in the configuration

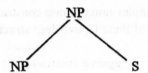

For example, elements in relative clauses are immune to questioning: *Mary* in *The boy who saw Mary came back* cannot be questioned to give **Who did the boy who saw come back?* The complex noun phrase constraint blocks this type of questioning because relative clauses stand in the illustrated configuration with their head noun.

This Complex Noun Phrase Constraint could explain why the subject-raising rule does not apply to factive clauses. This misapplication of the rule is excluded if, as we have assumed, factive clauses are associated with the head noun *fact*. If the optional transformation which drops this head noun applies later than the subject-raising transformation (and nothing seems to contradict that assumption), then the subjects of factive clauses cannot be raised. No special modification of the subject-raising rule is necessary to account for the limitation of infinitive complements to non-factive predicates.

Another movement transformation which is blocked in factive structures in the same way is NEG-raising (Klima, 1964), a rule which optionally moves the element

NEG(ATIVE) from an embedded sentence into the containing sentence, converting for example the sentences

> *It's likely that he won't lift a finger until it's too late*
> *I believe that he can't help doing things like that*

into the synonymous sentences

> *It's not likely that he will lift a finger until it's too late*
> *I don't believe that he can help doing things like that*

Since *lift a finger*, punctual *until*, and *can help* occur only in negative sentences, sentences like these prove that a rule of NEG-raising is necessary.

This rule of NEG-raising never applies in the factive cases. We do not get, for example:

> **It doesn't bother me that he will lift a finger until it's too late*

from

> *It bothers me that he won't lift a finger until it's too late*

or

> **I don't regret that he can help doing things like that*

from

> *I regret that he can't help doing things like that*

Given the factive deep structure which we have proposed, the absence of such sentences is explained by the complex noun phrase constraint, which exempts structures having the formal properties of these factive deep structures from undergoing movement transformations.[9]

Factivity also erects a barrier against insertions. It has often been noticed that subordinate clauses in German are not in the subjunctive mood if the truth of the clause is presupposed by the speaker, and that sequence of tenses in English and French also depends partly on this condition. The facts are rather complicated, and to formulate them one must distinguish several functions of the present tense and bring in other conditions which interact with sequence of tenses and subjunctive insertion. But it is sufficient for our purposes to look at minimal pairs which show that one of the elements involved in this phenomenon is factivity. Let us assume that Bill takes it for granted that the earth is round. Then Bill might say:

---

[9] We thought earlier that the oddity of questioning and relativization in some factive clauses was also due to the Complex Noun Phrase Constraint:

> **How old is it strange than John is?*
> **I climbed the mountain which it is interesting that Goethe tried to climb.*

Leroy Baker (1967) has shown that this idea was wrong, and that the oddity here is not due to the Complex Noun Phrase Constraint. Baker has been able to find a semantic formulation of the restriction on questioning which is fairly general and accurate. It appears now that questioning and relativization are rules which follow *fact*-deletion.

John claimed that the earth was (*is) flat

with obligatory sequence of tenses, but

John grasped that the earth is (was) round

with optional sequence of tenses. The rule which changes a certain type of present tense into a past tense in an embedded sentence if the containing sentence is past, is obligatory in non-factives but optional in factives. The German subjunctive rule is one notch weaker; it is optional in non-factives and inapplicable in factives:

Er behauptet, dass die Erde flach sei (ist)
Er versteht, dass die Erde rund ist (*sei)

The reason why these changes are in part optional is not clear. The exact way in which they are limited by factivity cannot be determined without a far more detailed investigation of the facts than we have been able to undertake. Nevertheless, it is fairly likely that factivity will play a role in an eventual explanation of these phenomena.[10]

5. INDIFFERENT AND AMBIGUOUS PREDICATES

So far, for clarity of exposition, only predicates which are either factive or non-factive have been examined. For this set of cases, the factive and non-factive complement paradigms are in complementary distribution. But there are numerous predicates that take complements of both types. This is analogous to the fact that there are not only verbs which take concrete objects and verbs which take abstract objects but also verbs which take either kind. For example, *hit* requires concrete objects (*boy, table*), *clarify* requires abstract objects (*ideas, fact*), and *like* occurs indifferently with both. Just so we find verbs which occur indifferently with factive and non-factive complements, *e.g., anticipate, acknowledge, suspect, report, remember, emphasize, announce, admit, deduce.* Such verbs have no specification in the lexicon as to whether their complements are factive. On a deeper level, their semantic representations include no specifications as to whether their complement sentences represent presuppositions by the

---

[10] This may be related to the fact that (factive) present gerunds can refer to a past state, but (non-factive) present infinitives can not. Thus,

> *They resented his being away*

is ambiguous as to the time reference of the gerund, and on one prong of the ambiguity is synonymous with

> *They resented his having been away.*

But in

> *They supposed him to be away*

the infinitive can only be understood as contemporaneous with the main verb, and the sentence can never be interpreted as synonymous with

> *They supposed him to have been away.*

speaker or not. Syntactically, these predicates participate in both complement paradigms.

It is striking evidence for our analysis that they provide minimal pairs for the subtle meaning difference between factive and non-factive complements. Compare, for example, the two sentences

> *They reported the enemy to have suffered a decisive defeat*
> *They reported the enemy's having suffered a decisive defeat*

The second implies that the report was true in the speaker's opinion, while the first leaves open the possibility that the report was false. This is explained by our derivation of infinitives from non-factives and gerunds from factives. Similarly compare

> *I remembered him to be bald* (*so I was surprised to see him with long hair*)
> *I remembered his being bald* (*so I brought along a wig and disguised him*)

Contrast *forget*, which differs from *remember* in that it necessarily presupposes the truth of its object. Although it is logically just as possible to forget a false notion as it is to remember one, language seems to allow for expressing only the latter. We cannot say

> **I forgot that he was bald, which was a good thing since it turned out later that he wasn't after all*
> **I forgot him to be bald*

There is another kind of case. Just as different meanings may accompany subjects or objects differing by a feature like concreteness, as in

> *The boy struck$_1$ me*
> *The idea struck$_2$ me*

so verbs may occur with factive and non-factive complements in different meanings. Compare

(a) *I explained Adam's refusing to come to the phone*
(b) *I explained that he was watching his favorite TV show*

In (a), the subordinate clause refers to a proposition regarded as a fact. *Explain*, in this case, means 'give reasons for'. When the object is a *that*-clause, as in (b), it can be read as non-factive, with *explain that S* understood as meaning 'say that S to explain X'. To account for the differences between (a) and (b), we might postulate two lexical entries for *explain* (not denying that they are related). In the entry appropriate to (a) there would be a presupposition that the subordinated proposition is true. This would require a factive complement (recall that the form of the complement has an associated interpretation) in the same way as the two verbs *strike$_1$* and *strike$_2$* would receive different kinds of subjects. The entry for (b) would have among its presuppositions that the speaker was not committing himself about the truth of the subordinated proposition, so that a factive complement would not fit. Thus, the meaning of the complement form is directly involved in explaining its occurrence with particular verbs.

6. PRONOMINALIZATION

The pronoun *it* serves as an optional reduction of *the fact*. It can stand directly before *that*-clauses in sentences with factive verbs:

> *Bill resents it that people are always comparing him to Mozart*
> *They didn't mind it that a crowd was beginning to gather in the street*

Although the difference is a delicate one, and not always clear cut, most speakers find *it* unacceptable in the comparable non-factive cases:

> **Bill claims it that people are always comparing him to Mozart*
> **They supposed it that a crowd was beginning to gather in the street*

This *it*, a reduced form of *the fact*, should be distinguished from the expletive *it*, a semantically empty prop which is automatically introduced in the place of extraposed complements in sentences like

> *It seems that both queens are trying to wriggle out of their commitments*
> *It is obvious that Muriel has lost her marbles*

Rosenbaum (1967) tried to identify the two and to derive both from an *it* which he postulated in the deep structure of all noun clauses. This was in our opinion a mistake. In the first place, the two *it*'s have different distributions. Expletive *it* comes in regardless of whether a factive or non-factive clause is extra-posed, and does not appear to be related to the lexical noun *fact*, as factive *it* is.

The relationship of factive *it* to the lexical noun *fact*, and its distinction from expletive *it*, is brought out rather clearly by a number of transformational processes. For example, the presence of factive *it* blocks the formation of relative clauses just as the lexical noun *fact* does:

> **This is the book which you reported it that John plagiarized*
> **This is the book which you reported the fact that John plagiarized*
> *This is the book which you reported that John plagiarized*

But expletive *it* differs in permitting relativization:

> *That's the one thing which it is obvious that he hadn't expected*
> **That's the one thing which the fact is obvious that he hadn't expected*

As Ross (1966) has shown, facts like these create seemingly insoluble problems for a system like Rosenbaum's, in which factive and expletive *it* are derived from the same source. We have not proposed an alternative in anything like sufficient detail, but it is fairly clear that a system of rules constructed along the general lines informally sketched out here, which makes exactly the required syntactic distinction, will not have inherent difficulties in dealing with these facts.

Direct comparison of factive *it* and expletive *it* shows the expected semantic difference. The comparison can be carried out with the verbs which are indifferent as to factivity:

> *I had expected that there would be a big turnout (but only three people came)*
> *I had expected it that there would be a big turnout (but this is ridiculous — get more chairs)*

The second sentence, with *it*, suggests that the expectation was fulfilled, whereas the first is neutral in that respect. On the other hand, expletive *it* adds no factive meaning, and the following sentence is ambiguous as between the factive and non-factive interpretation:

> *It was expected that there would be a big turnout*

This analysis makes the prediction that cases of *it* which cannot be derived from *fact* will present no obstacle to relativization. This is indeed the case:

> *Goldbach's conjecture, which I take it that you all know ...*
> *The report, which I will personally see to it that you get first thing in the morning ...*
> *This secret, which I would hate it if anyone ever revealed ...*

On the other hand, it is not too clear where these *it*'s do come from. Perhaps their source is the "vacuous extraposition" postulated by Rosenbaum (1967).[11]

The deep structures which we have posited for the two types of complements also explain the way in which they get pronominalized. In general, both factive and non-factive clauses take the pro-form *it*:

> *John supposed that Bill had done it, and Mary supposed it, too*
> *John regretted that Bill had done it, and Mary regretted it, too*

But the two differ in that only non-factive clauses are pronominalized by *so*:

> *John supposed that Bill had done it, and Mary supposed so, too*
> **John regretted that Bill had done it, and Mary regretted so, too*

These facts can be explained on the basis of the fairly plausible assumptions that *it* is the pro-form of noun phrases, and *so* is the pro-form of sentences. Referring back to the deep structures given in Section 3, we see that the only node which exhaustively dominates factive complements is the node NP. For this reason the only-pro-form for them is the pro-form for noun phrases, namely, *it*. But non-factive complements are exhaustively dominated by two nodes: NP and S. Accordingly, two pro-forms are available: the pro-form for noun phrases, *it*, and the pro-form for sentences, *so*.

[11]   Dean (1967) has presented evidence from German and English that extraposition is the general source of expletive pronouns.

7. ADDITIONAL NOTES ON FACTIVITY

We have dealt with the syntactic repercussions of factivity in sentential complementation. This is really an artificially delimited topic (as almost all topics in linguistics necessarily are). Factivity is relevant to much else in syntax besides sentential complementation, and on the other hand, the structure of sentential complementation is naturally governed by different semantic factors which interact with factivity. That is one source of the painful gaps in the above presentation which the reader will surely have noticed. We conclude by listing summarily a couple of possible additional applications of factivity, and some additional semantic factors which determine the form of complements, in order at least to hint at some ways in which the gaps can be filled, and to suggest what seem to us promising extensions of the approach we have taken.

(1) There is a syntactic and semantic correspondence between TRUTH and SPECIFIC REFERENCE. The verbs which presuppose that their sentential object expresses a true proposition also presuppose that their non-sentential object refers to a specific thing. For example, in the sentences

> *I ignored an ant on my plate*
> *I imagined an ant on my plate*

the factive verb *ignore* presupposes that there was an ant on my plate, but the non-factive verb *imagine* does not. Perhaps this indicates that at some sufficiently abstract level of semantics, truth and specific reference are reducible to the same concept. Frege's speculations that the reference of a sentence is its truth value would thereby receive some confirmation.

Another indication that there is a correspondence between truth of propositions and specific reference of noun phrases is the following. We noted in Section 1 that extraposition is obligatory for non-factive subject complements. Compare

> *That John has come makes sense* (factive)
> **That John has come seems* (non-factive)

where the second sentence must become

> *It seems that John has come*

unless it undergoes subject-raising. This circumstance appears to reflect a more general tendency for sentence-initial clauses to get understood factively. For example, in saying

> *The UPI reported that Smith had arrived*
> *It was reported by the UPI that Smith had arrived*

the speaker takes no stand on the truth of the report. But

> *That Smith had arrived was reported by the UPI*

normally conveys the meaning that the speaker assumes the report to be true. A non-factive interpretation of this sentence can be teased out in various ways, for example by laying contrastive stress on the agent phrase (*by the UPI, not the AP*). Still, the unforced sense is definitely factive. These examples are interesting because they suggest that the factive *vs*. non-factive senses of the complement do not really correspond to the application of any particular transformation, but rather to the position of the complement in the surface structure. The interpretation can be non-factive if both passive and extraposition have applied, or if neither of them has applied; if only the passive has applied, we get the factive interpretation. This is very hard to state in terms of a condition on transformations. It is much easier to say that the initial position itself of a clause is in such cases associated with a factive sense.

This is which the parallelism between truth and specific reference comes in. The problem with the well-known pairs like

> *Everyone in this room speaks two languages*
> *Two languages are spoken by everyone in this room*

is exactly that indefinite noun phrases such as *two languages* are understood as referring to specific objects when placed initially ('there are two languages such that...'). Again, it is not on the passive itself that the meaning depends. In the sentence

> *Two languages are familiar to everyone in this room*

the passive has not applied, but *two languages* is again understood as specific because of its initial position.

(2) We also expect that factivity will clarify the structure of other types of subordinate clauses. We have in mind the difference between purpose clauses (non-factive) and result clauses (factive), and different types of conditional and concessive clauses.

(3) There are languages which distinguish factive and non-factive moods in declarative sentences. For example, in Hidatsa (Matthews, 1964) there is a factive mood whose use in a sentence implies that the speaker is certain that the sentence is true, and a range of other moods indicating hearsay, doubt, and other judgments of the speaker about the sentence. While this distinction is not overt in English, it seems to us that it may be sensed in an ambiguity of declarative sentences. Consider the statement

> *He's an idiot*

There is an ambiguity here which may be resolved in several ways. For example, the common question

> *Is that a fact or is that just your opinion?*

(presumably unnecessary in Hidatsa) is directed exactly at disambiguating the statement. The corresponding *why*-question

> *Why is he an idiot?*

may be answered in two different ways, *e.g.*,

(a) *Because his brain lacks oxygen*
(b) *Because he failed this simple test for the third time*

There are thus really two kinds of *why*-questions: requests for EXPLANATION, which presuppose the truth of the underlying sentence, and requests for EVIDENCE, which do not. The two may be paraphrased

(a) *Why is it a fact that he is an idiot?*
(b) *Why do you think that he is an idiot?*

8. EMOTIVES

In the above discussion we rejected Rosenbaum's derivation of infinitive complements like

> *I believe John to have liked Anselm*
> *I forced John to say* cheese

from hypothetical underlying forms with *for–to*

> **I believe for John to have liked Anselm*
> **I forced John for John to say* cheese

This leaves us with the onus of explaining the *for–to* complements which actually occur on the surface:

> *It bothers me for John to have hallucinations*
> *I regret for you to be in this fix*

But once the spurious *for–to*'s are stripped away, it becomes clear that the remaining real cases occur with a semantically natural class of predicates. Across the distinction of factivity there cuts orthogonally another semantic distinction, which we term EMOTIVITY. Emotive complements are those to which the speaker expresses a subjective, emotional, or evaluative reaction. The class of predicates taking emotive complements includes the verbs of emotion of classical grammar, and Klima's affective predicates (Klima, 1964), but is larger than either and includes in general all predicates which express the subjective value of a proposition rather than knowledge about it or its truth value. It is this class of predicates to which *for–to* complements are limited. The following list illustrates the wide range of meanings to be found and shows the cross-classification of emotivity and factivity.

Factive examples	Emotive	Nonemotive
Subject Clauses	important	well-known
	crazy	clear
	odd	(self-evident)

	Emotive	*Nonemotive*
Subject Clauses	relevant	goes without saying
	instructive	
	sad	
	suffice	
	bother	
	alarm	
	fascinate	
	nauseate	
	exhilarate	
	defy comment	
	surpass belief	
	a tragedy	
	no laughing matter	
Object Clauses	regret	be aware (of)
	resent	bear in mind
	deplore	make clear
		forget
		take into account

Non-factive examples

	Emotive	*Nonemotive*
Subject Clauses	improbable	probable
	unlikely	likely
	a pipedream	turn out
	nonsense	seem
future { urgent		imminent
vital		in the works
Object Clauses	intend	predict
	prefer	anticipate
future {	reluctant	foresee
	anxious	
	willing	
	eager	
		say
		suppose
		conclude

We have proposed that infinitives are derived in complements whose verbs fail to undergo agreement with a subject. In the infinitives mentioned in Section 4, agreement did not take place because the subject was in one or another way eliminated by a transformation. There is a second possible reason for non-agreement. This is that the subject is marked with an oblique case. There seem to be no instances, at least in the Indo-European languages, of verbs agreeing in person and number with anything else than nominative noun phrases. Good illustrations of this point are the German pairs

> *Ich werde betrogen* (I am cheated)
> *Mir wird geschmeichelt* (I am flattered)
> *Ich bin leicht zu betrügen* (I am easy to cheat)
> *Mir ist leicht zu schmeicheln* (I am easy to flatter)

Presumably the same syntactic processes underlie both sentences in each pair. The accusative object of *betrügen* is changed into a nominative, whereas the dative object of *schmeicheln* stays in the dative. But from the viewpoint of agreement, only the nominative counts as a surface subject.

As the source of *for* with the infinitive we assume a transformation which marks the subjects in complements of emotive predicates with *for*, the non-finite verb form being a consequence of the oblique case of the subject.

We can here only list quickly some of the other syntactic properties which emotivity is connected to, giving an unfortunately oversimplified picture of a series of extremely complex and difficult problems. What follows are only suggestive remarks which we plan to pursue at a later time.

First of all, emotives may optionally contain the subjunctive marker *should*:

> *It's interesting that you should have said so*
> **It's well-known that you should have said so*

(We do not of course mean the *should* of obligation or the *should* of future expectation, which are not limited to emotives).

We assume that a future *should* is optionally deleted by a late rule, leaving a bare infinitive:

> *I'm anxious that he (should) be found*
> *It's urgent that he (should) be found*

Emotive complements can be identified by their ability to contain a class of exclamatory degree adverbs such as *at all* or (unstressed) *so, such*:

> *It's interesting that he came at all*
> **It's well-known that he came at all*

Finally, it seems that one of the conditions which must be placed on relativization by *as* is that the clause be non-emotive although many other factors are certainly involved:

> **As is interesting, John is in India*
> *As is well-known, John is in India*

9. CONCLUSIONS

Syntactic-semantic interrelationships of this kind form the basis of a system of deep structures and rules which account for the complement system of English, and other languages as well. The importance of a system successfully worked out along the general lines suggested above would lie in its ability to account not only for the syntactic structure of sentential complementation, but also for its semantic structure, and for the relationship between the two. Our analysis of presupposition in the complement system contributes a substantial instance of the relation between syntax and semantics, and enables us to correct an error which has been made in most past work on transformational syntax. The error is that different types of complements (*that*-clauses, gerunds, infinitives) have all been assumed to have the same deep structure, and hence to be semantically equivalent.[12] We have seen that there is good reason to posit a number of different base structures, each mapped by transformations into a syntactic paradigm of semantically equivalent surface structures. The base structures differ semantically along at least two independent dimensions, which express the judgment of the speaker about the content of the complement sentence.

This approach to a theory of complementation is not only more adequate from a semantic point of view. Its purely syntactic advantages are equally significant. It eliminates the need for marking each verb for compatibility with each surface complement type, that is, for treating complementation as basically irregular and unpredictable. We account for the selection of complement types quite naturally by our proposal that there are several meaningful base structures, whose choice is in large part predictable from the meaning of each predicate. These base structures are subject to various transformations which yield surface structures in which the relation between form and meaning is considerably obscured.

REFERENCES

Baker, Leroy,
    1967 "A Class of Semantically Deviant Questions" (unpublished).
Dean, Janet
    1967 "Noun Phrase Complementation in English and German" (unpublished).
Klima, Edward S.,
    1964 "Negation in English", in: Fodor and Katz, eds., *The Structure of Language* (Englewood Cliffs, N.J., Prentice-Hall).
Langendoen, D.T.,
    1966 "The Syntax of the English Expletive 'IT'", *Georgetown University Monograph Series on Languages and Linguistics*, No. 19: 207-216.
Lees, Robert B.,
    1960 *The Grammar of English Nominalizations* (The Hague, Mouton).

[12] The studies of Lees (1960) and Vendler (1964), however, contain many interesting semantic observations on sentential complementation and nominalization which still await formal description and explanation.

Matthews, G. H.,
  1964   *Hidatsa Syntax* (The Hague, Mouton).
Rosenbaum, P. S.,
  1967   *The Grammar of English Predicate Complement Constructions* (Cambridge, Mass., M.I.T.-Press).
Ross, John Robert
  1966   "Relativization in Extraposed Clauses (A Problem which Evidence is Presented that Help is Needed to Solve)" (= *Mathematical Linguistics and Automatic Translation*, Report No. NSF-17 to the National Science Foundation, Harvard University, Computation Laboratory).
  1967   "Constraints on Variables in Syntax" (Unpublished dissertation, M.I.T.).
Vendler, Zeno,
  1964   "Nominalizations" (Mimeographed, University of Pennsylvania).

ROBERT B. LEES

PROBLEMS IN THE GRAMMATICAL ANALYSIS
OF ENGLISH NOMINAL COMPOUNDS

Ten years ago, in a study of English nominal expressions, I attempted to contribute to the long and still continuing research on compounding.[1] At that time I conceived of the problem in the following terms: in English, German, Turkish, and other languages, the stock of nouns in the lexicon may be extended indefinitely by the creation of composite nouns, each characteristically of two members, themselves already *bona fide* words or compounds, the whole, a so-called NOMINAL COMPOUND, pronounced with the unifying stress-pattern typical of single-word nouns.

It is easy to see that such compound expressions are of indefinitely great internal complexity, for the members of a nominal compound may themselves be composite:

Pûre Fôod and Drúg Làw
ânti-Viêt Nâm wár dêmonstràtor
vîtamin defîciency disêase
súgar càne plantâtion ôwner

Thus, since ideally there can be no longest nominal compound in the language, *i.e.*, since the set of all well-formed nominal compounds of English must contain (countably) infinitely many members, one must suppose that a speaker's knowledge of WHICH composite nouns count as well-formed expressions of his language must be formulable only in terms of some grammatical RULES. My problem was to specify what rules suffice for the generation of English nominal compounds.

Since the grammatical structures which these rules would assign to the generated compounds must contribute essentially to a speaker-hearer's understanding or interpretation of each compound, I attempted to formulate the structure of each type of compound so that the syntactic relation between its parts would reflect that which occurs in some grammatically underlying expression, ultimately an independent sentence. For example, the internal organization of the compound *dráwbrìdge* can be

---

[1] Lees, R. B., *The Grammar of English Nominalizations*, Indiana Univ. Research Center in Anthropology, Folklore, and Linguistics, Publication No. 12, 1960; esp. Chapt. IV. [Abbrev. herein *GEN*].

assigned by construing it as a transform of the nominal expression *bridge for someone to draw*, itself a reduction of the relative-clause construction:

> *bridge which is for someone to draw*

and thus ultimately a derivative of a nominal which contains an embedded sentence

> *Someone draws the bridge*

Thus, the formal relation between the two parts *draw* and *bridge* was said to be just the syntactic relation between those two words in this underlying sentence, that is, the relation of a verb to its direct object. This compound is, of course, not an isolated instance, but it is drawn from a productive set: *blówpìpe, fláshlìght, púsh-bùtton sétscrèw, stópwàtch, tóuchstòne, wásh-drèss*, etc. Each is understood in terms of this Verb/Direct Object relation.[2]

The study revealed compounds of many internal structures and included the syntactic relations among the functional sentence-parts Subject, Predicate Nominal, Possessive Object, Verb, Direct Object, and Oblique (prepositional) Object. Different derivational rules might enumerate compounds of contrasting form but ones which reflect the same underlying syntactic relations. Thus, parallel to the infinitival *dráwbrìdge* type there would also be the gerundial type of *chéwing gùm, drínking wàter, réading matêrial, smélling sàlts, wéaring appàrel*, etc., which also reflect the Verb/Direct Object relation.[3]

Since the rules proposed for the analysis of compounds can be validated only if they comprise a functional part of a generative grammar of the language as a whole, and since such a grammar must provide primarily a description of whole sentences, the rules which generate nominal compounds not only synthesize them from their parts, but they must also serve to position each compound described just in those places inside of sentences where they may properly be used. For example, the compound *gRówing pàins* can be used in a sentence only where *plural* nouns may occur; similarly, *lócksmìth* is an *animate* noun, *stéambòat* inanimate, but *chátterbòx* is again animate. Thus, the rules always apply to both a so-called MATRIX-SENTENCE within which a given compound functions as a noun and also to an embedded sentence, the source of the compound's parts.[4]

A critic has recently pointed out that on this view the assignment of syntactic relations to certain compounds seems ambiguous.[5] In some, one member of the compound appears to be derived grammatically from an element of the embedded sen-

---

[2] These compounds were all described as the endocentric, infinitival V-O type of SETSCREW, in: Lees (1960: 152).
[3] Described as *for*-adverbial V-O type of EATING APPLE (from: *apple for eating*) in: Lees (1960: 153).
[4] Called "constituent sentence" in: Lees (1960: 153ff).
[5] C. Rohrer, Review of *GEN, Indogermanische Forschungen* 71 161 (1966).

tence, while in another type of compound the corresponding member appears to be derived from an element of the matrix-sentence.

Or conversely, for example, *éating àpple* is described as a transform of the nominal expression

> ... *apple which is for eating* ...

and the compound *clótting àgent* as a transform of

> ... *agent which causes clotting* (*of something*) ...

In both cases the head-noun in the compound appears to be a transform of a gerundial element in the embedded relative-clause sentence; yet *éating àpple* is characterized as reflecting the Verb/Direct Object relation, *clótting àgent* as exemplifying the relation of Direct Object/Subject! [6]

There is indeed some ambiguity in our use of such concepts as Subject, Object, *etc.*, for they refer now to the so-called grammatical subject or object, now to the so-called 'logical' subject or object. In sentences containing several echelons of successive embedding only a complex diagram can make clear the reference of these grammatical terms.

In other words, we must distinguish clearly between the superficial structure of expressions and their deeper syntactic organization, perhaps even at several levels of depth. The syntactic relations which the members of compounds were said to reflect are, of course, those definable only over the innermost embedded expressions underlying the compounds. If we represent this deeper syntactic structure abstractly in the form of a branching-diagram of constituency, then the contrast between the *éating àpple* and the *clótting àgent* cases becomes quite clear: [7]

---

[6] Described in *GEN*, p. 147, as of a small subclass of the O-S type of CAR THIEF in which the first member happens itself to be a gerund: *láughing gàs, sléeping pìll, snéezing pòwder*, etc.

[7] In these schematic derivations I make no strong claim about the detail of the transformational relation between the deepest structure and the compound itself. Thus, the underlying form might well be:

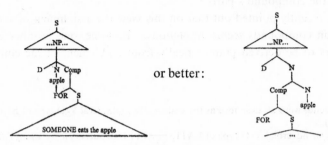

complicating the base-component of the grammar slightly but simplifying the transformational correspondingly.

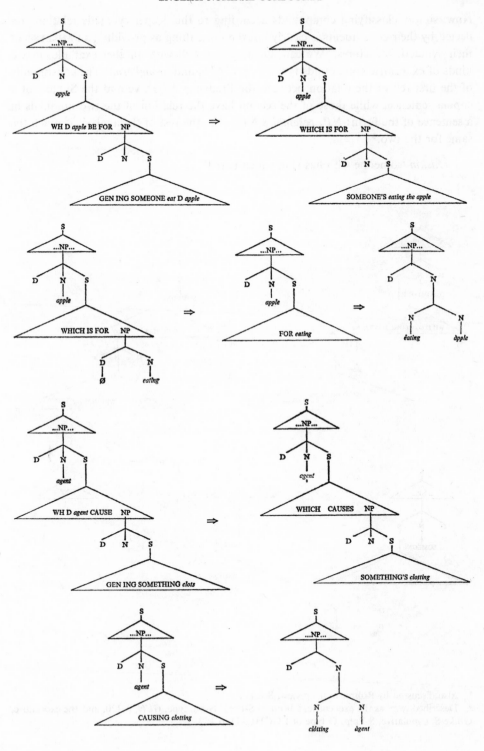

Now, simply classifying compounds according to the deeper syntactic relations reflected by their constituents is clearly not the same thing as providing an ANALYSIS of
their syntactic structures. We can illustrate this well with another example of two
kinds of exocentric compounds typified by *rédskìn* and *prónghòrn*.[8] The constituents
of the first reflect the relation between the Predicate Adjective and the Subject of a
copula sentence, while those of the second have the relation of the two nominals in
a sentence of the form: NP_1 *resembles* NP_2. Yet the rest of the analysis is much the
same for the two.[9]

    rédskìn 'someone who has skin which is red'

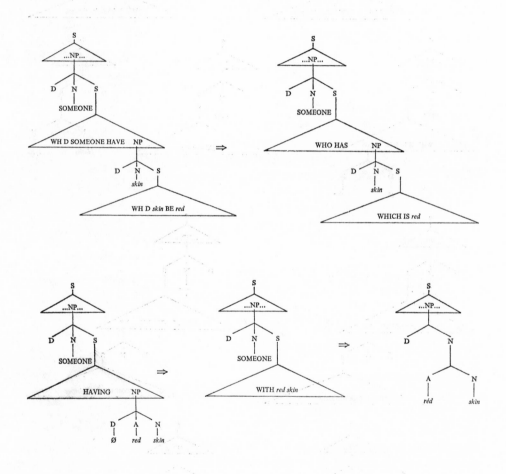

[8]   Also discussed by Rohrer in his review, Sec. IV.
[9]   Described resp. as the exocentric, adjectival S-Pred. Nom. type, *GEN*, p. 130, and the exocentric,
O-like-S, copulative, S-Prep. O type of EGGHEAD, p. 159.

prónghòrn 'something which has a horn which resembles a prong'

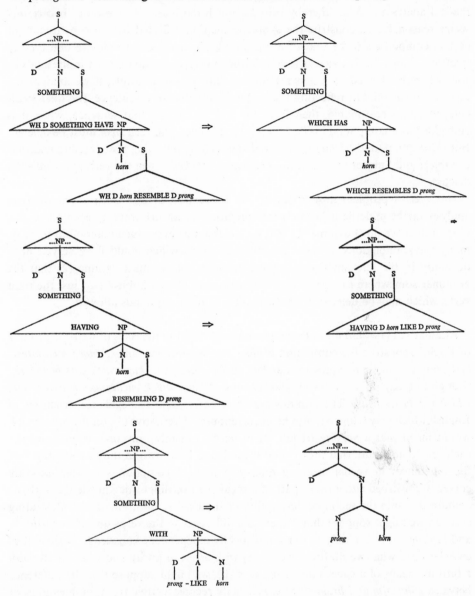

The efficacy, or explanatory power, of these analyses depends, of course, upon the generality and plausibility of the rules required to project from these abstract constituent-trees in each case to the pronounced compound expression itself, the surface-structure.[10]

[10] E.g., the major compound-generating rule of *GEN* was a generalized form of the rule T-86: $N_1 + P + N_2 \rightarrow \acute{N}_2 + \acute{N}_1$, pp. 133, 173-5.

The critic mentioned above has also pointed out another peculiarity of such grammatical analyses and has thereby raised a much more serious question. It certainly seems reasonable to construe the syntactic relation reflected by the constituents of certain compounds to be that of Subject and Direct Object, to choose one type in question. Now, on that view, the verb of the underlying sentence must in the analysis somewhere be deleted by a general rule of ellipsis. For example, if we analyze the compound *cár thìef* as reflecting the syntactic relations of a sentence *The thief steals cars*, as seems reasonable, then from the tree underlying that sentence, when it is embedded as a compound inside of a matrix-sentence, the verb *steal* must be deleted. But if the compound *bédbùg* is analyzed similarly as reflecting the syntactic relations of Object and Subject in a sentence *The bug infests beds*, then the verb *infest* must be deleted.

However, a problem now arises in our conception of how such a grammatical analysis might underlie a hearer's interpretation of an arbitrary compound of this type. Either we must assume (1) that he understands every such compound to be as many ways ambiguous as there are different verbs which could have served non-deviantly in the relevant deep-structure sentence, or we must assume (2) that the grammar somewhere associates explicitly with each Object/Subject pair just the right verbs which may be deleted in the formation of the compounds allowed.

Alternative (1) would mean that a person might, within the rules of well-formedness of English, construe the compound *bédbùg* as a version not only of *bug which infests beds*, but also of such expressions as *bug which steals beds*, *bug which eats beds*, etc., though not, say, of such deviant expressions as **bug which encourages beds* or **bug which purchases beds*. The non-deviant cases correspond to 'legal' constructions of English which may happen not to be in current use. Alternative (2), on the other hand, would mean that a very restricted set of verbs, possibly only one, would underlie each such compound, that they would thus always be known to the listener, and that the differences in verbal meaning among individual compounds in this class are correctly construed either (a) as part of a speaker's NON-linguistic knowledge or (b) as contained within the semantic description of the head-noun itself. Thus, illustrating case (a), we might suppose that if there is a difference in the verbs underlying *áshtrày* and *bírdcàge*, it is due only to our linguistically independent knowledge of the difference between what we do (in our culture) with ashes in a tray and what we do with a bird by means of a cage; illustrating case (b), we might suppose that the difference between *góldsmìth* and *bráin sùrgeon* is exactly reconstructible from the meanings of *smith* and *surgeon*.

In my opinion it is not easy to decide between these two alternative conceptions. But a more accurate and detailed analysis of compound expressions may yet render the conflict obsolete.

Now, for a number of good reasons several contemporary grammarians have been led to view the syntactic relations of Subject and Object as relatively superficial features of sentences.[11] In other words, the only difference between, *e.g.*, an active sentence and its corresponding passive version is the choice of whether the agent noun will be the 'topic of conversation' or the patient noun. Thus, the deepest representation of the structure of the sentence must contain choices for AGENT and PATIENT, not subject and object. The same superficial choice of topic may also distinguish the members of such sets of related sentences as:

(a) *I have an alligator in my room*
My room has an alligator in it
There is an alligator in my room

(b) *We filled the tank with tangerine juice*
The tank was full of tangerine juice
Tangerine juice filled the tank

(c) *They used a laser to carve the steak*
They carved the steak with a laser
It took a laser to carve the steak

From these and other considerations we are led to construct a deeper syntactic form for sentences directly in terms of noun-phrases which fulfill certain universal semantic functions, such as (human) agent, (human) patient, (non-human) instrument, location, time, purpose, or mere general, unspecified participant.[12] To these we must add a classification of verbs according to which of these noun-phrases they may obligatorily or optionally select as complements, as well as a set of transformational rules to map deep-structures onto surface-structures. These rules include those which choose from among the noun-phrases under specified conditions which will become Subject, which Object, *etc*.

Reapplied to the interpretation of nominal compounds, such an analysis permits a much finer distinction and a closer connection between the meanings of a compound and its deep syntactic structures. It may also afford a decision on the problem of indiscriminate verb ellipsis mentioned before.

For example, re-analyzing a large class of Subject/Object compounds including *windmìll* and *háy fèver*, we may isolate a productive set with the underlying structure:

Verb   General Complement Noun   Instrument Noun

that is, with the verb-phrase structure V-O-I. (In sentences with this selection of noun-phrases, normally the I-noun becomes Subject, the O-noun the Object.) But these compounds all fall into two subsets in such a way that the V of each member of one subset may be viewed as a variant of the verbs *impel, energize, activate, power, propel, etc.*, while the V of each of the others is a variant of *cause, engender, produce,*

[11]   E.g., C.J. Fillmore, J. Ross and G. Lakoff, J. Lyons, and M. A. K. Halliday.
[12]   This version of the proposal to deepen our picture of underlying syntactic structure is due to Fillmore (1968).

yield, etc. Thus, in the first set we find *wíndmìll, stéambòat, hýdrogen bòmb,* and in the second set *háy fèver, néttle ràsh, báttle fatìgue, etc.*

In other words, it may be possible to associate one, or a small number of generalized verbs with certain classes of compounds by fixed grammatical rule, so that the compounds in question need not be described by the grammar in such a way as to imply that they are indefinitely ambiguous. By 'generalized verb' I mean just the minimal set of semantic features which characterize all variants in the sets: *impel, propel, energize, activate, power, drive, actuate, etc.,* or: *cause, engender, produce, yield, …*

The case cited is not isolated. Another example arises within the class of compounds re-analyzed as exhibiting the syntactic relations of sentences whose verb-phrases contain:

Verb   General Complement   Agent   Locative,

that is, have the form V-O-A-L. Again there are two subsets whose verbs seem to be semantically characterizable. In one class, containing *bírd càge, pígpèn, dóg hòuse, sált cèllar* (!), *etc.,* the verbs are all variants of whatever underlies *keep, nurture, store, confine, house, etc.* In the other, including compounds such as *téa ròom, grócery stòre, lúnch còunter, banána pòrt, etc.,* the verbs are variants of whatever underlies *sell, deal in, service, handle, etc.*

It is by no means clear yet that all cases of compound types which contain as members two of the nouns of a verbal sentence can plausibly be analyzed in terms of only a few generalized verbs. Such compound types must include at least the following:

(1)   V-O-A → N_2 V-s N_1 → $\acute{N}_1 + \check{N}_2$
         | |
       $N_1 N_2$

  áirplàne pîlot   gúnsmìth
  brick màson   hórse dòctor
  cár thìef   pástry chèf

[These, as suggested above, require no special assumptions about the underlying verb since the latter is reconstructable from the meaning of the head-noun.]

(2)   V-O-I → N_2 V-s N_1 → $\acute{N}_2 + N_1$
         | |
       $N_1 N_2$

  (a) V = *energize, drive, power, actuate, propel, impel, …*
                áir rìfle   óil stòve
                álcohol làmp   stéambòat
                héat èngine   súction pùmp
                hýdrogen bòmb   wáter whèel
                mótor càr   wíndmìll

(b) V = *cause, yield, engender, emit, produce, ...*

báttle fatìgue	fínger prìnt	vírus disèase
blóod stàin	háy fèver	
cándle lìght	ínk blòt	
cóld sòre	néttle ràsh	
díaper ràsh	sáw dùst	
féver blìster	sóap sùds	

[Described above]

(3) V-O-A-I → A V-s N_1 with N_2 → $\acute{N}_1 + \grave{N}_2$

$$\begin{array}{cc} | & | \\ N_1 & N_2 \end{array}$$

(a) V *repel, prevent, reject, forestall, suppress, remove, ...*

búg sprày	héadache pìll
cóugh sỳrup	líghtning ròd
fíre èngine	mosquíto nèt
flý pàper	móthbàll
gás màsk	ráin càpe

(b) V = *preserve, ensure, protect, retain, foster, secure, ...*

chástity bèlt	lífebòat
chícken wìre	sáfety lòck

(c) V = *provide, vend, supply, afford, produce, ...*

cóke machìne	sóap òpera	wáter tòwer
eléctron gùn	tóne àrm	
pícture tùbe	wáter pìstol	

(d) V = *determine, measure, establish, ...*

defléction gàuge	distórtion mèter	hóur glàss

(e) V = *exhibit, portray, show, ...*

fáshion shòw	flówchàrt	wánt-àd

(f) [V as in (a)]

búg sprày	íon tràp
héat shìeld	mosquíto nèt
ínsect repèllant	nóise fìlter

[Perhaps reconstructible from head-noun, as in (1)]

(4) V-O-L → N_1 V-s in N_2 → $\acute{N}_2 + \grave{N}_1$

$$\begin{array}{cc} | & | \\ N_1 & N_2 \end{array}$$

V = *live, work, (in)fest, (in)habit, ...*

(a) animate endocentric

bédbùg	cáve màn

bóll wèevil	fíeld mòuse	
bánk tèller	hóspital òrderly	stóre clèrk
garáge mechànic	párlor màid	

(b) exocentric

gróund hòg	práirie dòg	wáter mòccasin
gúttersnìpe	séa-hòrse	

(c) inanimate

bódy flùids	hóuse dùst	spáce chàrge
gróund wàter	kídney stòne	

(5) $\text{V-O-A-L} \to \text{A V-s N}_1 \text{ in N}_2 \to \acute{\text{N}}_1 + \check{\text{N}}_2$
$\quad\quad\ \ |\quad\ |$
$\quad\quad \text{N}_1\quad \text{N}_2$

(a) V = *keep, nurture, put, raise, ...*

áshtràty	dóg hòuse	insáne asỳlum
bírd càge	dóvecòte	mádhòuse
bríef càse	dúck pònd	rábbit hùtch
búll pèn	flówer bèd	sált cèllar (!)
cár-bàrn	gréenhòuse	shéepfòld
cówshèd	ícebòx	síck bày

(b) V = *sell, deal in, service, ...*

banána pòrt	frúit màrket	téaròom
bárgain còunter	grócery stòre	
béauty shòp	hámburger jòint	
bíble bèlt	lúnch còunter	
bórscht cìrcuit	mílk bàr	
cóffee hòuse	stóck màrket	

(6) $\text{V-O-A-L} \to \text{A V-s N}_1 \text{ in N}_2 \to \acute{\text{N}}_2 + \check{\text{N}}_1$
$\quad\quad\ \ |\quad\ |$
$\quad\quad \text{N}_1\quad \text{N}_2$

V = *use, put, ...*

áircràft	móuthwàsh	táble wìne
cóffee crèam	nósedròps	
cúrry pòwder	pócketbòok	
éyewàsh	sándwich sprèad	
fíeld artìllery	séaplàne	
fóotwèar	schóol gràmmar	
gárden pàrty	shóe pòlish	
háirbrùsh	spaghétti sàuce	
hándcùff	stáge mòney	

(7) $V\text{-}O\text{-}A\text{-}Ab \rightarrow A$ V-s N_1 from $N_2 \rightarrow \acute{N}_1 + \grave{N}_2$

$\phantom{(7)\ V\text{-}O\text{-}A}| \quad |$

$\phantom{(7)\ V\text{-}O\text{-}}N_1 \quad N_2$

(a) $V = $ *get, obtain, derive, …*

cóal mìne	límestòne	rúbber trèe
fúr sèal	músk dèer	sílkwòrm
grável pìt	óil wèll	stóne quàrry
hóney bèe	ópium pòppy	súgarbèet

(b) $V = $ *make, prepare, concoct, …*

ápple sàuce	grápe wìne	wóod àlcohol
béet sùgar	óatmèal	
blóod sàusage	péanut bùtter	
chéese sprèad	potáto chìps	
cóal tàr	róotbèer	
físh càke	róse wàter	

There are, of course, still other large classes of compounds which may not reflect the syntactic relations of noun complements of a verb but rather those of the constituents of certain copula sentences, or those of the genitive constructions, *etc.* The following illustrative examples are a few of the types not yet fully investigated:

Object/Property	cóllar sìze, vápor prèssure
Whole/Part	árrowhèad, cártwhèel
	óyster shèll, ónionskìn
	cátgùt, whále bòne
Contents	múdhòle, pícture bòok
	sándbàg, áir pòcket
	gróund wàter, kídney stòne
Resemblance	búlldòg, háirsprìng
Form	bríck chèese, lúmp sùgar
	fírebàll, ráindròp
Material	tínfòil, páper mòney
	bútter còokie, shórtning brèad

More sophisticated analysis in the study of compounding provides some evidence for the view that the deepest syntactic structure of expressions is itself a more or less direct picture of their semantic descriptions!

In conclusion let me try to anticipate and meet a possible objection to this view. After struggling very hard to escape the obscurities of mentalistic philosophizing in the study of language, late 19th-century grammarians adopted a more and more rigidly empiricist doctrine on scientific rigor and validity in linguistics. This doctrine prescribed that an acceptable description of a language could contain nothing but direct generalizations from the spoken or written expressions themselves. Abstract, theoretical, or intervening variables were greeted with suspicion. Such a methodology left very little which could be said about the relation between sound and meaning. Its results contributed correspondingly little to our understanding of how a language user formulates what he wishes to say or interprets what others say to him. We have not yet entirely overcome the excesses of that empiricist or behavioristic period of development in the social sciences.

Thus, there may be some who would view the suggestions I have made, or have reviewed here, as an unfortunate return to pre-scientific classifying of expressions according to their supposed meanings, or to an undesirable semantically-based grammar. Others might feel that to re-iterate eternal verities, while not reprehensible as such, is hardly a contribution to our linguistic knowledge.

But contemporary grammatical analysis is not a mere re-discovery of the obvious or of what our ancestors have bequeathed to us. Scientific description is a continuing effort to render ever wider and deeper bodies of observations perspicuous and natural to our understanding. Replacing an older theory by a slightly improved modern one enables us to bring within its scope a larger variety of otherwise unconnected and *ad hoc* phenomena.

Accordingly, the value of these suggestions on compounding lies mainly in the way they serve to relate older and largely correct insights into universal semantic categories and deep syntactic structures to a wide spectrum of independently analyzed expressions within the framework of a unified conception of linguistic organization.

REFERENCES

Lees, Robert,
  1960 *The Grammar of English Nominalizations* (= *Indiana University Research Center in Anthropology, Folklore, and Linguistics, Publication* No. 12).
Rohrer, Christian,
  1966 Review of Lees (1960), *Indogermanische Forschungen* 71:161.
Fillmore, Charles J.,
  1968 "The Case for Case", in *Universals in Linguistic Theory* (New York, Holt, Rinehart and Winston, forthcoming).

A. R. LURIA AND L. S. TSVETKOVA

THE MECHANISM OF 'DYNAMIC APHASIA'

1. THE PROBLEM

Several years ago one of the authors (Luria, 1947, 1948, 1962, 1963) described a special form of speech disorder, which followed focal lesions of the anterior part of the left hemisphere, and which he called 'dynamic aphasia'. The syndrome of this aphasia, resembling the *Adynamie der Sprache* mentioned by earlier authors (Kleist, 1930, 1934; Pick, 1905; and others), could be described as follows. The patient had preserved sensory and motor speech; he could easily name objects and repeat words and even sentences. But he was unable to 'propositionize' and his active speech was severely disturbed. In cases of most massive brain destruction the patient was unable even to construct a simple phrase; in less massive cases, severe difficulties appeared when the patient tried to tell a story, to describe a situation or even to use his speech for verbal communication. Although his understanding as well as his motor speech were preserved, he did not use his speech for free communication, and remained practically speechless. When asked to describe a picture or tell a story he said: "...yes...and...how it can be said...Oh, gosh...I really don't know...". We remember a patient with a gunshot wound in the lower posterior part of the left frontal lobe who on attempting to give an oral composition on 'The North' could only say after 10 minutes: "There are bears in the North..." and after further stimulation added: "That's what I had to report...". Another patient with a similar syndrome tried to give an extended composition on 'The North', failed, and found a solution by reproducing M. Lermontov's well-known verse 'The North ...'.

Yet, the mechanisms of 'dynamic aphasia' are not clear. The purpose of this paper is to take some steps towards describing the basic disturbances underlying this form of verbal defect.

We shall give some examples of the disturbances of speech in patients with 'dynamic aphasia'; we shall then try to formulate a hypothesis and present experimental results to support it.

PATIENT MOR. (Neuro-Surgical Institute, case 36309), with an aneurism of the left anterior cerebral artery and hemorrhage in the posterior part of the left frontal lobe, was asked to tell the history of his own case.

"Well ... oh gosh ... I ... oh ... no ... that's the trouble ... no ..." (3'35")

"Will you please tell us where you are living, what you are doing, and how old you are?" "I'm ... oh ... that's the trouble ... no ..."

When concrete questions were posed, and when the psychologist started the answer, the patient was able to finish it.

"Where are you working?" "Oh ... yes ..." *"I'm working ..."* "I'm working as a horseman." *"How old are you?"* "Oh ..." *"I'm ..."* "I'm twenty-eight ..." *"Where are you leving?"* "Oh ... living ... living ..." *"I'm living ..."* "I'm living in a village ..." *"What do the horses do in the village?"* "Oh ... yes ... yes ..." *"They are transporting ..."* "They are transporting ... grass ..." *"Who is putting grass in the wagon?"* "Workers." *"Who pulls the carriage?"* "Horses ..." *"What is in the wagon?"* "Grass ..."

It is clear that the patient is unable to construct a sentence but has no great difficulty in finishing a sentence started by the psychologist. What is the basic disturbance leading to this defect of spontaneous formulation of a sentence? It can hardly be a naming defect: the patient has no difficulties in naming an object; it cannot be a general lack of activity: the patient tries very actively to find the verbal construction he needs, and shows clear symptoms of conflict and disappointment when the verbal structure he needs is not forthcoming.

2. DISTURBANCES OF PREDICATIVE FUNCTIONS

The basic deficit in cases of dynamic aphasia seems to us to be a disturbance of the *predicative function of speech.*

It has been suggested years ago that the process which is initiated by a thought and which ends in an extended phrase has as a transitional link, *inner speech*, abbreviated in its form and predicative in its structure (Vygotski, 1934). This inner speech is supposed to be a mechanism used by the subject for a transition from a preliminary idea to the extended verbal proposition. We hypothesize that this inner speech with its predicative function, which takes part in forming the structure or scheme of a sentence, is disturbed in cases of dynamic aphasia.

The first step to prove this hypothesis would be an experiment which could answer the question whether it is equally easy for patients with dynamic aphasia to find names of objects (substantives) and names of actions (verbs). If these patients really have a disturbance of the predicative function of speech, finding names of actions should be much more difficult than finding the names of objects. Fifteen patients with dynamic aphasia, and fifteen normal subjects took part in this experiment. With their eyes closed they were asked to give as many names of objects and of actions as they could during one minute.

Normal subjects had no difficulty in either task, and no marked differences in finding names of objects and names of actions could be observed. Patients with temporal (sensory) aphasia had severe difficulties both in naming objects and in naming actions.

Patients with dynamic aphasia could be divided into three groups. The first group consisted of patients with a massive syndrome of dynamic aphasia. They were unable to find either object or action names, and instead of giving a series of names, they only gave verbal stereotypes. The second group could find 9-10 names of objects in one minute, but was unable to give names of actions. The third group, which included patients with good recovery from dynamic aphasia, had no disturbance in naming objects, but marked difficulties in finding names of actions. Table I gives comparative data obtained in our experiments.

TABLE I

Finding names of objects and actions during one minute

		Number of names of objects	Number of names of actions
Patients with dynamic aphasia	15	10.3	2.7
Normal subjects	15	30	31

Table II gives some data obtained in a group of 6 patients with dynamic aphasia.

TABLE II

Finding names of objects and names of actions in group 2 of patients with dynamic aphasia

	Number of names of objects (1')	Number of names of actions (1')
1. Pim. (27237)	10	2
2. Mor. (36804)	8	2
3. Bog. (27715)	11	3
4. Kr. (33957)	12	2
5. Ilm. (33785)	9	4
6. Sklar (33755)	12	3
Total	62	16

We can see that in these patients finding of names of actions (verbs) is about 4 times as difficult as finding names of objects (substantives).

Here are several examples from our protocols:

PAT. PIM. (27237), 29-year old, graduate student of a university, removal of a tumor of the lower posterior part of the left frontal lobe, dynamic aphasia.

EXPERIMENT 1. Finding names of objects (1 minute period), "a circle…a camel…a horse… a cow…a lamb…green…blue…" "*You have to give only names of objects!*" "Objects… a table…a circle…sun…sky…rain…snow…"

EXPERIMENT 2. Finding names of actions (1 minute period), "…Oh…how is it…to go… to go by bus…to start to go…"

PAT. KR. (33957). 45-year old, bookkeeper, removal of tumor (meningioma) of the left premotor zone, dynamic aphasia.
EXPERIMENT 1. Finding names of objects (1 minute period), "Horses...a dog...a camel... a duck...a tree...an oak...a pinetree...a mapletree...apples...tomatoes...a cucumber... now...earth...earth...no, I can't..."
EXPERIMENT 2. Finding names of actions (1 minute period), "Oh (25″)...to work...oh, now...(35″)...to read..."
PAT. MOR. (36309), 28-year old, farmer, hemorrhage in the region of the left anterior cerebral artery, dynamic aphasia.
EXPERIMENT 1. Finding names of object (1 minute interval), "...yes...a fog...sky...oh... a window...a door...a frame...oh, yes a frame...I can't."
EXPERIMENT 2. Finding names of actions (1 minute interval), "...Oh...no (20″)...Oh no... (30″)...oh...I can't."

The facts presented here show that patients with dynamic aphasia are slow in finding. names of actions, and we propose that the *predicative structure of their speech is defective*.

We must now ask whether this defect is the most important cause of the difficulties in the free construction of propositions and, if so, the most important symptom of dynamic aphasia. To answer this question we have to construct a hypothesis and to test it in a special series of experiments.

3. DISTURBANCES IN THE SYNTACTIC SCHEME OF THE PROPOSITION

As noted, a difficulty in naming actions could be supposed to reflect a deeper disturbance — that of the predicative form of the inner speech.

One of the hypotheses of L. S. Vygotski was that inner speech, abbreviated in its structure and predicative in its function, is an important link between the initial thought and the final extended verbal proposition. If this predicative function of inner speech is disturbed, a deterioration in 'propositionizing' will follow. Is that the case in patients with dynamic aphasia? We can come nearer to the answer by examining a series of possible causes of the deficit of extended active speech in these patients.

As we have already said, it was not a disturbance of initial thought which was the cause of the patient's inability to engage in active extended speech. We could give them a starting idea (by giving them the general topic of the composition, for example 'North', or by giving them a picture they have to describe) and that did not make their propositionizing easier. It was not a disturbance of final expressive speech which was the cause of the defect: patients with dynamic aphasia had no trouble in motor organization of speech nor difficulties in naming objects. This leaves as the only candidate the deficit of the predicative function of inner speech and as a result a *disturbance of the 'linear scheme of the phrase'*, which was needed to find the way from the original idea to a verbal expression.

It seems to us that patients with dynamic aphasia could not find the scheme of the proposition they needed for a verbal formulation of the initial idea. They were unable to come to a preliminary scheme which contained knowledge of the number and sequence of the verbal elements included in the phrase needed. That is why they tried to single out separate words from the whole net of verbal connections and failed to find the needed scheme of the sentence. Hence it would appear that we are dealing with a disturbance of a kind of 'subjective grammar', the mechanisms of which are now in the center of interest of the most outstanding linguists (*cf.* Chomsky, 1957 and others). How could we prove this hypothesis?

Two ways of proving our hypothesis are possible: a negative and a positive one. The first test is to give to the patient all separate words, necessary for constructing the sentence, but not to give him the 'linear scheme of the phrase'. If that will not help him in constructing a proposition, we could conclude that the cause of the difficulties does not lie in the lack of needed words. The second test is positive: we could give to the patient a 'linear scheme of the phrase', not giving him a single concrete word. If this test will help the patient, it will be a positive proof that it is the scheme of the phrase which leads to a difficulty of active extended speech.

Let us describe both tests in greater detail.

(1) The patient with a syndrome of dynamic aphasia is presented with separate words and is asked to construct a whole sentence. As a rule he fails, and remains unable to do the task we require. He either tries to repeat separate words, or he finds another way and, instead of constructing a new sentence, he reproduces some ready-made pattern which he has only to remember.

PAT. MOR. (36309), with a tumor on the posterior part of the left frontal lobe, was given two words, 'house' and 'hen' and was asked to construct a sentence which included both words. After a long pause with unsuccessful efforts he utters: "House…oh…house…I can't…and hen…house…oh, dear me…it is house…and nothing…"

PAT. BOG. (27715), with a meningioma of the posterior part of the left frontal lobe, a scientist, was given the word 'thanks' and, in another experiment, the word 'fly', and was both times, asked to construct a sentence, containing the given word. During a long period (5-7 minutes) he tried to do so, repeating the given word, but was unable to construct a sentence. He then suddenly referred, in the first experiment, to a well-known part of a poem containing the word 'thanks', and, in the second experiment, to a nursery rhyme containing the word 'fly'.

The negative results of these experiments are clear. The patient with dynamic aphasia is unable to construct a sentence even when separate words are given to him. The problem does not evoke a scheme of the sentence needed, and the patient gives only references of separate words or turns to the reproduction of well-established verbal stereotypes.

(2) Let us now turn to what we called a 'positive proof'. The patient with a syndrome of dynamic aphasia is told to construct a phrase expressing his wish (*I am hungry* or *Give me some water*) describing a simple situation in a picture (*A woman is slicing bread*, *A boy is reading a book*).

After he proves unable to express an extended sentence as it was shown, a series of cues is placed upon the table. The cues have no specific meaning (pieces of paper, or buttons, or pennies can be used); a number of cues in a row reflects the number of words in the phrase required. The patient has to touch each cue, and pronounce the phrase needed.

That kind of experiment provides an *external linear scheme of the sentence*, not giving the patient any concrete word. The result of the experiment proved to be striking. The patient, previously helpless to construct a sentence, is suddenly able to accomplish this task, pointing with his finger to each successive cue; when the series of cues is removed he becomes helpless again and is unable to solve the problem. A successive linear scheme of the phrase becomes in many cases a way of compensating for the original defects. Let us show this in a series of examples.

PAT. MOR. (36309), with a pronounced form of dynamic aphasia, could easily name objects, repeat words and short sentences, but was unable to use his speech for free communication. Being questioned he echolalically repeated the question but was unable to find a phrase necessary for an answer. When he was shown a picture of a horse pulling a wagon with hay and asked to formulate the contents he tried to utter: "Oh...yes...oh, gosh...a horse..." "*And what else?*" "Oh, gosh..."
When three cues (pieces of white paper) were placed upon the table and the patient was ordered to point to each piece and to formulate a sentence, he said at once: "A horse (pointing to the first cue)...is driving (pointing to the second)...a carriage (pointing to the third)..." When four cues were placed before the patient and he was asked to tell what farmers are doing on their farm, he pointed successively to each cue and said: "Farmers are transporting hay...with horses." When the cues were removed and the patient was asked to answer the question once more, he was unable to do it, and tried to find the needed words, with no success. He was then asked to use the cues. He took separate pieces of white paper, placed five of them in a row on the table and, pointing to each cue, constructed a sentence: "Trucks...take...grain...to...the shed." Then he took one more cue and added: "and to the market!" He tried to say a sentence about the weather, but did not succeed: "The weather...oh...what is it...the weather...no!" Taking three cues and pointing to them he said: "The weather...today...is fine!"[1] The patient was asked to describe the contents of a picture (a boy in the forest). He said: "A boy...(a long pause)...a forest... no...I can't." He was given a series of cues. He placed them on the table, and pointing to every cue, told a story: "A boy...went...to the forest...for mushrooms...and was lost...he cried...and climbed a tree...", etc.

We shall not reproduce observation on other patients with the syndrome of dynamic aphasia, since *all* patients of our group showed in a more or less clear fashion the same compensatory role of this kind of help. We can conclude, therefore, that this experiment was a positive proof of our hypothesis.

The basic disturbance in dynamic aphasia can be described as a loss of the 'linear scheme of the phrase', which, so far as we know, can be due to a deterioration of inner speech with its abbreviated form and its predicative function.

---

[1] In Russian, this sentence consists of three words: no particles and no verbs ('is', 'are') are used.

4. REINFORCEMENT OF THE 'LINEAR SCHEME OF THE PHRASE' AND OVERCOMING OF PERSEVERATIONS

The recovery of the 'linear scheme of the phrase' by means of external cues provides an important help for overcoming the inertia of verbal stereotypes or of verbal perseverations, typical for disturbances of speech after lesions of the anterior parts of the brain. This is an additional result of great significance.

As was already mentioned by one of the authors (Luria, 1962, 1963, 1964) with regard to a series of animal studies, lesions of the anterior part of the brain have a double consequence: they disturb complex programs of actions, and they result in a pathological inertia of complex motor stereotypes.

The same can be seen in the pathology of speech: lesions in posterior parts of the left frontal lobe can result in marked perseverations in the expressive speech, and we have reason to believe that motor perseverations are among the most important mechanisms in the so-called 'efferent' or 'kinetic' form of motor aphasia (Luria, 1947, 1963, etc.).

Pathological perseverations can be easily observed in those cases of dynamic aphasia when the lesion is located in premotor zones and when subcortical motor ganglia are involved. In these cases which are related to 'efferent motor aphasia', troubles of active propositionizing are combined with perseverations of the words uttered.

It is one of the most important findings that in these cases the method of restitution of the 'linear scheme of the phrase' by means of external cues brings a double result: the restitution of propositionizing, and the overcoming of pathological perseverations. We shall give one example as an illustration.

PAT. Oss. (29558), 47, engineer, after removal of a tumor with a cyst in the left premotor zone. His movements were disautomatized, his speech was highly disturbed; no spontaneous active speech was observed, he was even unable to produce automatized series of words (counting, verses, etc.); he could give echolalic repetition of one or two words, but when a longer series of words was given, he was unable to repeat because of perseverations of the first word. Active speech was impossible; the patient was unable to give extended answers to questions, although his understanding of these questions remained unimpaired.
"*Please tell me your complaints.*" "Oh...yes...that's so...oh gosh...yes..." "*What work are you doing?*" "Oh...yes...that's so...oh...no."

A pen was shown to the patient, and he was told to ask someone to give him the pen. "Oh ...zd...da...zdar...z...darashku" (a contamination: instead of saying "daite ruchku" — "give me the pen" — the patient uttered a contamination of both words). External cues (two pieces of white paper) were given to the patient; they were placed on the table 15 cm apart. The patient was told to point to each cue and to say the phrase. The patient uttered: "Dai...ruchku!" ("Give me the pen!"). No perseverations or contaminations were observed. External cues were removed, and the patient was told to repeat the same proposition. "...Zdaruchku...oh...no...oh, dear me...Zdarusk...oh, gosh...".

Three pieces of white paper were placed on the table, 15 cm apart. The patient pointed to each cue and said:

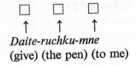

Daite-ruchku-mne
(give) (the pen) (to me)

He was very happy and smiled.

In this case external cues yield the double result we mentioned: they bring about a restitution of the scheme of the phrase, and simultaneously the help to overcome pathological perseverations.

We have here an example of the reorganizing role of the external cue and of the indirect (instrumental) organization of behavior which one of the present writers demonstrated long ago in a series of experiments (Luria, 1932, 1948).

5. SOME STEPS TOWARD A PHYSIOLOGICAL ANALYSIS

We have shown the role of external cues in the restitution of the 'linear scheme of the phrase' which was lacking in patients with dynamic aphasia, as well as the role of these cues in overcoming pathological inertia in the verbalization. Can we now take some steps towards a physiological analysis of the facts mentioned as well as towards an analysis of the mechanisms underlying dynamic aphasia?

Let us consider the mechanisms of speech disturbances in the cases of this particular form of aphasia. As was already said, we have every reason to believe that the disturbance of inner speech and its predicative function is the basic mechanism of dynamic aphasia. We could even suppose that it was the transition of the initial idea to the 'linear scheme of the phrase' which suffered in these cases. Could we not prove it in a more direct way? Could we really show that the transition to *verbal* processing was disturbed in this form of aphasia? To come nearer to its physiological mechanisms we conducted some physiological experiments.

It is well known that every intention provides a preliminary preparation for action, and that a preliminary SET is needed to make the action successful. In cases of preparation for verbal activity, such a preliminary set can be seen as a change of the electromyogram of the vocal tract. The pre-starting changes of initial background of the electromyogram of the tongue and lips in the period of preparation for speaking has been shown by a group of authors (Bassin and Beyn, 1958).

Could we use this technique for our purpose? Could we not show whether the disturbance of transition of the initial thought to the verbal propositionizing that we have seen in cases of dynamic aphasia are physiologically 'located' in the motor outlet of speech, or whether there is a kind of blocking of the process in some earlier links, where no transition to a verbalization of the initial thought can be seen? What kind of changes can be registered when we use the external cues we described above and when the external restitution of the 'linear scheme of the phrase' makes possible the verbaliziation of the initiative thought?

A technique already described by earlier authors (Bassin and Beyn, 1958) was used. Electromyograms of the lower lip (which proved to be representative for the transition from inner to external speech) was registered in patients with dynamic aphasia. This was done in both situations already described: when patients proved to be unable to construct verbal propositions, and when they overcame this difficulty by means of external cues of the 'linear scheme of the phrase'.

The patient was asked to be ready for a verbal answer, not giving aloud the pro-

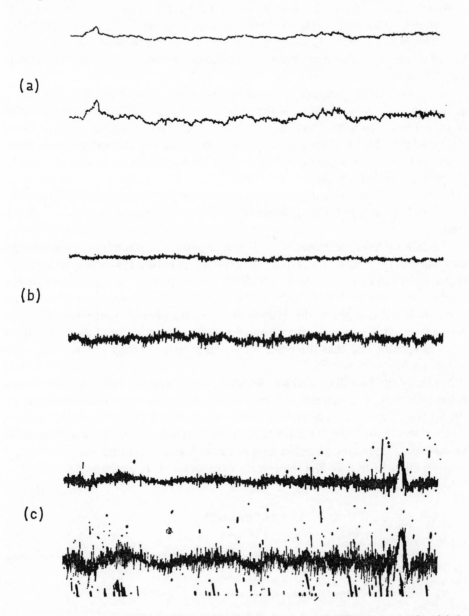

(a)

(b)

(c)

Fig. 1. Electromyogram of the lower lip of patient M. (a) Background (without any speech activity). (b) The attempts to recite a story (no bursts are seen). (c) The same, with a series of aids (paper showing the linear scheme of a phrase). (Active bursts by EEG are seen.)
Amplification: upper line 4 mV, lower line 6 mV

position required; and the EMG of the lower lip was recorded in both cases by means of the Alvar-Electroencephalograph with ink-pen. The results are shown in Figure 1 (a, b, and c).

We can clearly observe that in cases where a patient with dynamic aphasia tries to formulate a verbal expression, no changes in the EMG background are seen (Figure 1b). This proves that the disturbances in these patients are 'located' not in the motor link of verbal expression itself, but that a blocking of verbal impulses at a preliminary stage is present.

The EMG changes entirely in the second situation, that of external cues with a restitution of the 'linear scheme of the phrase'. In that case (Figure 1c) the intention to say a sentence (which is blocked by the instruction to remain silent) results in a total change of the EMG background: a pronounced increase of the voltage of the EMG takes place, and even separate bursts of EMG activity related to the components of the phrase prepared are seen.

It is clear that external cues do not only recover the 'linear structure of the phrase', but also open roads to the innervation of impulses to the motor apparatus of verbalization.

The data we have mentioned show that a important step towards a physiological evaluation of the mechanism of dynamic aphasia is possible. It may now be supposed that a distortion of inner speech with its predicative function is typical for dynamic aphasia; that this distortion results in a disturbance of the mechanism of transition from the initial thought to the 'linear scheme of the phrase'; that this disturbance makes it impossible to evoke the preliminary sets of innervations of the motor apparatus of speech; and that the defect of active propositionizing is a result of such disturbances.

A century ago Hughlings Jackson defined human speech as 'propositionizing', and half a century ago German neurologists made their first statement about the *Adynamie der Sprache*. Up to now, dynamic aphasia was supposed to be one of the strangest forms of speech disorders, a kind of 'aphasia without aphasia', as this syndrome could be described. Only now a combination of psychological, linguistic and physiological analyses allow us to take first steps in the description of its mechanisms.

Moscow

REFERENCES

Bassin, F.W. and E.S. Beyn,
    1958 *Electromyographic Studies of Speech* (Conference of Psychology, July 1-7, 1956, Acad. Pedag. Sci. Publish House, In Russian).
Chomsky, N.,
    1957 *Syntactic Structures* (The Hague, Mouton).
Jackson, H.,
    1884 "Evolution and Dissolution of the Nervous System", in *Selected papers*, II (London 1932).
Kleist, K.,
    1930 "Die alogischen Denkstörungen", *Arch. f. Psychiatr.* 1, 90.
    1934 *Gehirnpathologie* (Leipzig, Barth).

Luria, A. R.,
- 1932   *The Nature of Human Conflict* (New York, Liveright).
- 1947   *Traumatic Aphasia* (English revised edition, Mouton, 1969).
- 1948   *Restoration of Functions after Brain Trauma* (Moscow, Acad. Med. Sci. Press), in Russian (English edition: Pergamon Press, London 1963).
- 1962   *Higher Cortical Functions in Man* (Moscow, University Press), in Russian (English edition: Basic Books, New York, 1966).
- 1963   *Human Brain and Psychological Processes* (Moscow, Acad. Pedag. Sci. Press) in Russian (English edition: Harper & Row, New York, 1966).
- 1963   "Factors and Forms of Aphasia", in *Language Disorders* (London, CIBA Foundations).

Pick, A.,
- 1905   *Studien über motorische Aphasie* (Wien).

Vygotski, L. S.,
- 1934   *Thought and Language* (Moscow, Soc. Sc. Publish. House), in Russian (English edition: M.I.T. Press, Cambridge, Mass., 1962).

I. A. MEL'ČUK

TOWARDS A FUNCTIONING MODEL
OF LANGUAGE*

Only a very sketchy exposition of our theory can be given here; the interested reader is invited to get more information from references.

1. It is suggested that natural language be considered as a mechanism which transforms 'thought content' (= meanings) into texts and vice versa. A model of a (concrete) language should then be a logical device which does not simply generate sentences (along with their structural descriptions), but which instead converts any given meaning into all texts corresponding to, *i.e.*, conveying, it (SYNTHESIS) or which deduces from any given text its meaning (ANALYSIS).

EO IPSO A MODEL OF A LANGUAGE IS FOR US NOT A GENERATOR OF SENTENCES BUT RATHER A TRANSLATOR OF MEANINGS INTO SENTENCES AND VICE VERSA. Questions concerning the character of the 'meaning input' are beyond the range of the model: It can contain a false or contradictory assertion or even nonsense, but this is not relevant for the model (for the language); it is only necessary that any input (including nonsense) be translated into linguistically correct (grammatical) texts.

In other words, we would like to separate the problem of TRANSLATING any given meaning input into text (which we consider the main task of modern LINGUISTIC semantics) and the problem of ANALYZING the given meaning input, *e.g.*, hunting for inconsistencies, nonsense, *etc.* Such an analysis should be done not on natural sentences, but rather on their formulaic representation, and must therefore be excluded from linguistic semantics proper. We do not underestimate the importance of this analysis for linguistics — but still we would like to have the two above problems kept apart.

If this view is adopted, then the famous problem of grammaticality, or well-formedness, receives its solution in an obvious way: any sentence is LINGUISTICALLY well-formed (= 'grammatical') if and only if there is no better way to express in that language the given meaning. *Colourless green ideas sleep furiously* is linguistically

---

* It should be kept in mind that the paper has been written as a résumé for the X Intern. congress of linguists in early 1967. Since then the writer's views have undergone many modifications, but only references could have been slightly updated here. Yet, the conceptual core of our approach stands with no change.

quite correct and without the slightest deviance because such an odd meaning could not be converted into better, more idiomatic English; and the oddity of the meaning input itself does not interest English grammar nor English semantics either. All that is expected is that the language model be able to get from such a meaning to the quoted sentence, or from this sentence to its odd meaning. And as for the meaning as such, its study is quite another story. From these (indeed trivial) considerations it follows that, as a general rule,[1] linguistic well-formedness must be defined not on sentences, but on couples of 'sentence + its meaning'. So we cannot judge the well-formedness of the sentence *They have thrown an attack* until we are told what its meaning is: for, if the meaning is 'They have attacked', then this sentence is not well-formed — it should have *launched* instead of *thrown* (*to attack = to launch an attack*); on the other hand, if the intended meaning is 'They have thrown an attack', the sentence is perfectly all right (although its meaning is not). But here this topic cannot be developed any more.

Our model is intimately connected with two trends in modern linguistics: with the functional structuralism of the Prague School (the modelling of language from the point of view of its main function — as a means for the communication of meaning) and with the pioneering work of N. Chomsky ('active', functioning models in contradistinction to classificatory, taxonomic schemes); at the same time it represents a natural development of ideas put forth in the area of automatic text processing, above all in machine translation.[2]

2. For the transition meaning ↔ text the introduction of LEXICAL FUNCTIONS — certain meaning dependencies between words — turns out to be of high importance. A lexical function defines for any key-word i_0 (argument) a word or word collocation (value of the function; a lexical function can have several alternative values), expressing some specified meaning.

More exactly, a lexical function is (elementary enough) a meaning which satisfies the three following conditions:

(i) it can be semantically combined with many word meanings of the language under consideration (that is, it must be a very abstract and general meaning, like 'to cause' or 'large', *etc.*);

(ii) it has many (= hundreds) of linguistic expressions;

(iii) the choice of the appropriate one out of its synonymous expressions in a given context is determined only by the key-word i_0 (that is, this expression is phraseologically bound).

Nearly thirty lexical functions have been isolated so far, *e.g.*, *Conv* (converse) — the name of the inverse relationship of the type $R(a, b) = R^{-1}(b, a)$. (A regular way of forming converses is the passive).

---

[1]   With the exclusion of such phenomena as violated agreement laws or 'unsaturated' strong government, which bring about an absolute ill-formedness.

[2]   Paragraphs 2 through 6 draw heavily upon the results of the joint work by A. K. Žolkovskij and this writer: see Žolkovskij-Mel'čuk 1965, 1966, 1967a, 1967b, 1969, and also Mel'čuk 1967a.

i_0	иметь	страшить	знать	быть громче	быть начальником
$Conv\ (i_0)$	быть у	бояться	быть известным	быть тише	быть подчиненным

$Oper_1$ — typical name of what the subject of the situation 'i_0' does to i_0.

i_0	полномочия	пощечина	компромисс	ошибка	ущерб
$Oper_1\ (i_0)$	иметь, располагать	дать	идти на	делать, совершить, допускать	наносить, причинять

$Oper_2$ — typical name of what the object of the situation 'i_0' does to i_0.

i_0	полномочия	пощечина	поражение	сопротивление	ущерб
$Oper_2\ (i_0)$	входить в	получить	терпеть	встречать	нести

$Func_1$ — typical name of what i_0 itself does to the subject of the situation 'i_0'.

i_0	ответственность	заслуга	инициатива	преступление
$Func_1\ (i_0)$	лежать на	принадлежать	исходить от	быть делом рук

$Labor$ — typical name of what the subject of the situation does to its object by means of i_0.

i_0	допрос	тупик	список	кавычки	телефон
$Labor\ (i_0)$	подвергать	заводить в, ставить в	заносить в, включать в	брать в, ставить в	звонить по, связываться по

$Caus$ — 'to cause', bring about'.

i_0	кавычки	клякса	список	сквер	картина	состояние
$Caus\ (i_0)$	ставить	сажать	составлять	разбивать	писать	сколотить, нажить

$Magn$ — 'very', name of extreme degree for i_0.

i_0	брюнетка	отказ	клякса	спать	вооруженный	черный
$Magn\ (i_0)$	жгучая	категорический	жирная	крепко, сладко, без задних ног	до зубов	как смоль иссиня-

S_1 — typical name of the subject of the situation 'i_0'.

i_0	лесть, льстить	стрелять	много есть	лечить	стирать	паровоз
$S_1\ (i_0)$	льстец	стрелок	обжора	врач	прачка	машинист

Note also that many combinations of lexical functions are used: $CausOper_2$ (обязанность) = вменять в, $CausOper_1$ (заблуждение) = вводить в, $CausFunc_1$ (надежда) = вселять, $FinOper_1$ (повиновение) = выходить из, $IncepOper_2$ (власть) = попадать под, and so forth.

There are two interesting facts about lexical functions:

(a) They seem to be few in number — about fifty; yet such an inventory allows one to describe the vast majority of bound lexical collocations (maybe in any language). One is tempted to compare lexical functions to the twelve universal phonological differential features of R. O. Jakobson.

(b) There may exist certain meaning relationships between lexical functions; thus, all *Oper*'s and *Func*'s are inverse with respect to one another:

$$Oper_1 \qquad\qquad Oper_2$$

А нанес поражение В = В потерпел поражение от А, *etc.*

This property is exploited largely for the formulation of universal meaning equivalences — *i.e.*, for constructing a calculus of synonymous utterances in natural language (on the paraphrasing system, see below).

3. The values of lexical functions for every word are given in a special dictionary whose entries contain exhaustive information about the word: its declension or conjugation type, its derivational possibilities, saturation of its syntactic valencies (thus, Russ. угроза: 'subject' — N_{gen}/adjective/со стороны + N_{gen}; 'object' — N_{da} /в адрес, по адресу + N_{gen}; 'content': V_{inf}/N_{gen}; 'condition': в случае если ..., values of all its lexical functions (*i.e.*, its 'semantic declension' — similar to declension by cases) and so on. An essential property of the dictionary is the presence in the dictionary entries of so-called FILTERS — constraints and limitations on certain uses of the word (absence of its several forms, its non-combinability with certain derivational affixes, undesirability of using it in certain constructions, *etc.*).

The DICTIONARY plays a most important role in the framework of the model described and is viewed here AS ONE OF THE CENTRAL COMPONENTS OF THE (THEORETICAL) DESCRIPTIONS OF NATURAL LANGUAGES. Cf. Apresjan *et al.*, 1969.

4. In the process of transformation meaning↔text the superficial and deep representations of the text are distinguished (for the most part analogous to 'surface'/ 'deep structures' of transformational grammar). The superficial representation — or syntactic structure — is a tree whose nodes are filled with lexemes of the given sentence and whose branches correspond to formal-syntactic relationships (roughly speaking, the parts of the sentence); such phrases as *Гейл трактует* ... — *трактовка Гейла* — *трактовка Гейлом* — *гейловская трактовка* have different superficial representations. The deep representation — or lexico-syntactic structure (LSS) — is also a tree, representing the meaning of a sentence in terms of the DEEP SYNTAX (six relationships: four 'predicate' ones, *i.e.*, relationships between the predicate and its arguments — a subject and three objects; a general attributive relationship; and a conjunctive one) and of the DEEP LEXICON which includes independent words — *i.e.*, words not being correlates of other words — plus symbols of lexical functions; thus, for *упорное сопротивление, пристальное внимание,*

раннее утро, плотный, густой туман only one representative — *Magn* — is admitted into the deep lexicon. Not all words of the sentence need necessarily be represented in its LSS, but only those which have full meanings; on the other hand words can appear in the LSS which weren't in the sentence but which carry meaning, expressed in the text by a construction (*i.e.*, implicitly): *человек пять — приблизительно пять человек*. The above phrases have an identical deep structure:

$$\overset{1}{\text{трактовать}} \; \rightarrow \; \text{Гейл}$$

However, an LSS far from corresponds to ALL synonymous sentences: it represents only those synonymous sentences which happen to have a sufficiently similar syntactic structure: *победил врага* and *одержал победу над врагом* have different (but synonymous) LSS's —

$$\overset{2}{\text{победить}} \rightarrow \overset{2}{\text{врага}} \quad \text{and} \quad Oper_1 \rightarrow S_0 \quad \overset{2}{(\text{победить})} \rightarrow \text{врага}$$

The synonymy of such LSS's is taken care of by means of special rules — meaning preserving transformations, allowing one to get from any LSS to all other LSS's synonymous with it. One of all the synonymous LSS's, having the simplest structure (the concept 'simplicity' is not made precise here) is called the Basic LSS and acts as the representative of the whole set of synonymous LSS's. The chief properties of the Basic LSS are: (a) A B-LSS may include fictitious words introduced for symmetry and convenience of transformations (*преступать *vs.* совершать преступление as well as нападать *vs.* совершать нападение); (b) Not all 'independent' words of a language are used in B-LSS's but only a small quantity of specially selected words. IT IS PRECISELY IN THE TERMS OF BASIC STRUCTURES (B-LSS'S) THAT THE 'MEANING INPUT' FOR OUR MODEL OF LANGUAGE IS RECORDED. It should be emphasized that the B-LSS notation is by no means viewed here as an ultimate (deepest) representation of meaning. The writer is quite aware that a deeper and more explicit semantic notation is needed which must clearly and in a standard fashion state every relevant semantic difference and every relevant semantic relation (between all text items). Yet nothing definite can be said now about such a semantic language.

5. The transition from meaning (in B-LSS notation) to texts is fulfilled in three main steps:

(1) SEMANTIC SYNTHESIS — from a basic-structure to all corresponding syntactic structures;

(2) SYNTACTIC SYNTHESIS — from a syntactic structure to all strings of morphological codes (lexico-grammatical descriptions) implementing it;[3]

(3) MORPHOLOGICAL SYNTHESIS — from a lexico-grammatical description to the real word form. The steps of analysis are correspondingly inverse to the steps of synthesis.

---

[3]   For the time being the operations of B-LSS-to-syntactic structure transition are distributed between steps (1)-(2) in a different manner; but for the goals of this paper it does not seem of a vital significance.

6. SEMANTIC SYNTHESIS consists of two parts.

Part I — the Paraphrasing System — guarantees the transition from the initial Basic structure (or from any LSS) to all synonymous LSS's, *i.e.*, it implements the calculus of synonymous LSS's. The paraphrasing system includes:

(1) lexical rules — nearly fifty universal meaning equivalences, formulated in terms of the lexical functions, *e.g.*, $i_0 \leftrightarrow Oper_1 + S_0$ (i_0) (помогает $\leftrightarrow$ оказывает помощь), $Oper_1 \leftrightarrow Oper_2$ (Ему оказали прием $\leftrightarrow$ Он встретил прием), $Real_2 \leftrightarrow Adv_1$ $(Real_2)$ (Он выполнил приказ сдать книги $\leftrightarrow$ Он сдал книги в соответствии с приказом);

(2) syntactic rules, which provide for any lexical substitution the corresponding syntactic conversions. About thirty syntactic rules of the following kind are used:

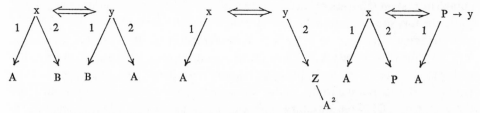

(double two-headed arrows mark transformations; single arrows, syntactic links).

All syntactic transformations are composed of elementary operations of only three types (transfer of a node, splitting of a node, lumping two nodes together); this makes it possible easily to construct a calculus of syntactic transformations. See Gladkij-Mel'čuk, 1969.

All rules of the paraphrasing system are applied without any constraint; the sifting out of those LSS's which cannot be converted into smooth Russian sentences is performed by means of FILTERS contained in the dictionary (lexical) entries (see above). A full description of the paraphrasing system is giving in Žolkovskij–Mel'čuk 1967.

Part II guarantees the transition from any LSS to all syntactic (surface) structures admitted for this LSS.

The model for semantic analysis has not yet been seriously studied.

7. SYNTACTIC SYNTHESIS consists of four parts.

Part I — DETERMINATION OF THE WORD ORDER in a simple sentence — fulfills its task in three steps.

(1) First of all, so-called Primitive Word Groups (PWG; elementary noun phrases, adjective phrases, adverb phrases, and verb phrases) are built up. The maximal 'pattern' of each PWG is specified; for instance, the pattern for primitive noun phrase in Russian is as follows:

1	2	3	4	5	6	7	8	9
или	не	из	всех	этих	трех	твоих	толстых	папок
or	not	from	all	these	three	your	thick	maps

The type of the head of the PWG, the type of the dependent and the type of syntactic connection between them uniquely determines the place of the dependent in the pattern and its morphological form.

(2) The primitive groups not immediately dependent on the predicate are connected into definitive word groups on the basis of rules which take into consideration the types and quantity of primitive groups combined. For example, three primitive groups ради скорейшего достижения, всеми участниками and поставленной цели are combined into one definitive group: ради скорейшего достижения поставленной цели всеми участниками.

(3) Finally, the definitive word groups are ordered. This is effected by four independent mechanisms: (A) ordering of the actants[4] (topics = subject and 'strong' complements) on the basis of their own properties and the properties of the predicate (other factors are not considered); (B) ordering of the circonstants[5] (adverbials of place, manner, time, *etc.*, and 'weak' complements) on the basis of their properties and the properties of the arrangement of the actants already obtained; (C) expression of logical emphasis (the logical subject, THEME, is shifted to the beginning, and the logical predicate, RHEME, to the end of the sentence; then more special permutations are executed); (D) 'Compensatory shift' employs a list of about twenty undesirable situations,[6] providing each with a 'mark' (an empirically chosen number which characterizes the degree of undesirability of the situation). Taking the sentence with the sum-total mark assigned to it, mechanism D tests in turn all possible rearrangements of definitive groups in order to get rid of as many undesirable phenomena as possible and thus raise the sum-total of the sentence.

The suggested mechanism for word order has the following properties:

(1) it works on the 'better-worse', and not 'yes-or-no' principle;

(2) it is based on the use of filters — compensatory shift is nothing but a set of filters;

(3) it consists of various independent mechanisms corresponding to different levels of language in the domain of word order;

(4) it belongs, to a significant degree, to stylistics (like the paraphrasing system which provides for the derivation of the set of synonymous variants and for the selection among them). For pertinent details see Mel'čuk 1965b.

Part II — DETERMINATION OF THE FORM OF THE WORDS — determines syntactically conditioned forms of the head of primitive and definitive groups (cases of the noun, number and person of verbs, *etc.*) judging by its properties and type of its syntactic connection with its head.

Part III replaces various phrases in resulting raw text by pronouns, introduces every kind of ellipsis, *etc.*

Part IV combines simple sentences related to one another into complex ones.

---

[4] L. Tesnière's term.

[5] L. Tesnière's term.

[6] For instance, a very short definitive word group not carrying any emphasis is located nearer to the end of the sentence than a longer group; there is no definitive word group to the left of the predicate while to the right of it there are more than two such groups.

Mechanism D is applied cyclically after each of the Parts I–IV, since undesirable situations can arise in principle at any stage of the construction of a sentence.

Syntactic analysis (for Russian) has already been described in detail in Mel'čuk 1964 and Iordanskaya 1967 and will not be touched upon here.

8. MORPHOLOGICAL SYNTHESIS consists of six autonomous mechanisms:

(I) Morphological rules. A — selection of morphemes (every string of lexico-grammatical indices resulting from the syntactic synthesis and representing a single word is replaced by a string of morphemes); B — selection of morphs (each previously selected morpheme is represented, *i.e.*, replaced, by its basic morph — a string of phonemes).

(II) Stress rules (determination of the place of stress).

(III) Morphonological rules (obligatory transformations on the resulting strings of phonemes applying only under explicitly stated MORPHOLOGICAL conditions).

(IV) Phonological rules (obligatory transformations on phonemic strings, but without taking into consideration morphological structure of these).

(V) Phonetic rules (transition from the phonemic transcription to the phonetic one).

(VI) Graphical-orthographic rules (transition from phonemic transcription to the conventional spelling).

For this a dictionary of root morphemes is used, each root represented by its basic morph and provided with all necessary information about its combinatorial properties.

Examples of construction of a word from:

SPANISH (verb):

Lexico-grammatical indices (semes):
| 'salir' | Pres | Subj | 1 pers | pl | →

morphemes
{'salir'} + {'base exponent'} + {'1 pl'} →

morphs
/sal/ + /a/ + /mos/ →

III, A_{increm}[7]

| *stress* | *morphonology* | *spelling* |

/sal/ + /á/ + /mos/ → /salg/ + /á/ + /mos/ = /salgámos/ → ⟨salgamos⟩

(For details see Mel'čuk 1965a, 1967b).

HUNGARIAN (noun):

Lexico-grammatical indices (semes):
| 'tükör' | pl | poss | 2 pers | pl | rel | sg | superes | →

---

[7] This is combinatorial information: III—*ir*-verbs; A_{increm} marks of such verbs as *conocer-conozco*, *tener-tengo*, etc.

morphemes
{'tükör'} + {'poss'} + {'2 pl'} + {'rel'} + {'sg'} + {'superess'} →

morphs
/tükör/ + /a/ + /i/ + /tok/ + /é/ + /n/ →
front, A_{cad}[8]

morphonology   *spelling*
/tükr/ + /e/ + /i/ + /tek/ + /é/ + /n/ → ⟨tükreitekén⟩
(Every detail can be found in Mel'čuk 1968).

An experimental variant of morphological analysis (for Russian) was described in Mel'čuk, 1961. At the present time a new, more general scheme of morphological analysis can be suggested presupposing the following:

(1) A list of basic morphs of the language.

(2) A list of alternations possible in this language ('meaningful alternations' of the type German *Mutter–Mütter* or Rumanian /čaškă/–/češt'/ and 'meaningless alternations' of the type Russian *г—ж* in *рог—рожок, луг—лужок etc.*).

(3) Each morph in the list must be provided with what is called main, or content information, *i.e.*, everything this morph contributes to the lexico-grammatical characterization of the word form in which it is included. Each morph in the list must be provided with auxiliary information, *i.e.*, every type of data which determine its combinatorial possibilities: (a) 'topological' information (about eventual discontinuity of the morph itself and/or of its neighbors: affix, infix, circumfix, transfix, see Mel'čuk, 1963), (b) 'geometrical' information (prefixes *vs.* postfixes and so on), (c) 'chemical' information (combinability with morphs of a concrete type), and also (d) information about alternations applying to the given morph under the given conditions.

9. As already noted, the suggested model has much in common with transformational grammar which is quite natural since both models are constructed with the same *Einstellung*, namely, to be functional. (Moreover, in elaborating the model described here the achievements of transformational grammar were deliberately exploited.) There are, however, essential differences. For a thorough comparison of both models a special study is needed; here we restrict ourselves to an indication of four specific properties of our model:

(1) its concern is not just the GENERATION of texts, but TRANSLATION of meaning into text and vice versa;

(2) it aims before and above all at the description of LINGUISTIC SEMANTICS;

(3) it uses extensively the '*deep*' *lexicon*, as well as 'deep' syntax;

(4) it makes a point of distinguishing MANY LEVELS of description corresponding to the multidimensionality of linguistic phenoma (thus, the rules of word order, *i.e.*, linearization of tree structures, are strictly separated from the rules of the transforma-

---

[8] Cf. footnote 7; front — the word belongs to the palatal series; A_{cad} — a base with unstable vowel ('beglyj glasnyj').

tion of such tree structures; *cf.* the division of each step effected by the model between several independent mechanisms).

The suggested model has also many essential points of contact with the well-known works by S. Lamb ('stratificational grammar') and P. Sgall ('multilevel generative linguistic description') which cannot be discussed here.

REFERENCES

Apresjan, Ju. D., I. A. Mel'čuk and A. K. Žolkovskij,
    1969   "Semantics and Lexicography: Towards a New Type of Unilingual Dictionary", In: *Studies in syntax and semantics* (Dordrecht), 1-33.
Gladkij, A. V. and I. A. Mel'čuk,
    1969   "Three Grammars (Δ-grammars)" (Stockholm), 7 pp. [Preprint No. 1 of Intern. Conference on Computational Linguistics.]
    1969a   "К построению действующей модели языка 'Смысл ↔ Текст'", *Машинный перевод и прикладная лингвистика*, вып. 11, 5-35.
Иорданская, Л. Н.,
    1967   *Автоматический синтаксический анализ*. Том II (Новосибирск, 231 стр.
Мельчук, И. А.,
    1961   "Морфологический анализ при машинном переводе (на материале русского языка)", *Проблемы кибернетики*, вып. 6, 207-276.
    1963   "О 'внутренней флексии' в индо-европейских и семитских языках", *Вопросы языкознания*, № 4, 27-40.
    1964   *Автоматический синтаксический анализ*, Том I (Новосибирск, 359 стр.
    1965a   "Об автоматическом морфологическом синтезе (на материале испанского языка)", *Научно-техническая информация*, № 4, 35-43.
    1965b   "Порядок слов при автоматическом синтезе русского текста (предварительное сообщение)", *Научно-техническая информация*, № 12, 36-41.
    1967a   "К вопросу о 'внешних' различительных элементах: семантические параметры и описание лексической сочетаемости", in: *To Honor Roman Jakobson. Essays on the occasion of his seventieth birthday* (The Hague).
    1967b   "Модель спряжения в испанском языке", *Машинный перевод и прикладная лингвистика*, вып. 10, 21-53.
    1968   "Модель склонения венгерских существительных", в кн.: *Проблемы структурной лингвистики*, вып. 3, 1967 (Москва), 344-373.
Жолковский, А. К. и И. А. Мельчук,
    1965   "О возможном методе и инструментах семантического синтеза", *Научно-техническая информация*, № 6, 23-28.
    1966   "О системе семантического синтеза. I. Строение словаря", *Научно-техническая информация*, № 11, 48-55.
    1967a   "О системе семантического синтеза. II. Правила перифразирования", *Научно-техническая информация*, 2-ая серия, № 2, 17-27.
    1967b   "О семантическом синтезе", *Проблемы кибернетики*, вып. 19, 177-238.

WOLFGANG MOTSCH

ANALYSE VON KOMPOSITA
MIT ZWEI NOMINALEN ELEMENTEN

1.   Jede grammatische Analyse hängt von der implizit oder explizit vorausgesetzten Grammatiktheorie ab. Die Grammatiktheorie bestimmt den Rahmen für die Formulierung von Aufgaben sowie für die mögliche Form der Analyse. In diesem Beitrag werden einige Probleme diskutiert, die sich bei der Analyse von Komposita mit zwei nominalen Elementen ergeben. Den theoretischen Hintergrund bildet die generative Transformationsgrammatik, als empirisches Beobachtungsmaterial dienen deutsche Komposita des genannten Typs. Ziel der Arbeit ist es, Aufgaben zu formulieren sowie mögliche Lösungswege zu skizzieren, miteinander zu vergleichen und im Hinblick auf ihre Konsequenzen zu untersuchen.

2.   Aus der Definition des Begriffs 'Tiefenstruktur' lassen sich Argumente ableiten, die für eine transformationelle Beschreibung von Komposita sprechen, das heißt Argumente, die einer Lösung, die die spezielle Struktur von Komposita nicht durch kategoriale Regeln direkt erzeugt, sondern durch Transformationsregeln, deren Grundlage explizite Tiefenstrukturen sind, den Vorzug geben. Zwei wesentliche Argumente stützen diese Annahme: (i) Die Mehrdeutigkeit von Komposita (Konstruktionshomonymie) kann mit syntaktischen Mitteln dargestellt werden, indem gezeigt wird, daß ein Kompositum auf verschiedene Tiefenstrukturen zurückgeht, die seine semantische Interpretation determinieren; (ii) Die 'syntaktische Verwandtschaft' (Konstruktionssynonymie) zwischen unterschiedlichen Oberflächenstrukturen ist explizit beschreibbar, indem gezeigt werden kann, daß verschiedene Strukturen auf eine Tiefenstruktur zurückgehen.
    Die Beispiele (1) und (2) erläutern (i) bzw. (ii):

(1) *Holzschuppen*
     Schuppen, in dem sich Holz befindet
     Schuppen, der aus Holz hergestellt ist
(2) *Holzschuppen*
     Schuppen aus Holz
     hölzerner Schuppen
     Schuppen, der aus Holz hergestellt ist

Die Vorteile der transformationellen Analyse werden deutlich, wenn man die Konsequenzen einer alternativen Lösung betrachtet. Es wäre möglich, Regeln im kategorialen Teil der Basis zu formulieren, um Strukturen der Form 'lexikalische Kategorie dominiert lexikalische Kategorien' zu erzeugen. Eine Analyse dieser Form ist im Rahmen taxonomischer Theorien ohne Transformationsregeln die einzig mögliche. Eine Beschreibung der Fakten, für die die Beispiele (1) und (2) gewählt wurden, müßte in der semantischen Komponente der Grammatik erfolgen. Wie eine semantische Komponente beschaffen sein muß, die auf einer Syntax ohne Transformationsteil aufbaut und die den genannten Fakten Rechnung trägt, wurde bisher nicht gezeigt. Dagegen wurden instruktive Vorschläge über Aufgaben und Form einer semantischen Komponente im Rahmen einer generativen Transformationsgrammatik unterbreitet, die zugunsten der transformationellen Analyse sprechen.[1] Ohne eine Entscheidung über die Adäquatheit der Transformationsgrammatik zu fällen, darf behauptet werden, daß sie gegenwärtig bessere Voraussetzungen für eine Analyse von Komposita bietet, als Grammatiktheorien ohne Transformationsteil.

3.   Aus den Annahmen der Transformationsgrammatik über die Erzeugung von Komposita ergibt sich, daß Komposita als verkürzte syntaktische Ausdrücke aufzufassen sind, denen explizitere Strukturen mit umfangreicheren grammatischen Informationen zugrundeliegen. Damit wird auf der Grundlage einer fundierten Grammatiktheorie eine bereits im 19. Jahrhundert diskutierte Hypothese wieder aufgegriffen. K. Brugmann, einer der hervorragendsten Vertreter der Sprachwissenschaft des 19. Jahrhunderts, vertrat gegen H. Paul, W. Wilmanns u.a. mit Nachdruck die Auffassung, Komposita seien als verkürzte Sätze zu interpretieren, die in einen Satz eingebaut sind, das heißt, die Relationen zwischen den Gliedern eines Kompositums seien auf syntaktische Relationen in Sätzen zurückzuführen.[2] Spätere Forscher haben sich dieser Auffassung angeschlossen. So K. Bühler:

Man trifft nicht weit am richtigen vorbei mit der These, daß tabellarisch aufgenommen im Schoße des indogermanischen Kompositums schon alle syntaktischen Momente zu finden sind, die im Satze wieder zum Vorschein kommen.[3]

---

[1]   J. J. Katz und P. M. Postal, *An Integrated Theory of Linguistic Descriptions* (Cambridge, Mass. 1964) und N. Chomsky, *Aspects of the Theory of Syntax* (Cambridge, Mass. 1965), haben ausführlich gezeigt, wie eine semantische Komponente in eine generative Transformationsgrammatik zu inkorpieren ist. Nach den in diesen Arbeiten entwickelten Vorstellungen, kann der Zusammenhang zwischen Syntax und Semantik am einfachsten dargestellt werden, wenn die semantische Komponente lediglich auf Tiefenstrukturen operiert. Die semantische Interpretation von Komposita setzt demnach eine Rückführung von Ausdrücken dieses Typs auf Tiefenstrukturen voraus. Je geringer der Aufwand bei der Formulierung von Tiefenstrukturen ist, umso geringer ist auch der Aufwand an Regeln in der semantischen Komponente, die Tiefenstrukturen semantisch interpretieren. Das bedeutet, daß die Grammatik insgesamt genereller formuliert werden kann, wenn viele verschiedene Oberflächenstrukturen auf möglichst wenige Tiefenstrukturen zurückführbar sind.

[2]   Vgl. K. Brugmann, "Über das Wesen der sogenannten Wortzusammensetzung. Eine sprachpsychologische Studie", *Sächs. Ak. Ber. Phil.-hist. Cl.* (1900), S. 359 ff.

[3]   K. Bühler, *Sprachtheorie* (Jena 1934), S. 326.

Auch in moderneren Arbeiten über Komposita, die nicht von Standpunkt einer generativen Grammatik verfaßt wurden, spielt diese Hypothese eine tragende Rolle. H. Marchand vertritt folgende Auffassung:

Morphologic composites (= compounds, suffixal derivatives, prefixal derivatives) are 'reduced' sentences in substantival adjectival or verbal form and as such explainable from 'full' sentences.[4]

H. Pauls Ansichten[5], die in der Germanistik fast ausschließlich befolgt wurden (vgl. die zusammenfassende Darstellung von W. Henzen)[6], basieren auf historischen und psychologischen Argumenten, die heute schwerlich als relevant bezeichnet werden können. Gegen die historische Begründung der Analyse von Komposita wandte bereits Brugmann ein:

Ob ein Typ in vorhistorischer oder in historischer Zeit aufgekommen ist, ist also gleichgültig. Nicht auf die Schicksale, welche die fertigen Komposita erfahren haben, kommt es uns an, sondern auf den Kompositionsprozeß selbst, auf die Komposition als Urschöpfungsakt.[7]

Brugmann weist hier auf ein grundlegendes Problem hin. Es ist notwendig zwischen dem Prozeß der Bildung von Komposita und im Lexikon existierenden Bildungen zu unterscheiden, anders ausgedrückt: zwischen den grammatischen Regeln, die potentielle Komposita erzeugen und lexikalisierten Bildungen, die als Ausdrücke in das Lexikon einer Sprache aufgenommen wurden und nur in beschränktem Maße systematisch analysiert werden können. Lexikalisierte Bildungen können eine lange Geschichte haben, in deren Verlauf Eigenschaften hinzukommen, die als idiosynkratisch zu bezeichnen sind. Wir setzen diese Unterscheidung voraus und untersuchen nur die grammatischen Eigenschaften potentieller Komposita.[8]

H. Pauls Charakterisierung von Komposita entspricht in ihren wesentlichen Zügen einer im Rahmen der Konstituentenstrukturgrammatik (*Phrase Structure Grammar* bzw. *Immediate Constituent Grammar*) möglichen Analyse. Komposita werden im Hinblick auf die lexikalischen Kategorien ihrer Konstituenten beschrieben. Dazu kommen Angaben über grammatische Relationen, die aus historischer Sicht motiviert werden. So nimmt Paul einen Typ 'genitivische Zusammensetzungen' an. Eine solche Klasse, die sich u.a. auf morphologische Indizien beruft, ist leicht als irrelevant nachzuweisen. Einerseits ist der Genitiv selbst der Analyse bedürftig und andererseits gibt

---

[4] H. Marchand, "On the analysis of substantive compounds and suffixal derivatives not containing a verbal element", in: *Indogerm Forschungen*, 70 (1966), 117-145. Die Frage, ob alle Wortbildungstypen transformationell zu behandeln sind, ist nach meiner Auffassung nicht entschieden. Andere Möglichkeiten, Wortbildungsfakten im Rahmen der Grammatik zu repräsentieren, sind denkbar und in bestimmten Fällen empirisch sinnvoller. Vgl. W. Motsch, "Der kreative Aspekt in der Wortbildung", unveröffentliches Manuskript.
[5] H. Paul, *Principien der Sprachgeschichte*, 2. Aufl. (Halle 1886), S. 274 ff.
[6] W. Henzen, *Deutsche Wortbildung* (Halle 1947).
[7] K. Brugmann, *Über das Wesen der sogenannten Wortzusammensetzung*, S. 361.
[8] Die Unterscheidung zwischen lexikalisierten und potentiellen Wortbildungen wird ausführlich behandelt in: W. Motsch, "Der kreative Aspekt in der Wortbildung", unveröffentlichtes Manuskript.

es in der deutschen Gegenwartssprache (die Paul untersucht) eine beträchtliche Anzahl von Komposita, die morphologisch als 'genitivische Zusammensetzungen'
charakterisiert werden müßten, jedoch nicht auf Ausdrücke mit Genitiv zurückgeführt werden können. Eine historisch motivierte Betrachtung geht also an den Fakten,
die in der Gegenwartssprache zu beobachten sind, vorbei. Für die Analyse der Relationen, die zwischen den Konstituenten von Komposita mit zwei nominalen Elementen bestehen, hat Paul keine theoretische Grundlage. Er begnügt sich mit Angaben,
deren Gültigkeit bestenfalls intuitiv geprüft werden kann. Paul charakterisiert zum
Beispiel Typen von Komposita durch folgende Umschreibungen:[9]

(3) Das erste Glied bezeichnet den Stoff: *Darmsaite, Filzhut, Goldring*, usw.
     Das erste Glied bezeichnet einen Teil des Stoffes, aus dem das zweite gebildet
     ist: *Apfelbaum, Rosenbusch, Hornvieh*, usw.

     Das erste Glied bezeichnet den Raum, an dem sich das zweite befindet oder für
     den es wenigstens bestimmt ist: *Bergbahn, Fußbank, Feldblume*, usw.
     Das erste Glied bezeichnet den Gegenstand, für den das zweite bestimmt ist:
     Bierfaß, Weinglas, Obstmesser, usw.

Die hinter solchen verbalen Umschreibungen verborgenen Fakten müssen durch
eine fundierte grammatische Analyse explizit beschrieben werden. Der Weg, den die
Transformationsgrammatik anbietet, entspricht offensichtlich den Voraussetzungen
der Brugmannschen Hypothese. Pauls Weg kann dagegen mit den Auffassungen
L. Bloomfields verglichen werden (abgesehen von den historischen Gesichtspunkten),
der Komposita als syntaktische Konstruktionen beschreibt, deren Konstituenten
Elemente bestimmter lexikalischer Kategorien sind. Die Relationen zwischen den
Konstituenten bestimmter Konstruktionstypen müßten nach Bloomfield durch 'Konstruktionsbedeutungen' charakterisiert werden. Eine strengere Fassung des Begriffs
'Konstruktionsbedeutung' bleibt uns Bloomfield allerdings schuldig.

   Der Disput zwischen Brugmann und Paul kann demnach im Rahmen modernerer
Vorstellungen auf die Frage zurückgeführt werden, ob Komposita direkt durch
Regeln der kategorialen Komponente zu erzeugen sind oder durch Transformationsregeln, die auf expliziteren Tiefenstrukturen, in denen Sätze vorkommen, operieren.

4.   Die transformationelle Analyse von Komposita mit ausschließlich nominalen
Konstituenten ist mit Problemen verbunden, die nun näher untersucht werden sollen.
Es handelt sich in erster Linie um die Frage, wie Informationen zu repräsentieren
sind, die aus den der Beobachtung leicher zugänglichen strukturellen Eigenschaften
solcher Komposita nicht direkt ablesbar sind, anders ausgedrückt: wie sind Informationen über die der semantischen Interpretation zugrundeliegenden Relationen
zwischen den Nomen dieser Komposita in der syntaktischen Analyse zu repräsentieren?

---

[9]   H. Paul, *Deutsche Grammatik*, Band V, Teil IV (Halle 1920), S. 9f.

Wir beschränken die Diskussion auf sogenannte Determinativkomposita, die auf Basisstrukturen folgender Form zurückgeführt werden können:[10]

(4)

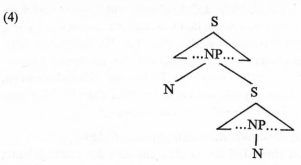

Verbal ausgedrückt besagt (4): das zweite Glied des Kompositums geht auf das direkt von einer NP, die eine beliebige (grammatisch mögliche) Satzposition besetzt, dominierte Nomen zurück; das erste Glied auf ein Nomen, das an einer bestimmten Stelle in einem eingebetteten 'Attributssatz' steht. Diese Analyse bietet die Möglichkeit, das erste Glied eines Kompositums als ein spezielles Attribut zu behandeln. Andere Formen von Attributen sind in Beispiel (2) angegeben. Für Strukturen der Form (4) gilt die generelle Bedingung für Attributssätze: sie müssen ein Nomen enthalten, das mit dem Nomen, das Co-Konstituente des Attributssatzes ist, referenz-identisch ist.

Auf der Grundlage von (4) können die uns interessierenden Probleme präziser formuliert werden. Sie lauten nunmehr: welche Verben liegen dem eingebetteten Satz zugrunde und welche Positionen nehmen die Nomen der zu beschreibenden Komposita in ihm ein? Man könnte, um ein Beispiel zu nennen, die Komposita *Bienenhonig* und *Honigbiene* auf Strukturen zurückführen, die einen Attributssatz mit dem Verb *erzeugen* enthalten. Dann ginge *Bienenhonig* auf (5) und *Honigbiene* auf (6) zurück:

(5) $((Honig)_N (Bienen\ erzeugen\ Honig)_S)_{NP}$
(6) $((Biene)_N (Biene\ erzeugt\ Honig)_S)_{NP}$

Im ersten Fall geht das zweite Kompositionsglied auf das direkte Objekt des eingebetteten Satzes zurück, das erste auf dessen Subjekt; im zweiten Fall geht das zweite Glied auf das Subjekt des eingebetteten Satzes zurück, das erste auf das direkte Objekt.

Probleme dieser Art sind nicht allein mit der Analyse von Komposita verbunden, sondern sie sind auch in Zusammenhang mit einer transformationellen Beschreibung bestimmter Typen von Genitivattributen, präpositionaler Attribute sowie gewisser Typen von derivierten Adjektiven zu lösen. Vergleiche folgende Beispiele:

(7) *Das Haus des Nachbarn*
     Die Praxis des Amtsarztes

---

[10] Die Unterscheidung zwischen 'restriktiven' und 'appositiven' Relativsätzen, die in den Basisstrukturen ihren Niederschlag finden muß, wird hier vernachlässigt.

Das Haus neben der Schule
Die Dame mit dem Hund
Handschuhe aus Leder
Spielzeug für Kinder
Die väterliche Wohnung
Die hölzerne Harke
Der bucklige Mann

In vielen Fällen kann eine vorausgesetzte Tiefenstruktur in mehrere Oberflächen-strukturen umgewandelt werden. Entsprechende Regelmäßigkeiten müssen bei der Formulierung von Transformationsregeln berücksichtigt werden.

5.   Wir dürfen voraussetzen, daß die Frage, welche Positionen die Nomen in dem eingebetteten Satz einnehmen können, zum Teil durch die Merkmale der strikten und selektionalen Subkategorisierung des angenommenen Verbs beantwortet wird. Informationen dieser Art muß die Grammatik unabhängig von der Analyse der Komposita zur Verfügung stellen. Damit wäre die Tatsache, daß zum Beispiel das Kompositum *Holzpferd* nicht als 'Pferd, das durch Holz erzeugt wird' interpretiert werden kann, durch die Selektionsbedingungen für das Verb *erzeugen* im Hinblick auf Subjekts- bzw. Objektsnomen erklärbar.

Das bedeutet jedoch noch nicht, daß mit der Erzeugung von Komposita keinerlei zusätzliche Beschränkungen für den eingebetteten Satz verbunden sind. Eine Reihe von Fakten legt den Schluß nahe, daß die Möglichkeit, in Attributssätzen enthaltene Konstituenten zu eliminieren, nicht beliebig ist. Mit anderen Worten, nicht jeder korrekte Attributssatz kann als Grundlage für die Ableitung eines Kompositums dienen. Die Annahme, daß bei der Formulierung von Transformationsregeln, die Komposita erzeugen, spezielle Beschränkungen zu berücksichtigen sind, wird zum Beispiel durch die Beobachtung gestützt, daß negierte Attributssätze nicht reduzierbar sind. Beispiel (8) verdeutlicht diese Behauptung:

(8)   *Fischfrau ≠ Frau, die keine Fische verkauft*
      Holzhaus ≠ Haus, das nicht aus Holz hergestellt ist

Ferner muß genauer untersucht werden, ob Beschränkungen für Tempora, modale Elemente sowie für die Determination des Nomens, das zum ersten Glied des Kom-positums umgewandelt wird, notwendig sind. Kann zum Beispiel *Wasserglas* inter-pretiert werden als 'Glas, in dem sich zum Zeitpunkt des Sprechaktes Wasser befindet' und *Fischfrau* als 'diejenige Frau, die soeben die fünf Fische verkauft, die ich vorhin erwähnte'? Mir scheint, daß Komposita tatsächlich als Abkürzungen solcher Aus-drücke verwendet werden können. Beschränkungen des Tempus und der Determina-tion sind lediglich für lexikalisierte Bildungen charakteristisch. Potentielle Bildungen werden normalerweise zu Termini und damit zu Bestandteilen des Lexikons einer Sprache, wenn sie auf Strukturen mit Attributssätzen zurückgehen, deren Nomen

nicht-partikulär determiniert sind. Da häufig nur lexikalisierte Komposita berücksichtigt werden, entsteht der Eindruck, als bestünden im Hinblick auf die Determination des Nomens, das zum ersten Glied eines Kompositums werden kann, grammatische Beschränkungen. Bezieht man dagegen die spontane Verwendung von Komposita in das Untersuchungsmaterial ein, so erweist sich diese Annahme als fragwürdig.

Eine weitere Frage, die hier nur gestellt, jedoch nicht beantwortet werden kann,
ist folgende: muß das erste Glied eines Kompositums eine Konstituente des Attributssatzes sein oder kann es Konstituente eines in den Attributsatz eingebetteten Satzes
sein? Wird der zweite Teil der Frage positiv beantwortet, so kann weiter gefragt
werden: welcher Einbettungsgrad ist zulässig? Denkbar wäre zum Beispiel eine Analyse,
die Komposita wie *Obstmesser, Geflügelschere* auf Strukturen zurückführt, die den
Ausdrücken 'Messer, das man benutzt, um Obst zu schneiden' bzw. 'Schere, die man
benutzt, um Geflügel zu zerschneiden' zugrunde liegen. Problematischer ist dagegen
eine Entscheidung der Frage, ob der Ausdruck *der Mann, der eine Fabrik besitzt,
in der Maschinen stehen, die benutzt werden, um Autos zu lackieren* vom Standpunkt
der Grammatik mit dem Kompositum *der Automann* korrespondiert.

6.   Die mit der Festlegung geeigneter Verben verbundenen Probleme können prinzipiell von zwei Voraussetzungen aus untersucht werden.

(V-1) Es wird angenommen, daß die Relationen zwischen Komposita mit ausschließ-
       lich nominalen Konstituenten auf der Grundlage positiv spezifizierter Verben
       oder Verbklassen beschrieben werden müssen. Das bedeutet: nicht jedes be-
       liebige Verb, das bezüglich der Nomen die Bedingungen der strikten und
       selektionalen Subkategorisierung erfüllt, darf vorausgesetzt werden. Man
       nimmt vielmehr an, daß auf der Grundlage von einzelnen Verben oder von
       Verbsubklassen Typen von Komposita unterschieden werden müssen.

(V-2) Es wird angenommen, daß die vorauszusetzenden Verben keine speziellen Be-
       dingungen für die Analyse von Komposita festlegen, sondern daß lediglich
       allgemeine Bedingungen für die Reduktion von Tiefenstrukturen existieren.
       Das bedeutet, daß jeder grammatisch korrekte Satz, der die Bedingungen für
       Attributsätze und zusätzliche Bedingungen für die Reduktion von Tiefen-
       strukturen erfüllt, zugelassen ist.

Bisher was es üblich, von (V-1) auszugehen.[11] Damit ist jedoch keine Entscheidung
über die Zulässigkeit von (V-2) verbunden. Wir wollen zunächst Lösungswege
skizzieren und besprechen, die von (V-1) ausgehen und kommen dann auf (V-2)
zurück.

---

[11] Auf der Grundlage dieser Voraussetzung werden in der traditionellen Forschung Typen von
Komposita unterschieden. Vgl. auch: R.B.Lees, "Problems in the Grammatical Analysis of English
Compounds", in vorliegendem Sammelband, H.Marchand (Anm. 4).

7.   Wenn (V-1) zu einer generellen Analyse führen soll, so muß die Zahl der durch Verben charakterisierten Typen von Komposita möglichst gering sein. Je mehr Verben bzw. Verbklassen vorausgesetzt werden, um so weniger generell werden die Aussagen über die Bildung entsprechender Komposita. Dies vorausgesetzt, können auf der Grundlage von (V-1) folgende Lösungswege beschritten werden:

(L-1) Es besteht die Möglichkeit, Verben wie *erzeugen, besitzen, sich befinden, etwas tun mit, haben* u.a. anzunehmen. Die Anzahl solcher Verben muß gering und ihre Bedeutung entsprechend allgemein sein. Dieser Lösungsweg wurde in anderem Zusammenhang bereits vorgeschlagen, so bei der Analyse possessiver Genitive, die auf Attributsätze mit dem Verb *haben* zurückgeführt wurden. Die Wahl geeigneter Verben könnte dadurch motiviert werden, daß sie auch bei der transformationellen Beschreibung anderer Konstruktionen benötigt werden. So können zum Beispiel die Verben *besitzen* und *sich befinden* bei der Erzeugung von derivierten Adjektiven verwendet werden. Vgl. *das väterliche Haus* und *der steinige Acker*.

(L-2) Man nimmt die Existenz von Verben an, die keine phonologische Matrix haben, sondern nur durch ein komplexes Symbol repräsentiert werden, das alle syntaktischen und semantischen Eigenschaften der vorausgesetzten Relation charakterisiert. Dieser Lösungsweg ist auch für die Beschreibung von Nominalisierungen denkbar. *Nomina agentis* wie *Briefträger* können (unter Auslassung der Details) wie folgt analysiert werden:

(9)

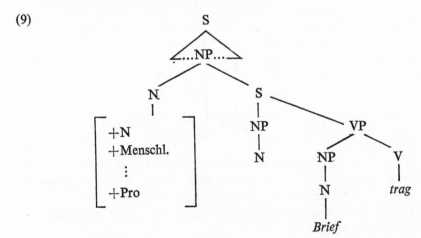

Das komplexe Symbol unter N muß alle Informationen enthalten, die *nomina agentis* charakterisieren. Für andere Typen von Nominalisierungen wären entsprechende Angaben notwendig. Das Merkmal [+ Pro] wird benötigt, um die Einsetzung von Lexikoneintragungen zu verhindern.

Alternative Lösungen zu (9), die die Annahme der Existenz phonologisch nicht repräsentierter Elemente vermeiden, sind denkbar. Man könnte die Suffixe von Verbalnomen als Lexikoneintragungen behandeln, die u.a. die Merkmale [+N] und [+____S] enthalten. Dieser Lösungsweg führt jedoch nur scheinbar zu einer Vermeidung der Annahme, daß die Grammatik phonologisch nicht repräsentierte Elemente enthalten kann, da Nominalisierungen ohne Suffix möglich sind. *Fischkoch* ist zum Beispiel eine Bildung, die in der gleichen Weise analysiert werden sollte wie *Briefträger*. Um das zu erreichen, müßte das Lexikon Eintragungen (in diesem Falle Suffixe) enthalten, die keine phonologische Matrix besitzen; das Problem wäre demnach nicht beseitigt. Einen Ausweg könnte man darin sehen, daß *Fischkoch* auf *Fischkocher* zurückgeführt wird. Die Annahme von Regeln, die Suffixe wieder eliminieren, wäre im vorliegenden Fall jedoch unplausibel.[12]

Eine zweite Alternative zu (9) könnte von speziellen Pronomen ausgehen, zum Beispiel von *jemand*. Alle in Frage kommenden Pronomen legen jedoch Determinationen fest, eine unerwünschte Konsequenz, da die Determination der *nomina agentis* frei sein muß. Überlegungen dieser Art unterstützen (L-2).

Wenn die in (9) für nomina agentis vorgeschlagene Analyse als zulässig betrachtet wird, so können Komposita wie *Briefbote, Zeitungsjunge, Milchmann* analog behandelt werden:

(10)

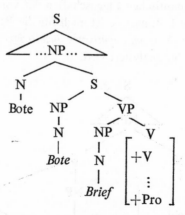

Der Unterschied zwischen (9) und (10) bestünde dann lediglich darin, daß im ersten Fall ein phonologisch nicht repräsentiertes Nomen angenommen werden muß, jedoch ein normales Verb vorhanden ist, während im zweiten Fall ein phonologisch nicht repräsentiertes Verb vorausgesetzt werden muß, jedoch ein normales Nomen existiert.

(L-3) Statt individuelle Verben anzugeben, können Verbklassen charakterisiert wer-

---

[12] Angenommen, man würde eine Regel formulieren, die in bestimmten Fällen das generell eingeführte Suffix *-er* wieder eliminiert. Diese Lösung setzt voraus, daß das komplexe Symbol von Wörtern wie *Koch* das idiosynkratische Merkmal [+ Regel (*-er*-Eliminierung)] enthält. Das heißt, der nichtsystematische Charakter von *nomina agentis* ohne Suffix wird durch eine Regel und durch ein idiosynkratisches Merkmal beschrieben. Sinnvoller ist eine Lösung, die in den fraglichen Fällen von vornherein die Wahl eines Suffixes verhindert.

den. Formal kann dies durch die Festlegung von Bedingungen für die strukturelle Beschreibung von Transformationsregeln erreicht werden. Solche Bedingungen wären durch die Angabe von Merkmalen zu formulieren, die ein Verb neben anderen enthalten muß, um die Regel durchlaufen zu können. Demnach schaffen die mit der Formulierung von Transformationsregeln verbundenen Bedingungen Klassen von Verben. Jedes Verb, das zu dieser Klasse gehört, kann zusätzliche syntaktische und semantische Informationen enthalten. So könnten zum Beispiel Komposita wie *Zeitungsjunge, Briefbote, Milchmann, Fischfrau* durch eine Transformationsregel erzeugt werden, deren strukturelle Beschreibung Verben wie *austragen, vertreiben, verkaufen, fortschaffen* u. a. m. erfüllen. Mit dieser Analyse wäre die Behauptung verbunden, daß *Zeitungsjunge* u. a. auf Tiefenstrukturen zurückgeht, die folgenden Ausdrücken zugrundeliegen:

(11)   *Junge, der Zeitungen austrägt*
      Junge, der Zeitungen verkauft
      Junge, der Zeitungen vertreibt
      Junge, der Zeitungen fortschafft

(L-1) und (L-2) verlangen die Angabe individueller Verben. (L-1) setzt im Lexikon existierende Verben voraus, während (L-2) die Existenz phonologisch nicht repräsentierter Verben postuliert. Die phonologische Seite der Verben ist für die Analyse von Komposita des hier besprochenen Typs jedoch unwesentlich. In syntaktischer und semantischer Hinsicht sollten sich die durch (L-1) oder durch (L-2) erzielten Ergebnisse der Analyse nicht wesentlich unterscheiden. Die Wahl zwischen (L-1) und (L-2) hängt demnach in erster Linie davon ab, ob man phonologisch nicht repräsentierten Einheiten einen selbständigen Status in der Syntax einräumen darf. Wenn diese Frage positiv entschieden wird, so brigt (L-2) eine Reihe von Vorteilen mit sich. Die Ausarbeitung von (L-1) verlangt zum Beispiel Entscheidungen, die offensichtlich willkürlich sind. Man könnte mit dem gleichen Recht entweder *erzeugen* oder *produzieren* wählen, muß sich aber festlegen. In anderen Fällen sind die in Frage kommenden Verben mehrdeutig, und es ist notwendig, die gewünschte Bedeutung festzulegen. Ferner ist eine Reihe von möglichen Verben mit morphologischen und syntaktischen Eigenschaften idiosynkratischer Natur verbunden, zum Beispiel: *sich befinden, etwas tun mit*. Schwierigkeiten dieser Art treten in Zusammenhang mit (L-2) nicht auf. Stattdessen ergeben sich aus (L-2) weitreichende theoretische Konsequenzen. Dieser Weg wird möglicherweise nur dann sinnvoll, wenn das Verhältnis zwischen Tiefenstrukturen und semantischen Strukturen so charakterisiert wird, daß eine entsprechende Analyse theoretisch zulässig ist. Versuche, die kategoriale Komponente der Basis so zu formulieren, daß sie mit der als universell zu betrachtenden semantischen Struktur zwischen Lexikoneintragungen eines Satzes zusammenfällt, wurden in jüngster Zeit unternommen. Eine Klärung dieses Problems wurde jedoch nocht nicht erreicht.

Mit allen drei Lösungswegen sind unterschiedliche Auffassungen über die Bildung von Komposita verbunden. Es handelt sich demnach nicht nur um technische Alternativen, sondern um verschiedenartige Interpretationen der Fakten. (L-1) und (L-3) lassen die Möglichkeit offen, die vorausgesetzten Tiefenstrukturen entweder zu Nominalphrasen mit Relativsätzen umzuformen oder zu Komposita bzw. anderen Formen reduzierter Attributssätze. Im Gegensatz dazu, verlangt (L-2) obligatorische Reduktionsregeln. Der eingebettete Satz kann in diesem Fall, da er kein phonologisch repräsentiertes Verb enthält, nicht zu einem Relativsatz entwickelt werden. Vom Standpunkt der Regeln, die Attributssätze in Relativsätze und durch Reduktion entstehende Formen von Attributen umwandeln, entstehen aus (L-2) Sonderbedingungen, die sich in nicht-generellen Beschränkungen äußern. Mit (L-1) ist die wenig plausible Annahme verbunden, daß nur Sätze mit den spezifizierten Verben die Grundlage für die Erzeugung von Komposita bilden. Sätze mit synonymen (oder weitgehend synonymen) Verben können zwar in der semantischen Komponente als Paraphrasen charakterisiert werden, dürfen aber nicht als Grundlage der Erzeugung von Komposita dienen. Hat man sich zum Beispiel für *erzeugen* entschieden, so könnte die Tiefenstruktur von *Honig, den Bienen erzeugen* zu *Bienenhonig* umgeformt werden, nicht aber die Tiefenstruktur von *Honig, den Bienen produzieren*. Sowohl die unerwünschten Konsequenzen von (L-1), als auch die mit (L-2) verknüpften, können durch (L-3) vermieden werden. Mir scheint deshalb, daß (L-3) unter Voraussetzung von (V-1) der beste Lösungsweg ist.

In jedem Falle sind die Besonderheiten der Lexikalisierung auszuklammern. Ginge man von lexikalisierten Bildungen aus, so müßte die Menge der vorauszusetzenden individuellen Verben so umfangreich sein, daß generelle Aussagen nur in beschränktem Maße möglich wären. Da (L-3) Subklassen von Verben voraussetzt, ist die Möglichkeit, generelle Aussagen zu formulieren größer. Angenommen, die strukturelle Beschreibung einer Transformationsregel läßt Verben wie *austragen, verkaufen, vertreiben, verteilen*, u.a. zu. Dann müßten Komposita, die durch diese Regel erzeugt werden, genau so viele Mehrdeutigkeiten aufweisen, wie die in der strukturellen Beschreibung postulierte Verbsubklasse Verben enthält. Da die gleichen Nomen unter Umständen auch in Attributssätzen mit anderen Verbklassen vorkommen können, erhöht sich die Mehrdeutigkeit entsprechend. Mir scheint, daß diese Konsequenz mit den beobachtbaren Fakten verträglich ist.[13] Eine Einschränkung der Mehrdeutigkeit

[13]   Tatsächlich sind Komposita in einem hohen Grade mehrdeutig, so daß die '*recoverability*' in diesem Falle nicht garantiert werden kann. (Vgl. dazu: N.Chomsky, *Aspects*, S.144f.) In einer Rezension zu R.B.Lees, *The Grammar of English Nominalizations*, vertritt Ch.Rohrer (Indogerm. Forschungen, 71 (1966)) die Auffassung, die '*recoverability*' von Komposita müsse garantiert werden: "Das Kompositum *oil well* müßte genau so viele Bedeutungen haben, wie es transitive Verben gibt, denn das Symbol *Vtn* kann ja durch jedes transitive Verb der englischen Sprache ersetzt werden. Der normale Sprecher empfindet jedoch ein Kompositum wie *oil well* nicht als unendlich mehrdeutig. Die Regel zur Elidierung des transitiven Verbes in den Komposita vom Typ Subjekt-Objekt ist folglich falsch und muß neu formuliert werden." Diese Argumentation verdeutlicht die Konsequenzen, die entstehen, wenn nicht zwischen potentiellen und lexikalisierten Bildungen unterschieden wird. Nur vom Standpunkt lexikalisierter Bildungen ist die Argumentation gerechtfertigt. Der Prozeß der Lexikalisierung ist nach unserer Auffassung jedoch bei der Formulierung grammatischer Regeln nicht relevant.

von Komposita erfolgt durch die Lexikalisierung, nicht durch die grammatischen Regeln. Die Tatsache, daß *Fischfrau* normalerweise als 'Frau, die Fische verkauft' interpretiert wird, *Zeitungsfrau* aber als 'Frau, die Zeitungen austrägt' hängt mit terminologischen Konventionen zusammen, die nicht Gegenstand der grammatischen Regeln sein können, die potentielle Komposita erzeugen. Die potentielle Bildung *Zeitungsfrau* kann durchaus als 'Frau, die Zeitungen verkauft' interpretiert werden, ebenso wie *Fischfrau* als 'Frau, die Fische austrägt' interpretierbar ist. Daß die zuletzt genannte Interpretation weniger wahrscheinlich ist, hängt von unseren Kenntnissen sozialer Gewohnheiten ab, die schwerlich die grammatische Korrektheit der Bildung mit dierser Interpretation einschränken. Unter Voraussetzung von (L-3) könnte eine Form der Lexikalisierung darin bestehen, daß die Mehrdeutigkeit durch eine konventionelle Festlegung bestimmter Verben beschränkt wird. Wählt man (L-1) oder (L-2) so müßten entsprechende Lexikalisierungsprozesse umständlicher formuliert werden.

8.   Auf die vorangegangenen Überlegungen über den Status der Verben in der Tiefenstruktur von Komposita des behandelten Typs, folgen nun einige Beispiele für möglicherweise zu unterscheidende Verbklassen sowie für die Klärung der Frage, welche grammatische Funktion die Nomen ausfüllen können. Die Verbsubklassen werden durch eine Umschreibung charakterisiert. Eine präzisere Beschreibung setzt umfangreiche Studien über die Subklassifizierung von Verben voraus. Stünden die notwendigen Informationen zur Verfügung, so müßte der Gehalt der verbalen Umschreibung als ein Komplex strukturierter Merkmale repräsentiert werden. Welche Merkmale benötigt werden und wie die Struktur komplexer Symbole beschaffen sein muß, ist gegenwärtig sowohl empirisch als auch theoretisch ungewiß.

Ein Typ von Komposita könnte auf Tiefenstrukturen zurückgehen, deren Attributsatz Verben enthält, die durch 'Subjekt tut etwas mit Objekt' umschrieben werden können. Verben dieser Klasse verlangen ein direktes Objekt. Je nach der grammatischen Funktion der Nomen in Attributssätzen dieses Typs, sind folgende Arten von Komposita unterscheidbar:

(i)   Das erste Glied geht auf das Subjekt des Attributsatzes zurück, das zweite auf das Objekt: *Pferdewagen, Windmühle.*

(i') Das erste Glied geht auf das Objekt zurück, das zweite auf das Subjekt: *Droschkenpferd, Zeitungsjunge.*

(ii) Das erste Glied geht auf das Objekt, das zweite auf ein Lokaladverbial zurück. Das Subjekt wird in diesem Falle eliminiert: *Schuhladen, Buchgeschäft.*

(ii') Das erste Glied geht auf eine Lokalphrase zurück, das zweite auf das Objekt: *Gebirgsschuhe, Strandanzug.*

(iii) Das erste Glied geht auf das Objekt, das zweite auf ein Richtungsadverbial zurück: *Fußbank, Kopfkissen.*

(iii') Das erste Glied geht auf ein Richtungsadverbial zurück, das zweite auf das Objekt: *Tischtuch, Kaffeesahne.*

(iv) Das erste Glied geht auf das Objekt zurück, das zweite auf ein Instrumentaladverbial: *Heugabel, Obstmesser.*

(iv') Das erste Glied geht auf ein Instrumentaladverbial zurück, das zweite auf das Objekt: *Gabelbissen.*

(v) Das erste Glied geht auf das Objekt zurück, das zweite auf ein Temporaladverbial: *Bierabend, Fischtag.*

(v') Das erste Glied geht auf ein Temporaladverbial zurück, das zweite auf das Objekt: *Nachthemd, Winterkleid.*

Ein zweiter Typ soll durch die Umschreibung 'Subjekt erzeugt Objekt' charakterisiert werden. Diese Relation entspricht den 'Verben mit effiziertem Objekt' der traditionellen Grammatik. Der zuvor genannten Relationen entsprechen 'Verben mit affiziertem Objekt'. Eine syntaktische Besonderheit der 'Verben mit effiziertem Objekt' besteht darin, daß sie 'Stoffbezeichnungen' wie *aus Eisen, aus Holz, aus Blei* usw. als Ergänzung zulassen. Folgende Typen sind möglich:

(i) Das erste Glied geht auf das Subjekt zurück, das zweite auf das Objekt: *Bienenhonig, Hühnerei.*

(i') Das erste Glied geht auf das Objekt zurück, das zweite auf das Subjekt: *Honigbiene, Kostümschneider.*

(ii) Das erste Glied geht auf das Objekt zurück, das zweite auf ein Lokaladverbial: *Brotfabrik, Spielzeugstadt.*[14]

(ii') Das erste Glied geht auf ein Lokaladverbial zurück, das zweite auf das Objekt: *Fabrikbrot, Landbutter.*

(iii) Das erste Glied geht auf das Objekt zurück, das zweite auf ein Instrumentaladverbial: *Nuthobel, Strumpfmaschine.*

(iii') Das erste Glied geht auf ein Instrumentaladverbial zurück, das zweite auf das Objekt: *Messerwunde, Hobelspäne.*

(iv) Das erste Glied geht auf das Objekt zurück, das zweite auf eine Stoffergänzung: *Kuchenmehl, Hutfilz.*

---

[14] Die Beispiele können auch anders interpretiert werden, nämlich: 'Fabrik, die Brot erzeugt' bzw. 'Stadt, die Spielzeug erzeugt', sie wären in diesem Fall unter (i') aufzuführen. Wir begegnen hier einem Problem, mit dem sich Ch.J.Fillmore in: "A Proposal Concerning English Prepositions", *Monograph Series on Languages and Linguistics*, No.19 (Georgetown University 1966), und in: "Toward a Modern Theory of case", *The Ohio University Research Found. Proj. on Linguistic Analysis*, Report No.13 (1966), ausführlicher befaßt. Fillmore zweifelt die semantische Relevanz der Begriffe 'Subjekt' und 'Objekt' an und damit ihre Berechtigung in der Tiefenstruktur. Einige Konsequenzen aus Fillmores Ansichten für die Analyse von Komposita zieht R.B.Lees in vorliegendem Sammelband.

(iv') Das erste Glied geht auf eine Stoffergänzung zurück, das zweite auf das Objekt: *Mehlsuppe, Filzhut.*

(v) Das erste Glied geht auf das Objekt zurück, das zweite auf ein Temporaladverbial: so zu interpretieren wäre etwa *Kuchentag* (belegte Bildungen sind mir nicht bekannt).

(v') Das erste Glied geht auf ein Temporaladverbial zurück, das zweite auf das Objekt: Belegte Bildungen sind mir nicht bekannt, der Typ ist jedoch nicht auszuschließen. Ein Bäcker könnte zum Beispiel Brötchen, die er am Morgen bäckt, *Morgenbrötchen* nennen.

Weitere Verbklassen könnten zum Beispiel umschrieben werden durch 'X ist Teil von Y' (*Automotor, Pferdekopf, Hauswand*) sowie durch 'X befindet sich + lokale Präposition Y' (*Feldstein, Waldblume, Wandbild*). Wie die Beispiele zeigen, können Subjekt, Objekt und eine Reihe von Adverbialen zu Gliedern eines Kompositums werden und zwar sowohl erstes als auch zweites Glied. Im Gegensatz zum Subjekt darf das Objekt nicht eliminiert werden. Verben der ersten Klasse lassen Richtungsadverbiale zu, Verben der zweiten Klasse Stoffergänzungen. Diese syntaktischen Eigenschaften müssen in einer genaueren Charakterisierung der Verbklassen berücksichtigt werden. Da die Verhältnisse in beiden Fällen systematischer Natur sind, können die Bedingungen für reduzierbare Tiefenstrukturen sehr generell formuliert werden. Man benötigt nur eine Regel mit verschiedenen Bedingungen.

9.   Die bisherigen Überlegungen gingen von der Gültigkeit der Voraussetzung (V-1) aus. Wir wollen diese Hypothese nun genauer prüfen. Wir hatten darauf hingewiesen, daß möglichst wenige Verbklassen gefunden werden müssen, um generelle Aussagen über die Bildung von Komposita zu ermöglichen. Je genereller die Angaben über Verbsubklassen sind, um so stärker wird der Verdacht, daß letzten Endes alle Verben durch die geforderten Subklassen erfaßt werden. Bestätigt sich dieser Verdacht, so wäre eine Angabe spezieller Verbklassen in der strukturellen Beschreibung von Transformationsregeln, die Komposita des diskutierten Typs erzeugen, vom grammatischen Standpunkt überflüssig. Damit wäre (V-2) gerechtfertigt. Eine Begründung von (V-1) müßte zeigen, daß es Verbklassen gibt, die nicht als Grundlage der Interpretation von Komposita aus zwei Nomen gewählt werden dürfen. Aber selbst dann, wenn solche Klassen angegeben werden können, könnte es sinnvoller sein, die auszuschließenden Klassen in der strukturellen Beschreibung anzugeben statt die zugelassenen Klassen positiv aufzuzählen. Die Relevanz solcher Klassen wird fragwürdig, wenn man bedenkt, daß ein Kompositum nicht nur auf Verben einer Klasse zurückgehen muß. Das geht aus Beispiel (2) hervor. Die Bevorzugung von (V-1) ist — wie mir scheint — durch die Untersuchung lexikalisierter Komposita motiviert worden. Wenn man von der Bildung potentieller Komposita in der spontanen Kommunikation ausgeht, so wächst die Plausibilität von (V-2). Es mag der Fall sein, daß die Lexikalisierung einer potentiellen Bildung in Anlehnung an bereits lexikalisierte Bildungen mit gleich-

artigen konventionellen Beschränkungen erfolgt. Eine formale Darstellung dieses Gedankens geht offensichtlich über die Grammatik hinaus, mit anderen Worten, die Frage, unter welchen Bedingungen potentielle Bildungen lexikalisiert werden können und durch welche Faktoren ihre Akzeptabilität bestimmt wird, ist durchaus legitim, sie kann jedoch nicht allein mit grammatischen Begriffen beantwortet werden.[15]

Unter Berücksichtigung der Tatsache, daß Lexikalisierungs- und Akzeptabilitätsprobleme in der grammatischen Analyse von potentiellen Komposita nicht beschrieben werden können, bietet (V-2) eine bessere Grundlage als (V-1). (V-2) ist jedenfalls besser geeignet, die Frage zu klären, welche Klassen von Verben auszuschließen sind. Mit einiger Sicherheit darf dies von privativen Verben behauptet werden. Das Kompositum *Autoreifen* kann als potentielle Bildung in vielfacher Weise interpretiert werden, jedoch nicht als 'Reifen, der einem Auto fehlt'. Die einschränkende Bedingung für die Reduktion von Attributssätzen, auf die weiter vorn hingewiesen wurde, erfaßt demnach nicht nur Satznegationen, sondern auch Verben mit privativer Bedeutung. Mit großer Wahrscheinlichkeit trifft die Annahme zu, daß eine Formulierung der Bedingungen, unter denen Attributssätze zu Komposita verkürzt werden können, einfacher wird, wenn nur Angaben über auszuschließende Klassen notwendig sind.

Geht man von (V-2) aus, so hat die grammatische Analyse von Komposita mit ausschließlich nominalen Konstituenten folgende Fragen zu beantworten:

(i) Welche Grundstrukturen sind anzunehmen? Erfaßt die Grundstruktur, die wir für Determinativkomposita angenommen haben, alle Fälle?

(ii) Darf das erste Glied Konstituente von in den Attributssatz eingebetteten Sätzen sein? Wenn ja: Ist der Einbettungsgrad determiniert?

(iii) Welche Bestandteile des Attributssatzes dürfen eliminiert werden, oder — anders ausgedrückt — welche Beschränkungen grenzen die Reduktion expliziterer Ausdrücke ein?

---

[15] Ein Versuch, diesen Gedanken zu präzisieren, müßte in folgender Richtung erfolgen: Ausgehend von strukturellen Informationen über im Lexikon repräsentierte Bildungen werden Regeln für die Erzeugung neuer Wörter geschaffen. Die Regeln gehören also nicht zur Grammatik, sondern sie werden im Zusammenhang mit der Absicht, ein neues Kompositum zu bilden auf der Grundlage grammatischer Informationen erzeugt. Regeln dieser Art sind nur zum Teil genereller Natur, denn jedes neue Wort hat von Anfang an idiosynkratische Eigenschaften. Die Erzeugung neuer Komposita (und Derivationen) wäre demnach ein bei weitem komplizierterer Prozeß als die Bildung anderer sprachlicher Ausdrücke, die in der Grammatik existierende Regeln voraussetzen. Da die Erzeugung neuer Regeln als eine Erscheinung des Lernprozesses aufzufassen ist, müßte die Bildung neuer Komposita und Derivationen als ein Prozeß verstanden werden, der Mechanismen der Spracherlernung einschließt.

Obwohl Prozesse dieser Art in der Wortbildung nicht ausgeschlossen sind, scheint es uns in der Mehrzahl der Fälle sinnvoller zu sein, generelle grammatische Regeln für die Bildung von Komposita anzunehmen. Ein potentielles Kompositum, das durch grammatische Regeln erzeugt wird, kann dann lexikalisiert werden, das heißt die generelle Analysierbarkeit wird durch Konventionen eingeschränkt. Diese Konventionen finden ihren Niederschlag in den lexikalisierten Bildungen, die zum Lexikon der Sprache gehören. Die Motivierung solcher Konventionen sowie — falls das überhaupt möglich ist — eine systematische Darstellung gehört nicht zu den Aufgaben der Grammatik, sondern zu denen einer Theorie der Sprachverwendung.

Es ist zu erwarten, daß Frage (iii) nicht nur für die Beschreibung von Komposita und Attributen berechtigt ist, sondern für alle Arten von Reduktionen. Deshalb kann eine Beantwortung dieser Frage zu Erkenntnissen über allgemeine Bedingungen für die Reduzierung expliziterer sprachlicher Ausdrücke führen.

Die hier vorgetragenen Überlegungen sind sehr allgemeiner Natur. Als Ergebnis haben wir zunächst nur ein Forschungsprogramm anzubieten. Mir scheint jedoch, daß Betrachtungen dieser Art ein neues Licht auf die Frage werfen, wie der kreative Aspekt von Komposita zu studieren ist. Eine konsequente Unterscheidung zwischen lexikalisierten und potentiellen Komposita erweist sich offensichtlich als notwendig. Das bedeutet wiederum, daß die Voraussetzung (V-1), die bisher die Behandlung des Themas bestimmte, ihre scheinbare Plausibilität verliert, da sie letzten Endes von lexikalisierten Bildungen ausgeht. Die grammatischen Möglichkeiten, neue Komposita des hier diskutierten Typs zu bilden, sind nach unserer Auffassung nicht durch positiv spezifizierte Verbklassen determiniert. Das schließt nicht aus, daß im Zusammenhang mit der Lexikalisierung potentieller Bildungen bevorzugte Typen charakterisiert werden können, die auf Klassen von Verben beruhen. Dabei handelt es sich jedoch um eine Fragestellung, die im Rahmen einer Theorie der Sprachverwendung (*Performance*) zu klären ist.

E. V. PADUČEVA

ANAPHORIC RELATIONS AND THEIR REPRESENTATION IN THE DEEP STRUCTURE OF A TEXT

1. This paper deals with a problem widely discussed in mathematical logic, though some modifications appeared necessary in the course of mutual readjustment of the logical and linguistic approach to the linguistic facts. Using the terms familiar to logicians rather than to linguists we shall say that sentences (or, in the general case, texts) of a natural language express propositions about OBJECTS, properties of objects, and interrelations between objects; linguistic expressions which make it possible to speak about objects will be called NAMES of objects; objects are DENOTATA of their names; reference of names to objects is carried out through the MEANINGS of names.

The notions of object and name are vague: everything that has a name is an object, while the use of names is not independent of the language. Take the trivial example whereby one and the same situation is most commonly described in Russian as *Идет дождь*, where rain is treated as an object, and in English as *It rains* where it is not; and take, then, the example of W. Quine [11], where the sentence **It rabbits* is, in general, one of the possible linguistic means of describing the situation 'Rabbit!'. According to W. Quine, a linguistic expression is understood as a name of an object, if it is naturally associated with the idea of identification and quantification. Indeed, the Russian sentence *Идет дождь* allows for a direct question: *Это тот же самый дождь или другой?* (Is it the same rain [as before] or a new one?). While in English such a question can be formulated only if we describe the situation of rain in some other terms.

In logic it is accepted that sentences are but a special type of names, and logicians suggest that the denotatum of a sentence is one of the two abstract objects — truth or falsity. Then it is natural to expect that the following relations will hold between the notions just mentioned:

Thesis (1) The substitution of a name by a name with the identical meaning (*i.e.*, by a synonymous name) does not change the meaning of the initial expression.

Thesis (2) The substitution of a name by a name with the identical denotatum does not change the denotatum of the initial expression.

The first relation is, apparently, really universal; while the second thesis, as is known, when applied to natural languages encounters difficulties, which led to the logical notion of the oblique context. Take the classical example of oblique context (the example belongs to B. Russell): the names *Scott* and *the author of 'Waverley'* have the same denotatum; still the sentence *George IV wished to know whether Scott was the author of 'Waverley'* is true, while the sentence *George IV wished to know whether Scott was Scott* is not. The explanation of this class of exceptions, given by logicians (*cf.* [6]), do not seem satisfactory to a linguist; and the thesis itself is, perhaps, not interesting for a linguist, who has usually nothing to do with the truth or falsity of sentences. Meanwhile some modification of the problem of substitution of names enables one to attack the facts derived from the most vital aspects of language usage. Namely, there is another kind of substitution of names which belongs to the operations practically implemented by the users of language.

2.   In natural languages there are cases when names with the identical denotata and different meanings can be substituted for one another with no effect not only on the truth of the text but even on its meaning. In order to get this effect we need only to take a text where one object is mentioned several times (which is almost inevitable in a coherent discourse [3], [4]). In this case the object, when mentioned for the second time, can be referred to by a great variety of non-synonymous names which are substituted for one another without changing the integral meaning of the text, *e.g.*: (1) *The English writer Walter Scott was born in Scotland. His father* (= *the father of Walter Scott,* = *the father of the writer*) *was a baronet.* The name corresponding to the first reference to an object in a given text will be called the INITIAL name; names corresponding to all the other references, will be called DERIVED names. Thus instead of the thesis (2), about the substitutability of names preserving the truth-value of the sentence, another thesis can be suggested, about the substitutability of non-synonymous derived names preserving the meaning of the sentence.

However, the substitutability of derived names is only one side of the problem. This kind of substitution of names cannot be studied independently of another group of facts — these are the facts of differentiation between the derived names of some object and its initial name. For example, the role of the initial name of an object can be fulfilled by its proper name, and the corresponding derived name may be a pronoun; if the initial name is a noun phrase including a detailed description of the properties of the object, then the corresponding derived name may consist of the syntactically principal noun of this phrase: (2) *A woman with blue eyes and black hair came into the room. The woman looked upset.* Sometimes this differentiation of names is not obligatory, *e.g.*: (3) *Mary returned home in the evening. Mary* (= *she*) *looked upset.* But there are derived names that can never be used as initial ones (*e.g.*, 3rd person pronouns); and there are initial names that can never be used as derived ones, *e.g.*, the name *a woman with blue eyes and black hair* in (2).[1]

---

[1]   W. Quine [13] calls attention to the distinction between the ANTECEDENT of a pronoun and its SUBSTITUTE; the phrase *a woman with blue eyes and black hair* can be the former and not the latter;

The relation between the names of a given text that have identical denotata may be called an ANAPHORIC RELATION (this term is employed *e.g.* in [14]).

3.   In a logical formula every reference to an object corresponds to a certain occurrence of a variable associated with that object. According to W. Quine [12], the role of variables in mathematical and logical formulae consists in identifying and differentiating the objects referred to.   It is natural to suppose that names of objects in a strict sense of a word are exactly those symbols (or expressions) that provide their identification and differentiation; no properties of an object must be included in its name: they must be stated separately.   In this case the true name of an object in the deep structure of a sentence (*i.e.*, the 'deep name' of an object) must look like a variable in a logical formula, *i.e.*, like some kind of identification index. *Cf.* W. Quine [13]:

We can systematically so paraphrase our sentences that the only definite singular terms [= names, E.P.] to survive are variables used pronominally in apposition with indefinite singular terms, like the variables 'x' and 'y' in *Every region* x *contains a region* y *smaller than* x.

In the surface structure of a sentence naming of objects usually is not separated from stating their properties.[2]   Thus in the surface structure of a sentence it is not the surface name of an object that is an equivalent to the deep name of this object, but an anaphoric relation between the surface names.   In other words, in the course of transition from the deep structure of a sentence to its surface structure, variables are eliminated and substituted by anaphoric relations between surface names (unambiguously expressed in every stylistically adequate text).   It might be useful to note that this problem can also be formulated as a problem of describing the synonymity relation that holds, *e.g.*, between the sentences

> *Every region* x *contains a region* y *that is smaller than* x

and

> *Every region contains a region smaller than itself*

The aim of this paper is to describe possible structural relationships between the names connected by anaphora.   It is most convenient to present such a description in the form of a set of rules that yield all possible derived names of an object, given its initial name.   These rules must not be confused with the transformations that obtain surface names of objects form their deep names.   The deep name of an object does not coin-

---

the same is true for the corresponding Russian phrase *женщина с голубыми глазами и черными волосами*, though Russian has no articles.
[2]   *Pronoun* is the only kind of name that can be regarded as a true name in this sense; even proper names serve not only to refer to an object but also to point to some constant property of that object; *e.g.*, John means 'a person who responds to a call *John*!'.   A variable differs from a proper name in that it names a given object only in a given text and thus does not confer any interesting property of that object.   Perhaps it would be more reasonable (though less consistent) to use in the deep structure variables of different domains, *cf.* [5]; in this case properties of the corresponding domain of variables will be included in the deep name of the object.

cide with the first member of an anaphoric relation; the deep name must be transformed into the initial name if it corresponds to the first mention of a given object in a
given text; otherwise it will be transformed into a derived name.

Initial names can also vary without changing the meaning of the text, though this
variation is never reduced to mere substitution of names, because it must be accom-
panied by some other syntactic changes. Thus, (1) *I found a ripe red apple* is synonymous to (2) *I found an apple; it was ripe and red*, and even to (3) *I found an object;
it was an apple; it was ripe and red*. The representation of objects by means of variables makes the deep structure a convenient basis for a formal description of such kinds
of transformations.

4.   Thus we conclude that the linguistic problem differs from its logical formulation
first of all in that we do not deal with denotata of sentences but only with their meaning. On the other hand, we study substitutability not for all kinds of non-synonymous
names, but only for the derived names: for the initial names it does not exist. The
third point of difference is that substitutability of derived names is not studied by
itself but together with free and contextually bound differences between initial and
derived names: substitutability of derived names is a mere consequence of the fact
that one and the same initial name may have more than one corresponding derived
name.

We shall treat the anaphoric relation as binary; *i.e.*, if there are more than two
references to a certain object in a certain text then all the derived names are treated as
anaphorically connected only with the initial name, the relations of the derived names
with each other not being taken into consideration. Certainly this is a simplification
of the real situation. If the derived names were not related to each other, then, in
particular, each of them could have been used independently of all the others. Meanwhile repetition of identical derived names is as undesirable as any repetition. Besides,
for some of the derived names repetition is specially prohibited — when repeated they
are conceived as written with a capital letter, *i.e.*, they behave like proper names (*cf.*
the examples in [10]). But this is primarily a stylistic problem which, it may be hoped,
can be studied separately.

5.   Here are some examples of expressions that function as initial names. (I) Proper
name (*Napoleon, John*). (II) Definite description (*the natural satellite of the Earth, the
present King of Denmark*). (III) In many cases the initial name of an object consists of
a general term + a word or expression (perhaps, only implied) equivalent to an existential quantifier (strictly speaking, this is rather a quantifier of 'introducing an object',
cf. [8], because in natural languages the existential quantifier is used in a somewhat
constructivist sense: the object in question must be pointed to); example: *A young
woman came into the room.* (IV) It is not altogether clear how to analyse the noun
phrases that contain a universal quantifier (explicit or implied). Normally such an
expression cannot be treated as a name of an object; in particular, it cannot be the

first member of anaphora: (1) *If every man had two wives he would have made many women unhappy*; (2) *If the point A belongs to every set, then the point B belongs to this set* (cf. [13]). But there are exceptions: (3) *Every man thinks about it, especially if he is twenty.* (V) The initial name often contains 'egocentric particulars' (B. Russell [15]), *i.e.*, its meaning essentially depends upon the reference to a given act of speech; thus *I* = 'a person who pronounces this token of the word *I*'; *this table* = 'the table pointed to by a gesture, accompanying the pronounciation of this token of the word *this*', and so on. It should be noted that a reference to a given act of speech is what makes many other names (like *John*) unambiguous; but for the present this fact can be ignored. (VI) Sometimes initial names are not independent of one another, because they include auxiliary differentiators; example: *One line crosses the two other lines.* These initial names cannot serve as the derived ones.

It may be the case that the same set of objects is treated in one part of the text as one object, and in another — as several different objects: (4) *John met Mary and they went to the cinema*; (5) *The boys arranged to meet at six, but John came in time while Peter was late*; (6) *The boys arranged to meet at six, but only one of them came in time while all the others were late.* Questions of this kind must be treated separately.

6.   A derived name can be presented as consisting of two parts — the lexical component and the identifier. Accordingly, in order to construct a derived name we must find its lexical component and its identifier.

The lexical component of a derived name is defined by a set of transformations of the lexical component of the initial name. Some transformations are obligatory. Thus, introduction of reflexive pronouns is obligatory wherever it is possible; the name which is left unchanged under these conditions, is interpreted as the name of a different object: *word after word* = *one word after another*.

In other cases the choice of transformations is either free, or it is regulated by the following general tendencies: (I) UNAMBIGUITY of the anaphoric relation; (II) ECONOMY of the means of expression, which requires ridding text of unnecessary repetition of semantic elements; (II) DIVERSITY of the means of expression, which requires avoiding the repetition of words even if they correspond to necessary repetition of semantic elements.

These tendencies may contradict each other. Thus, the tendency towards economy has the effect of reducing the length of the text, while the tendency towards unambiguity gives the opposite result. In different styles one tendency may prevail over another. Thus for the scientific texts the requirement of diversity is not so important as for newspaper texts. Sometimes these tendencies turn into grammatically obligatory requirements; thus in (1) it is necessary to follow the requirement of economy, while in (2) — the requirement of unambiguity:

(1)   *The English writer Walter Scott was born in Scotland. Having graduated from a university the English writer Walter Scott attended the bar ⇒ ... Having graduated from the university Walter Scott attended the bar*

(2)   *An exterior angle of a triangle is greater than its interior angle not contiguous
to this angle ⇒ An exterior angle of a triangle is greater than its interior angle
not contiguous to this exterior angle

Transformations generating the lexical component of the derived name can be divided
into two groups. The tranformations of the first group are purely syntactical:
(1) substitution of a noun phrase by a pronoun, e.g., Napoleon ⇒ he, himself, cf. [1],
[2]; (2) substitution of a noun phrase by the syntactically principal noun in that
phrase, e.g., a beautiful young woman with blue eyes and black hair ⇒ woman, cf. [5],
where this transformation is formally described for a fragment of Russian.

Transformations of the second group are essentially semantic, i.e., they are based
on some kind of semantic analysis of the text. These transformations sometimes increase the amount of information contained in the name, and do not diminish it, as
in the previous case. The allowed sources for this increase of information are only
the preceding text and the information which can be supposed to be a part of the
language competence of a language user.

Examples of this kind of transformation.

The first case is the introduction of classifiers (the term of H. Hiż [9]):

linguistics ⇒ (this) science
Peter's daughters ⇒ the girls

The second can be illustrated by the following text:

A boy was sitting on the bench. Suddenly the door opened and another boy entered
the room. Then the boy who had been sitting stood up and went away.

Another example:

Jane was the daughter of Peter. Jane adored her father.

The process of synthesizing the name her father is as follows: Initially, the second sentence sounds like Jane adored Peter. But the first sentence is synonymous to Peter
was father of Jane. Thus Peter can be substituted by father of Jane ⇒ her father.
It is not clear, however, to what extent such transformations preserve the meaning of
the text. Probably sometimes it is the question of different deep structures. Take
the following convincing example:

I have seen the portrait of John Booth, and John Booth has killed Lincoln; consequently I have seen the portrait of the murderer of Lincoln.

Though it is known from the text that the murderer of Lincoln = John Booth, still
the substitution of the latter name for the former would not have preserved the meaning of the sentence.

Classifiers can also be substituted for the names of facts:

Mathematics studies not things but relations. This peculiarity of mathematics
explains why...

It can be assumed that the second sentence in this text is synthesized in the following way: the first sentence is reduced to a more abstract form, *i.e.*, to its classifier:

Mathematics has some peculiarity

After this everything is the same as in the previous examples.

Classifiers vary from sentence to sentence:

Gradually the pupil gets accustomed to all the requirements. The teacher must quicken this process.

The classifier for the first sentence is

Some process takes place

7.   Let us now turn to the identifiers. The meaning of the identifier in a derived name always implies a reference to the text: (1) *this* (*object*) means '(object) that was mentioned in the previous text'; (2) *the latter* (*the former*) means 'that which was mentioned last (first)'. In the language of science letters are often used as identifiers: *the set M* means 'the set which in this text will be called M'.

In languages with articles the definite article is one of the possible identifiers. In languages without articles, as Russian, the identifiers are often omitted. The use of identifiers in Russian depends upon the structure of the lexical component of the derived name and upon the context. In (1) both variants are admissible: (1) *Я написал статью. Статья* (= *эта статья*) *посвящена морфонологии* (I wrote an article. [The] article [= this article] deals with morphonology). In other cases strict but complex rules of complementary distribution come into play. Example of a simple rule: if the lexical component consists of a pronoun, or a proper name, or a definite description, then the derived name can contain no demonstrative pronoun: **this he*, **this Eifel tour*, **this Napoleon's mother*, **this space of my room*; cf. *this science* and **this linguistics*. Examples of restrictions that are not easy to understand: (2) *You shall see a boy and a girl. You must give a doll to the girl and a car to the boy*; (3) *A woman came into the room. I saw this woman at my friend's house.* In (2) the demonstrative pronoun must be absent, and in (3) it must be present. The Russian sentence (4) *Я видел человека, и ты видел человека* (I saw [a] man and you saw [a] man) is unambiguously understood as having no anaphoric relations between lexically identical names.

Such identifiers as *such*, *the same* obey special rules; perhaps they must be represented in the deep structure in a different way.

8.   Up till now nothing was said about the derived names containing descriptive modifiers, as in (1) *Mary went out at six. The young woman decided to go to the market.* Here the derived name of an object contains information about its qualities never mentioned before. The use of derived names with descriptive modifiers is a complex stylistic problem, because such names are often stylistically inadequate or at least not

neutral: (2) *Я нашел в чулане чайник; у жестяного чайника была отломана ручка* (I have found [a] tea-pot in the cellar; [a/the] tin tea-pot had a broken handle). This sentence is interpreted either as stylistically defective or as speaking of two different tea-pots: a modifier precludes the noun-phrase from being interpreted as a derived name.

This restriction is even more definite for such modifiers as quantifiers and numerals: (3) *На углу стояли девочки. Две девочки кого-то ждали* (There were girls standing at the corner. [ø/the] two girls were waiting for somebody); (4) *Он поедет в деревню. В любой деревне он будет чувствовать себя лучше* (He will go to [a] village. In any village he will feel better). In (3) and (4) lexically identical names are not understood as connected by the anaphoric relation. The limits in which the use of derived names with descriptive modifiers is admissable must be studied separately.

Note that the border-line between descriptive and non-descriptive modifiers is not absolute. *Cf.*, (5) *Mildred is in bed. She is ill.* For the reader who doesn't know that *Mildred* is a feminine name *she* will contain new information.

9. The fact that non-synonymous derived names can be substituted for one another with no effect upon the meaning of the text deserves special explanation, because in general if we change the meaning of one component of a text, the meaning of the whole text also changes. It may be supposed that the derived names have the same meaning, *i.e.*, the same 'absence of meaning', because their role is reduced to a mere mention of some object. But if we follow the definition of meaning belonging to G. Frege [7], that the meaning of a name is the way in which it refers to its denotatum, then the meanings of the names *he* and *the writer* in the first example of paragraph 2 are different: *he* means 'the male person mentioned before' while *the writer* means 'the writer mentioned before'. Preservation of the meaning of the text is due to the fact that all the differences in the meaning of names concern the amount of features included in the name all of which have already been mentioned; thus the choice of a derived name influences not the meaning of the text but only the level of its redundancy — *cf.*, the Russian sentence *Маленькие дети спали*, where the idea of plural is expressed three times, with its English equivalent *Little children slept*, where it is expressed only once.

The importance of anaphoric relations in the deep structure of the text makes us draw one important conclusion concerning the theory of generative grammar. The noun phrases in a text (as well as in a sentence) are not independent of one another as to their lexical and syntactic structure — *e.g.*, articles, quantifiers, numerals and some adjectives normally cannot be inserted into a noun phrase irrespectively of its being an initial or a derived name. This means that lexical characterization of a sentence cannot be carried out after its syntactic structure is wholly defined: syntactical and lexical derivations must take place simultaneously — as it is the case *e.g.* in formation rules of logical languages.

REFERENCES

Шумилина, А. Л.,
  1961 "Вопросы анализа личных местоимений 3-го лица", *Лингвистические исследования по машинному переводу* (Москва), 142-149. [1]
Иорданская, Л. Н.,
  1964 "Об одной проблеме автоматического синтеза: употребление личного местоимения 3-го лица в русском языке", *Научно-техническая информация*, 10, 27-32. [2]
Белецкая, И. П.,
  1966 *Об одном методе изучения структуры связного текста.* Канд. Дисс. (Москва). [3]
Падучева, Е. В.,
  1965 "О структуре абзаца", *Тартуский Гос. Университет. Труды по знаковым системам*, т. II (Тарту), 284-292. [4]
  1967 Выражение тождества упоминаемых объектов как одна из проблем синтеза языкового текста", *Труды третьей всесоюзной конференции по информационно-поисковым системам и автоматической обработке информации* (Москва), 101-132. [5]
Смирнова Е. Д. и Таванец, П. В.,
  1967 "Семантика в логике", *Логическая семантика и модальная логика* (Москва), 3-53. [6]
Черч, А.,
  1960 *Введение в математическую логику*, пер. с англ. (Москва). [7]
Шрейдер, Ю. А.,
  1965 "Об одной модели семантической теории информации, *Проблемы кибернетики*, вып. 13 (Москва), 233-240. [8]
Hiż, H.,
  1965 "Style and grammar", *Reports at the conference on semiotics in Kazimiers* (*Poland*). [9]
Wierzbicka, A.,
  1965 *Descriptions or quotations?, ibid.* [10]
Quine, W. O.,
  1960 *Word and object* (New York–London). [11]
  1960 "Variables explained away", *Proc. Amer. philos. soc.*, v. 104, p. 343-347. [12]
  1961 *Logic as a source of syntactical insight, Structure of language and its mathematical aspects* (Providence, 1961). [13]
Tesnière, L.,
  1959 *Eléments de syntaxe structurale* (Paris). [14]
Russell, B.,
  1951 *An inquiry into meaning and truth* (London). [15]

DAVID M. PERLMUTTER

ON THE ARTICLE IN ENGLISH[1]

Studies of the English articles *the* and *a* within the framework of generative grammar have treated the two articles in a parallel manner. Chomsky (1962) treated *the* and *a* as constituents of the symbol *T*, which had itself been introduced as a constituent of NP by a phrase structure rule. Lees (1960) likewise introduced *the* and *a* as an expansion of the cover symbol *T*, whose other expansions included such prenominal constituents as *this, many, both,* and *all.* In Chomsky (1965) the category 'Article' is introduced as a constituent of *Det* and then undergoes the rule: Article → [± Definite]. Allusion is then made to rules that realize Definite as *the* and non-Definite as null before a following non-count or plural noun, and presumably as *a* or *an* before a following singular count noun. Postal (1966) does not introduce the category 'Article' by a phrase structure rule, but rather makes use of a 'segmentalization rule' which spells out various bundles of syntactic features of the head noun of an NP as articles. The definite and indefinite articles both arise in this way as segmentalizations of what are syntactic features in deep structure.

In each of these analyses, the indefinite article has the same kind of origin in deep structure as the definite article. In this paper I will present evidence to show that although the definite and indefinite articles have the same status in surface structures, the indefinite article is represented in deep structure not as an article but as the numeral *one.* Its deep structural origin must therefore be the same as that of other numerals.

English noun phrases with numerals have different possibilities of occurrence, depending on whether the numeral or the noun is stressed:

[1] This is a revised and expanded version of a paper presented at a seminar in syntax at Harvard University in February, 1967. This work was done in part during the summer of 1966, when I was a summer student associate at the System Development Corporation in Santa Monica (California), and in part during 1966-1967, when I was a graduate student at M.I.T., supported by a graduate fellowship in linguistics from the American Council of Learned Societies. I am grateful to both SDC and ACLS for their support. I am also indebted to Adrian Akmajian, Stephen Anderson, Leroy Baker, George Bedell, Noam Chomsky, Jay Keyser, Susumu Kuno, George Lakoff, John Olney, Neil Smith and especially Paul Postal and Haj Ross for many valuable criticisms and suggestions. Errors are of course my own. For secretarial assistance beyond the call of duty, I am indebted to Ellie Dunn.

(1) (a)　　*There are only twó boys in the room, not five*
　　(b)　　*There are only two bóys in the room, not any girls*

But the numeral *one* does not occur unstressed before a noun; instead we find the indefinite article *a*:

(2) (a)　　*There is only óne boy in the room, not five*
　　(b)　　**There is only one bóy in the room, not any girls*
　　(c)　　*There is only a bóy in the room, not any girls*

This suggests that English has a rule which obligatorily converts unstressed proclitic *one* to *an*, with the final *n* later dropping before a consonant. If this is correct, we would expect that various facts about the distribution of the indefinite article which would otherwise have to be stated by means of *ad hoc* rules will follow automatically from certain distributional facts concerning numerals in general and the numeral *one* in particular. As we will see below, this is indeed the case.

Earlier generative treatments have had to state in an *ad hoc* way that the indefinite article is null with plural nouns. Since it must be stated anyway that the numeral *one* occurs only with singular nouns, if the indefinite article is derived from *one* the fact that it does not occur with plural nouns is accounted for automatically.

Similarly, it has heretofore been necessary for the grammar to state that the indefinite article is null with non-count nouns. It has had to state this in addition to stating that non-count nouns do not occur with numerals. Thus we do not get

(3) (a)　　*one blood
　　(b)　　*two bloods
　　(c)　　*three bloods

and so on. However, if the indefinite article is derived from the numeral *one*, as proposed here, then the fact that we do not have

(4)　　　*a blood

follows directly from the fact that *(3a) is ungrammatical, which in turn follows from the fact that non-count nouns cannot in general occur with numerals.[2]

Aside from its ability to explain the paradigm of (2), a grammar which derives the indefinite article from the numeral *one* does not need a rule to state that the indefinite article is realized as *a* or *an* with singular count nouns and as null with plural nouns and with non-count nouns. These facts follow automatically from the distribution of numerals in general and from that of *one* in particular. In this sense, such a grammar *explains* why it is that the 'indefinite article' has this distribution rather than,

---

[2]　Non-count nouns sometimes occur with numerals, in which case they have a somewhat different meaning. Compare, for example, *coffee* and *three coffees*. Just as we may have *three coffees* and *one coffee*, we may also have *a coffee*. And *a coffee* has the meaning which *coffee* has when used with numerals. The occurrence of the indefinite article with mass nouns under these circumstances, then, is exactly what we would expect if *a* is derived from *one*.

say, being realized as *a* or *an* with plural nouns and null with singular nouns, or as *a* or *an* with Animate nouns, *glup* with Abstract nouns, and null elsewhere, or any other logically possible distribution.[3]

The hypothesis that the indefinite article is derived from a numeral is further supported when we note that it occurs in environments in which *only* numerals occur. One such environment is in fractions. We find

(5) (a)   *one seventh*
   (b)   *three sevenths*
   (c)   *six sevenths*

but not

(6) (a)   **some sevenths*
   (b)   **all sevenths*
   (c)   **few sevenths*

and so on. The grammaticality of

(7)   *a seventh*

is explained if it is a variant of (5a) in which unstressed *one* has become *a*.[4]

That *one* is the source of the indefinite article can be seen in expressions where *one* and *a* are the *only* possibilities.

(8) (a)   *It was one hell of a mess*
   (b)   *It was a hell of a mess*

(9) (a)   *I didn't like it at all — not one bit*
   (b)   *I didn't like it at all — not a bit*

Here stressed *one* alternates with unstressed *a*. Numerals, quantifiers, the definite article, and anything else one might try to use instead of *one* and *a* here will result

---

[3] An earlier analysis of the indefinite article, due to Chomsky, postulated a deep structural indefinite article which was realized as *a/an* with singular count nouns and as unstressed *some* (which I will write *s'm*) with plural and non-count nouns, seeking to account in this way for the fact that *a/an* and *s'm* are in complementary distribution. Under the analysis presented here, this complementarity is accidental, just as it is accidental that *a/an* is in complementary distribution with *enough*. Although the issue is far from clear, the very thorny problem of generic sentences, to be discussed in footnote 10 below, provides some evidence that the complementary distribution of *a/an* and *s'm* is indeed accidental. If they were both manifestations of a single underlying 'indefinite article,' differing only in that some low-level morphological rule gives them different phonological shape, there would be no way to account for the fact that *a/an* occurs in generic sentences while *s'm* does not.

[4] We have seen that in sentences like *(2b) the stress obligatorily goes on the noun, leaving *one* unstressed and thereby producing (2b). It is often the case, however, that stress on the numeral is optional, with the result that both *one* and *a/an* are grammatical. The grammaticality of both (5a) and (7) is an instance of this. I have no explanation for the seeming optionality of numeral stress in such cases, which turn up repeatedly — see, for example (8), (9), (24), and the examples cited in footnotes 2 and 5.

in ungrammaticality. If *a* is derived from *one*, the fact that it can occur where *one* is the *only* possibility follows automatically.

The derivation of *a* from *one* in the manner proposed automatically accounts for certain other phenomena which would otherwise require special treatment. If *the* and *a* were both articles in deep structure, we would expect to find, alongside such expressions as

(10) (a) *the three cows*

    (b) *the one book that was interesting*

similar expressions with *a* instead of *the*. But such expressions are ungrammatical, because *a* derives from a numeral and numerals cannot precede one another in these contexts.

We would also expect to find the ungrammatical **a one* in sentences where *one* is a pro-form which shows up as a substitute for a deleted NP. This pro-form *one* is presumably distinct from the numeral *one*.[5]

(11) (a) *Svetlana has two red masks and Guido has a green one*

    (b) *Svetlana has two grotesque red masks and Guido has a beatific one*

Here *one* has replaced *mask* in (11a) and either *mask* or *red mask* in (11b). We would likewise expect *one* to replace *red mask* in sentences like

(12)   **Svetlana has two red masks and Guido has a one too*

Instead we find

(13)   *Svetlana has two red masks and Guido has one too*

It would appear that we need a special rule to delete *a* before *one* in sentences like this.

If *a* is derived from *one*, however, such a rule is not necessary. Note that the *one* in (11) and (13) is always unstressed. And alongside

(14)   *Svetlana sells red masks and Guido sells green ones*

if we have a numeral instead of an adjective we get

(15) (a) **Svetlana sold three masks and Guido sold four ones*

    (b) *Svetlana sold three masks and Guido sold four*

That is, this unstressed pronominal element *one(s)* is deleted after a numeral.[6] Since

---

[5] This pro-form *one* must be distinct from the numeral *one*, for the two can co-occur: *Svetlana has two red masks and Guido has one green one*. The pro-form *one* and the numeral *one* have therefore been treated as distinct in the past and are so treated here. Still, the fact that the pro-form *one* shows up only with count nouns suggests that its resemblance to the numeral *one* is not entirely accidental.

[6] This rule seems to be more general, operating after possessive pronouns and perhaps other constituents of what has been called the 'determiner'. Thus *my flag and hers one* would be reduced to

a is derived from *one*, at some stage in its derivation (12-13) will be:

(16)   *Svetlana has two red masks and Guido has one one too*

The *second* instance of *one*, being after a numeral, will be deleted by the same rule that deletes *ones* in (15). The first *one*, which remains, will not be an unstressed proclitic, and so it will not be reduced to *a*. The result is (13).

There are a few expressions which at first seem to constitute an exception to the rules posited here. For example, in answer to the question

(17)   *Have you seen any C.I.A. agents today?*

one might answer

(18)   *Not a one*

But note that the stress falls on *one*. It is not clear why it is stressed, but it is clear that stress must be assigned to this otherwise unstressed *one* at some point in the derivation. We will then have:

(19)   *Not one óne*

Now the rule which deletes unstressed pronominal *one(s)* after a numeral in sentences like (15) will not apply. As a result, the first *one* will be an unstressed proclitic and will reduce to *a*, yielding (18). Expressions like *not a one*, *such a one*, *nary a one*, then, are not counterexamples to the analysis proposed here.

Without any additions, the rules proposed account for the following paradigm:

(20) (a)   *three villages in Greece and four villages in Yugoslavia*
     (b)   *three villages in Greece and four in Yugoslavia*

(21) (a)   *a village in Greece and a village in Yugoslavia*
     (b)   **a village in Greece and a (an) in Yugoslavia*
     (c)   *a village in Greece and one in Yugoslavia*

The derivation of *a* from *one* also explains why the indefinite article cannot occur with certain gerundive nominalizations.[7]

(22) (a)   *I observed the shooting of the hunters*
     (b)   **I observed a shooting of the hunters*

---

my flag and hers by the same rule. Another rule would be necessary to convert *hers* to *her* in proclitic position — perhaps in the same environment in which *one* is converted to *an*. We cannot regard *her* as basic and *hers* as an amalgam of *her one* or *her ones* because of phrases with non-count nouns such as *my blood and hers*, where the putative source **my blood and her one* is ungrammatical. The same problem would arise in the attempt to generate *my scissors and hers*. Even if this extension of the rule to the environment after possessive pronouns is not correct, however, note that the *one(s)*-deletion rule, which is presumably a syntactic rule, must make reference to the stresslessness of the morpheme which is to undergo deletion — a situation which seems to be unique in terms of linguistic discussion if not in terms of linguistic reality.

[7]   This fact was pointed out by Dean (1966).

*(22b) is ungrammatical because this nominalization cannot in general occur with numerals.

(23)   *I observed two shootings of the hunters

Nominalizations which can occur with numerals also occur with the indefinite article.

(24) (a) I observed two changings of the guard
     (b) I observed one changing of the guard
     (c) I observed a changing of the guard

The derivation of the indefinite article from stressless proclitic *one* enables us to see that the inability of subjects with the indefinite article to occur with certain stative predicates[8] is only a particular instance of a more general phenomenon. That is, the fact that such sentences as

(25)   *A boy is tall

are ungrammatical results from the fact that when the subject of such predicates has a numeral the stress goes on the numeral.

(26) (a) Síx boys are tall
     (b) *Six bóys are tall

When *one boy* is subject of *tall* the stress will likewise go on *one*, so that *(25) cannot arise.

The situation is essentially the same with what Warshawsky (1965a and 1965b) has called 'picture nouns'.

(27) (a) Tén pictures were of me
     (b) *Ten píctures were of me

The numeral *one* will likewise be stressed in such sentences, and as a result

(28)   *A picture was of me

is ungrammatical.

It would seem that instances of the 'indefinite article' with predicate nominals in such sentences as

(29)   He's a doctor

cannot be derived from the numeral *one*, since the source sentence

(30)   *He's one doctor

is itself ungrammatical. This difficulty is only apparent, however. Note that in general in this construction the stress cannot fall on a numeral.

---

[8]   For a discussion of the feature [± Stative] in English, see Lakoff (1968).

(31) (a)   *They are six dóctors*
    (b)   **They are síx doctors*

In the derivation of *(30), then, the stress will go on *doctor*. As a result, *one* will be unstressed and will be obligatorily converted to *an*. We end up with (29) rather than *(30).

There is a variety of evidence, then, which indicates that the so-called 'indefinite article' is simply the result of a phonological rule which obligatorily converts unstressed proclitic *one* to *an*.[9] If this is correct, the 'indefinite article' is not a special indicator of indefiniteness. Noun phrases like *a muskrat* are indefinite for the same reason that *twelve muskrats, six muskrats, one muskrat*, and so on are. There is no underlying 'indefinite article' at all, and no special rules are needed to spell it out.[10]

[9] It is interesting to note that in "The Owl and the Nightingale", a late twelfth-century poem brought to my attention by S. J. Keyser, both *one* and *an* occur as forms of the 'indefinite article'. The first line of the poem is exemplary in this respect:

An hule and one nihtingale

The reason why we find *an* with *hule* but *one* with *nihtingale* becomes apparent when we note the location of the stress maxima which define the meter:

An húle and óne nihtingále

It seems that at that time instances of *one* in metrically stressed position did not reduce to *an*, while those in unstressed position did. In contemporary English, on the other hand, it is only the output of the rule which reduces *one* to *an* which can be used as the basis of meter.

[10] Although there is strong evidence for deriving the indefinite article from the numeral *one*, it is clear that not all instances of the indefinite article can be so derived. A notable exception is the 'generic' indefinite article which appears in sentences like

(i)   *A beaver builds dams*

Since the corresponding sentence with *one*,

(ii)   *One beaver builds dams*

is not a generic sentence, but rather a statement about a particular beaver, (ii) cannot be the source of (i). Generic sentences with the indefinite article are only one form of generic sentences in English. Alongside (i) we have

(iii)   *The beaver builds dams*

and

(iv)   *Beavers build dams*

Sentences like

(v)   *The beavers build dams*

with a definite plural subject, are not generic in English.

A study of the properties shared by (i), (iii), and (iv) would take us into a full study of genericness, which is well beyond the scope of this paper. Of interest here is the appearance of the indefinite article in sentences like (i). We will proceed by systematically setting aside the properties shared by all generic sentences (which we will assume to belong to the study of genericness), and concentrate on facts which make (i) different from (iii) and (iv). We shall see that these facts provide some evidence for an underlying *any* in the subject NP of sentences like (i). We will also observe that there is some evidence that the numeral *one* is present in the deep structure of sentences like (i). We will conclude rather inconclusively that the deep structure of (i) may be something like

(vi)   *Any one beaver builds dams*

but we will not pursue this analysis any further.

Let us now turn to the question of the status of the definite article in English. Noting paradigms like

(32) (a) *The nine men were silent*

    (b) *The two men were silent*

    (c) **The one man was silent*

    (d) *The man was silent*

we are led to postulate a rule which deletes the numeral *one* when preceded by the definite article. Without such a rule we would have to resort to some ad hoc constraint to block the ungrammatical *(32c).

Generic sentences like (iii) and (iv) can be conjoined with *and,* yielding sentences like

(vii)   *The beaver and the otter build dams*

(viii)   *Beavers and otters build dams*

For (i), however, this is impossible

(ix)   **A beaver and an otter build dams*

On the other hand, we find that, unlike (iii) and (iv), (i) may be conjoined with *or*:

(x)   *A beaver or an otter builds dams*

These properties are shared with *any*:

(xi)   (a) **Any beaver and any otter build dams*

                                   (b) *Any beaver or any otter builds dams*

If the *a* in (i) is derived from an underlying instance of *any*, these facts will follow automatically.

   Second, note that whereas (iii) and (iv) passivize, yielding

(xii)   (a) *Dams are built by the beaver*

                                   (b) *Dams are built by beavers*

(i) yields no such passive.

(xiii)   **Dams are built by a beaver*

If the generic indefinite article is derived from *any*, this will follow as an automatic consequence of the fact that in general *any* does not occur in the *by*-phrase of passive sentences:

(xiv)   **Dams are built by any beaver*

   The generic NP's of (iii) and (iv) can occur in *of*-phrases as in:

(xv)   (a) *I said of the beaver that it builds dams*

                                   (b) *I said of beavers that they build dams*

This is not the case with indefinite singular NP's:

(xvi)   **I said of a beaver that it builds dams*

The same is true of *any*:

(xvii)   **I said of any beaver that it builds dams*

   A fourth piece of evidence for deriving generic *a* from *any* comes from the inability of both to occur with predicates which require non-conjoined plural subjects and which predicate something of the entire group or class rather than of any individual in it. Not only the plural generic NP of (iv), but also the definite singular generic NP of (iii) can occur with predicates of this kind.

(xviii)   (a) *The beaver is found in Canada*

                                   (b) *Beavers are found in Canada*

(xix)   (a) *The beaver is increasing in numbers*

                                   (b) *Beavers are increasing in numbers*

To show that the rule we are positing which converts *(32c) to (32d) is not itself *ad hoc*, we must first note that the definite article can be added to the antecedent NP of a relative clause in the process of relativization. For example, proper nouns such as *Paris* cannot in general occur with either article, but with relative clauses we find

(33) (a) *the Paris that I love*
    (b) *the Paris of the nineteenth century*

Since the definite article can occur with such proper nouns *only* in the presence of a relative clause, the presence of the definite article must be due to relativization. The obverse of this argument leads to the same conclusion: since it is impossible to

---

(xx)   (a) *The beaver is extinct*
                            (b) *Beavers are extinct*

The generic indefinite article cannot occur in such sentences

(xxi)   (a) **A beaver is found in Canada*
                            (b) **A beaver is increasing in numbers*
                            (c) **A beaver is extinct*

Neither can *any*.

(xxii)   (a) **Any beaver is found in Canada*
                            (b) **Any beaver is increasing in numbers*
                            (c) **Any beaver is extinct*

Deriving generic *a* from *any* will make it unnecessary to state these facts twice.

Although we usually do not have generic sentences when the verb is in the progressive, the sentence is generic if we add an adverbial like *these days*.

(xxiii)   (a) *The beaver is building dams these days*
                            (b) *Beavers are building dams these days*

This is not the case with the generic *a*

(xxiv)   **A beaver is building dams these days*

any likewise cannot occur with the progressive, even with *these days*.

(xxv)   **Any beaver is building dams these days*

A similar situation exists with verbs in the past tense. These ordinarily do not yield generic sentences by themselves, but they do with appropriate adverbials.

(xxvi)   (a) *The beaver built dams in prehistoric times*
                            (b) *Beavers built dams in prehistoric times*

Again the unacceptability of the sentence with *a*

(xxvii)   **A beaver built dams in prehistoric times*

is paralleled by that of the sentence with *any*:

(xxviii)   **Any beaver built dams in prehistoric times*

In addition to this evidence for an underlying *any* in the deep structural subject NP of sentences like (i), we find that there is also some evidence that the indefinite article in (i) derives from an underlying numeral *one*, just like the non-generic instances of the indefinite article in English.

First, note that this 'generic indefinite article' occurs only with singular count nouns. We have already seen that this distribution of the indefinite article results automatically if it is derived from *one*.

Second, we note that the occurrence of the indefinite article in generic sentences such as (i) is not a peculiarity of English, but also happens in other languages in which either the numeral *one* or a have a restrictive relative clause on *Paris* without adding an article, the addition of the article must be due to relativization. Note that it will not do to say that relativization adds the feature [+ Definite], since proper nouns like *Paris* are [+ Definite] anyway, and if there is indeed a feature [+ Definite] which is segmentalized as *the* along the lines suggested by Postal, then the segmentalization rule, which does not segmentalize the [+ Definite] feature on Paris in sentences like

(34)   *Paris is ours*

as *the* will not be able to do so in examples like (33) either. In other words, relativization must add the article *the* itself, rather than a definiteness feature.[11]

---

stressless or reduced form of it known as the 'indefinite article' is used much as in English, in non-generic sentences.

Third, in British English, in which collective nouns may be either singular or plural

(xxix)   (a) *The government is responsible for the welfare of the unemployed*
                          (b) *The government are responsible for the welfare of the unemployed*

in generic sentences with the 'indefinite article' which correspond to plural generics like

(xxx)   *Governments are responsible for the welfare of the unemployed*

we find that the verb must be singular.

(xxxi)   (a) *A government is responsible for the welfare of the unemployed*
                          (b) **A government are responsible for the welfare of the unemployed*

All of these facts will be accounted for if the generic indefinite article, like the instances of the indefinite article we have already considered, derives from underlying instances of the numeral *one*.

It would seem that we have reached a contradiction, having shown evidence for deriving the generic indefinite article both from *any* and from *one*. Consider, however, the following paradigm.

(xxxii)   (a) *Any six beavers either build dams or hunt rodents*
                          (b) *Any two beavers either build dams or hunt rodents*
                          (c) **Any one beaver either builds dams or hunts rodents*

Whereas *(xxxii-c) is ungrammatical, we find that both

(xxxiii)   *Any beaver either builds dams or hunts rodents*

and

(xxxiv)   *A beaver either builds dams or hunts rodents*

are grammatical. It is possible that *one* drops after *any* to produce (xxxiii), and that *any* then reduces to *an*, yielding (xxxiv). Alternatively, it may be the case that *any* is deleted before *one*, leaving *one* to reduce to *an* by the rule that has already been established. I will not explore these possibilities here, however, because the problem of genericness is so difficult and wide-ranging and so little is known about it at present that, despite the evidence I have presented for a deep structure like *(xxxii-c) for (xxxiv), this deep structure for this sentence is almost certainly incorrect. I therefore propose no solution to the problem of the generic indefinite article here, having contented myself with pointing out some of the facts that any solution must account for and leaving the entire question of genericness for future study.

[11] This can be seen even more clearly in French, where alongside such examples as

(xxxv)   (a) *le Paris que j'aime*
                          (b) *le Paris du dix-neuvième siècle*

which are completely analogous to (33), many speakers also accept

(xxxvi)   (a) *le La Haye que j'aime*
                          (b) *le La Haye du dix-neuvième siècle*

To show that the rule which deletes *one* after *the* is not *ad hoc* for cases like (32), we will examine cases in which an NP with indefinite determiner has *the* added by relativization, with resultant deletion of the indefinite article (or its underlying *one*) after *the*.

Because indefinite singular count nouns cannot occur without the numeral *one* which reduces to *a* we have

(35) (a)   *There was a problem*
    (b)   **There was problem*

Because the *there*-insertion rule applies only in the presence of an indefinite NP we do not get

(36)   **There was the problem*

Now consider NP's like

(37)   *the problem that there was*

The underlying NP in the relative clause which undergoes relativization must be *a problem*, as (35) and (36) show. On the assumption that the matrix NP is the same, the structure of (37) after a *there*-insertion has applied in the relative clause must be

(38)   [$_{NP}$ *a problem* [$_S$ *there was a problem*]$_S$]$_{NP}$

Relativization adds the definite article to the matrix NP, and the indefinite article or its underlying *one* is deleted after *the*. The result is (37). However, it is not yet clear that the matrix NP in (38) is indeed *a problem* rather than *the problem*, and consequently we have not yet shown that the definite article is added as a consequence of relativization. To see this, consider the sentence

(39)   *In England there was never the problem that there was in America*

(xxxvii)   (a) *le Le Caire que j'aime*
                  (b) *le Le Caire du dix-neuvième siècle*

where it is clear that as a result of the relative clause an article has been added in addition to whatever article the proper noun already bears. The same thing must also happen in English, to account for the fact that we get neither

(xxxviii)   **the The Hague that I love*

nor

(xxxix)   **the Hague that I love*

That is, in the course of relativization a definite article must be added to *The Hague*, producing (xxxviii). An output condition on the structure of the noun phrase must then discard the resulting NP as ungrammatical for having two instances of the definite article. Since output conditions on the structure of the noun phrase have not yet been investigated, their content can only be guessed at. It is possible that there will be some variation in the exact form of the output condition for different speakers, producing differing judgments on (xxxviii) and (xxxix) in English and (xxxvi) and (xxxvii) in French. For a justification of output conditions in syntax, see Ross (1967), pp. 51-73, and Perlmutter (1968).

In (39) the *there*-insertion rule has applied in the presence of the NP that ends up as (37). As *(36) shows, such NP's must be indefinite. Hence (38) must underlie (37). Hence the definite article in (37) must have been added as a result of relativization. Hence the indefinite article (or its underlying *one*) in (38) must have been deleted once it was after the definite article. This supports the rule we postulated to account for the ungrammaticality of *(32c).

A similar argument for deletion of *one* or the indefinite article after *the* could be made on the basis of such sentences as

(40) (a) *The book of John's that I borrowed is in the bathtub*
     (b) *The seventh of the rice that I gave you was wasted*

The subject NP's of these sentences cannot bear a definite article without a relative clause

(41) (a) *A book of John's is in the bathtub*
     (b) **The book of John's is in the bathtub*

(42) (a) *A seventh of the rice was wasted*
     (b) **The seventh of the rice was wasted*

As a result we could argue that the definite articles in (40) are added in the course of relativization, and that *one* or *a* is deleted after *the*.[12]

We can determine whether it is *one* or *a* that is deleted after the definite article by noting what happens to the expression *a few*[13] when *the* is added as a result of relativization. To distinguish *a few* from *few* we will use a verb like *dribble in*, which requires a plural subject.

(43) (a) *Some customers dribbled in in the late afternoon*
     (b) **A customer dribbled in in the late afternoon*

NP's with *a few* can be the subject of such verbs, while NP's with *few* cannot.

(44) (a) *A few customers dribbled in in the late afternoon*
     (b) **Few customers dribbled in in the late afternoon*

Now, *the few customers* is ungrammatical in

(45)   **The few customers dribbled in in the late afternoon*

but with a relative clause it is grammatical.

---

[12] Unlike (37), however, the subject NP's of (4) do not allow *there*-insertion. I have no explanation for this difference.

[13] *a few*, like *a certain* and *a lot of*, is a fixed expression in which the indefinite article cannot be replaced by *one*. These expressions are counterexamples to the claim made here that the indefinite article is derived from *one*. Since these expressions are few in number and unvarying in form, however, they can be listed in the lexicon just as they are and will not cause further difficulties for our analysis.

(46)   *The few customers that came by dribbled in in the late afternoon*

Since neither *few customers* nor *the few customers* can be the underlying subject here, as *(44b) and *(45) show, we must have here an instance of *a few customers* to which *the* has been added in the course of relativization. The indefinite article has been deleted after this *the*. Since we do not get *one few*,[14] it must be the indefinite article rather than its underlying *one* that is deleted in all the sentences we have been discussing. This means that in *(32c), for example, *one* is first reduced to *an* and is then deleted after *the*. The grammaticality of sentences like (46) constitutes evidence for this deletion rule.

There are some apparent exceptions to this deletion rule, such as the phrase *the one man* in

(47)   *I spoke with the one man who had been there*

However, the morpheme *one* in this NP receives some special stress which would prevent it from reducing to *an* and would thereby prevent it from undergoing the deletion rule. Furthermore, such NP's must constitute some kind of special phenomenon, unlike the usual cases in (32), because they differ syntactically from the NP's in (32) in at least three respects.

First, as the difference in grammaticality between *(32c) and (47) shows, NP's like *the one man* can occur only with relative clauses.

Second, a relative clause on such an NP may contain the *any* whose occurrence is familiar in negative environments and questions. This differentiates *the one man* from *the two men* and *the man*

(48) (a)   *He was the one man who had anything interesting to say*
    (b)   **They were the two men who had anything interesting to say*
    (c)   **He was the man who had anything interesting to say*

Third, the relative clause on such NP's may be reduced to an infinitival complement.[15]

(49) (a)   *He was the one man to have visited Cochabamba in winter*
    (b)   **They were the two men to have visited Cochabamba in winter*
    (c)   **He was the man to have visited Cochabamba in winter*

In all three respects NP's like *the one man* behave like NP's with *only* such as *the only two men* and *the only man*. They constitute a special phenomenon that is not understood at present. The ordinary cases of *the one man* that we would expect to find alongside (32a) and (32b) are absent. We have seen evidence that the *one* in

[14]   See footnote 13.
[15]   The fact that NP's like *the one man* can occur only with relative clauses constitutes evidence that these infinitival complements are derived from relative clauses. Note also the appearance of *any* in these complements:

He was the one man to say anything interesting

such NP's first reduces to *an* and is then deleted after *the*, explaining the gap in the paradigm.

If this is correct, the relation between the definite article and the indefinite article in English in quite different from what has been generally supposed. Grammarians have worked on the assumption that NP's may bear either a definite or an indefinite article, and that the two constitute some sort of opposition. If the analysis given here is correct, however, the indefinite article is simply a numeral like all other numerals, and the occurrence or non-occurrence of the definite article is a completely independent phenomenon. NP's may or may not have a definite article *in addition to* the numeral *one*, but there is no question of their having it *instead of* the numeral *one*. The relevant opposition, then, is not between the definite and indefinite articles, but rather between the presence and absence of the definite article.

Within this framework, there is no motivation for an Article node in either deep or surface structure. In fact, if the indefinite article is derived from the numeral *one* as proposed here, there is good reason *not* to have such an Article node. If we assume that the traditional classification of *the* and *a/an* as 'articles' is correct, then it is the task of linguistic theory to define the notion 'article' such that the definition will make *the* and *a/an* 'articles' in English. If the notion 'article' is defined as a category in deep structure, then *a/an* will not be articles in English because in deep structure they will not be dominated by Article for the same reason that other numerals will not be. If one were to maintain that the notion 'article' is reconstructable in terms of an Article node in surface structure, *a/an* will still not be characterized as articles in English. Consideration of examples like (32a) and (32b) makes it clear that if there were an Article node, numerals would not be dominated by it. In order to define the notion 'article' in terms of domination by an Article node, then, it would be necessary to make the rule which reduces *one* to *an* remove this constituent from its place in the tree and put it under the Article node. There is no motivation for this other than an *a priori* commitment to the idea that the notion 'article' must be defined in terms of domination by an Article node. We must therefore reject this proposal. The proposed definition of 'articles' becomes even more unpalatable when we recall that the rule which would have to move *an* under the Article node is a PHONOLOGICAL rule that must refer to stress. For a phonological rule to perform operations of this kind is unheard of. We must conclude, then, that there is good reason not to have Article nodes in either deep or surface structure.

In fact, it is not clear whether the notion 'article' has any substantive meaning in syntax. No transformations are known that must refer to 'articles', and there do not seem to be any significant generalizations that cannot be stated without recourse to the notion 'article'.[16] It is possible that there is an 'article slot' in the output condition

---

[16]   I know of only one exception to this statement. It concerns the addition of articles to the antecedent NP under relativization. We have already noted that the definite article must somehow be

alluded to in footnote 11, but even if this is the case the notion 'article' will not have been shown to have any reality in the transformational component itself, but only at the post-transformational level of output conditions. The properties that articles share are statable only in terms of surface structure. They are usually stressless clitic elements on the noun phrase. This holds not only of the definite and indefinite articles in many languages, but also of the so-called 'personal articles' in such languages as Catalan and Maori and of *s'm* in English. What is more striking is the fact that just as there are languages in which sentence-clitics that are repositioned go to 'second position' in the sentence, so is the article in some languages moved into second position in the noun phrase. This is the case, for example, in Bulgarian. Because the possibility of some definition of 'article' in terms of such surface structure properties remains open, the notion may turn out to have some reality in surface structure. But if the notion 'article' has any real meaning with respect to deep structure or transformational derivations, that remains to be shown.

REFERENCES

Chomsky, Noam,
  1962   "A transformational approach to syntax", reprinted in J. Fodor and J. Katz (eds.), *The Structure of Language: Readings in the Philosophy of Language* (Englewood Cliffs, Prentice-Hall, Inc., 1964).
Chomsky, Noam,
  1965   *Aspects of the Theory of Syntax* (Cambridge, The M.I.T. Press).
Dean, Janet,
  1966   "Determiners and relative clauses" (Unpublished paper, M.I.T.).

---

added to the antecedent NP in examples like those in (33). There are also cases where it is the indefinite article that is added.

(xl)   *He left a Paris that had become cold and impersonal*

Something must be added to the proper noun antecedent of a restrictive relative, and it can only be *the* or *a/an*. To say that an 'article' must be added is to state a generalization.

   The same argument can be made with respect to certain mass nouns which cannot occur with articles by themselves.

(xli)   (a) *He greeted me with warmth*
                (b) **He greeted me with a warmth*
                (c) **He greeted me with the warmth*

As was the case with proper nouns, with a restrictive relative clause an article *must* be added.

(xlii)   (a) **He greeted me with warmth that was puzzling*
                (b) *He greeted me with a warmth that was puzzling*
                (c) **He greeted me with the warmth that was puzzling*

(xliii)   (a) **He greeted me with warmth that was expected*
                (b) **He greeted me with a warmth that was expected*
                (c) *He greeted me with the warmth that was expected*

Depending on the content of the relative clause, we get either *the* or *a/an* on the antecedent. The relevant generalization is again that an article must be added to the antecedent.

Lakoff, George,
  1968 "Stative verbs and adjectives in English", in T. Bever and W. Weksel (eds.), *Readings in the Psychology of Language*.
Lees, Robert B.,
  1960 *The Grammar of English Nominalizations* (The Hague, Mouton and Co.).
Perlmutter, David M.,
  1968 *Deep and Surface Structure Constraints in Syntax* (Ph.D. dissertation, M.I.T.).
Postal, Paul M.,
  1966 "On so-called 'pronouns' in English", in F. Dinneen (ed.), *Report of the 17th Annual Round Table Meeting on Linguistics and Language Studies* (Washington, Georgetown University Press).
Ross, John R.,
  1967 *Constraints on Variables in Syntax* (Ph.D. dissertation, M.I.T.).
Warshawsky, Florence,
  1965a "Reflexivization I" (Unpublished paper, M.I.T.).
  1965b "Reflexivization II" (Unpublished paper, M.I.T.).

JOHN ROBERT ROSS

GAPPING AND THE ORDER OF CONSTITUENTS*

There are many examples in the literature of generative grammar which show how greatly the superficial structures of sentences can differ from the abstract structures which underlie them. Deep structures can contain elements or even whole clauses which do not appear in surface structure, and the order in deep structure of elements which appear in both levels of representation may be far different from the surface structure order of the same elements. Furthermore, it seems to be the case that even in apparently simple sentences, the transformational mapping between deep and surface structure is extremely complex — far more so, in fact, than has previously been thought.[1] These facts make it extremely difficult to ascertain the nature of deep structure, and necessitate the use of long chains of inference to this end. This paper, which is devoted to discovering the deep structure order of subject, verb, and object (hereafter S, V, and O), is centered on several such chains of inference.

In his important paper, "Some universals of grammar",[2] Joseph Greenberg divides the languages of the world into three major types, based on the position of the verb in the 'basic' or 'dominant' order of constituents. He does not explain which phenomena he takes as critical in deciding which of the many orders of S, V, and O that can be observed in a language is basic, but some examples of each of his three types will illustrate what he means. Type I languages have the verb in the first position in their basic order — VSO: Arabic is an example. Type II languages, like English, exhibit SVO order, and Type III languages, like Japanese, SOV order.

It now appears doubtful that one of Greenberg's universals — that subject precedes

* This work was supported in part by the U.S. Air Force (ESD Contract AF19(628)-2487) and the National Institutes of Health (Grant MH-13390-01).

A version of this paper was presented at the Tenth International Congress of Linguists at Bucharest, August 28-September 2, 1967. I would like to thank Susumu Kuno, George Lakoff, and David Perlmutter for many helpful comments, and especially Manfred Bierwisch, who not only commented on this paper but actually presented it for me at Bucharest.
[1] Many arguments to this effect will be presented in *The Abstractness of Underlying Structure*, by George Lakoff and John Robert Ross (in preparation).
[2] Cf. pp. 73–113, and especially p. 76, in *Universals of Language*, Joseph Greenberg (ed.), first paperback edition, M.I.T. Press, Cambridge (1966).

object in the basic order — can be maintained: Paul Schachter has informed me that the basic order in Tagalog and related languages is VOS; Ives Goddard that the unmarked order in Algonkian is OVS; and Guy Carden that the basic order in Aleut is OSV. But whether or not all six possible orders must be assumed to exist in deep structure is not my concern here. My aim is the more modest one of providing a way of deciding when a language is Type II or Type III.

With this goal in mind, let us consider the English rule of GAPPING, which converts structures underlying such sentences as those in (1) into those underlying the corresponding sentences in (2).

(1) (a) *I ate fish, Bill ate rice, and Harry ate roast beef*
   (b) *Tom has a pistol, and Dick has a sword*
   (c) *I want to try to begin to write a novel, and Mary wants to try to begin to write a play*

(2) (a) *I ate fish, Bill rice, and Harry roast beef*
   (b) *Tom has a pistol, and Dick a sword*
   (c) *I want to try to begin to write a novel, and*

$$Mary \begin{bmatrix} to\ try\ to\ begin\ to\ write\ a\ play \\ to\ begin\ to\ write\ a\ play \\ to\ write\ a\ play \\ a\ play \end{bmatrix}$$

This rule operates to delete indefinitely many occurrences of a repeated main verb in a conjoined structure. The problem of formulating the rule so that it will convert (1c) into any of the sentences in (2c) has not been solved, and seems to require an *ad hoc* abbreviatory convention: I know of no other rules which make use of this convention. There are many other problems that are connected with GAPPING: note, *e.g.*, that the sentences in (3) cannot be converted into those in (4).

(3) (a) *I didn't eat fish, Bill didn't eat rice, and Harry didn't eat roast beef*
   (b) *They have been arrested, and we have been being followed*
   (c) *I want Bob to shave himself, and Mary wants Bob to wash himself*

(4) (a) **I didn't eat fish, Bill rice, and Harry roast beef*
   (b) **They have been arrested, and we (been) being followed*
   (c) **I want Bob to shave himself, and Mary to wash himself*

But since an exact formulation of the rule of GAPPING is not my main concern in this paper, I will sidestep these problems here.

Note that GAPPING operates only forward in English — that is, in *n* conjoined sentences, it is the leftmost occurrence of the identical main verb that causes the *n-1* following occurrences to be deleted. In Japanese, an SOV language, exactly the posite opis the case — it is the rightmost verb among *n* identical verbs that is retained. Thus (5a) becomes (5b).

(5) (a) *watakusi wa sakana o tabe, Biru wa gohan o tabeta*
      I (prt) *fish* (prt) *eat, Bill* (prt) *rice* (prt) *ate*
    (I ate fish, and Bill ate rice)

  (b) *watakusi wa sakana o, Biru wa gohan o tabeta*
      I (prt) *fish* (prt), *Bill* (prt) *rice* (prt) *ate*
    (I ate fish, and Bill rice)

Schematically, sentences of the form (6a) are converted to sentences of the form (6b), and sentences of the form (7a) are converted to sentences of the form (7b).

(6) (a) SVO + SVO + SVO + ... + SVO ⇒
  (b) SVO + SO + SO + ... + SO

(7) (a) SOV + SOV + SOV + ... + SOV ⇒
  (b) SO + SO + ... + SO + SOV

Given these facts, an obvious hypothesis suggests itself:

(8)   The order in which GAPPING operates depends on the order of elements at the time that the rule applies; if the identical elements are on left branches, GAPPING operates forward; if they are on right branches, it operates backward.

This hypothesis finds further support in a language like Russian, where word order is freer than it is in English or Japanese, and where sentences both of form (6a) and of form (7a) occur.

(9) (a) *ja pil vodu, i Anna pila vodku*
    (I drank water, and Anna drank vodka

  (b) *ja vodu pil, i Anna vodku pila*
    I water drank, and Anna vodka drank
    (I drank water, and Anna drank vodka)

As the hypothesis predicts, (9a), which is of form (6a), can be gapped forward to produce (10a); and (9b), which is of form (7a), can be gapped backward to produce (10b).

(10) (a) *ja pil vodu, i Anna vodku*
     (I drank water, and Anna vodka)

   (b) *ja vodu, i Anna vodku pila*
     I water, and Anna vodka drank
     (I drank water, and Anna vodka)

Leaving aside, for the time being, the problem of whether Russian has SVO or SOV order in deep structure, it is clear that these Russian facts of gapping can be accounted for if the rule of GAPPING follows SCRAMBLING, the rule which optionally permutes major elements of a clause, subject to various conditions which need not concern us here. That is, the two rules must be ordered as shown in (11)

(11)   SCRAMBLING OPTIONAL
         GAPPING OPTIONAL

But there is a third sentence, of a type not found in English or Japanese, which can be derived from the deep structure underlying the sentences in (9).

(12)   *ja vodu   pil,   i   Anna vodku*
         I water drank, and Anna vodka
         (I drank water, and Anna vodka)

This sentence is of the schematic form shown in (13):

(13)   SOV + SO + SO + ... + SO

At least superficially, (12) provides counterevidence for the hypothesis stated in (8), for GAPPING has operated forward, despite the fact that the verb is on the right branch of the first conjunct. Must the hypothesis then be abandoned?

I think not, for the Russian facts can be explained in another way. And if (8) is abandoned entirely, how can it be explained that, to my knowledge, no language in the world has sentences of the schematic form shown in (14)?

(14)   *SO + SO + ... + SO + SVO

Below, I will provide an explanation for the universal impossibility of sentences of this form — an explanation which makes crucial use of (8).

Let us now return to the problem of accounting for the Russian sentence in (12). If we assume that Russian has the deep structure order SVO, and that GAPPING is an 'anywhere rule' — *i.e.*, a rule that can apply at any point in a derivation[3] — then

---

[3]   There is independent evidence that this convention of rule application is necessary, regardless of how the problems posed by sentences involving GAPPING are dealt with. In his "Deep and Surface Grammar" (unpublished Harvard mimeograph, 1967), George Lakoff argues that such sentences as

Mary is said to be tall, but I don't believe it

require that the rule of S DELETION, which deletes under identity a sentence immediately dominated by an NP whose head noun is the pronoun *it*, must apply pre-cyclically to the whole tree before the cyclically ordered rules of IT REPLACEMENT and PASSIVE can apply. If this same rule of S DELETION is to produce also such sentences as

John condescended to kiss the bishop's foot, but I wouldn't agree to it

it can be seen that S DELETION will have to follow the cyclic rule of EQUI NP DELETION, the rule which deletes the subject of the clausal objects of *condescend to* and *agree to* in the above sentence, for prior to the application of this rule, these embedded clauses are not identical, and S DELETION will not apply. Since S DELETION thus must sometimes apply pre-cyclically, and sometimes after the application of a cyclic rule, Lakoff has proposed that it be allowed to apply at any point in a derivation. So far, no countercases due to this extremely strong hypothesis have been found. I will thus assume that GAPPING can be another such 'anywhere rule'.

Various problems involving the ordering of syntactic transformational rules will be examined in detail in George Lakoff and John Robert Ross, *The Transformational Component* (in preparation).

sentences like (10a), (10b), and (12) will be derivable from the deep structure underlying the sentences in (9), but no sentence of the form (14) will be. For if GAPPING
is an anywhere rule, it will be able to apply before and after SCRAMBLING, as shown
in (15), and the derivations of (10a), (10b) and (12) will proceed as shown in (16).

(15)   GAPPING   OPTIONAL
       SCRAMBLING OPTIONAL
       GAPPING   OPTIONAL

                            Forward
                            Gapping
(16) (a) Base: SVO + SVO   ⇒   SVO + SO [=(10a)]

                                              Backward
                            Scrambling   *Gapping*
     (b) Base: SVO + SVO   ⇒   SOV + SOV   ⇒   SO + SOV
                                                          [=(10b)]
                    Forward
                    Gapping   *Scrambling*
     (c) Base: SVO + SVO   ⇒   SVO + SO   ⇒   SOV + SO [=(12)]

It should be evident that (14) cannot be derived by the rule ordering shown in (15),
if the deep structure order of constituents is SVO. For in (14), GAPPING has operated
backwards, which is only possible, on hypothesis (8), if all conjuncts have the order
SOV. But if the basic order was SVO, the order SOV can only have resulted through
SCRAMBLING. But then, if backward gapping occurs after SCRAMBLING, the last conjunct
will remain in the SOV order of sentence (10b), not the SVO of (14), for SCRAMBLING
has been passed in the ordering, and cannot reapply.

   However, if the basic order were SOV, rules ordered as in (15) could derive (14),
as the derivation in (17) shows.

                    Backward
                    Gapping   *Scrambling*
(17)   Base: SOV + SOV   ⇒   SO + SOV   ⇒   *SO + SVO [=(14)]

Thus we can see that one long chain of inference is necessary to establish that Russian
has the deep structure order SVO, and not SOV. More inferences of the same sort
will follow.

   It might be objected that it is wrong to collapse the two rules which effect what I
have called forward gapping and backward gapping, on the grounds that they perform different operations on trees. Thus while it seems intuitively reasonable to claim
that SVO input structures are gapped by merely deleting the last *n-1* instances of the
verb, as in the conversion of (18a) into (18b),

(18) (a)

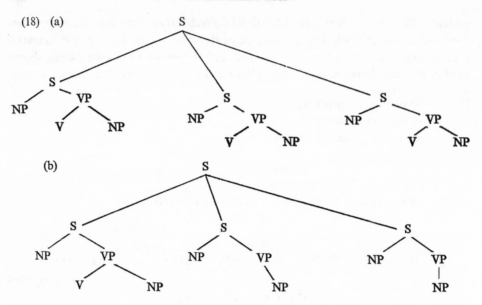

(b)

it may seem wrong to merely delete the first *n-1* occurrences of the verb in backward gapping, as shown in the conversion of (19a) into (19b).

(19) (a)

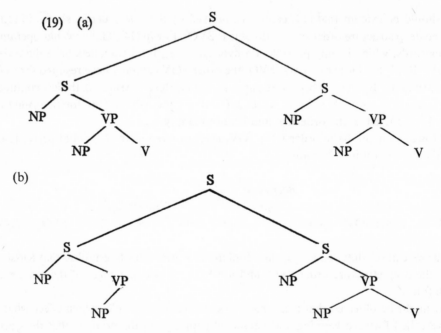

(b)

For some speakers feel that the largest constituent break in sentences in which Gapping has proceeded backward, such as (5b) or (10b), should be directly before the verb, a fact which (19b) does not reflect. For these speakers, a more reasonable derived constituent structure, after (19a) has been gapped, would be that shown in (20).

(20)

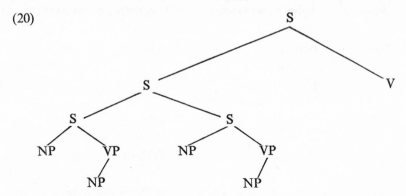

Speakers of different languages disagree about the constituency of sentences which result from backward gapping, but if structures like (20) are ever necessary, there is an independently necessary rule of conjunction reduction which could convert (19a) into (20).[4] Nonetheless, despite the fact that the formal operations involved in converting (18a) into (18b) are quite different from those which would be involved in changing (19a) into (20) I still feel that the rules which effect these changes should be collapsed. For note that in (10b), in which backward gapping has occurred, the verb *pila* 'drank' has the feminine ending *-a*, agreeing with the gender of the subject NP, *Anna*, of the right conjunct of (9b). Thus it is the rightmost verb that has been kept in backward gapping, even if it has been raised out of its VP to become a sister to the conjoined S-node as in (20). I believe this similarity to outweigh the dissimilarity of the operations involved, and I will therefore continue to speak of two varieties of gapping, and to consider that GAPPING is an anywhere rule. This may be a wrong decision on my part, but I do not believe it will affect the argument below one way or the other.

In (21), I have put into one list all the four logically possible outputs of GAPPING. There are, of course, many more outputs if other orders than just SVO and SOV, to which this study is restricted, are taken into consideration.

(21) A. SVO + SO + SO + ... + SO } *Forward Gapping*
    B. SOV + SO + SO + ... + SO

    C. SO + SO + ... + SO + SOV } *Backward Gapping*
    D. *SO + SO + ... + SO + SVO

Type *A* is the same as (6b), type *B* the same as (13), type *C* the same as (7b), and type *D* is the same as the impossible (14). As I showed above, Russian exhibits all of the three possible output structures, Japanese only type *C*, and English only type *A*. In (22), I have taken all eight logically possible subsets of these first three output types and listed them at the heads of columns. The names of languages under them

---

[4] This rule will be discussed in detail in Lakoff and Ross, *The Transformational Component*.

exhibit just those output types at the top of the column. If a column heading is starred, it means that I know of no language which exhibits all and only the output types it lists.

(22) *None*   *Only A*   *Only B*   *Only C*

	Only A		*Only C*
	English	*Only B*	Japanese
	French		Siouan
	German (main clauses)		

Only AB	*Only AC*	BC	ABC
		Hindi	Russian
		Turkish	Latin
		German	
		(subordinate clauses)	

How can the strange distribution of facts in (22), and the fact that no language exhibits outputs of type *D*, be accounted for? As far as I can see at present, they can be accounted for only if hypothesis (8) — that the direction in which GAPPING operates is universally determined by the input phrase structure configuration — is assumed to be correct and added to the theory of language. The strongest indications that (8) must be correct come from the predicted nonexistence of languages exhibiting type *D* outputs, and from the nonexistence of languages exhibiting only outputs of type *B*. Inspection of (22) reveals that every language exhibiting type *B* also exhibits type *C*. I will attempt an explanation of this fact presently: here it is sufficient to note that hypothesis (8) correctly allows for the existence of such languages as English and Japanese, whose grammars do not contain the rule of SCRAMBLING, and which gap only forward or only backward, respectively, while excluding SOV languages which gap only forward, and languages which exhibit type D outputs.

I know of no language which exhibits no gapping behavior of any kind [hence the asterisk before *None* in (22)], but even if such languages should prove to exist, hypothesis (8) would not be refuted. If it is assumed that GAPPING must be an any-where rule in any language in whose grammar it occurs, the nonexistence of lan-guages exhibiting only output types *AB* or *AC* can be explained. A language would exhibit only types *A* and *B* if it had underlying SVO order and could gap before SCRAMBLING but not after, and a language would exhibit only types *A* and *C* if it could gap only after SCRAMBLING. I must emphasize, however, that even if languages ex-hibiting only *AB* or only *AC* can be found, hypothesis (8) can be maintained: it is only the claim that forward and backward gapping are effected by one anywhere rule that would have to be abandoned.

Now let us return to the question of languages which exhibit only the output types *B* and *C*. With the exception of German, to which I will return below, these languages would be classified as SOV languages by Greenberg. What then differ-entiates *BC* languages, like Hindi, from *C* languages, like Japanese, which were both classified as SOV languages by Greenberg (*cf.* op. cit. p. 107)?

The answer to this question that I propose is the following: C languages, which gap only backward, have SOV order in deep structure, whereas BC languages, which gap in both directions, have underlying SVO order. In other words, despite the fact that verbs appear only clause-finally in both Japanese and Hindi, I would argue that in Hindi, verbs start out before their objects, and then, after GAPPING has had a chance to apply forward, they are obligatorily moved to the end of their VP, where backward gapping will subsequently also be able to apply. That is, despite the superficial similarity of BC languages to C languages, I would analyze the former as being deeply similar to ABC languages, where an obligatory rule has prevented A type outputs from appearing.

There is one other piece of evidence which separates C languages from BC languages: the former languages appear not to have rules of the form shown in (23), while BC languages always have such rules.

$$(23) \qquad \ldots A \ldots X$$
$$\qquad\qquad 1 \quad 2 \Rightarrow 0 \quad 2+1$$

In other words, while the grammars of BC languages in particular, and in general of all languages whose deep structure order is SVO, can contain rules which permute elements rightward around a variable, the grammars of C languages cannot contain such rules.

An English example of a rule of the form of (23) is the rule of EXTRAPOSITION FROM NP, which I have stated in following:

$$(24) \qquad \textit{Extraposition from NP}$$
$$\qquad\qquad X - [NP - S]_{NP} - Y$$
$$\qquad\qquad 1 \quad 2 \quad 3 \quad 4 \quad \Rightarrow$$
$$\qquad\qquad 1 \quad 2 \quad 0 \quad 4+3$$

This rule converts the structures underlying such sentences as those in (25) to the structures underlying the corresponding sentences in (26).

(25) (a) A woman who was wearing a fur coat came in
    (b) I gave a pistol which I had found in my soup to the inspector

(26) (a) A woman came in who was wearing a fur coat
    (b) I gave a pistol to the inspector which I had found in my soup

That the grammar of German, which exhibits only SOV order in subordinate clauses, must also contain rule (24) can be seen from the fact that both the sentences of (27) are grammatical.

(27) (a) *Wir gafften, weil eine Frau, die einen Pelzmantel trug, herein-*
        We gawked because a woman, who a fur coat was wearing in
        gekommen war
          come had

(We gawked, because a woman who was wearing a fur coat had come in)

(b) *Wir gafften, weil eine Frau hereingekommen war, die einen Pelzmantel trug*
     (We gawked, because a woman had come in who was wearing a fur coat)

Neil Smith has informed me that Hindi also appears to have some rule of extra-position, of the form shown in (23), although it appears to be much more limited than the German and English rules. And Greenberg (*op. cit.*, fn. 10) points out that in Turkish, a dative or locative noun phrase can follow the verb. Both these languages, although Greenberg classifies them as SOV languages, gap in both directions, and are therefore *BC* languages.

As far as I know, a language will gap only backwards, if and only if its grammar contains no rules of the form shown in (23). I propose that it is just these languages which should be analyzed as having SOV order in deep structure, and that principle (28) be added to the theory of grammar.

(28)   If a language has SOV order in deep structure, it is a VERB-FINAL LANGUAGE: its grammar can contain no rule which moves verbs to the left, nor any rule of the form of (23).

If this principle is right, it will occasion a sweeping revision of the analyses of Hindi and Turkish, which must be analyzed as being SVO, and not SOV, languages. And similarly, German, which exhibits SVO order in main clauses, but SOV order in subordinate clauses, cannot be derived from deep structures manifesting SOV order, as has been assumed in previous generative analyses.[5] Both the fact that German contains rules of the form of (23), as can be seen from the grammaticality of (27b), and the fact that GAPPING can operate in either direction in subordinate clauses [thus (29) can be converted into (30a) or (30b)] indicate that German should be considered to be an SVO language in deep structure.

(29)   *Weil ich das Fleisch aufass, und meine Mutter den Salat aufass, wurden*
        Because I the meat up ate, and my   mother the salad up ate, became
        wir beide krank
        we both sick
        (Because I ate up the meat, and my mother ate up the salad, we both got sick)

(30) (a) *Weil ich das Fleisch, und meine Mutter den Salat aufass, wurden wir beide krank*

     (b) *Weil ich das Fleisch aufass, und meine Mutter den Salat, wurden wir beide krank*

If my proposed analysis of German and Hindi as SVO languages is correct, it will have deep consequences for the comparative syntax of Indo-European, for it will mean that Proto-Indo-European was an SVO language also. For all other non-free

---

[5] Cf. e.g. Manfred Bierwisch, *Grammatik des Deutschen Verbs*, (*Studia Grammatica*, II) Akademie Verlag, Berlin, 1963.

word-order languages which descended from it seem clearly to be SVO languages, except for these two and Dutch, which is closely related to German.

To recapitulate briefly, I have attempted to account for the nonexistence of sentence structures of the form shown in (14), and for the distribution of facts in (22), by the following set of four hypotheses:

(31) (a) Hypothesis (8) — the direction of GAPPING depends on the input phrase-structure configuration.

(b) Hypothesis (28) — Languages whose deep structure order is SOV always have the verb in clause-final position.

(c) GAPPING is an anywhere rule in any language in whose grammar it appears.

(d) GAPPING is a universal rule: it is to be stated in its most general form in the theory of language, and by convention, every grammar will be able to make use of it in some form. (It is of course to be expected that some grammars may impose language-particular conditions on this rule.)

If the facts are as I have asserted in (22), I know of no simpler explanation for them than this set of hypotheses.

In conclusion, note that although hypothesis (8) and principle (28) are fairly abstract hypotheses, it is easy to prove them wrong. If further research on syntax confirms them, however, their use in the above discussions about what the deep structure order of subject, verb, and object is, in languages like Russian, Japanese, and German, provides a good example of the complexity of arguments which often must be brought to bear in trying to increase our knowledge of deep structure.

RUDOLF RUŽIČKA

DIE BEGRIFFE "MERKMALHALTIG" UND "MERKMALLOS" UND IHRE VERWENDUNG IN DER GENERATIVEN TRANSFORMATIONS-GRAMMATIK

ILLUSTRATIONEN UND BEISPIELE VOR ALLEM AUS DEM MODERNEN RUSSISCHEN

0. Die generative Transformationsgrammatik ist so angelegt, daß sie linguistische Einsichten verschiedenster Herkunft aufnehmen kann, auch verstreute, die zu keiner grammatischen Theorie in Beziehung gesetzt wurden. Um so mehr Aufmerksamkeit schenkt sie Hypothesen, die über die grundsätzliche Beschaffenheit linguistischer Fakten angestellt werden und gewissen theoretischen und formalen Ansprüchen genügen. So konnte es nur eine Frage der Zeit sein, daß Anhänger der Transformationsgrammatik ihr Interesse an den linguistischen Vorstellungen bekundeten, die mit der Verwendung der Begriffe 'merkmalhaltig' und 'merkmallos' zusammenhängen, also an den Merkmalkorrelationen, die in erster Linie der Prager Schule zu verdanken sind. Wenn sich die Transformationsgrammatik nicht sogleich dieser Hypothesen annahm, die in den Fakten zahlreicher Sprachen relativ sicheren empirischen Halt finden,[1] dann nur deshalb, weil sie vordringlich von der Errichtung ihres eigenen Fundaments in Anspruch genommen war.

Das weitere Zögern, Merkmalkorrelationen auf ihre Verwendbarkeit in der Transformationsgrammatik zu prüfen, hat sachliche Gründe: Trotz ihres Anspruchs, das ganze sprachliche System zu durchdringen, blieb die Markiertheitshypothese Teilstück, ein unvermitteltes theoretisches Fragment. Ihrer Bedeutung konnte man nicht gerecht werden, wenn sie einer globalen linguistischen Theorie angeheftet wurde; die Markiertheitshypothese kann den präzisen theoretischen Status, der ihren tiefen Einsichten gerecht wird, nur gewinnen, wenn sie einer zusammenhängenden linguistischen Theorie unterworfen wird. Die generative Transformationsgrammatik erscheint mir geeignet, der Markiertheitshypothese den notwendigen theoretischen Status zu geben und sie in den Begründungszusammenhang einer linguistischen Theorie einzuordnen.

0.1. Im Rahmen der erwähnten Theorie erheben sich vor allem diese Fragen hinsichtlich der Begriffe 'merkmalhaltig' und 'merkmallos':

[1] Eine glänzende aber theoretisch unverpflichtete Zusammenschau zahlreicher solcher Fakten der Phonologie, Morphologie, Syntax und Semantik gibt Joseph H. Greenberg in seiner Arbeit "Language Universals", in: *Current Trends in Linguistics*, Volume III, Theoretical Foundations, ed. by Thomas A. Sebeok (The Hague-Paris, 1966), S. 61-112. Vgl. dazu die kritische Rezension von M. Bierwisch in "Current Anthropology" Vol. 9, No. 2-3, April-June 1968, p. 134-136.

(1) Welchen theoretischen Status erhalten die Begriffe in der linguistischen Beschreibung, d.h. wie werden sie zu anderen Begriffen, Kategorien, Merkmalen
und Regeln der Theorie in Beziehung gesetzt? Im besonderen:

(2) Ist der implizierte Anspruch der Markiertheitshypothese, durchgängige oder
weitgehende Gültigkeit in natürlichen Sprachen zu besitzen, gerechtfertigt und
rechtfertigt er ihre Zuordnung zu den substantiellen und/oder formalen Universalien?[2]

(3) Gilt ihre Anwendbarkeit (a) für alle Ebenen oder Komponenten einer grammatischen Theorie oder nur für eine oder einige, etwa nur für die phonologische,
nicht für die syntaktische, und ist (b), wenn sie für mehrere oder alle Ebenen
gilt, die theoretische Handhabung des Begriffspaars in den verschiedenen Ebenen
verschieden und in welcher Weise?

(4) Ist es ein entscheidender Aspekt der theoretischen Lösung des Markiertheits-
problems, wenn vorausgesagt werden kann "...*a priori, regarding any specific
set of categories, when given their definitional specifications, what the relations of
marked and unmarked would be among them*"?[3]

0.2. Die folgenden Erörterungen werden sich innerhalb dieser Fragestellungen
bewegen, zunächst auf eine vorgezeichnete Lösung hinweisen (1), dann auf strittige
Probleme eingehen (2 und 3). Im Abschnitt (4) werden einige Beziehungen des
Begriffspaars 'merkmalhaltig' und 'merkmallos' zu linguistischen Ebenen diskutiert;
schließlich wird nach einer Zusammenfassung (Abschnitt 5) versucht, an mehreren
Problemen der modernen russischen Grammatik ein theoretisches Konzept für die
Anwendung der Begriffe 'merkmalhaltig' und 'merkmallos' zu erproben (6).

1.0. N. Chomsky, M. Halle und P. Postal haben Vorschläge gemacht, wie die
Markiertheitsrelation in einer Transformationsgrammatik zu behandeln sei.[4] Sie
betreffen vorwiegend die phonologische Komponente, vereinzelt auch die syntaktische. Weil die frühere generative Phonologie alle phonologischen Elemente (Merkmale) gleichsetzte, sei sie außerstande gewesen, so erklärt Lakoff, eine Reihe wesentlicher Fakten zu erklären, z.B. warum bei der Neutralisation von Verschlußlauten
der stimmlose Konsonant viel öfter als der stimmhafte erscheint (a.a.O., S. C-1).

---

[2] Zum Begriff der Universalien vgl. Jerrold J. Katz, Paul M. Postal, *An Integrated Theory of Linguistic Descriptions* (Cambridge, Mass., 1964), S. 159 ff.; Das Verhältnis der Begriffe 'merkmalhaltig' und
'merkmallos' zu den formalen und substantiellen Universalien ist angedeutet bei M. Bierwisch, a. a. O.,
und Verf., "Aufnahme von Merkmalkorrelationen in eine generative Transformations grammatik",
in: *Abstracts of Papers, Xth International Congress of Linguists* (Bucharest, 1967), S. 311.

[3] Greenberg, *a. a. O.*, S. 77.

[4] Dieser Vorschlag befindet sich in der bei Manuskriptabfassung noch nicht erschienenen Arbeit
von N. Chomsky und M. Halle *The Sound Pattern of English*. Ich stütze mich auf G. Lakoff's und
M. Bierwischs Wiedergaben: George Lakoff, *On the Nature of Syntactic Irregularity* (The Computation Laboratory of Harvard University, Cambridge, Mass., 1965), besonders S. C-1 bis C-10. Hier
wird auch auf P. Postals Anregungen verwiesen. M. Bierwisch, "Syntactic Features in Morphology:
General Problems of So-called Pronominal Inflection in German"; in: *To Honor Roman Jakobson*
(The Hague–Paris, 1967), S. 244 f., 267 ff.

Die Prager Schule hatte dieser Tatsache Rechnung getragen, indem sie den stimm-losen Konsonant als 'merkmallos' gegenüber dem 'merkmalhaltigen' stimmhaften in einer privativen phonologischen Opposition charakterisierte. Der positive Wert (Bedeutung) eines Merkmals, in diesem Beispiel der Stimmbeteiligung [+ stimmhaft], bestimmt die Charakterisierung als 'merkmalhaltiges' Glied, der negative Wert des-selben Merkmals, also Abwesenheit der Stimmbeteiligung [− stimmhaft], bestimmt die Auszeichnung *merkmallos*. Die Werte der übrigen beteiligten Merkmale, z.B. [+ palatalisiert], sind in der privaten Opposition in beiden Gliedern gleich und kommen in ihrer Kombination nur diesen beiden in Opposition stehenden Gliedern zu. Die Verkettung des positiven Werts eines Merkmals mit dem Begriff 'merk-malhaltig' löst sich bei der Anwendung der Merkmalkorrelationen außerhalb der Phonologie (vgl. 3.2.0.), aber auch hier bleibt die Charakterisierung *merkmalhaltig* mit einem bestimmten Wert ('+' oder '−') des Merkmals verhaftet. Chomsky und Halle haben diese Festlegung der Markiertheitshypothese der Prager Schule auf-gehoben. Die Werte '+' und '−', die den Merkmalen gegeben werden, sind von deren Markiertheit in der Weise getrennt, daß ein und dasselbe Merkmal in Abhängigkeit vom Kontext sowohl mit positiver wie mit negativer Bedeutung 'merkmalhaltig' und 'merkmallos' sein kann.

In this theory [Chomsky's und Halle's, R.R.], the phonological representation of an item in the lexicon is a distinctive feature matrix, but not with plus and minus values for the features; rather, each feature may be *marked* or *unmarked*. The unmarked form represents the 'normal' state of the feature with respect to that segment; the marked form of a feature represents the 'non-normal' state. Thus, vowels will be unmarked for voicing in most languages. Since vowels in their normal state are voiced, there would be a universal rule stating that a vowel unmarked for voicing is voiced (G. Lakoff, a.a.O., S. C-2).

Die Markierungen fallen bei der Bewertung der Grammatik ins Gewicht:

In the evaluation procedure which is part of this theory Chomsky and Halle propose that *m*'s should be counted, but that *u*'s should not be counted. Thus, a grammar which has more marked features, more deviations from the 'normal' state, would be valued less than a gram-mar that had fewer deviations from the 'normal' state (G. Lakoff, a.a.O., S. C-2/C-3).

Freilich bleibt ausschlaggebend, ob sich die Beschreibung mit hypothetischen Mar-kierungen als empirisch angemessen erweisen wird. Aber die Hypothese wird dadurch nicht fragwürdig, daß "... it is not immediately obvious that it will lead to the choice of empirically correct grammars" (a.a.O., S. C-3), sondern interessanter, da sie mehr Tiefe besitzen kann. Durch universelle oder einzelsprachliche Regeln werden die Symbole *m* (merkmalhaltig) und *u* (unmarked; merkmallos) in + oder − überführt. Ein Regelbeispiel von G. Lakoff (a.a.O., S. C-2):

$$[\text{u voice}] \rightarrow [+\text{voice}] / [\_\_\_\_, +\text{vocalic}, -\text{consonantal}]$$

In Sprachen mit stimmlosen Vokalen würden diese Vokale als *merkmalhaltig* hin-sichtlich der Stimmbeteiligung ausgezeichnet werden und durch eine universelle Regel als 'stimmlos' interpretiert werden (Regel nach G. Lakoff, a. a. O., S. C-2):

[m voice] → [− voice] / [____, + vocalic, − consonantal]

Ob ein Merkmal im Lexikon mit *m* oder *u* gekennzeichnet wird in dem Bemühen, möglichst wenig *m*'s zu gebrauchen[5] und ob *m* oder *u* die Bedeutung + oder − erhält, hängt also vom simultanen oder linearen Kontext ab, in der Phonologie von der Segment- oder Sequenzstruktur nach der Terminologie R. Stanley's.[6]

1.1. Ich verlasse den Bereich phonologischer Merkmale und Regeln und wende mich der Markiertheitshypothese in anderen Bereichen der Grammatik zu. Zur Illustration verwende ich vor allem das moderne Russische. Dabei halte ich an dem Binaritätsprinzip fest, daß jedes Merkmal entweder den Wert '+' oder den Wert '−' annimmt. Die theoretischen Vorteile dieses Prinzips liegen auf der Hand. R. Jakobson und A. V. Isačenko haben es streng befolgt, wenn auch nicht, wie wir noch sehen werden, im Sinne zweier alternativer Bedeutungen '+' und '−'.[7] Das Binaritätsprinzip hat noch keine lückenlose empirische Rechtfertigung erfahren,[8] aber die Bemühungen, seine empirische Unangemessenheit nachzuweisen, sind bisher fehlgegangen. Behauptungen, daß die Dichotomie künstlich sei und das "reale Bild der Sprache nicht widerspiegle", sind wissenschaftstheoretisch nicht haltbar.[9] Daß der binären Interpretation die Kategorien entgegenstünden, die aus mehr als zwei Gliedern bestehen (z. B. 'Tempus' und die Kategorie 'Person' im Russischen), ist ein nachhaltiges Mißverständnis:

Всем известно, какие трудности пока вызывает общеприемлемая трактовка таких категорий, как, напр., категория числа, вида и нек. др., основанных на противопоставлении двух членов и могущих, т. о., послужить идеальным примером пар,

---

[5] Die Verwendung der Begriffe 'm' und 'u' soll unter anderem die 'Natürlichkeit' phonologischer Elemente erklären. Die 'Natürlichkeit', die sich etwa in der 'merkmallosen' Charakterisierung des Merkmals [Stimme] bei Sibilanten [s'] reflektiert und als 'Natürlichkeit' oder Einfachheit der Artikulation verstehen läßt, bleibt in der phonetischen Repräsentation, die der Artikulation näher steht, nicht grundsätzlich bestehen. Die systematische phonologische Repräsentation des russischen Wortes просьба ist vereinfacht [pros'ba] d. h. das vierte Segment ist über [u Stimme] → [− Stimme] repräsentiert. Die systematische phonetische Repräsentation ist [pròz'ba]. In der Neutralisation erscheint das stimmhafte, also kompliziertere Element. Dies könnte zum Teil vermieden werden, wenn in den Sequenzstruktur-Regeln festgelegt würde, daß in Gruppen von Geräuschkonsonanten das Merkmal [Stimme] nur beim letzten Konsonant als 'merkmalhaltig' oder 'merkmallos' charakterisiert wird. Analoge Beschränkungen gelten hinsichtlich der Palatalitätsassimilation.

[6] Richard Stanley, "Redundancy Rules in Phonology" (Manuskript, MIT 1966).

[7] R. Jakobson, "Zur Struktur des russischen Verbums", in: *Charisteria Guilelmo Mathesio Quinquagenario...* (Prag, 1932); dass. auch in: *A Prague School Reader in Linguistics*, Compiled by Josef Vachek (Bloomington 1964); ders., *Shifters, Verbal Categories, and the Russian Verb, Russian Language Project* (Harvard University, 1957); ders., "Beitrag zur allgemeinen Kasuslehre", in: *TCLP VI*; ders., "морфологические наблюдения над славянским склонением", *American Contributions to the Fourth International Congress of Slavistics* ('s-Gravenhage, 1958). A. V. Isačenko, "Бинарность, привативные оппозиции и грамматические значения", in: *Вопросы языкознания*, 2 (1963). S. 39-56.

[8] Vgl. auch M. Bierwisch, *Syntactic Features...*, S. 243.

[9] Vgl. A. V. Isačenko, *a. a. O.*, S. 43 ff.

отличающихся друг от друга наличием или отсутствием сигнализации признака. Тем
больше затруднений связано с интерпретацей категорий, представленных больше чем
двумя членами, хотя напр. А. В. Исаченко вслед за Р. Якобсоном доказывает, что
разложение многочленной системы в бинарные оппозиции всегда возможно и только
оно и отражает действительное функционирование данной категории в языке ... В
научной литературе было уже отмечено, что нельзя свести к бинарным оппозициям,
напр., отношения между членами категории времени в русском языке.[10]

Die Schwierigkeiten, für zweigliedrige Kategorien wie Aspekt und Numerus eine
"allgemein annehmbare Behandlung" zu finden, haben nichts mit dem Binaritätsprinzip zu tun. Sie entstehen bei dem Versuch, für den Aspekt z.B. nur EIN semantisches Merkmal aufzuwenden, und generell aus der Suche nach geeigneten theoretischen Elementen der Beschreibung. Was die Kategorien mit mehr als zwei Elementen betrifft, so berühren sie nicht die Möglichkeit der Zweiwertigkeit ('+', '—')
ihrer Merkmale. Für Kategorien mit mehr als zwei Elementen muß lediglich mehr
als EIN Merkmal aufgewendet werden. Der Einwand richtet sich nicht gegen den
binären Wert der Merkmale, sondern stellt die empirische Angemessenheit der
binären hierarchischen Klassifikation von Kategorien mit mehr als zwei Elementen
in Frage. In einer solchen Klassifikation würden z.B. bei drei Elementen zwei dem
dritten gegenübergestellt werden, und zwar in der Weise, daß entweder zwei Elemente, vereint durch den gemeinsamen Wert eines Merkmals, dem dritten, das
diesen Wert desselben Merkmals nicht aufweist, gegenübergestellt werden oder umgekehrt eins der drei Elemente mit einem bestimmten Wert eines Merkmals den
beiden anderen, die diesen Wert nicht haben. So wird z.B. das Präteritum mit dem
positiven Wert des Merkmals "prior to speech event" (Jakobson, 1957) dem Präsens
und Futurum, die diesen Wert des Merkmals nicht haben, in binärer Opposition
entgegengestellt. Es handelt sich also um Binarität der Gliederung, der hierarchischen
Klassifikation von Untermengen der Elemente einer Kategorie (vgl. das Schema des
russischen Tempus auf S. 266).

Es scheint, daß die Einwände gegen solche Hypothesen durch den Verdacht genährt
werden, die Konstruktion der Merkmale und die Zuordnung ihrer Werte sei der
Absicht untergeordnet, eine binäre Klassifikation dieser Art zu erzielen. Ein solcher
theoretischer Plan wäre jedoch durchaus gerechtfertigt. Die Zweckmäßigkeit dieses
Konzepts ist nicht wegen theoretischer Vorgefaßtheit in Zweifel zu ziehen, sondern
weil eine Kreuz-Klassifizierung (*cross-classification*) dieser hierarchischen Klassifi-
zierung und binären Verzweigung vielleicht ebenso vorgezogen werden muß wie die
Kreuz-Klassifikation der Nomina ihrer Einführung durch Ersetzungsregeln und der
dabei erforderlichen Hierarchie von Merkmalen, die nicht gefunden werden kann.[11]
Wo andererseits eine Kategorie aus zwei Elementen besteht, die durch die binären
Werte EINES Merkmals charakterisiert werden können, wird dieses Minimum auch

[10]   Helena Křížková, "Привативные оппозиции и некоторые проблемы анализа многочленных
категорий (на материале категорий лица в русском языке)", in: *Travaux linguistiques de Prague*, 1
(Prag, 1964), S. 203.
[11]   Vgl. N. Chomsky, *Aspects of the Theory of Syntax* (Cambridge, Massachusetts, 1965), S. 79 ff.

für ausreichend gehalten, die intensionale, semantische Beschreibung der zwei Elemente zu bewältigen. Der minimale Aufwand, um zwei morphologische Klassen auseinanderzuhalten, wird mit dem notwendigen Aufwand an Merkmalen für die semantische und syntaktische Charakterisierung verwechselt. So wird z.B. der slavische Aspekt mit seinen beiden Elementen durch EIN Merkmal charakterisiert: "absolute Grenze der Handlung" (R. Jakobson, 1932), "Ganzheit" oder "unteilbare Ganzheit" (неделимая целостность)[12] der Handlung, u.a. Der Scharfsinn ist vielleicht verschwendet. Mit nur einem Merkmal können die beiden Aspekte nicht ausreichend semantisch interpretiert werden. Außerdem hat die Beschränkung auf EIN Merkmal den Nachteil, daß die Semantik des slavischen Aspekts unvergleichbar wird und einer Tiefenstruktur, die Universalität anstrebt, entzogen ist. Denn die Eigenart des slavischen Aspekts besteht vor allem darin, eine zusammenfassend einheitliche morphologische Repräsentation syntaktischer und semantischer Merkmale zu bieten, die in den meisten nichtslavischen Sprachen anders und vor allem uneinheitlich ausgedrückt werden. Es erscheint deshalb zweckmäßig, erst durch Transformation je ein morphologisches Merkmal für den perfektiven und den imperfektiven Aspekt einzuführen, und zwar nach Maßgabe von Merkmalen, die in der Ableitung verstreut plaziert sein können und die einen der beiden Aspekte oder bei 'freier' Aspektwahl keinen determinieren.[13]

2.0. Die beträchtliche Modifikation der Markiertheitshypothese der Prager Schule erstreckt sich auch auf Morphologie, Syntax und Semantik.

Given the concept of markedness, we can easily state the generalization that adjectives are normally stative and verbs normally non-stative ... We can then mark the abnormal cases, the stative verbs and non-stative adjectives, with the feature [m Adjectival], and leave the normal cases unmarked.

	hit	*know*	*noisy*	*tall*
Adjectival	u	m	m	u [14]

Dann gibt es Regeln, die diese Markierungen *m* (= merkmalhaltig) und *u* (= merkmallos) als einen der zwei Werte (Bedeutungen) der Merkmale in Abhängigkeit von einem bestimmten (Merkmal) Kontext interpretieren:

---

[12] Ю. С. Маслов: *Роль так называемой перфективации и имперфективации в процессе возникновения славянского глагольного вида: Доклады IV Международного съезда славистов* (Москва, 1958).

[13] Untersuchungen in dieser oder ähnlicher Richtung sind von Brigitte Haltof "Die Aspekte des modernen Russischen; Versuch einer semantischen und distributiven Modellierung", in *ZfSl*, XII (1967) und Anthony L.Vanek (On Some Problems in the Phonology of Czech Conjugation, (Manuskript), Vortrag auf dem X.Internationalen Linguistenkongreß in Bukarest) begonnen worden. Es ist deshalb auch eher ein theoretischer Vorzug als ein Nachteil, wenn Isačenko in seiner Tempusbeschreibung *Tempis und Aspekt* "vermischt" (s. 3.1.). Vgl. A. В. Исаченко, *Грамматический строй русского языка в сопоставлении с словацким, морфология, часть вторая* (Братислава, 1960), S. 419ff.

[14] G.Lakoff, *a.a.O.*, *S.* C-9, C-10.

(a) [u Adjectival] → [− Adjectival] / [___, − stative]
(b) [u Adjectival] → [+ Adjectival] / [___, + stative]
(c) [m Adjectival] → [+ Adjectival] / [___, − stative]
(d) [m Adjectival] → [− Adjectival] / [___, + stative][15]

Die abschließende Bermerkung G. Lakoffs erscheint soweit berechtigt:

Thus, our use of the concept of markedness reveals that this case in syntax is exactly parallel to a case in phonology.[16]

Die Divergenz zu den asymmetrischen Merkmalkorrelationen R. Jakobsons wird hier beträchtlich. Die Bedeutungen (Werte) der Merkmale dieser Korrelationen werden nach der folgenden grundsätzlichen Feststellung Jakobsons so verstanden, daß es zunächst kaum möglich scheint, die Charakterisierung als *merkmalhaltig* nicht mit dem positiven Wert des betreffenden Merkmals zu verknüpfen:

The general meaning of a marked category states the presence of a certain property A; the general meaning of the corresponding unmarked category states nothing about the presence of A and is used chiefly but not exclusively to indicate the absence of A (R. Jakobson 1957).[17]

Diese Auffassung schließt das Nebeneinander von Interpretationsregeln wie (a), (b) und (c), (d) aus. Die 'Nichtsignalisierung von A' kann im Rahmen der Zweiwertigkeit nur als weder 'plus' noch 'minus' verstanden werden, dem dritten Wert phonologischer Merkmale ähnlich:

Примером универсальной классификации может служить классификация фонем с помощью различительных признаков, предложенных Р. Якобсоном (при условии, что значение "ни плюс ни минус" признается особым, третьим значением всякого признака).[18]

In den morphologischen asymmetrischen Korrelationen Jakobsons ist dieser dritte Wert der zweite. Es gibt keinen 'minus'-Wert. Die Asymmetrie '+':'∓' oder '+': *weder* '+' *noch* '−' ist gerade das entscheidende Charakteristikum der Merkmalkorrelationen im Verständnis Jakobsons und Karcevskis.[19]

3.0. Im folgenden werden drei diesem theoretischen Konzept immanente Probleme diskutiert (3.0.—3.2.). Das erste Problem entsteht, wenn Kategorien, bzw. Elemente von Kategorien als *merkmalhaltig* oder *merkmallos* charakterisiert werden sollen,

---

[15] Siehe Fußnote 14.
[16] Siehe Fußnote 14.
[17] Dies ist eine Paraphrasierung seiner früheren Formulierung: "In Wirklichkeit verteilen sich die *allgemeinen Bedeutungen* der korrelativen Kategorien anders: falls die Kategorie I. das Vorhandensein von A ankündigt, so kündigt die Kategorie II. das Vorhandensein von A nicht an, d.h. sie besagt nicht, ob A anwesend ist oder nicht. Die allgemeine Bedeutung der Kategorie II. im Vergleich zu der Kategorie I. beschränkt sich auf den Mangel der 'A-Signalisierung'. Falls in einem gewissen Kontext die Kategorie II. das Nichtvorhandensein von A ankündigt, so ist es bloß eine der Anwendungen der gegebenen Kategorie; die Bedeutung wird hier durch die Situation bedingt..." (Jakobson, 1932).
[18] А. А. Зализняк, *Русское именное словоизменение* (Москва, 1967), S. 7.
[19] S. Karcevskij, "Du Dualisme Asymétrique du Signe Linguistique", in: *TCLP* I, S. 33-38.

zu deren Beschreibung mehr als *ein* Merkmal gebraucht wird. Es besteht darin, auf welches Merkmal sich die Charakterisierung beziehen soll, wenn der Wert nicht nur *eines* der Merkmale unterschiedlich ist. R. Jakobson beschreibt z.B. die russischen Kasus mit Hilfe von drei semantischen bzw. syntaktischen Merkmalen.

Acht Kasus werden vorausgesetzt (R. Jakobson 1936 und 1958, vgl. Fußnote 7).

(a)

	1 направленность Gerichtetheit	2 периферийность 'peripher', 'Rand-'	3 объемность 'Umfang-'
Nom			
Akk	+		
Dat	+	+	
Gen I	+		+
Gen II			+
Präpositiv I	+	+	+
Präpositiv II		+	+
Instrumental		+	

In der Matrix sind nur die positiven Werte der Merkmale angegeben. Die Werte der Merkmale in den freigelassenen Feldern erörtere ich in (3.2.1.). Die Konstellation der Merkmalbedeutungen in (1) ergibt eine typische *cross-classification*, keine hierarchisch-binäre Gliederung: der Akkusativ ist gegenüber dem Instrumental hinsichtlich des Merkmals 1 *merkmalhaltig*, hinsichtlich des Merkmals 2 *merkmallos*. Der Instrumental ist gegenüber dem Genitiv I hinsichtlich des Merkmals 2 *merkmalhaltig*, hinsichtlich der Merkmale 1 und 3 *merkmallos*.

Der L (Lokativ = Präpositiv R. R.) ist also gegenüber dem N, I, A und D als Umfangskasus und gegenüber dem N, A und G als Randkasus 'merkmalhaltig' (Jakobson 1936, S. 276).

Es bestehen isomorphe Beziehungen hinsichtlich jeweils *eines* Merkmals, z.B.: Instr.:Nom = Dat:Akk = Präp II:Gen II; hinsichtlich zweiter Merkmale: Präp II:Nom = Präp I:Akk. Aber das Prinzip einer binären hierarchischen Gliederung mußte aufgegeben werden. Es ist in einigen neueren Arbeiten auch bei der Beschreibung ursprünglich binär klassifizierter Kategorien nicht aufrechterhalten worden.[20]

3.1 Das zweite Problem kann entstehen, wenn durch eine entsprechende Ausstattung mit Merkmalen und Werten eine hierarchisch-binäre Klassifikation erzielt worden ist. Ich wähle als Beispiel Isačenkos Beschreibung des "Systems der aspektlich-

[20] Vgl. die ausgezeichnete Analyse der Kategorien des russischen Verbs: А. В. Бондарко, Л. Л. Буланин, *Русский глагол, под редакцией профессора Ю. С. Маслова* (Ленинград, 1967).

temporalen Formen des aktiven Genus im Russischen" (Isačenko 1960, Tabelle 2, vgl. Fußnote 13):

(b)

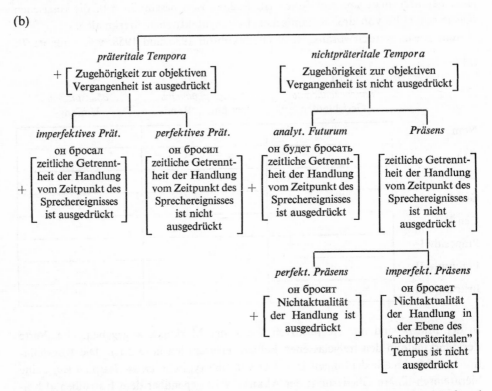

Eine andere hierarchisch-binäre Gliederung wäre erzielt worden, wenn das Merkmal 'zeitliche Getrenntheit der Handlung vom Zeitpunkt des Sprechereignisses' an die erste Stelle und das Merkmal 'Zugehörigkeit zur objektiven Vergangenheit' an die zweite Stelle gesetzt worden wäre. Die gewählte Reihenfolge oder Hierarchie der Merkmale, auch wenn sie, wie in diesem Beispiel, intuitiv einsichtig ist, bedarf prinzipiell einer theoretischen Rechtfertigung in allen Fällen binärer Kategorisierung.

3.2.0. Das dritte, gewichtigere Problem bezieht sich auf die Bedeutungen (Werte) der Merkmale und ihre Relation zur Charakterisierung *merkmalhaltig* und *merkmallos*. Die Auffassung, daß Neutralität gegenüber dem Besitz eines Merkmals oder 'Nichtausdruck' eines Merkmals als 'merkmallos' zu gelten habe, hat dazu geführt, daß eindeutiger Besitz und auch eindeutiger (invarianter) Nichtbesitz eines Merkmals als *merkmalhaltig* ausgezeichnet werden. Ohne diese letzte Annahme (Negation eines Merkmals, Signalisierung von 'Nicht-A') hätte auf manche Korrelation verzichtet werden müssen, z.B. auf die zwischen den Präsensformen des Russischen in (b) angenommene. In den hierarchisch-binären Klassifikationen wird also mit drei Werten der Merkmale operiert. In der Fassung 'Signalisierung von *A*' soll *A* zwar nur als '+ A' verstanden sein, aber hinter diesen [+ A] kann sich ein [− B] verbergen, wo

B ein Merkmal ist. Die Markiertheit ist in der Konstruktion binärer Hierarchien auch mit dem negativen Wert ZWEIER Merkmale verknüpft worden:

Nomina neutra bilden also eine merkmalhaltige Kategorie gegenüber den Nicht-Neutra, die den Sexus bezeichnen können und somit keine "Asexualität" ankündigen (Jakobson 1932, S. 80).

Diese Korrelation läßt sich durch Merkmalwerte redundant reflektieren: [— Asexualität, + Maskulinum], [— Asexualität, + Femininum], [+ Asexualität]; eine nicht redundante Reflektierung wäre [— Maskulinum, — Femininum] für die Neutra.

3.2.1. Auf besondere Schwierigkeiten stößt die Umformulierung der Jakobsonschen Kasuskorrelationen in Merkmalwerte. Die in der Matrix (a) offengelassenen Werte sind uneinheitlich.

Der tatsächliche Gegensatz des A-s und N-s besteht bloß darin, daß der A ankündigt, auf den Gegenstand sei eine Handlung gerichtet, wogegen der N an sich weder das Vorhandensein noch das Nichtvorhandensein eines Bezugs zu einer Handlung angibt. Die *Angabe des Vorhandenseins eines Bezugs* ist also das *Merkmal des A im Gegensatz zum N*; es ist mithin angebracht, den A als das merkmalhaltige, bzw. den N als das merkmallose Glied einer *Bezugskorrelation* zu betrachten (Jakobson 1936, S. 249).

Wenn das Merkmal des Akkusativs umgedeutet wird als positiver Wert des Merkmals *Bezug*, also [+ Bezug], kann dem Nominativ in seiner 'Gesamtbedeutung' der Wert '±' dieses Merkmals, in seiner 'spezifischen' Bedeutung der Wert '—' zugesprochen werden:

Wenn die Gesamtbedeutung des N-s im Gegensatz zum A nicht angibt, ob der bezeichnete Gegenstand irgendeiner Handlung unterworfen ist (Nicht-Signalisierung von α), so gibt die *spezifische Bedeutung* dieses Kasus an, daß die Aussage von einer solchen Handlung nichts weiß (Signalisierung von Nicht-α) (Jakobson 1936, S. 252/253).

Eine analoge Interpretation ist für die 'Umfangskorrelation' nicht angängig:

... wir können ... den Gegensatz des G-s, der die Umfangsverhältnisse anzeigt, und derjenigen Kasus, die keine Umfangsverhältnisse anzeigen (N, A), als eine *Umfangskorrelation* bezeichnen (Jakobson 1936, S. 255).

Den merkmallosen Nominativ und Akkusativ kann ebensowenig wie den peripheren Kasus Dativ und Instrumental — diese beiden stehen den peripheren Umfangskasus Präpositiv I und II gegenüber — der Wert '∓' für das Umfangsmerkmal zukommen. Sie haben dieses Merkmal in keinem Falle, also die Bedeutung [— Umfang]. Außer den drei Werten '+', '—', '∓' scheint noch ein vierter gebraucht zu werden:

Was den Gegensatz der Signalisierung und Nichtsignalisierung einer auf den bezeichneten Gegenstand gerichteten *Handlung* betrifft, ist dieser Bedeutungsunterschied im G *aufgehoben*, und der fragliche Kasus kann ebensogut einen von einer Handlung betroffenen oder einen unabhängigen Gegenstand bezeichnen (Jakobson 1936, S. 255).

Als vierte Bedeutung kommt 'O' oder 'blank' in Frage. Der 'Bezugsgegensatz' gilt

z. B. als aufgehoben in syntaktisch homonymen Nominalphrasen mit Subjekts- oder Objektsgenitiv:

(1)   *посещение писателя*

Der Nominativ ist hinsichtlich des Bezugsmerkmals anders gekennzeichnet. Er befindet sich in der Bezugskorrelation, die also für ihn nicht aufhebbar ist; aber in den Sätzen:

(2) (i)   *рабочие строят дом*
    (ii)   *дом строится рабочими*

kombiniert der Nominativ ebenso wie der Genitiv Subjekts- und Objektsfunktion im Sinne des Merkmals *Gerichtetheit* (*Bezug*). Der hier angetroffene Widerspruch läßt sich jedoch vermeiden (vergl. 4.1.).

Das Merkmal, das die Umfangskorrelation trägt, ist hinsichtlich seiner Werte dem Merkmal der Stellungskorrelation analog (Peripherität, Randstellung).

... bezeichne ich den I und D als Randkasus und den N und A als Vollkasus, und für den Gegensatz der beiden Gatrungen verwende ich im folgenden die Benennung *Stellungskorrelation* (Jakobson 1936, S. 262).

Zu den peripheren Kasus gehört als dritter der Präpositiv, bzw. die beiden Präpositive. Den vier 'Vollkasus' Nominativ, Akkusativ, Genitiv I und II kann nur die Bedeutung '—', nicht '干' für das Merkmal *peripher* zugeordnet werden. Der Wert '干' kommt auch nicht in Betracht, wenn *peripher* als morphologisches Merkmal zur Reflektierung des Kasus(teil)synkretismus verwendet wird.

4.0. Wir wollen in diesem Abschnitt zeigen, daß die Annahme von Merkmalen und Merkmalbedeutungen eine klare Grenzziehung zwischen linguistischen Ebenen voraussetzt. Merkmale werden für bestimmte Ebenen oder Komponenten der grammatischen Theorie verliehen und sind für diese gültig. Sie können Konsequenzen für andere Ebenen haben. Im Rahmen des generativen Transformationsmodells können Merkmale durch Formationsregeln, durch Transformationsregeln und in den Lexikoneintragungen eingeführt werden. Sie sind nach verschiedenen Kriterien klassifizierbar.[21]

4.1. Der Nominativ kann den plus-Wert des Merkmals *Gerichtetheit* nur erhalten, wenn Passiv-Transformation oder eine ähnliche vorgenommen wurde. In der Tiefenstruktur des aktivischen (21) wie des passivischen Satzes (2ii) gehört das Merkmal *Gerichtetheit* einem bestimmten (demselben) Nomen an, das die Transformationsregeln verschieden behandeln, und zwar so, daß der Nominativ durch die Passivtransformation vorbestimmt wird. Das Merkmal *Gerichtetheit* braucht die Permutation der

---

[21]   Im theoretischen Rahmen der generativen Transformationsgrammatik stellt Bierwisch (*Syntactic features*..., S. 241 ff.) drei Klassifikationen der nichtphonologischen Merkmale auf, und zwar (1) nach dem semantischen Wert der Merkmale, (2) nach ihrer Herkunft im Verlaufe der Derivation und (3) nach ihrer Funktion im Derivationsprozeß.

Nominalphrase nicht mitzumachen. Die neue Stellung der Nominalphrase determiniert den Nominativ.

Komplizierter noch sind die Beziehungen zwischen Tiefen- und Oberflächenstruktur, wenn die Negationstransformation das den Genitiv determinierende Merkmal [+ Umfang] einführt und eine Passivtransformation dessen Wert zu '—' ändert:

(3)   *мы читаем газеты*
        мы не читаем газет
        газеты *нами не читаются*

In anderen Fällen, vermutlich bei Nomina mit dem Merkmalwert [−konkret], der damit syntaktischen Charakter erhält, behält das Merkmal [+ Umfang] bei Passivtransformation seinen Wert:

(4)   *мы не наблюдали* изменений
        изменений *нами не наблюдалось*[22]

Hier bietet sich — ich greife vor — eine relativ klare Möglichkeit, das bei Negation gegebenenfalls einzuführende Merkmal [Umfang] als *merkmalhaltig* und *merkmallos* zu kennzeichnen und diese Charakterisierung in Abhängigkeit vom Kontext als 'plus' oder 'minus' zu interpretieren.

(c) $[u \text{ Umfang}] \rightarrow [- \text{Umfang}] / \begin{bmatrix} + \text{konkret} \\ + \text{passiv} \underline{\qquad} \end{bmatrix}$

        $[u \text{ Umfang}] \rightarrow [+ \text{Umfang}] / \begin{bmatrix} - \text{konkret} \\ + \text{passiv} \underline{\qquad} \end{bmatrix}$

Die Empfindlichkeit der Merkmale und Merkmalwerte gegenüber der Tiefen- und Oberflächenstruktur zeigt sich auch an dem bereits erwähnten Verhalten des Merkmals *Gerichtetheit* beim Akkusativ-Nominativ einerseits und beim Genitiv andererseits (vgl. 3.2.1.). Jakobsons intuitive Unterscheidung zwischen der Aufhebung der Bezugskorrelation im Genitiv, die als Wert 'O' für das Merkmal *Bezug* verstanden werden kann, und der Beteiligung des Nominativs an dieser Korrelation, eines Kasus, der wie der Genitiv *Gerichtetheit* (Objekt) und *Nichtgerichtetheit* (Subjekt) bezeichnet (als Wert [∓ Bezug] interpretierbar), kann wie folgt expliziert werden. Der Genitiv hat in ein und derselben Oberflächenstruktur negativen wie auch positiven Wert des Merkmals *Bezug* (*Gerichtetheit*):

(5)   *Посещения писателя*

Der Nominativ hat in ein und derselben Oberflächenstruktur (nach Passiv-Transformation) nur positiven Wert dieses Merkmals. Wenn der Wert '∓', den der Nominativ für das Merkmal *Bezug* hat, durch Unterscheidung von Ableitungsebenen auf den Wert '—' reduziert wird, so ist die Bedeutung 'O' (blank) dieses Merkmals für

---

[22] Vgl. dazu Verf., "Versuch einer Modellierung des genus verbi moderner slavischer Sprachen im Rahmen der generativen Transformationsgrammatik", in: *ZfSl*, XIII 2 (1968).

den Genitiv hinfällig, weil die Werte '+' oder '−' in der Tiefenstruktur festzulegen sind, so daß es keinen Sinn hat, sie danach, wenn 'Genitiv' in der Oberflächenstruktur formiert wird, als *unbestimmt* anzugeben. Die Nutzung des Merkmals *Gerichtetheit* scheint am ehesten nützlich als Synonym für 'direktes Objekt', aber es ist unbrauchbar, wenn Tiefen- und Oberflächenstruktur nicht streng geschieden werden.[23]

4.2. Ganz anders verhält es sich mit dem Merkmal *peripher*. Es ist unabhängig von der Unterscheidung zwischen Tiefen- und Oberflächenstruktur; von ihm kann z. B. nicht gesagt werden, wie vom Merkmal *Gerichtetheit*, daß es ein und demselben Kasus in der Oberflächenstruktur zukommt, in der Tiefenstruktur aber nicht. Es kann nicht neutralisiert werden wie das Bezugsmerkmal im Genitiv und ist unabhängig von der Konstituentenstruktur. Der Akkusativ verliert das Bezugsmerkmal in der Adverbialphrase:

(6)   он работал всю ночь

Jeder Instrumental, Dativ und Präpositiv, welcher Struktur immer sie sind, besitzt positiven Wert des Merkmals [+ peripher] und jeder andere Kasus hat negativen Wert [− peripher]. Das Merkmal [+ peripher] ist vorwiegend ein morphologisches, besser vielleicht ein syntaktisches mit ausschließlich morphologischen Konsequenzen. Was der Instrumental sonst 'bedeutet' muß anders dargestellt werden (vgl. z. B. 6.1.). Das Merkmal reflektiert den (Teil)Synkretismus des Instrumental mit dem Dativ und die Ähnlichkeit des paradigmatischen Inventars der Instrumentalendungen. Die zwei Merkmale, die in der Interpretation Jakobsons den Dativ charakterisieren, sind eine äußerst heterogene Kombination.

4.3. Das Merkmal *Umfang*, das für Genitiv und Präpositiv positiven Wert hat, läßt sich, soweit es den Genitiv betrifft, in mindestens drei unabhängige Merkmale verschiedener Ebenen zerlegen: als morphologisches Merkmal reflektiert es den (Teil) Synkretismus mit dem Präpositiv; als syntaktisches Merkmal wird es durch Transformation eingeführt und setzt ein syntaktisches Merkmal und ein semantisches voraus (vgl. 4.1. und 6.2.).

---

[23] Das Merkmal 'Gerichtetheit' könnte nicht unabhängig von der semantischen Charakterisierung des Verbums behandelt werden und müßte dann weiter differenziert werden:

> *er schreibt ein Buch*; *er erzählt eine Geschichte*;
> *er schlug seine Kinder*; *Devrient spielt den Hamlet*
> (*Der Hamlet des Devrient*) u. a.

Allen Verben, die ein direktes (Akkusativ) Objekt 'regieren', ist eine in der strikten Subkategorisierung aufzuführende Nominalphrase gemeinsam, deren Struktur und Funktion durch die Formationsregeln bestimmt sind. Auf diese Nominalphrase, d. h. ihr Kern-Nomen, werden durch Transformationsregeln Merkmale aus der Merkmalmatrix des Verbums übertragen, die den Akkusativ determinieren. Die Beziehungen zwischen diesen morphologischen Merkmalen und den semantischen Merkmalen des Verbums sind nicht klar. Eine semantische Determinierung des Akkusativs kann nur angenommen werden, wenn mindestens EIN semantisches Merkmal allen den Akkusativ 'regierenden' Verben gemeinsam ist.

(7)   *снегу кругом*[24]

Schließlich wird es als idiosynkratisches syntaktisches Merkmal für eine Klasse von Verben in den entsprechenden Wörterbucheintragungen geführt:

(8)   *бояться, остерегаться*
        лишать кого-л. чего-л.

4.4. Jakobson hat in den 'морфологические наблюдения ...' (1958) das russische Kasussystem anders interpretiert als im 'Beitrag...' (1936). Die Verschiedenheit der Interpretation reflektiert *implicite* die Bevorzugung verschiedener Ebenen bei der Zuweisung von Merkmalen und Merkmalwerten. Es handelt sich um die beiden Genitive und die beiden Präpositive, bzw. Lokative. Genitiv auf -*u* und Präpositiv auf -*ú* werden im 'Beitrag...' als merkmalhaltig interpretiert:

Der G II und der L II sind im Verhältnisse zu G I und zu L I *merkmalhaltige* Kategorien. Sie besagen im Gegensatz zu den merkmallosen G I und L I, daß der bezeichnete Gegenstand nicht als Gestalt, sondern als etwas *Gestaltendes oder zu Gestaltendes* im Sachverhalte der Aussage fungiert. Man kann dementsprechend den G II und den L II als *Gestaltungskasus* und ihr Verhältnis zum G I und L I als *Gestaltungskorrelation* bezeichnen (S. 278).

Hier ist ein viertes Merkmal aufgewendet, um die beiden Kasus G II und L II (снегу, в снегу́) als merkmalhaltige den merkmallosen Kasus G I und L I (снега, в снеге) gegenüberzustellen. In der späteren Arbeit wird das Verhältnis umgekehrt:

Собственно, каждый из четырех падежей Р. I, П. I, В. и Д., в отличие от Р. II, П. II, И. и Т., наделяет предмет свойством или состоянием, вытекающим из направленного на предмет действия, и соответственно может быть назван падежом наделительным (S. 22/23).

Genitiv I (= Р. I) und Präpositiv I (= П. I) sind wie Akkusativ (= В.) und Dativ (= Д.) mit positivem Wert des Merkmals *Gerichtetheit* ausgestattet. Vier Kasuspaare sind mit Hilfe *eines* Merkmals in eine isomorphe Relation gesetzt: Nom: Akk, Instrumental: Dat, Gen II: Gen I, Präpos II: Präpos I.

Таким образом все восемь падежей русского склонения составляют трехмерную систему (S. 23).

Durch die Modifikation der früheren Interpretation wird mit der Differenzierung von acht Kasus die optimale Leistung dreier Merkmale erzielt. Aber es verbirgt sich mehr dahinter. Die frühere Interpretation hatte vorzüglich Merkmalhaltigkeit der morphologischen Ebene, d.h. die außergewöhnlichen, abweichenden Endungen auf -*u* und -*ú* gegenüber den normalen -*a* und -*e*, berücksichtigt ungeachtet der Verschleierung als Gestaltungskorrelation. In der späteren Arbeit tritt Merkmalhaltigkeit der semantischen Ebene mit akzessorischer Ökonomie der Merkmale in den Vordergrund.

---

[24] Beispiel aus R. Jakobson 1958; vgl. auch Verf. "О трансформационном описании так называемых безличных предложений в современном русском литературном языке", in: *Вопросы языкознания*, 3 (1963), S. 24.

5.0. Aus der vorausgegangenen Diskussion lassen sich die folgenden zusammenfassenden Feststellungen über die bisherige, vor allem in der Prager Schule geläufige Verwendung der Begriffe 'merkmalhaltig' und 'merkmallos' außerhalb der Phonologie gewinnen:

(1) Durch die Begriffe 'merkmalhaltig' und 'merkmallos' werden nicht Merkmale sondern (Teil)Kategorien, bzw. Elemente mehrgliedriger Kategorien, z.B. die schiedenen Tempora, die beiden Aspekte, charakterisiert.

(2) Als *merkmalhaltig* wird die Kategorie ausgezeichnet, die für ein bestimmtes Merkmal die Bedeutung (den Wert) '+' oder '—' hat, während die merkmallose Charakterisierung der Zuweisung eines Wertes '∓' gleichkommt; dieser Wert kann als allgemeine Reflektierung der 'Nichtsignalisierung von A' (= *merkmallos*) gegenüber der 'Signalisierung von —A' (= *merkmalhaltig*) gelten. Als ein vierter Wert 'O' könnte die Aufhebung eines Merkmalgegensatzes interpretiert werden.

(3) Kategorien mit mehr als zwei Elementen werden hypothetisch hierarchischen Klassifikationen unterworfen auf Grund fortlaufender Gegenüberstellung *zweier* Untermengen ihrer Elemente (Teil- oder Unterkategorien), von denen der einen, der Untermenge der jeweils 'merkmalhaltigen' Kategorie(n), der Wert '+' oder der Wert '—' eines bestimmten Merkmals, der anderen der Wert '∓' für das gleiche Merkmal zugeordnet ist.

(4) Die hierarchische Klassifikation von Untermengen der Elemente einer Kategorie ist nicht als generelles theoretisches Ordnungsschema aufrechtzuerhalten. Dem Prinzip der *cross-classification* scheint hier ebenso der Vorzug eingeräumt werden zu müssen wie z.B. bei der Merkmalspezifizierung von Nomina, wo die Überkreuz-Klassifikation den Versuchen hierarchischer Kategorisierung in der anfänglichen Version der generativen Transformationsgrammatik entgegengesetzt wurde. In der Nachfolge der Prager Schule gibt es bereits mehrere Beschreibungen, die sich der *cross-classification* bedienen.[25]

(5) Die in Punkt (2) erwähnte Überschreitung der Binarität der Merkmalwerte erweist sich in mehreren Fällen als vermeidbar, wenn die linguistischen Ebenen auseinandergehalten werden.

(6) Wenn der Merkmalwert '+' ebenso wie '—' die Charakterisierung *merkmalhaltig* und der Wert '∓' ebenso wie '—' die Charakterisierung *merkmallos* erhalten kann, liegt die Frage nahe, ob die beiden Markierungen der Merkmale nicht grundsätzlich von den Werten der Merkmale getrennt werden können, so daß einem als *merkmalhaltig* oder *merkmallos* gekennzeichneten Merkmal positiver oder negativer Wert in Abhängigkeit vom simultanen oder linearen Kontext vermittels Regeln zugewiesen wird.

Ebendies ist ein Grundgedanke der Markiertheitshypothese von Chomsky

[25] Vgl. z.B. die unter Fn. 20 zitierte Arbeit von А. В. Бондарко und Л. Л. Буланин und den unter Fn. 10 angegebenen Aufsatz von H. Křížková; weiter А. В. Исаченко, "трансформационный анализ кратких и полных прилагательних", in: *Исследования по структурной типологии* (Москва, 1963), S. 61-93.

Halle, Postal und Lakoff, deren theoretische und formale Klarheit eine empirische Erprobung lohnend erscheinen läßt. Es erweist sich freilich schnell, daß damit nur ein Ausgangspunkt gegeben ist. Im folgenden versuche ich, Möglichkeiten sinnvoller Verwendung der Begriffe 'merkmalhaltig' und 'merkmallos' im Rahmen dieses theoretischen Konzepts in einer Beschreibung des modernen Russischen zu entwickeln und zu erörtern, und zwar (a) in Beziehung auf Merkmale, (b) unter möglichst strenger Trennung linguistischer Ebenen und (c) unter Beschränkung auf die zwei Bedeutungen (Werte) '+' und '−'.

6.0. Als erstes komme ich auf einige idiosynkratische Fakten im Kasusgebrauch des Russischen zu sprechen, darunter (6.2) auch solche, die bisher nicht als Erscheinungen der Kasus-Struktur angesehen wurden und darauf zurückführbar schienen.

6.1.0. Subtile Feststellungen Jakobsons (1936) beziehen sich auf semantische Unterschiede, die zwischen Nominativ und Instrumental in Kopulasätzen oder in Sätzen, denen in der Tiefenstruktur eine Kopula-Struktur zugrunde liegt, bestehen. Der Nominativ (des sogenannten Prädikatsnomens) wird verwendet

Falls ... eine ständige, urtümliche, unabschaffbare Eigenschaft des Gegenstands gemeint wird, oder mindestens die Absicht nicht besteht, den episodischen Charakter dieser Eigenschaft zu kennzeichnen ... (S. 265).

Der Instrumental wird verwendet, wenn

... es sich um eine Sonderfunktion des Gegenstands, um eine vorübergehende, gelegentliche (erworbene bzw. veräußerliche) Eigenschaft handelt (S. 265).

Einige illustrative Beispiele Jakobsons:

(9) *Все они были греки; будь татарином!*
     он был титулярный советник, она генеральская дочь ...
     он вернулся больной; он вернулся больным. (S. 265-266)

Mit dieser Unterscheidung steht in einem Zusammenhang, der leicht erklärbar zu sein scheint, die starke Einschränkung des Instrumentals bei präsentischem Tempus des Verbs und die etwas geringere des Nominativs bei Nichtpräsens und Nichtpräteritum. Im Präteritum sind beide Kasus gleichmäßig vertreten.[26] Wenn für die von Jakobson paraphrasierten Bedeutungsunterschiede das Merkmal *statisch* und für die erste Bedeutung (Nominativ) der Wert '+', für die zweite (Instrumental) der Wert '−' festgesetzt und in die Merkmalmatrix des (Kopula)Verbums aufgenommen wird, lassen sich die Begriffe 'merkmalhaltig' und 'merkmallos' in folgender Weise verwenden:

(d) $[\text{m statisch}] \rightarrow [-\text{statisch}] / \left[\begin{array}{c} +\text{präsens} \\ \underline{} \end{array} \right]$

'm' = *merkmalhaltig*; 'u' = *merkmallos*.

[26] Vgl. J. Bauer, R. Mrázek, S. Žaža, *Příruční mluvnice ruštiny* II, skladba (Praha, 1966), S. 277 ff.

Diese Interpretationsregel reflektiert mit Hilfe der Regel (g) die Außergewöhnlichkeit von Instrumental-Konstruktionen wie

(10)   *Я снова посудником на пароходе 'Пермь'*[27]

                                    (Горький)

(e)   [m statisch] → [+ statisch] / $\begin{bmatrix} -\text{präsens} \\ -\text{präteritum} \end{bmatrix}$

(e) reflektiert zusammen mit (g) ungewöhnliche Konstruktionen wie

(11)   *О, милый мой, ты будешь* царь
         ... будь сильный *до последнего дыхания!*[28]

                                    (Фадеев)

(f)   [u statisch] → [+ statisch] / $\begin{bmatrix} +\text{präsens} \end{bmatrix}$

        [u statisch] → [− statisch] / $\begin{bmatrix} -\text{präsens} \\ -\text{präteritum} \end{bmatrix}$ von (e) impliziert.

'+ präsens' steht provisorisch für Merkmale, die Präsensformen determinieren; '− präsens' und '− präteritum' läßt Futurum, Imperativ, Konditional übrig. Das Merkmal *statisch* befindet sich, wie erwähnt, in der Merkmalmatrix des (Kopula)-Verbs und wird in der Merkmalmatrix des (Prädikats)Nomens doubliert, um mit Merkmalen, die den Instrumental determinieren, in Beziehung gesetzt zu werden:

(g)   [+ statisch] → [− peripher]
        [− statisch] → [+ peripher]

Es ergibt sich die Konsequenz, das (Kopula) Verb im Wörterbuch sowohl mit [m statisch] wie mit [u statisch] auszustatten. Eine der beiden Charakterisierungen wird dann mit dem Verbum in den Phrasensignator (*phrase-marker*) eingeführt. Die Behandlung des Merkmals bei Präteritum ist mir unklar.

6.1.1. Einen Sonderfall stellt die Klasse der Verben dar, die explizite ein Werden, eine Mutation bezeichnen, vor allem das Verbum стать/становиться. Sätze mit diesem Verbum können grob in folgender Weise abgeleitet werden, wobei hier auf spezielle Probleme der Derivation des Kopulaverbs nicht eingegangen werden kann und eine provisorische Lösung gegeben wird.[29]

(12)   *Борис стал учителем*

[27] Beispiel aus dem in Fn. 26 zitierten Werk.
[28] Beispiele aus dem in Fn. 26 zitierten Werk.
[29] Vgl. insbesondere John Robert Ross, "Adjectives as Noun Phrases" (Manuskript); offen ist vor allem das Problem der unterschiedlichen Derivation von *John is hungry* (Prädikatsadjektiv) und *John is a teacher* (Prädikatsnomen); vgl. auch Verf., "Studien zur Theorie der russischen Syntax", *Sitzungsberichte der Deutschen Akademie der Wissenschaften, Klasse für Sprachen, Literatur und Kunst*, Jahrgang 1966, Nr. 1.

(h)

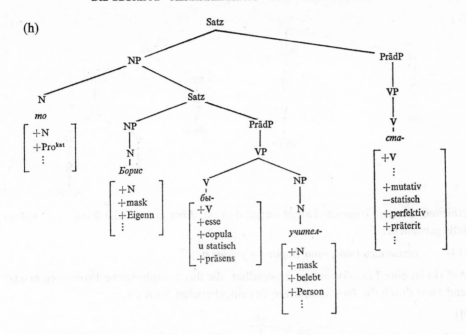

In Verbindung mit стать/становиться kann nur der Instrumental verwendet werden.

… In solchen Fügungen wie *stal sudjej* ist die Randstellung bloß semantisch, nicht aber syntaktisch fundiert: bei der Aussage *on stal* ist die Frage *kem, čem* [I] unentbehrlich (Jakobson 1936, S. 265).

'Syntaktisch nicht fundiert' erscheint die Randstellung, weil keine Opposition zum Nominativ hier stattfindet. Wenn wir den hier wesentlichen Aspekt der Semantik des Verbums *stat'* mit dem Merkmal [+mutativ] kennzeichnen, kann die Redundanzregel syntaktischer Merkmale

(i)   [+mutativ] → [−statisch]

aufgestellt werden, die in (h) berücksichtigt ist.

Im ersten Transformationszyklus (für den eingebetteten Satz) erfolgt keine Transformation. Im zweiten Zyklus wird eine Extrapositionstransformation vorgenommen[30] mit dem Ergebnis (k).

Eine fakultative Permutation von *NP* und *PrädP* kann die Derivation eines Satzes

(13)   *стало то, что Борис — учитель[31]

---

[30] Vgl. Peter Steven Rosenbaum, "The Grammar of English Predicate Complement Constructions", (Manuskript, Doktordissertation, Massachusetts Institute of Technology, 1965, S. 11).
[31] Zur Grammatikalität von (13) vgl. einen Satz wie
                Что он тогда говорил, то и стало (*Николаева*)
Beispiel aus: *Словарь русского языка*, том IV (Москва, 1961).

(k)

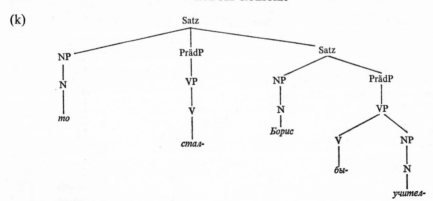

einleiten, dessen Grammatikalität anfechtbar ist. Aber eine solche Regel wird jedenfalls gebraucht:

(14)   *оказалось (то), что Борис — учитель*

Auf (k) ist eine Transformation anwendbar, die das kataphorische Pronomen ersetzt
und zwar durch die Nominalphrase des eingebetteten Satzes.[32]

(l)

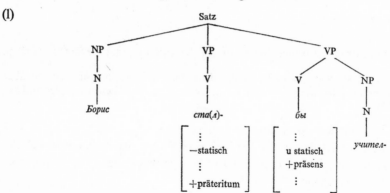

Hier ist nun eine weitere Transformationsregel notwendig, die ein Kopulaverb ESSE
unter bestimmten Bedingungen, u.a. bei linker Nachbarschaft bestimmter anderer
Verben und bei der Markierung [+präsens] tilgt. Dann wird auch [u statisch] in der
Merkmalmatrix des Kopulaverbums entfernt, so daß [−statisch] des Verbums *ста-*
im Merkmalbereich des Nomens *учител-* doubliert wird und nach (g) zum Instrumental
führt.

    6.1.2. Eine analoge aber kompliziertere Struktur mit merkmalhaltigem Nominativ
bietet folgender Satz:

(15)   *А еще первые бойцы улицы считаетесь, котята!*[33]

                                                                (Горький)

---

[32]   Diese Transformation entspricht der *Pronoun Replacement Transformation* Rosenbaums, *a.a.O.*,
S.12.
[33]   Beispiel aus J.Bauer, R.Mrázek, S.Žaža, *a.a.O.*, S. 229.

Von dieser (vereinfachten) Tiefenstruktur kann ausgegangen werden:

(m)

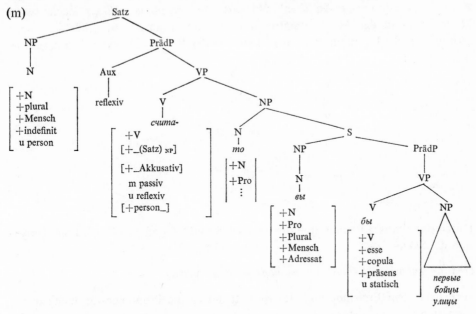

Hierzu gelten die Interpretationsregeln (n), (vgl. auch 6.4.):

(n) $[\text{u person}] \rightarrow (-\text{person}_1, -\text{person}_2) / \begin{bmatrix} \text{indefinit} \\ \underline{\hspace{1.5cm}} \end{bmatrix}$

$[\text{m passiv}] \rightarrow [-\text{passiv}] / \begin{bmatrix} +\underline{\hspace{1cm}}\text{Akkusativ} \\ \underline{\hspace{2cm}} \end{bmatrix}$

$[\text{u reflexiv}] \rightarrow [+\text{reflexiv}] / \begin{bmatrix} +\underline{\hspace{1cm}}\text{Akkusativ} \\ \underline{\hspace{2cm}} \end{bmatrix}$

und Regel (f).

Nach Reflexiv-Passiv-Transformation[34] liegt folgender — wiederum stark vereinfachter und teilweise weitergeführter — Phrasensignator vor:

(o)

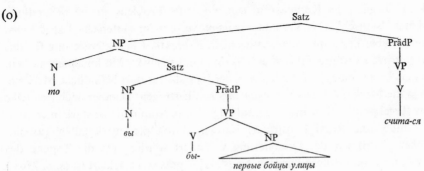

---

[34] Vgl. Verf., "Versuch einer Modellierung des *genus verbi* moderner slawischer Sprachen im Rahmen der generativen Transformationsgrammatik", in: *ZfSl*, 2 (1968).

In (o) sind noch andere Transformationen vorausgesetzt, die Tilgung des unspezifizierten 'unbestimmt-persönlichen' Nomens, des Symbols *reflexiv* nach seiner Doublierung in der Merkmalmatrix des Verbums *счита-* und schließlich seine morphologische Repräsentation. (o) ist sodann der Extrapositionstransformation zu unterziehen:

(p)

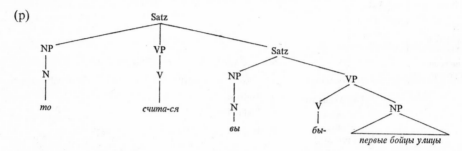

Durch (fakultative) Permutation der linken NP und VP (vgl. S. 277) wird die Derivation des Satzes

(16)   *считается (то), что вы первые бойцы улицы*

vorbereitet. Zur Erzielung von (15) ist statt dessen die Pronomen-Ersetzungstransformation vorzunehmen:

(q)

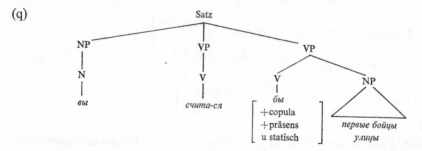

Die Derivation von (15) verläuft analog zur Derivation von (12). Es entsteht aber mit der analogen Tilgung des Kopulaverbs ESSE ein neues Problem für die Behandlung des Merkmals 'statisch'. Das Verbum *считать* verfügt im Unterschied zu *стать/ становиться* über keine inhärente, sei es auch indirekte, Charakterisierung für das Merkmal *statisch*. Es wäre sinnlos, dieses Verbum mit so einem Merkmal zu versehen. Am zweckmäßigsten ist es, vor der Tilgung der Kopula das dort befindliche Merkmal [statisch] in die Merkmalmatrix von *считать* zu übertragen. Da aber nach *считать* (*ся*) in der Regel prädikativer Instrumental folgt — der Nominativ ist stark 'merkmalhaltig' — muß eine Regel konstruiert werden, durch die 'merkmallos' (*u*) und 'merkmalhaltig' (*m*) vor der Doublierung verändert werden. Da die Tilgung des Kopula-Verbums nur erfolgen kann, wenn es als [+ präsens] markiert ist (s. S. 276f.) würde [m statisch] als [− statisch] und [u statisch] als [+ statisch] nach Regel (d) und (f) interpretiert werden. Die Konsequenz ist nach (g) im ersten Falle Instrumental, im zweiten Falle Nominativ. Die Merkmalhaltigkeit und -losigkeit der Kasus ist bei Nichtcopula-Verben wie *считать* und vielen anderen gerade umgekehrt. Der Doublierungsregel des Merkmals *statisch* muß demnach die folgende Regel vorausgeschickt werden, die hier unzureichend formuliert ist:

(r) $[\alpha \text{ statisch}] \rightarrow [\sim\alpha \text{ statisch}] / [\underline{\quad} + \text{copula}]$
wo $\alpha = m$ oder u und $u = \sim m$, $m = \sim u$

Das Ergebnis dieser Regel ist sofort nach (d) und (f) zu interpretieren. Erst dann findet Doublierung [+ statisch] oder [− statisch] statt. Regel (r), die Doublierungsregel und die Tilgungsregel für das Kopulaverb sind ein zusammenhängender Regelblock. Alle drei Regeln sind jeweils gemeinsam anzuwenden. Eine sehr große Zahl Konstruktionen mit Einbettungen von Kopulasätzen sind hier betroffen.

6.2. Eine singuläre Eigenart des heutigen russischen Kasussystems scheint durch Markiertheitsangaben eine schärfere Erklärung, nicht nur schmückendes Beiwerk zu erhalten. Es handelt sich um den in einem Paradigma vorliegenden Genitiv auf betontes oder unbetontes *-u* und um den im gleichen Paradigma vorhandenen Präpositiv auf betontes-*u*. Beide Kasus haben neben sich einen 'normalen', der die übliche Endung des Paradigmas zeigt. Von den Substantiven, die diesem Paradigma angehören, haben einige sowohl den Genitiv auf *-ú* wie den Präpositiv auf *ú* (*снег, сок, спирт*), andere nur den Genitiv auf *-u* (*творог, сор*) und einige wiederum nur den Präpositiv auf *-ú* (*берег, стог*). Schließlich gibt es Nomina, die keinen von beiden haben (*хлеб*). Von der Gemeinsamkeit des Deklinationstyps abgesehen, müssen Genitiv und Präpositiv unabhängig behandelt werden. Über den Genitiv hat Šachmatov die klarste Feststellung mit den Worten getroffen, daß der Genitiv auf *-u* von Substantiven gebildet werden kann, die nichtzählbare Gegenstände bezeichnen.[35] Der Genitiv auf *-u* ist semantisch zu interpretieren, so daß die ihn beschreibenden Merkmale in der Tiefenstruktur anwesend sein müssen.

(17)   *народ собрался; народу собралось*

Als ein solches Merkmal soll hier gelten: *quant(itativ)*. Es charakterisiert die Einstellung auf die Quantität der bezeichneten Sache. Gleichzeitig wird es als syntaktisches Merkmal weiter verwendet, das im Rahmen einer Transformation die Formierung des Genitivs zur Folge hat: es signalisiert die Einführung der Merkmale [+ Umfang], [−peripher] derer ich mich hier in rein morphologischem Sinne bediene. Da die Zugehörigkeit der Substantiva zu einem Deklinationstyp im Lexikon verzeichnet ist, bedeutet die Kombination [+ quant] mit den hinzukommenden Merkmalen [+ Umfang] und [− peripher] die Formierung des Genitivs auf *-u* z.B. für *narod*, den Genitiv auf *-y* für *vody*. Im zweiten Falle operiert [+ quant] als syntaktisches Merkmal, indem es die genannte Einführung signalisiert, morphologisch operiert es leer, weil es in diesem Paradigma nur EINEN Genitiv, nämlich auf *-y* gibt. Als semantisches Merkmal wird es ebenso wie bei *narodu* zur Interpretation gebraucht. Es erscheint mir zweckmäßig,

---

[35]   А. А. Шахматов, *Очерк современного русского литературного языка*, 4-е изд. (Москва, 1941).

auch das Merkmal *quant* als 'merkmallos' und 'merkmalhaltig' zu charakterisieren und so in die Merkmalmatrizen der Nomina im Wörterbuch einzuführen. Die Markierungen werden dann so interpretiert:

(s) $\quad [\text{u quant}] \rightarrow [+\text{quant}] \,/\, \begin{bmatrix} -\text{zählbar} \\ +\text{Stoff oder} + \text{Kollektiv} \\ \rule{3cm}{0.4pt} \end{bmatrix}$

(t) $\quad [\text{m quant}] \rightarrow [-\text{quant}] \,/\, \begin{bmatrix} -\text{zählbar} \\ +\text{Stoff oder} + \text{Kollektiv} \\ \rule{3cm}{0.4pt} \end{bmatrix}$

(u) $\quad [\text{m quant}] \rightarrow [+\text{quant}] \,/\, \begin{bmatrix} \text{zählbar} \\ \rule{1.5cm}{0.4pt} \end{bmatrix}$

(v) $\quad [\text{u quant}] \rightarrow [-\text{quant}] \,/\, \begin{bmatrix} \text{zählbar} \\ \rule{1.5cm}{0.4pt} \end{bmatrix}$

Diese Regeln sind nicht nur Ausdruck dessen, daß bei Stoff-, Masse- und Kollektivbezeichnungen die Einstellung auf die Quantität als das 'Normale', 'Gewöhnliche' angesehen wird, bei zählbaren Gegenständen dagegen nicht, so daß etwa in

(18)   *писем накопилось*

der Genitiv aus merkmalhaltigem [m quant] und in (17) aus merkmallosem [u quant] hervorgeht. Sie stellen den negativen Wert des Merkmals *quant* als 'merkmalhaltig' bei Massebezeichnungen hin und lösen damit den Widerspruch zwischen der geringeren morphologischen Spezifizierung und der 'merkmalhaltigen' Semantik, die bei solchen Substantiva gerade durch die fehlende Einstellung auf Quantität markiert ist. Der Genitiv ist eine bloße Funktion bestimmter Transformationen:

(19)   *он не любил снега*
          пугался снега; разговор коснулся
          коньяка; цвет снега, красота снега[36]

Der morphologisch spezifiziertere Genitiv, der des positiven Merkmals [+ quant] zu seiner Determinierung bedarf, wird bei Masseobjekten kraft seiner durch [+ quant] reflektierten Einstellung auf Menge und Quantität als 'merkmallos' begriffen.

(20)   *снегу кругом*

Da alle Quantitätsdeterminierungen wie *много, мало, (не)сколько*, auch der in der semantischen Beschreibung verwendbare und auf syntaktische Merkmale abbildbare negierte Existentialoperator ('Nulldosis') 'merkmallos' hinsichtlich der ihnen inhärenten 'Quantität' sind ([u quant]) und jedes auf sie folgende Nomen den Genitiv *-u* hat, sofern es diesen überhaupt haben kann, findet die hier gebotene transformationelle Doublierung des Merkmals [u quant] im Nomen ohne Änderung der 'Merkmallosigkeit' statt.

[36]   Beispiele u.a. aus Jakobson (1958).

Bezeichnungen zählbarer Objekte erfahren durch (u), (v) eine umgekehrte Behandlung. Für sie ist positiver Wert [+quant] die Interpretation der Merkmalhaltigkeit. kein Nomen für zählbare Objekte verfügt prinzipiell über die Genitiv-Doublette *-a:-u.*[37]

Die Quantität kann durch Zahlen spezifiziert werden und ist dann eine deutliche zusätzliche Charakterisierung zählbarer Objekte. Daraus erklärt sich Regel (u). Endgültige Entscheidungen darüber, ob die Interpretationsregeln (s)-(v) akzeptabel sind, können erst getroffen werden, wenn eingehendere semantische Interpretationen der Substantiva vorliegen.

6.2.1. Eine ähnliche Beschreibung kann die Doublette des Präpositivs finden. Hier ist neben dem mechanischen silbenzählenden Kriterium, nach dem nur einsilbige Substantiva und zweisilbige mit Polnoglasje (*берег*) diese Doublette aufweisen können — leicht umgangssprachliches *в отпуску* ausgenommen — der Zusammenhang mit anderen semantischen und/oder syntaktischen Merkmalen aufzuklären, was etwa die Tatsache erhellen könnte, daß es zwar *на берегу́* aber nicht *в городу́* gibt.[38]

6.3. Weitere syntaktische Idiosynkrasien des Russischen lassen die Verwendung des Markierungspaars angebracht erscheinen. Im Russischen gelten folgende Sätze als korrekt:

(21) *Командующий просил меня приехать*
      и тебя с собой, взять

(22) *И приказав, чтоб ему позвонили ...*
      положил трубку

(23) *Серпилин сел за стол и приказал соединить* себя *с медсанбатом*

(24) *Когда Бережной и*
      Пикин ушли, он, приказав
      Птицыну разбудить себя *ровно*
      через три часа, разобрал койку[39]

(25) *Я извиняюсь за то, что я*
      заставил себя *ждать*

In den letzten drei Sätzen erfolgt reflexive Pronominalisierung des Nomens *Серпилин* [in (24) als Pronomen *он* vertreten] bzw. *я*, obwohl keine Identität mit dem Subjekt des gleichen (eingebetteten) Satzes vorliegt. In der Tiefenstruktur (24) ist *Птицын* Subjekt des eingebetteten Satzes und *Серпилин* (→ *себя*) Objekt. In (23) liegt unbestimmt-persönliches Subjekt ('*man*') des eingebetten Satzes vor, dessen direktes

---

[37] Präpositionalphrasen wie *из ле́су* : *из леса, из дому* : *из дома, со стра́ху* (*от страха*) sind individuell-idiosynkratische Formen und im Lexikon zu vermerken.

[38] Ich habe hier unerwähnt gelassen, daß der doppelte Präpositiv auch im Paradigma der 'i-Stämme' anzutreffen ist, als bloße Akzentunterscheidung: *в степи́* : *в сте́пи; в тени́* : *в те́ни; в грязи́* : *в грязи.*

[39] Alle Beispiele außer dem letzten aus К. Симонов, *Солдатами не рождаются.*

Objekt *Серпилин* (→ *себя*) ist. Analoge Beziehungen bestehen in (25), wo *себя* anstelle von *меня* erscheint. In (21) ist die reflexive Pronominalisierung auf Grund der Identität mit dem Subjekt des eingebetteten Satzes vorgenommen (*с собой*), in (22) ist wegen Nichtidentität bloße anaphorische Pronominalisierung (*Серпилину* → *ему*) erfolgt. Die genaueren Bedingungen für die den üblichen Regularitäten zuwiderlaufende[40] reflexive Pronominalisierung sind keineswegs klar. Es scheint jedoch gewiß, daß es sich um Verbal- oder Objektkomplemente mit infinitivischer Formierung handeln muß und natürlich um Verben, deren Subjekt mit ihrem Objekts-nomen nicht identisch ist [vgl. (25)]. Offensichtlich ist die reflexive Form nicht an-gängig, wenn der eingebettete Satz durch Konjunktion eingeleitet wird. Will man den außergewöhnlichen Sachverhalt mit Hilfe der 'Merkmalhaftigkeit' reflektieren, könnte sich eine Charakterisierung, etwa [m reflexiv-anaphorisch], nur auf die Transforma-tionsregeln beziehen, die reflexive Pronominalisierungen zyklisch vollzieht, und diese Regeln in besonderer Weise modifizieren: Hinsichtlich der Norm zyklischer Anwen-dung innerhalb von Satzgrenzen. Die Modifikation hebt die Anwendung innerhalb der Satzgrenze(n) der Tiefenstruktur auf und weist ihr einen anderen Anwendungs-bereich zu.

(26)   *Борис заставил Бориса* (*ждать*)

(26) bietet den normalen (als Endkette veranschaulichten) Struktur-index für die reflexive Pronominalisierung. Aber sie würde durch [m reflexiv-anaphorisch] ver-hindert. Der Satz

(27)   *Борис заставил себя ждать*

entsteht nicht aus (26), sondern aus

(28)   *Борис заставил кого-то ждать Бориса*

Dies ist gerade die Voraussetzung der Struktur des Satzes (25). Somit würde das Merkmal [m reflexiv-anaphorisch] bei einem Verbum bedeuten, daß Identität mit SEINEM Subjekt, nicht mit dem des Einbettungssatzes, also des Satzes, zu dem das zu pronominalisierende Nomen gehört, Grundlage der reflexiven Pronominalisierung wird.[41]

Es ist aber ungewiß, ob Störungen der Anwendungsnormen von Transformations-regeln gewissen Verallgemeinerungen zugänglich sind, und mit den Begriffen 'merk-malhaltig' und 'merkmallos' sinnvoll charakterisiert werden können.

6.4. Zahlreiche Möglichkeiten, das Begriffspaar der Markiertheit anzuwenden, erscheinen demgegenüber nicht als zweifelhaft. Von den vielen Einzelfällen in bezug auf das Russische sei noch einer angeführt: Die Verba, die direktes (Akkusativ) Objekt aufweisen, werden zweckmäßig durch [m passiv] charakterisiert, wenn sie nicht von der Passivtransformation erfaßt werden können:

[40]   Vgl. R.B.Lees, E.S.Klima, "Rules for English Pronominalization", *Lg.*, 39 1 (1963).
[41]   Vgl. Verf., "On Pronominalization in Slavic Languages" (im Druck).

(w) $[m\ passiv] \rightarrow [-passiv] \, / \begin{bmatrix} +\underline{\quad}Akkusativ \\ \underline{\hspace{3cm}} \end{bmatrix}$

Verba, die kein direktes (Akkusativ) Objekt haben, werden als [m passiv] charakterisiert, wenn sie von der Passivtransformation betroffen werden.

(x) $[m\ passiv] \rightarrow [+\ passiv] \, / \begin{bmatrix} -\underline{\quad}Akkusativ \\ \underline{\hspace{3cm}} \end{bmatrix}$

$[m\ passiv] \rightarrow [\sim\alpha\ passiv] \, / \begin{bmatrix} \alpha\underline{\quad}Akkusativ \\ \underline{\hspace{3cm}} \end{bmatrix}$

7. Die Versuche zur Anwendung des Begriffspaares 'merkmalhaltig' und 'merkmallos', die hier angestellt wurden, haben provisorischen, manchmal nur illustrativen Charakter. Viele Fragen bleiben offen, wenn auch die grundsätzliche Möglichkeit und Zweckmäßigkeit der Verwendung dieser Begriffe nicht mehr als fragwürdig zu erscheinen braucht. Kaum in Zweifel zu ziehen ist auch, daß die Kennzeichen m und u nicht nur für die im Lexikon fixierten Merkmale zutreffende Charakterisierung sind. Von den im Abschnitt 0.1. gestellten Fragen konnten die ersten drei nicht klar beantwortet, jedoch vielleicht einer Antwort nähergebracht werden. Die Markierungshypothese, wie sie hier illustriert wurde, sollte weiter erprobt werden, um ihr schließlich einen gesicherten theoretischen Status anweisen zu können, der auch ihre Gültigkeit in den linguistischen Ebenen klarstellt. Es erscheint mir sicher, daß diese Hypothese Aspekte substantieller und auch formaler Universalien zeigt. Völlig unklar bleibt weiterhin die entscheidende theoretische Frage der Prädiktabilität der Charakterisierung von Merkmalen als 'merkmalhaltig' oder 'merkmallos' [Frage (4) in 0.1.].

SANFORD A. SCHANE

PHONOLOGICAL AND MORPHOLOGICAL
MARKEDNESS

The notion of markedness as developed with Praguian phonology, and more recently
within generative phonology, allows phonological segments to be differentiated by
means of the presence or absence of a particular phonological feature.[1] For example,
two segments, such as /p/ and /b/, may differ only to the extent that the former is
UNMARKED for voicing, whereas the latter is MARKED for this feature. Implicit in the
notion of markedness is the assumption that the unmarked member represents the
less complex or normal state. On the other hand, to mark a segment for a feature is to
impose something additional on that segment. Thus, voicelessness is the normal state
for obstruents, and to obtain voiced obstruents, voicing is a feature which must be
added.

Among related segments which differ in markedness, it has been noted that the
unmarked member generally has a higher frequency of occurrence. Also, it is the
unmarked member which is most likely to occur first in the acquisition of language
and to be found in the phonological systems of a wide variety of languages.[2] Finally,
it is the unmarked member which often appears in neutralized environments — for
example, the occurrence of voiceless obstruents in word final position in Russian.

The unmarked member may play a dual role. In those environments where there
is a contrast — for example, whenever in a particular environment both /p/ and /b/
can occur — the unmarked segment, *e.g.* /p/, is opposed to the marked segment, *e.g.*
/b/. In such cases, the absence of a feature is directly in opposition to its presence.
This type of opposition is analogous to the + or − values attached to features in a
binary system, where, for example, /p/ would be indicated as [− voiced] whereas /b/
would be indicated as [+ voiced]. However, in those environments in which neutralization takes place, and where the neutralized segment is represented as unmarked,

[1] For discussion and reference, see N.S.Troubetzkoy, *Principes de Phonologie* (Paris, Klincksieck,
1949), pp. 80-87, 246-260; N. Chomsky and M. Halle, *Sound Pattern of English* (New York, Harper-
Row, 1968).
[2] Concerning the acquisition of phonological segments, see R.Jakobson, "Kindersprache, Aphasie,
und allgemeine Lautgesetze", *Selected Writings I* (The Hague, Mouton, 1962), pp. 328-401; also "Les
Lois Phoniques du Langage Enfantin", pp. 317-327.

the unmarked feature is not found in opposition to its marked counterpart, but rather it represents the absence of any phonological opposition. Although the neutralized unmarked feature may nonetheless still represent the absence of a particular feature, the absence of this feature is no longer opposed to its presence. In a sense, this situation is analogous to the use of blanks or zeros in the binary system. Thus, the unmarked member may, in some environments, be in contrast with, or be opposed to, the marked member, while in other environments, no such contrast or opposition is found, and instead, the unmarked member represents merely the neutralized or non-contrastive state.[3]

In phonological representations, instead of having matrices of distinctive features containing pluses and minuses, the matrices can contain M's and U's, for marked and unmarked respectively. Yet, it is important to understand how the notion of markedness differs from that of distinctiveness, and to realize that the use of M's and U's is not just a notational variant for pluses and minuses. The marked segment is phonologically more complex since it is equivalent to the unmarked segment plus something additional. In this system, /d/, for example, is considered to be more complex than /t/. In the binary system, on the other hand, segments, such as voiceless and voiced, are treated as being of equal complexity. They are opposed to each other as opposite values of a given attribute. In evaluating the number of features utilized in a matrix, pluses and minuses are counted equally. However, in the system of markedness only M's are counted in determining complexity. This means that /t/ and /d/ would not be of equal complexity, but rather /d/ would be evaluated as more complex since it contains an M for voicing, which is otherwise unmarked for /t/.

Having established some preliminary notions concerning the nature of markedness in phonology, I should now like to extend the idea of markedness to the morphological and syntactic-semantic aspects of language. The majority of examples will be drawn from French.[4]

As for the morphological forms of adjectives in French, they can be either masculine or feminine, and either singular or plural. Before investigating the morphosyntactic

[3] To be sure, the phonetic realization in the position of neutralization may be intermediate between that exibited elsewhere by the terms entering into the opposition. In such cases it may happen that more than one feature is being neutralized. To cite an example from Troubetzkoy (p. 168), in English there are contrasting pairs of stops at the same point of articulation, the contrast being between tense voiceless and lax voiced. However, after /s/ this opposition is neutralized, the neutralized segment being lax and unvoiced. Although the neutralized segment is phonetically intermediate between the two terms of the opposition, it is nonetheless still the unmarked segment *par excellence*; viz., the tense voiceless stop is unmarked for voicing but marked for tenseness; the lax voiced stop is marked for voicing but unmarked for tenseness; whereas the stop after /s/ is unmarked for both voicing and tenseness. Although two features are involved, the features are not independent. Given a value for either one of the features, the value for the other feature is, of course, predictable.

[4] I have not had the opportunity to explore in any depth how this notion of morphological markedness could be extended to other languages. The French examples are particularly revealing since what is morphologically more complex is also generally so phonologically.

aspects of French adjectives, it will be necessary to consider their morphological and phonological structure in greater detail.[5]

A masculine adjective such as *petit* has two allomorphs — /pəti/ and /pətit/ — the former occurring before words beginning with a consonant sound, the latter before words beginning with a vowel sound; *e.g. petit garçon* /pəti garsõ/ 'little boy' versus *petit ami* /pətit ami/ 'little friend'. If we set up the prevocalic form (*i.e.*, the form of the adjective which terminates in a consonant) as the BASIC or UNDERLYING form, then we can derive the variant which terminates in a vowel if there is a rule which deletes a final consonant whenever the following word also begins with a consonant. In this way, the masculine singular adjective always has a consistent underlying representation — *e.g.* |pətit#ami#| and |pətit#garsõ#|. The latter is then converted to /pəti garsõ/ by the rule which deletes final consonants before other consonants.[6]

In the masculine plural one finds the forms /pəti/ and /pətiz/, the former occurring before words beginning with a consonant sound, the latter before words beginning with a vowel sound — *e.g., petits garçons* /pəti garsõ/ 'little boys' versus *petits amis* /pətiz ami/ 'little friends'. On the basis of the prevocalic form, if we set up |z| as the mark of the plural morpheme and continue to represent the underlying form of an adjective such as *petit* with the same representation as was established for the singular — *i.e.* |pətit|, the plural then being |pətit+z#| — we can account for both variants of the masculine plural adjective with only a slight modification of the consonant deletion rule. We shall extend the generality of this rule by applying it to morpheme final consonants as well as to word final consonants. With this extension, the underlying |t| and |z| of |pətit+z#garsõ#|[7] will be deleted, yielding /pəti garsõ/: in the underlying form the final |t| of |pətit+z#| is followed by a boundary — the morpheme boundary — plus a consonantal segment (i.e. the plural |z|); the |z| also is followed by a boundary — the word boundary — plus a consonantal segment (i.e. the initial consonant of |garsõ#|). As for the underlying |pətit+z#ami#|, only the final |t| of |pətit+z#| will be deleted, since this is the only consonant followed by a boundary plus another consonant.

In the feminine singular, the final |t| of |pətit| is not deleted — *e.g. petite fille* /pətit fij/ 'little girl' and *petite amie* /pətit ami/ 'little friend'. Since the |t| appears through-

---

[5] For a detailed analysis of the adjective paradigm from the point of view of generative phonology, see S. A. Schane, *French Phonology and Morphology* (Cambridge, Mass., M.I.T. Press, 1968).
[6] Phonetic representations are given between diagonal bars whereas underlying phonological representations are given between vertical bars. In underlying representations + indicates morpheme boundary and # indicates word boundary. In actuality nasalized vowels and schwa would not appear in underlying representations, the former being derived from sequences of oral vowel plus nasal consonant, the latter from various underlying vowels. Since these details are not relevant for the problems considered here, I have chosen for ease of exposition to indicate nasalized vowels and schwas in the underlying phonological representations. For a detailed treatment on the source of French vowels, see S. A. Schane, *French Phonology and Morphology*, Chapter 2.
[7] The plural marker |z| also occurs with plural nouns; it would be deleted by a rule which truncates word final consonants in phrase final position. I have not indicated the plural marker in nouns since it is not crucial for the problems considered here.

out the paradigm of the feminine, this segment must be followed by a vowel, which protects it from deletion. (Recall that morpheme or word final consonants are deleted only when the following morpheme begins with a consonant.) The vowel in the underlying representation of the feminine is the morpheme which indicates feminine gender in adjectives, represented phonologically as schwa — that is, the French 'e muet': — e.g., |pətit+ə#fij#| and |pətit+ə#ami#|. It is the feminine schwa which protects the stem final consonant from deletion. However, since the schwa does not usually appear in derived forms, it may subsequently be deleted — but, of course, only after the rule for consonant deletion has been applied.[8]

The derivations of the feminine plural forms /pətit/ and /pətitz/ — e.g., *petites filles* /pətit fij/ 'little girls' versus *petites amies* /pətitz ami/ 'little friends' — are straightforward. The underlying representations are |pətit+ə+z#fij#| and |pətit+ə+z#ami#| respectively. In the former, the plural |z| is deleted before the following consonantal segment; the feminine schwa may then subsequently be deleted. In the latter, the consonants are not deleted since they are not followed by other consonants; the feminine schwa may, of course, subsequently be deleted.

Underlying representations exhibit structural regularities which are not necessarily apparent in the derived phonetic forms. Thus, in the preceding examples, the morpheme {petit} has a consistent underlying representation — i.e., |pətit| — wherever it occurs; similarly, in the underlying structure, the plural morpheme is a constituent of all plural forms, and the feminine morpheme is a constituent of all feminine forms, even though these morphemes may not always be realized phonetically.[9] The abstract or underlying form is related to the concrete or derived form by rules such as the rules for consonant deletion and schwa deletion. The rules serve to explain the particular variants which appear.

In the underlying representation, the masculine singular is represented simply as the STEM OR BASE form of the adjective — there is no overt marker for masculine gender or for singular number. The masculine plural is represented as stem plus plural morpheme — again there is no overt marker for gender but there is a marker for number. The feminine singular is represented as stem plus feminine morpheme — like the masculine singular, there is no overt marker for number, but unlike the masculine singular, the feminine singular does have a marker for gender. The feminine plural is represented as stem plus feminine morpheme plus plural morpheme. It has markers for both gender and number.

Considering the morphological system in terms of markedness, we can say that the French adjective has the following structure: the masculine singular is UNMARKED FOR BOTH GENDER AND NUMBER; the feminine singular is MARKED FOR GENDER but

---

[8] There are other structural reasons, in addition to the adjective morphology, for positing underlying schwas in French, even thought the schwas are not always phonetically realized. See S. A. Schane, "On the Abstract Character of French 'E Muet'", *Glossa* 2 (1968).

[9] In the case of adjectives, the standard French orthography clearly reveals the morphological structure. Our underlying representations are practically identical to the orthography.

UNMARKED FOR NUMBER; the masculine plural is UNMARKED FOR GENDER but MARKED FOR NUMBER; and the feminine plural is MARKED FOR BOTH GENDER AND NUMBER.

Within phonology, we have seen that the unmarked member is considered to be more basic, more simple; the marked member, on the other hand, entails the presence of an additional feature. Within morphology, we can note the same phenomenon. The masculine singular is the most basic form, whereas the plural or the feminine is phonologically equivalent to the masculine singular plus something else — *i.e.*, the plural morpheme and/or the feminine morpheme.[10] In phonology, the unmarked member may also function as a neutralized segment, which, in that particular environment, is not in contrast with the marked segment. In order to see how neutralization or noncontrast applies to morphological markedness, it is necessary to consider the syntactic and semantic aspects of gender and number.

Adjectives in French agree with the nouns they modify in gender and number. Consider the following two forms.

> *Le garçon est petit*   (The boy is small)
> *La fille est petite*   (The girl is small)

Here, unmarked gender is in direct opposition with marked gender. The form of the adjective reveals whether the quality of 'smallness' is attributed to an entity which is grammatically masculine or to one which is grammatically feminine.

A similar situation holds for the following pair.

> *Le garçon est petit*   (The boy is small)
> *Les garçons sont petits*   (The boys are small)

Here, unmarked number is in direct opposition with marked number. The form of the adjective reveals whether the quality of 'smallness' is attributed to an entity which is grammatically singular or to one which is grammatically plural.

A plural adjective must be used with coordinate singular noun phrases.

> *Le garçon et son père sont petits*   (The boy and his father are small)

Here, marked number is to be expected, since the quality of 'smallness' is attributed to more than one entity. This is reflected in the form which the adjective takes.

If both of the coordinate noun phrases are feminine, then the adjective is feminine plural.

> *La fille et sa mère sont petites*   (The girl and her mother are small)

Marked gender and marked number are both to be expected, since the quality of 'smallness' is attributed to more than one entity, both of which are grammatically feminine.

---

[10]   Just as the masculine singular adjective is the form morphologically unmarked for gender and number, within the verb conjugation it is the present tense which is morphologically unmarked for tense. Note that it is the present which is used for generic statements; *e.g., J'aime les pommes* 'I like apples'; *La terre est ronde* 'The earth is round'.

The interesting case is where one coordinate member is masculine and the other one is feminine. The adjective is then masculine plural.

Le garçon et la fille sont petits   (The boy and the girl are small)

Although, morphologically, the form of the adjective is masculine, it is not the case that there is a uniquely masculine attribution, since 'smallness' is, in fact, attributed to a feminine entity as well as to a masculine one. Hence, in this environment the adjective DOES NOT reflect a masculine-feminine distinction, but only a plural one. In other words, the masculine-feminine contrast has become neutralized in this environment. What is significant is that THE NEUTRALIZED FORM IS EQUIVALENT TO THE MORPHOLOGICALLY UNMARKED FORM. Although this form looks like a masculine plural on the surface, it is not to be regarded as masculine in its function. This ambivalent behavior of the 'masculine plural' — that is, that at times it modifies nouns which are uniquely masculine, and at other times it modifies nouns of both genders — has a natural explanation within a theory of markedness. It is the UNMARKED member which in some environments is in contrast with the marked member, whereas in other environments, it is not in contrast, but instead represents the neutralized state.

The importance of environment in determining the function of the unmarked member is borne out by the next two examples.

Les Américains sont sérieux   (Americans are serious)

Here the nounal adjective *Américains*, although it is morphologically masculine plural, is not so semantically, since what is claimed here is that all Americans, both male and female, are serious. Note the different interpretation imposed on this same sentence in another context.

Les Américaines sont frivoles, mais les Américains sont sérieux

(American women are frivolous, but American men are serious)
Here the form *Américains* can only mean American men, since it has been placed in contrast with the feminine *Américaines*. That is, whenever the form which is morphologically unmarked for gender (*e.g.*, *Américains*) is contrasted with a form morphologically marked for gender (*e.g.*, *Américaines*), the semantic interpretation of unmarked gender is 'masculine', since it is opposed semantically to the marked gender, whose interpretation is always 'feminine'. However, when the unmarked gender is not opposed to the marked gender, then the semantic interpretation of the unmarked gender may be neutralized, *i.e.*, 'mixed' gender.[11]

---

[11] The use of the 'masculine plural' for mixed gender is common in all the Romance languages including Latin. In Spanish this device is used heavily in kinship terms: *e.g.*, *padre* 'father', *madre* 'mother', *padres* 'parents'; *hermano* 'brother', *hermana* 'sister', *hermanos* 'brothers' or 'brothers and sisters'; *tío* 'uncle', *tía* 'aunt', *tíos* 'uncles' or 'uncles and aunts'; *etc.* In Spanish, as in French, the plural is phonologically marked whereas the singular is not: *tío* 'uncle' *vs.* *tíos* 'uncles', or *tía* 'aunt' *vs.* *tías* 'aunts'. However, unlike French, the masculine and feminine seem to be equally complex phonologically — at least on the surface, where the masculine ending is usually -*o* and the feminine one is -*a*. A deeper analysis might indicate, however, that the feminine ought to be |tío + a|; the |o|

This type of neutralization in the plural is also exhibited by the third person personal pronouns when they are anaphoric, that is, when they refer back to a single noun phrase or a coordinate one.[12]

> *Voilà Jean. Il est intelligent*
>   (There is John. He is intelligent)
> *Voilà Marie. Elle est intelligente*
>   (There is Mary. She is intelligent)
> *Voilà Jean et George. Ils sont intelligents*
>   (There are John and George. They are intelligent)
> *Voilà Marie et Susanne. Elles sont intelligentes*
>   (There are Marie and Susan. They are intelligent)
> *Voilà Jean et Marie. Ils sont intelligents*
>   (There are John and Mary. They are intelligent)

There is no inherent logical reason for the masculine plural form to be used for 'mixed' gender. (I exclude from consideration such extralinguistic explanations as the patriarchic nature of Indoeuropean society.) Granted that a SINGLE plural form of the adjective is to be used with 'mixed' gender, it is just as reasonable for the feminine to be employed for this purpose as for the masculine. After all, the feminine plural in French at least has the advantage of being morphologically richer. However, when the theory of markedness is brought into the picture we can then understand why the feminine plural form would be the less desirable one. The fact that the feminine plural is morphologically richer means that it is morphologically more complex. Yet, as we have seen, in cases of neutralization there is a tendency for the less complex, rather than the more complex, of the forms to become the surface

---

is then deleted before the vowel of the feminine ending. Such a deletion rule is independently needed in any case. Certain surface forms, however, show that the masculine is phonologically less complex: e.g., *Inglés* 'Englishman', *Inglesa* 'English woman'; *Francés* 'Frenchman', *Francesa* 'French woman'. It remains to determine the extent to which there is a relation between morphological markedness and phonological complexity. French is particularly interesting in that there is a very evident correlation.

[12]   Whenever subjects of 'mixed' person are coordinated, the verb, which agrees in number with the subject, is, of course, plural in form. However, the particular ending which the verb takes will depend on the persons being coordinated. If a first person pronoun is present the verb form will be in the first person; if a first person pronoun is not present but a second person pronoun is, then the verb form will be in the second person; only if all subjects are third person will the verb be in the third person.

Toi et moi (*nous*) *partons*	'You and I are leaving'
Jean et moi (*nous*) *partons*	'John and I are leaving'
Jean et toi (*vous*) *partez*	'John and you are leaving'
Jean et Marie partent	'John and Mary are leaving'

This might suggest that in addition to markedness operating with the gender and number systems, it also functions in the person system. These examples would lead one to suspect that the first person should be the least marked form. However, the evidence is scant. Also there is no correlation here between morphological complexity and the complexity of the phonological manifestations.

realization. An explanation is then available for the appearance of the masculine plural with 'mixed' gender — of the two possible plural forms which can occur in French it is the less complex.

The notion of markedness explains why interrogative and indefinite pronouns APPEAR to be masculine singular in French (and in most other languages).

Qui est heureux?	(Who is happy?)
Qu'est-ce qui est beau?	(What is beautiful?)
Quelqu'un est heureux	(Someone is happy)
Quelque chose est beau	(Something is beautiful)
Personne n'est heureux	(No one is happy)
Rien n'est beau	(Nothing is beautiful)

Syntactically, an interrogative pronoun such as *qui* is masculine singular since the adjective must agree with it. Yet, semantically, there is no basis for maintaining that *qui* is masculine singular. If *qui* were really masculine singular, it should be the case that anyone answering the question would be required to supply the name of a masculine singular individual. But this, of course, is false, since in answer to the question *qui est heureux?*, one is perfectly free to supply the name of a feminine individual or even of any number of individuals of either or both genders. Since the question may elicit either gender or number, the interrogative word itself must be neutral — that is, it is unmarked for gender and for number. Since it is unmarked, the adjective which agrees with it superficially resembles — although it does not function like — the masculine singular.

The fact that INDEFINITE PRONOUNS MUST BE UNMARKED explains the nonoccurrence of *quelqu'une* 'feminine someone' as opposed to *quelqu'un* 'someone'. It also explains why forms such as *quelque chose* 'something' and the negative *personne* 'no one' — composed of lexical items which, when they function as nouns, are feminine, *i.e.*, *une chose* 'a thing', *une personne* 'a person' — appear to be masculine when indefinite.

Quelque chose est beau	(Something is beautiful)
Cette chose est belle	(That thing is beautiful)
Personne n'est heureux	(No one is happy)
Cette personne est heureuse	(That person is happy)

Finally, we note that unmarked gender and number are uniquely used with impersonal pronouns and adjectives.

Il fait beau	(It's nice weather)
Il est certain qu'il va pleuvoir	(It is certain that it is going to rain)
C'est certain	(It's certain)
C'est bon	(That's good)

In these examples the pronoun *il* is not an anaphoric pronoun; that is, it does not refer back to any noun phrase with which it must agree in gender and number.

The adjectives *certain* and *bon* are the predicates of the impersonal pronouns *il* and *ce*. These pronouns are functioning here as neuters. However, in French there do not exist special neuter forms for the personal pronouns and the adjectives. Morphologically, French has only marked and unmarked gender. It is then the unmarked form which once again is used for these neuters. Thus the semantic interpretation of *unmarked* may also be 'neither masculine or feminine'.

A. SCHWARTZ

ON INTERPRETING NOMINALIZATIONS

The title of this paper is an unfortunate one in a few respects: the topic really goes much beyond the area of nominalizations; the term 'nominalization', at least for a transformational audience, has a firm connection with Lees' work (1960), and will tend to be understood in the way the concept was explicated in that monograph; the term is, I believe, quite misleading, and prejudices any analysis of the phenomena usually covered by it. I will therefore, for the remainder of this paper, try to avoid use of the term, although the circumlocutions pressed into service will, at times, be more ungainly than the word itself.

The topic, broadly conceived, is that of derivational morphology. This phenomenon is sufficiently widespread so that we can assume the problems discussed here are not peculiar to English, Germanic, or Indo European. Many languages manifest root morphemes that appear in various functions with various affixes: the verbal form might convey a 'causative' or 'iterative' or 'privative' sense; the nominal form might convey the sense of an 'abstract quality' or the 'agency of an action' or the 'thing performed', and so on. Very often it is not clear whether the root can be assigned to a lexical category; but even if most of the dictionary entries were to be unclassifiable, in this sense, the problem would not be affected — the root, being that abstraction we take from varying surface forms to serve as a basis for derivatives, would still be susceptible to modification, and these modifications, in turn, modifiable.

It may also be the case that when a base form appears in a sentence 'as something else' it may or may not require any morphological sign (*e.g.*, the verb *tree*, the noun *walk*, etc.). We might also note that the form-class of the root need not change when it appears 'as something else': so, the nouns *sister* and *man* appear in the nouns *sisterhood* and *manhood*; the adjectives *simple* and *long* appear in the adjectives *simplistic* and *longish*; the verbs *look*, *think*, and *vary* appear in the verbs *overlook*, *rethink*, *co-vary*.[1] Finally, we should observe that some affixes allow others to attach

---

[1] At first glance, such verbs as *overlook*, *rethink*, and *co-vary* do not seem to be instances of the same process as, say, forms like *simplify* or *darken*. However, when one considers the specifics of affixation, particles like *co-* and *-ify* demand the same kind of information and in the same way.

(*tree + less + ness*) while others do not (**dark + ness + less*); and in some cases, the process can go on and on, the same affixes recurring: *con + tain + er + ize + er + ...*; *nat + tion + al + ize + (a)tion + ...*; *etc.*

When we say that the base form re-appears in the same form-class, we mean that the secondary or complex form shows the same set of co-occurrence relations as the root: thus, if *think* admits a following complement (say, *the problem*) and may be preceded by a modal (say, *would*), so does *rethink*; if *sister* can be preceded by *the* and followed by *that is least popular*, so can *sisterhood*; if *simple* appears in a construction *as simple as...*, so can *simplistic*; *etc.*[2] Moreover, the affix may determine other properties of the secondary form: thus, all nouns ending in *-hād* in Old English are masculine in gender, and are treated exactly as basic masculine nouns are. The masculine gender of a noun in *-hād* has no reference to the inherent gender of the root that appears in the complex form: *e.g.*, *wīf* 'woman, wife' is a neuter noun, but *wīf-hād* 'womanhood' is masculine. Moreover, if a base form must have, in its lexical characterization, some special information (with regard to, say, plural formation; or ablaut series; *etc.*), this information is typically rendered unnecessary if the base form appears in a secondary formation: thus, although *mann* 'man, person' requires some indication of the kind of plural suffix it should admit in order to realize as the plural *menn*, the information required to account for this particular form of the root is not needed for the secondary form *mannhād* since the form *mennhād never occurs; *settan* 'to set, establish' is a weak verb, but this requirement of a dental suffix as a sign of the preterite has no relevance for the noun *set + l* 'seat, throne'. To all intents and purposes, then, such information may be erased when the root enters into its secondary form. But if *man* (say, in *manly*) is shorn of its syntactic and/or morphological idiosyncrasies, and *man + XXX* may or may not show co-occurrence relations typical of the form-class 'noun', what is left of the 'noun' in *man* when it appears in forms like *manhood, mannish, manikin, mankind, manliness, etc.*? It does not seem too extravagant to observe that what we may call the 'semantic' (and, of course, the phonological) content of the form is what remains, for the most part.

I have taken some time to repeat what is familiar and obvious simply to re-establish the facts in an un-biassed manner. It seems to me we must accept as the reality here the fact that while *tree* may appear as the complement to *climb* or *plant* or *prune*, the form *treeless* may not; and that the complete loss of the inherent syntactic character of the root is the typical situation. It must be added that with the acquired function, there is some new element of meaning, and that this increment will be carried over into further formations. So, from *nerve*, there is *nerv + y*, *nerv + ous*, *nerve + less*; and these bear semantic and phonological resemblance to *nerviness*, *nervousness*, and *nervelessness*, respectively. As with the root and its secondary form, the syntactic

---

[2]   Some interesting qualifications should be made here (the peculiarity of *very toothless*; *as longish as...*; *rethink over again*; *manhoods*; *etc.*), but I regard these as semantic qualifications and of independent interest.

character of *-ous*, *-less*, *etc.* is nullified by the dominant function of *-ness*. 'Dominant function', in fact, has to be understood precisely as the category node given by the base expansion rules. One can imagine redundancy rules (*e.g.*, N → [± no], [± def]) which would distribute over the class *N* of the language those values of number and definiteness which, in part, define the notion 'noun' for that language. Such rules can be visualized as coming last in the base, and as supplementing the feature-composition of any one particular form with these features common to the form-class. Notice that these redundancies are relevant to FUNCTION, and so do not appear (typically) in the lexicon.

An adequate description of this phenomenon must, then, involve the syntactic character of the 'surface' form (the dominating function), laid over the semantic increments of 'prior' formations. It is not quite true to limit the residue to 'semantics' since the information of form-class is also retained: in, for example, *deliberateness*, from the verb *de + liber + âte* ⇒ the adjective *de + liber + ăte*, the adjectival sense and form are present in the nominal function, even though it has no syntactic value. So, it seems as if the bracketing is not superfluous: there is, in a sense, a 'derivation' here — [$_N$[$_A$[$_V$*de + liber + ate*]]*ness*]. Traces of 'past performance' persist, and one has the same dual sense of 'deep' and 'surface' structure as with any composition.

I think it is easy to underestimate the latent significance of the process. One might have quite reasonably supposed that natural language, because of memory limitations, would indeed extend its stock of primitives by some such 'transference' of meaning and function (roughly, 'metaphorical'). But it would have been unreasonable to imagine that this process could, in any one formation, go beyond the first step. That is, *mud* functioning in some role as modifier is not an exorbitant request. But that these derived forms should then become the basis for further development is indeed surprising. And even more surprising is the retention of the SUCCESSION of these 'past performances' in the surface form. In the phrase, *a muddying encounter*, the word *muddying* is adjectival, but there is a clear sense that by stripping away the *-ing*, one gets at the verb (*to*) *muddy*, and that this verb is causative in meaning and is somehow a derivative of the adjective *muddy*, and finally that by stripping away the *-y*, one arrives at the root noun *mud*. A more plausible invention would have been the 'obliteration of the past' with each increment, so that, while perhaps there are morphological traces of substrata, the 'past' is obscure — there may or may not have been adjectives and verbs involved in the formation of *muddying*: all we know 'at this point' is that the form means 'that which soils'. But in fact, such masking would have defeated the attempt to maximize the limited stock of primes; and, as in normal sentence formation, the information is sequential and recoverable: *i.e.*, 'regular'.

Now, what has been sketched up to this point is, as I see it, the typical situation. There is a development out of this simplest process, however, in which some of the complement structure of the root is retained. So, the root *tend* may function as a verb, and admit various prefixes: *pre-*, *sub-*, *ex-*, *etc.* One such prefix is *ad-*, which after assimilation yields *attend*; and this verb in one of its uses in Modern English must appear with the preposition/particle *to*:

> *he attended to all the details*

This verb, like many others, appears in an adjectival function (with the affix *-ive*): *attend+ive*. But its basic capacity to govern, let us say, the *to*-case persists:

> *he was attentive to their wives*

Even so, this persistence of the verbal character into adjectival form and function is still not too unusual: many adjectives, base included, admit noun complements — so that it is not as if a 'transitive' adjective were an anomaly. However, when we also find structures like *attentiveness to detail, attentiveness to women, etc.*, where the adjunct to the noun *attentiveness* still shows the primitive nature of *attend*, we confront the real problem of derivational morphology: the accommodation of derived constituent structure (surface bracketing) to basic complement structure (root properties).

I do not believe these relationships (*attend to* : *attend+ive to* : *attend+ive+ness to*) can be handled in a generative-transformational way. Consider the simpler case of *toothless* : *without (a) tooth*. One can observe a considerable semantic and distributional match between N + *less* and *without* + N:

she was hopeless	*she was without hope*
it was useless	*it was without use*
the affair was loveless	*the affair was without love*
they were penniless	*they were without a penny*
they were childless	*they were without (a) child*
the plan was senseless	*the plan was without sense*
etc.	*etc.*

On the basis of co-occurrence relations, a transformational statement can be posited — 'transformational' in Harris' sense, where 'co-occurrence relation' depends largely on selectional restrictions. For example, in Harris (1957: 330, 337), we find a transformational relation proposed for *Mary has a fate* and *Mary's fate*, partly on the basis of paraphrase, but mostly on the basis of the selectional features of *Mary, have*, and *fate*. (This same relation is proposed in Smith (1964: 44-5) and in Katz and Postal (1964: 137), and would, I assume, lead to accepting *have no N* as a third member of the N + *less* : *without* N correspondence since the 'have' relation can be viewed as equivalent to the 'be + with'.) Note that in Harris' work, a transformation is given in linear terms, and so is typically symmetrical. Transformational in the generative sense involves dominance relations, and is asymmetrical throughout, as is emphasized in Chomsky (1964: 83, n. 29). A generative statement of the active-passive relation [as for example in Chomsky (1962: 136)] is superficially like Harris' (1957: 325); but the requirement that a (generative) transformation provide derived constituent structure, *i.e.*, proper bracketing (= dominance relations) for subsequent operations

— both syntactic and phonological — is the critical difference. It is not difficult to formulate a rule that will take *be with + NEG N* to *be N + less*; the problem is to account for the subsequent unitary character of *so careless, so useless, etc.*, as is manifest in the WH-fronting of such complexes (*how careless, how useless, etc.*).[3]

How then may we provide, within the generative framework, for (1) the sense of 'derivation' discernible in *muddying*; and (2) the problem of root complement structure that appears in surface bracketing? Consider, like *muddying*, the form *ocean-going* which can function as an adjunct to a noun: *ocean-going vessel*. It is a complex form, obviously, and reflects the same relation we find in the 'ordinary' predication *go (on) ocean*, that is, an intransitive verb of motion followed by a directional noun complement (*cf.* the transitive relation in *grave-digging*, the copulative relation in *sick-looking*, and so on). We are led to suppose, then, that while *muddying* reflects the fact that a verb (*to muddy*) can function as an adjective (*muddy + ing*), that an adjective (*muddy*) can function as a verb (causative *muddy*), and that a noun (*mud*) can function as an adjective (*mud + y*), the form *ocean-going* indicates that a verb phrase may also function as an adjective: *to muddy* is to *muddying* as *go + ocean* is to *ocean + going*. I have emphasized the relation 'as a' in order to recall the original motivation behind the positing of phrase-structure rules. A rule like NP → (D) N (S) is a compact expression of the fact that sequences of strings like *Joe*; *the boy*; *the correct amount*; *people who lie*; *etc.* behave similarly, and can be manipulated as units if we hypothesize that every one, however simple or complex, can be identified 'as an' NP.

While it is true enough that the rule is a compression of a number of statements (*e.g.*, NP → D N; NP → N S; *etc.*), one of the interesting questions that arises from such a conception is whether the expansion NP → N is really an 'expansion' since

(1)

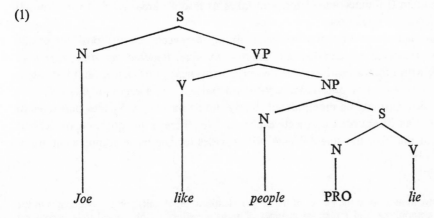

---

[3] To account for the different bonds between the term of degree and *without + N* before and after transformation, one would have to revamp linguistic theory in the direction of particles and valences: the constellation now abbreviated as *A* would have a value that required incorporation of degree-modifiers; the constellation now abbreviated as *N* would not, but would require expression of object-definiteness (*e.g.*, degrees of foolishness *vs.* the state of being a fool).

there is no question of multiple constituency (henceforth, by 'branching' I mean multiple branching). In recent work, I have adopted the constraint that phrasal nodes that do not branch are, by convention, erased [the idea is an extension of Ross (1965), and was suggested to me by M. Freeman]. This metarule operates throughout a derivation, both on base expansion and on transformational output. The base representation for the sentence *Joe likes people who lie* would then be as in (A), and illustrates both V and VP, N and NP.[4]

In the formalization of a notion like 'a verb can function as an adjective' as well as the notion 'a verb phrase can function as an adjective', the rule A → VP, given the convention on phrase-node erasure, appears to be an adequate expression of both, and would lead to configurations like

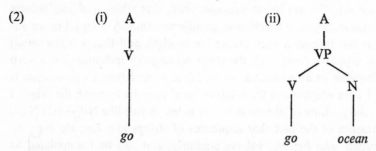

(2)   (i)   A   (ii)   A
                  | |
                  V   VP
                                                  / \
                                                 V   N
                  | | |
                 go   *go* *ocean*

which are then 'legitimized' by an adjectival affix (*e.g.*, *-ing*). [It is in this sense that I said at the outset that 'nominalization' is misleading: one can view it either as a morphological process that 'permits' (is anterior to) the use of some form as a noun; or, one can view it as an expression of the use, a (convenient but not obligatory) signal of the transferred function.] This formulation still leaves the re-ordering of constituents in (ii) unaccounted for, and takes us into an area which, to my knowledge, is relatively unexplored.

The re-ordering, at first glance, seems simply a reversal of the position of the segments. However, expressions like *salt-free, tax-free, lint-free, rent-free, care-free, etc.* (and, with other adjectives, *world-weary*; *sea-worthy*; *girl-crazy*; *etc.*) indicate a different outcome. For one thing, *salt-free*, if indeed it is a reflex of *free (of) salt*, 'is an' adjective (it can be manipulated as any simple base A by T-rules that refer to A) that has as its source an adjective phrase. So, there is no question of derived function or the like: the rule AP → A NP provides for the basic complement structure of *free*:

[4]   The convention leads to the matter of the proper identification of units and unit-sequences in the structural descriptions and structural changes of transformations. One immediately encounters 'difficulties' if, for example, one attempts to retain the notion NP throughout as a generic for the class of sequences *Joe*; *the boy*; *the correct amount*; *etc.* NP could, of course, be 'read back in' by convention, under the appropriate conditions. But rather than do that, and rather than interpret the 'difficulty' as an invalidation of the convention on the erasure of phrasal nodes, I have taken it tentatively as a questioning of the validity of NP in T-rule specification of segments.

(3)   (i)

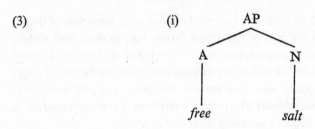

But *salt-free* is obtained 'as an' A only if we assume that the re-ordering, rather than simply a permutation of constituents, is an incorporation into the head of the phrase. ['Head' may be (meta)defined as the obligatory constituent of an expansion rule, and 'modifier' as any optional constituent of such a rule.] Not only does this assumption permit *salt-free* to be an A, but it accounts for the inability of the complex A to admit another complement: **salt-free of the powder*; **world-weary of travelling*; **girl-crazy about dating*; *etc.* Re-ordering, in this case, then, yields the sequence of structures —

(3)   (iii)   (ii)

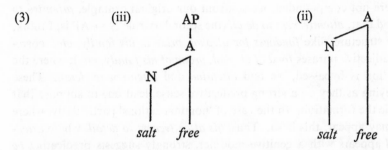

(3ii) the result of incorporation, (3iii) the result of phrase-node erasure.

A few comments on this particular example and the process illustrated before we return to 'nominalization' proper: the structure (iii) appears to express the sense of the form more nearly than would a pre-posing, pure and simple — *i. e.*, it seems to be a 'kind of *-free*' that is being talked about. In this respect, *salt-* seems to be a prefix such as *over-* or *pre-*, as in *over-do* or *pre-heat*. Secondly, the incorporation itself —

$$[_{AP}X \quad \langle A \rangle \quad N]$$
$$\begin{array}{ccc} 1 & 2 & 3 \rightarrow \\ 1 & 3+2 & \emptyset \end{array}$$

(where angle brackets indicate a segment indentified by feature, and where the notation '+' means adjunction of segments so that their immediate domination by the same node results), focusses on the segmental character of the head, thus contrasting with complex adjectives like *snow-white*, *freezing-cold*, *filthy rich*, *etc.*, which are not like *salt-free* in formation. The AP expansion rule given above should be, I believe, AP → (NP) A (NP), where the first NP is the term of degree. This structure can be realized by simple N or A, as in *boiling hot* or *wondrous fair* (but typically, in Modern English, the A in its function as a 'nominal of degree' is marked by *-ly*), or by a clause

(*so cold that the paint cracked*; *as cold as it ever was*). When such nominals of degree
are reduced in position (or, in the case of the simple forms, kept in their base order),
a 'complex' A appears to result. However, one should note the stress contrast between
hòpping mád and *móney-màd*, and that *hopping* already expresses the degree of anger
(**very hopping mad, *quite hopping mad*) but not a complement (*hopping mad about
the results*), whereas *money-mad* already expresses a complement (**money-mad about
the results*) but not a term of degree (*so money-mad that* ...).[5]

We see, then, that it is possible to express the sense of 'derivation' behind a form
like *muddying* by allowing secondary rules like V → A and A → V to interact with
a primary rule like VP → V AP; and to express the same complement structure for
both *go* (*on*) *ocean* and *ocean-going* by extending these secondary substitutions to
V → AP, A → VP, and the like. Again, I think the compounding (incorporation) of
structures like $[_A[_{VP}[_V go]\ [ocean]]]$ is probably the unmarked condition. *Ocean-going*,
by the account just given, should emerge as an adjectival kind of verb whose meaning
has been delimited by a noun used as a prefix: *i.e.*, $[_A[_V[_N ocean]\ go]ing]$. But when
such structures are not compounded, we confront our original example, *attentive to
detail*; and beyond that, *attentiveness to detail* (the secondary rule N → AP is, I think,
substantiated by structures like *fondness for alcohol, pride in his family*, *etc.*, corresponding to the adjective phrases *fond of alcohol, proud of his family, etc.*); where the
A → VP substitution is bypassed, we find *attention* and *attention to detail*. These
structures, conveying as they do a strong predicative sense, lead one to suppose that
an S may underlie the formation. In the case of 'nominalizations' particularly, where
a quasi-subject may appear, this is so. Thus, *his attentiveness to detail*, where *attentiveness to detail* appears with a genitive modifier, strongly suggests predicating *be
attentive to detail* of the subject *he*. However inviting this relationship between the
S and the 'nominalization' may be, there are a number of observations that militate
against the hypothesis. First, consider the cogency of that hypothesis if the sentence

> *his attentiveness to detail, if we asked him to, was impressive*

were acceptable. There would be no answering the argument that a deletion of the
copula (plus adjective complement) had taken place; and one would then proceed
to order the derivation so that the ellipsis would precede the 'nominalization' of the
dominant clause. But, in fact, the sentence is not acceptable. Second, consider the
fact that *attend*, in the sense being used here, is a strict transitive verb: yet note that
the structure *his attentiveness* (*was impressive*) is perfectly acceptable. One might
have granted such a nullification of transitivity in the form *attention* (which seems
«more nominal' than, say, *attending*); but even here, a complement (*to detail*) is

---

[5] The form *scot-free*, because its stress pattern contradicts the typical one for the class to which
it probably belongs (*i.e., free* (*of*) *scot*, may no longer be derivable, that is, 'regular'). In order to
provide for the stress pattern that is manifested in Modern English, *scot* would have to be listed in
the lexicon with the class *very, quite, rather, plumb*, *etc.* This reanalysis may not be inappropriate
to the sense with which it is used.

admissible. The implication, then, is that the 'basic complement structure' need not appear in such secondary formations: in other words, there is the option N → V as opposed to N → VP. I would suppose that the affix permitted correlates with the degree to which the 'verbal force' (the amount of complement structure) of the root is retained: *e.g.*, *-ing* versus *-ment*. Other facts (for example, the acceptability of the *when*-clause in

> *his leaving when Congress had just convened surprised everyone*

as opposed to the unacceptable

> *his announcement when Congress had just convened surprised everyone*

the latter 'understood' acceptably when the clause is interpreted as *at a time when...* and then *made at a time when...*: that is, when the nominal character of *announcement* is respected in terms of a relative clause) also indicate that one would have to erase 'verbal information' by degrees; and that such a gradation would explicate the notion 'verbal force'.[6]

So much for the 'optional' complement of something like a strict transitive verb. On the matter of the implied subject, it should be noted first that the 'subject' need not appear at all, in contrast to normal sentence formation in which the subject of a finite verb must appear (excluding sentences involving first and second person subjects, *e.g.*, *Gotta go now.*; *Why worry?*; *etc.*). Again, it is easy to underestimate this 'option': only when one considers the reverse — *i.e.*, that the subject must be present in all secondary formations — and the force that fact would have had for an 'underlying' S-hypothesis, does one appreciate the 'aberration' of a subjectless 'predicate':

> *attentiveness to detail* (*attention to detail*) *is a rare quality these days*

We may note, further, that even if an underlying subject were to be posited (obligatorily present in the base representation, and subsequently deleted), we would be hard put to account for the following:

$$
\textit{dissecting ants} \left\{
\begin{array}{l}
\textit{strikes him as a sign of immaturity} \\
\textit{interested the late chancellor} \\
\textit{causes her to suffer} \\
\textit{gives me a headache} \\
\textit{makes your eyes tear} \\
\textit{etc.}
\end{array}
\right.
$$

where there is a 'variable' sense of a subject-relation between some human agent mentioned in the predicate and the verb-like noun at the front of the sentence. Notice also that the same variability obtains regardless of the 'verbal force' of the noun:

---

[6] The time-adverbial *yesterday* that appears in the sentence *his announcement yesterday surprised everyone* does not argue for the 'verbal' character of *announcement*. Such adverbials appear to be deflected genitives (*cf.*, *yesterday's rain*, *next Monday's class*; *etc.*), and not at all peculiar to verb-like nouns. Neither are they sentence-adverbials: *cf.*, *this morning's type will be re-classified at 3 o'clock*.

the dissection of ants; *the pursuit of truth*; *etc.* Finally, a sentence like

    one's being at the game is half the fun

is peculiar enough (if thought of as a 'more explicit' version of *being at the game is half the fun*) to suggest that some formations may even preclude the appearance of a 'subject'.

    Understandably, a number of characteristics of such secondary formations conspire to suggest 'sentential predication'. We noted, first, that the notion 'derived' cannot be limited to a single-step process; and that like other processes in natural language, if more-than-one is allowed, then (barring the limitations of the mind's processing of information) there is 'no end to it'. Since recursiveness has typically been limited to the reappearance of S in the base rules, an S seems the likely source for such repeated formations. Moreover, since the secondary formations were not limited to simple substitutions but involved also the introduction of phrasal structure, the predicative force of, say, adjective-plus-complement or verb-plus-complement would suggest an S as the basis for the 'refracted proposition'. Finally, the system — by way of 'datives of interest' (or reference) and genitive noun-adjuncts — allows for the possibility of implied subjects: it is not difficult to see how a sequence like infinitive + dative as in

    Geneva is a good place to live for one interested in the growth of the child's mind

could be re-arranged in 'proper' sentential order (*for one ... to live ...*) — especially when datives of person tend to precede abstract clausal complements, whether genitive or accusative. When the various devices of natural language are summed with respect to their contribution to 'felt' predication, the move from a 'logical' sentence to a syntactic S is a natural one.

    The problems that now arise — if what has been sketched above approximates the actual nature of derivational morphology — are formidable. There are certainly limitations on the interaction of rules like A → VP, N → AP, *etc.*: even with a liberal application of compounding to reduce the amount of structure, the monstrous involutions that quickly emerge suggest that severe constraints operate somewhere and somehow to keep the process in check. But perhaps this delimitation is no more a syntactic problem than the degree of self-embedding; what is a problem is the refinement of notions like 'verbal force' and 'implied subject'. I have avoided the more familiar constructions in which verb-like nouns appear (with and without complementation), since I do not have solutions for these difficult areas: a view of the topic from the angle of adjective + complement has been used because it is less familiar and so less prejudiced, and because the verb in Modern English (that is, in its non-indicative forms, and non-finite forms; in its modal structure, and aspectual structure) is among the most complex areas of the grammar. I offer this perspective in the hope that some clues to a more manageable account of 'nominalizations' may be forthcoming; and that a general consideration of derivational morphology may provide such guidelines.

REFERENCES

Chomsky, N.,
  1962 "A Transformational Approach to Syntax", *Third Texas Conference on Problems of Linguistic Analysis in English* (Austin; The University of Texas).
  1964 "Current Issues in Linguistic Theory", *The Structure of Language*, eds. J. Fodor and J. Katz (Englewood Cliffs, Prentice-Hall).
Harris, Z.,
  1957 "Co-occurrence and transformation in linguistic structure", *Language* 33, 283-340.
Katz, J. and P. Postal,
  1964 *An Integrated Theory of Linguistic Descriptions* (Cambridge, Mass., M.I.T. Press).
Lees, R. B.,
  1960 *The Grammar of English Nominalizations* (The Hague, Mouton & Co.).
Smith, C. S.,
  1964 "Determiners and relative clauses in a generative grammar of English", *Language* 40, 37-52.

ANTHONY L. VANEK

A CASE FOR SYNTACTICALLY ORIENTED PHONOLOGICAL ANALYSIS*

0.0. The question of derivational morphology has been plaguing transformationa analysis for a long time. As has been pointed out by Lightner, "part of the difficulty in doing derivational morphology lies in the absence of syntactic and semantic analysis which could be used to help solve questions of derivation ...".[1] For instance, phonologically oriented analysis does not seem to shed light on the difference in syntactic information expressed by phonetically identical segments, *e.g.*, *í* in *sedíme–sázíme–posadíme* 'we are sitting–we are setting out–we will seat' and *hloubíme–prohloubíme* 'we are deepening–we will deepen', nor does it account for vowel alternation (*ablaut*) within the same root, *e.g.*, *sed–sáz–sad*, *hloub–hlub* (in *prohlubujeme* 'we are deepening'), in any non *ad hoc* way.

This paper will attempt to investigate exactly this type of problem. In particular, it will seek to determine the correlation between phonological segments which are appended to the lexical entry (LE) of Czech verbs and the syntactic information which those segments contain. The necessity of syntactic analysis for this investigation is apparent.

0.1. Syntactic analysis encompasses three basic tasks: determination of the appropriate deep constituent structure of a sentence S, postulation of transformational rules (T-rules), and utilization of these rules in the conversion of the deep constituent structure (d.c.s.) into the surface structure which is the output of the syntactic component. Each T-rule has a definite structural index or description SD that must be met by the input structure in order for the rule to apply, and a specified structural change SC which converts the input constituent structure into the derived structure which is the output of that rule. Transformational rules are mutually ordered and apply cyclically, first to the most deeply embedded sentence.[2]

* A revised and expanded version of a paper entitled "On Some Problems in the Phonology of Czech Conjugation", which was presented at the *Tenth International Congress of Linguists*, Bucharest, Roumania, 1967.
[1] T.M.Lightner, "On the Use of Minor Rules in Russian Phonology", to appear in *Journal of Linguistics* (1968).
[2] Cf. N.Chomsky, *Aspects of the Theory of Syntax* (Cambridge, MIT Press, 1965); N.Chomsky, *Current Issues in Linguistic Theory* (The Hague, Mouton & Co., 1964); J.J.Katz and P.M.Postal,

Similarly, phonological analysis requires the investigator to determine the underlying phonological representations (UR) of the linearly arranged constituents of an S, to postulate phonological rules which are mutually ordered and have a specified SD and SC, and to apply these rules to the UR to obtain the phonetic derived representation that is the output of the phonological component.[3]

0.2. *A syntactically oriented phonological analysis* requires that the investigator look beyond the UR. It implies correlation of the output of the syntactic component to the input into the phonological component. This correlation can be achieved by means of associating the individual syntactic feature sets of the surface structure (the final derived P-marker) with their appropriate phonological matrices (PM) which, in turn, constitute the underlying phonological representations. It seems that only then can phonological analysis achieve an effective link-up with syntactic analysis.

0.3. Section 1 concentrates on the basic questions encountered in syntactic analysis of inflection. Section 2 endeavors to ascertain the nature of the relationship between the output of the syntactic component and the input into the phonological component, and section 3 focuses on specific problems of derivation.

1.0. In this section I will suggest a syntactic analysis that is concerned primarily with the phenomenon of inflection. Because of space limitations I am confining my discussion to only a portion of the derivation, and consequently the postulated deep constituent structures as well as the transformational rules should be viewed as tentative and approximate. What is at issue here is primarily the basic derivation of verbal suffixes, and the relationship of the feature composition of these derived suffixes to the input into the phonological component. Only a more detailed and complete analysis can yield a more general and definitive proposal.[4]

1.1. The majority of languages, and certainly all Slavic languages, contain in their lexicon verbs which express inchoation, causation, action, duration, and completion, *e.g.*, respectively, in English *to become, to cause, to do, to continue, to cease*; in French, *devenir, causer, faire, continuer, cesser*; in German, *werden, verursachen, tun, (fort)-dauern, aufhören*; in Russian, *stanovit'sja, pričinjat', delat', prodolžat', prekpaščat'*;

An Integrated Theory of Linguistic Descriptions (Cambridge, MIT Press, 1964); G. Lakoff, *On the Nature of Linguistic Irregularity*, Mathematical Linguistics and Automatic Translation Report NSF-16 (Computational Laboratory, Harvard University 1965); recent studies have also argued for the existence of pre- and post-cyclical transformational rules, cf. G. Lakoff, "Precyclical and Post-cyclical Transformational Rules", *LSA* (Winter, 1966), (mimeo).

[3] Cf. Chomsky, *Aspects*; Chomsky, *Current Issues*; M. Halle, "Phonology in Generative Grammar", *Word* 18 (1962), 54-72; M. Halle, "A Descriptive Convention for Treating Assimilation and Dissimilation", Research Laboratory of Electronics Quarterly Progress Report QPR 66 (Cambridge, MIT, 1962), 295-6; T. D. Langendoen, "Assimilation and Dissimilation in Generative Phonology", 19th University of Kentucky Foreign Language Conference, 1966 (mimeo); T. M. Lightner, *Segmental Phonology of Modern Standard Russian*, unpublished Ph. D. Dissertation, MIT, 1965.

[4] A. L. Vanek, *Syntactically Oriented Phonological Analysis* (tentative title), Ph. D. dissertation: University of Illinois (in preparation).

in Czech, *státi se, způsobiti, dělati, pokračovati, přestati.* Each of these verbs is idiosyncratically marked in the lexicon with respect to selectional restrictions, command of case, and applicability of specific T-rules. In all cases mentioned above, only verbs expressing causation and action are transitive verbs, all others are intransitive.

1.2. There exist sentences, however, in which causation and/or inchoation, for instance, is expressed by a verb other than those mentioned (*cf.* 1.1.) above. The occurrence of this type of sentence is restricted in languages like English, French and German, but is a common phenomenon in many Slavic languages. Thus, for example, the following pairs of sentences are synonymous:

(1) (a)   *The throng became noticeably* $\left\{ \begin{array}{l} sad \\ sadder \end{array} \right\}$ *at that news*

     (b)   *The throng sadd*ENed *noticeably at that news*

(2) (a)   *That explosion caused John to become temporarily deaf*

     (b)   *That explosion deaf*ENed *John temporarily*

(3) (a)   *La réaction chimique a causé la substance de devenir solide*

     (b)   *La réaction chimique a solid*IFIé *la substance*

(4) (a)   *Die Studenten wurden ersichtlich* $\left\{ \begin{array}{l} fröhlich \\ fröhlicher \end{array} \right\}$ *als die Ferien sich näherten*

     (b)   *Die Studenten fr*EUten *sich ersichtlich als die Ferien näherten*

(5) (a)   *Grigorij stal gluxim*

     (b)   *Grigorij oglux*NUl

In sentences (a), the causative and/or inchoative verbs are followed by embedded adjectives: *sad (sadder), deaf, solide, fröhlich(er), gluxim.* In sentences (b), however, no overt verbs of causation and/or inchoation are present, and the adjective has become a true verb which expresses causation and/or inchoation either by the presence of the capitalized suffixes in (1b, 2b, 3b, 5b) or by the *ablaut* in (4b). The relationship between the absence of the causative and/or inchoative verb and the presence of a 'verb-forming suffix' is quite clearly evident in the following Czech sentences which, again, are synonymous:

(6) (a)   *Ta explose způsobila to, že Jan se stal přechodně hluchým*
         (That explosion caused it that John became temporarily deaf)

     (b)   *Ta explose způsobila to, že Jan přechodně ohluchnul*
         (That explosion caused it that John temporarily deafened

     (c)   *Ta   explose   Jana   přechodně   ohlušila*
         That explosion John temporarily deafened
         (That explosion deafened John temporarily)

In (6a) both causation and inchoation are expressed by overt verbs *způsobil* and *se stal*; in (6b) only causation is thus expressed, inchoation being expressed by the suffix *-nu-* in *ohluchnul*; in (6c) both causation and inchoation are expressed by the suffix *-i-* in *ohlušil*. These facts suggest that the verbs *ohluchnul* and *ohlušil* contain the features [+ Causative] and/or [+ Inchoative]. The phenomenon can be accounted for in one of two ways. Either these two verbs are two separate lexical items and contain these syntactic features inherently, or they share the same lexical entry which is devoid of either of these syntactic features [and which underlies the adjective *hluchým* in (6a) as well] and the syntactic features are introduced into the lexical entry in the course of derivation.

If we claim that the three constituents *hluchým*, *ohluchnul* and *ohlušil* are three separate lexical entries, then we likewise have to claim that the following sets of constituents, *e.g.*, *mladý–omládnouti–omladiti* 'young–become young–make young', *ležeti–položiti* 'to lie–to lay down', *hustý–zhoustnouti–zhustiti* 'thick–to thicken–to thicken', *viseti–pověsiti* 'to hang–to hang up', *etc.*, have separate lexical entries. But it is evident that (a) each set of constituents shares a common root and (b) that each set is closely related semantically. In fact, the difference in meaning that exists between the members of each set can be traced to the presence or absence of causative and/or inchoative information. Thus to claim that we are dealing with separate lexical items is to miss the fact that the constituents of each set can be differentiated on the basis of the same syntactic features, and that this phenomenon can be dealt with in a general way. Moreover, a large set of verbs which express causation share the same 'verb-forming suffix' *-i-*, *e.g.*, *omladiti*, *pověsiti*, *bíliti* 'to whiten', *ohlušiti*, *rozpustiti* 'to dissolve', *etc.*; this fact suggests that there exists some kind of relationship between the presence of the feature [+ Causative] and this suffix, *i.e.*, that this suffix may be the overt expression of causation.

1.3. It appears, therefore, that if the presence of the features [+ Causative] and/or [+ Inchoative] in the suffix could be accounted for derivationally, the generality of this phenomenon could be captured. The fact that the sentences in (6) are synonymous suggests that they share the same or nearly the same deep constituent structure (d.c.s.). Sentence (6a) must contain true verbs of causation and inchoation, as well as the adjective *hluchý*. If the presence of the features [Causative] and [Inchoative] is to be accounted for by a transfer of those features to the adjective *hluchý* by a transformational rule, then the d.c.s. of (6b) and (6c) must contain some constituent which contains these features. I venture to propose that the d.c.s. of the sentences in (6) are identical up to the feature [Pro] of the causative and inchoative verbs, and that a transformational rule can be postulated which obligatorily transfers a duplicate of the syntactic features of a verb which carries the feature [+ Pro] (henceforth referred to as Pro verb) to the verb or adjective of the embedded S that carries the feature [− Pro] (henceforth referred to as true verb or adjective). The fact that no overt verbs of causation and/or inchoation are present in the surface structure of (6b) and (6c) can be accounted for by a rule which obligatorily deletes any Pro verb. It is then possible to propose the approximate structures (7a) and (7b) (or rather portions of these, since higher sentences are not at issue here and S_{n+2} has already undergone derivation)[5] to underlie (6a) and (6c).

(7) (a)

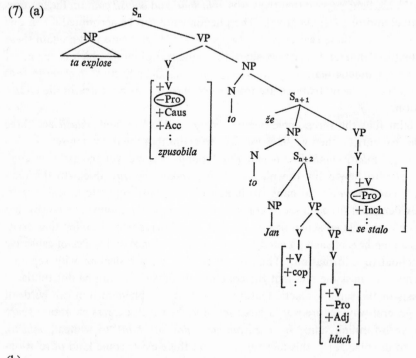

(b)

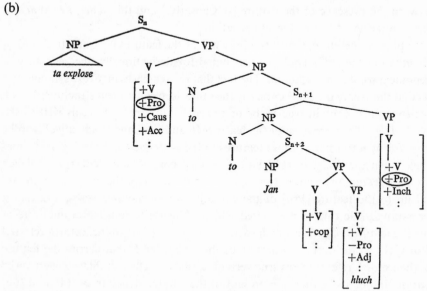

[5] For this derivation, see J.R.Ross, "Adjectives as Noun Phrases", *LSA*: (Winter, 1966), (mimeo, Eric/Pegs).

The structures (7a) and (7b) are identical up to the circled feature [Pro]. It should be noted that the true verbs of inchoation and causation are paralleled by their Pro verb counterparts with respect to transitivity and intransitivity. In the case of the true and Pro verbs of causation, they both command the accusative case. If the Pro verbs are taken to be lexical entries, a fact that their presence in the d.c.s. implies, then it follows that they do not necessarily parallel their true verb counterparts as to all their idiosyncratic markings. Thus, they may differ from their true verb counterparts with respect to selectional restrictions (*cf*. 1.5.) and with respect to the complementizers they take.[6]

1.4. The facts discussed in the preceding section require us to consider the structure of the deep constituent structure in general. If Pro verbs of causation and inchoation do occur in d.c.s., then it may be indicated that there exist also other Pro verbs which are present in the d.c.s. of sentences in which the corresponding true verb does not occur in the surface structure. Thus, for instance the Czech sentences

(8) (a)   *My ležíme v posteli*
           (We are lying in bed)
    (b)   *My si leháme do postele*
           (We are lying down in bed)

are closely related; in (8a) the action of 'lying' is one of protracted duration, while in (8b) the action is one of limited duration which at the same time implies intended completion. The difference in the 'durative' information imparted by the verbs *ležíme* and *leháme* is contained in the different suffixes *-í-* and *-á-*, respectively. Since the durative and completive verbs *pokračujeme* and *přestaneme* (*cf*. 1.1.) are not overtly realized in the surface structure, we may assume that the structures that underlie (8a, b) contain at some point of their derivation, or in the d.c.s., Pro verbs of duration and completion. A parallel analysis can be given that accounts for the presence of a Pro verb of action in d.c.s., although a much more detailed analysis needs to be undertaken in that case.[7]

1.4.1. It appears that both (8a) and (8b) are derived from d.c.s. that contain the Pro verb of duration, *i.e.*, a Pro verb which carries the feature specification [+ Duration]. It appears, however, that only (8b) contains in its d.c.s. a Pro verb which carries the feature specification [+ Completion]. But it is not possible to state that the d.c.s.

---

[6] See note 21.

[7] Although the feature [± Action] has been utilized in this paper, it appears that the feature [± Stative] might be more appropriate (cf. G. Lakoff, "Stative Adjectives and Verbs in English", Mathematical Linguistics and Automatic Translation Report NSF-17 (Computational Laboratory: Harvard University, 1966)); verbs bearing the feature [—Stative] may then be further specified with respect to the feature [± Action] e.g. *poslouchati* 'to listen', *dívati se* 'to look' being specified [—Action], *nositi* 'to carry', *choditi* 'to go', *psáti* 'to write', *seděti* 'to sit', [+ Action]; additional feature specification is necessary to distinguish between verbs which imply manipulation, e.g. *nositi*, *psáti*, and those which do not, *e.g.*, *choditi*, *seděti*, on the one hand, and those which imply locomotion, *e.g.*, *nositi*, *choditi*, and those which do not, *e.g.*, *psáti*, *seděti*, on the other hand. It is probable that additional feature specification will also be necessary for [+ Stative] verbs.

of (8a) contains a Pro verb which is simply not specified with respect to the feature [Completion], or that this verb is absent in the d.c.s. of (8a), since (a) the notion of 'protracted duration' implies absence of completion, and (b) the difference in the 'verb-forming suffix' clearly suggests that there must exist some feature that accounts for this difference, since both (8a) and (8b) do contain a Pro verb of duration. I venture to propose therefore that the d.c.s. that underlies (8a) does contain a 'completive' Pro verb, but that this Pro verb carries the feature specification [— Completion]. In fact, due to the close interrelationship of the features of [Duration] and [Completion] I propose that there exists only a single durative Pro verb which is specified with respect to both these syntactic features.[8] This proposal makes then the theoretical claim that in the theory of grammar there exist Pro verbs which may contain both positively and negatively specified syntactic features.

1.4.2. This claim may be further supported by consideration of the following facts. The Czech sentences

(9) (a)   *My si sedáme*
          (We are sitting down)
    (b)   *My se posazujeme*
          (We are seating ourselves)

are closely related as to the information they convey. If the reflexive clitics *si* (dative) and *se* (accusative) are replaced by an NP which is not identical to the Subject NP *my*, as in (10a) and (10b)

(10) (a) **My sedáme Petrovi*
          (We are sitting down Peter)
     (b) *My posazujeme Petra*
          (We are seating Peter)

we see that (10a) is not permissible. The non-permissibility of (10a) is directly related to the fact that (9a) does not express causation, but merely a change of state, while (9b) expresses causation of that change. Since inchoation cannot refer to an NP which is not identical to its Subject NP while causation can of course do so, the non-permissibility of (10a) is apparent.

The clitics *si* and *se* derive from the reflexive pronouns *sobě* and *sebe*, respectively. In order for a reflexive pronoun to be derived, the structures underlying (9a) and (9b) must contain a constituent which is identical to the Subject NP *my*. Up to this time the surface realization of the clitic *si* in sentences like (9a) has eluded analysis, and verbs like *sedati si* 'to be sitting down' have been referred to as '*reflexiva tantum*'. It seems to me that the presence of the clitic *si* in (9a) can be accounted for if the following approximate structures (11a) and (11b) are postulated to underlie (9a) and (9b):

[8]   Additional feature specifications will in all probability need to be assigned to this Pro verb, among them the features [Inception] and [Momentariness].

(11) (a)

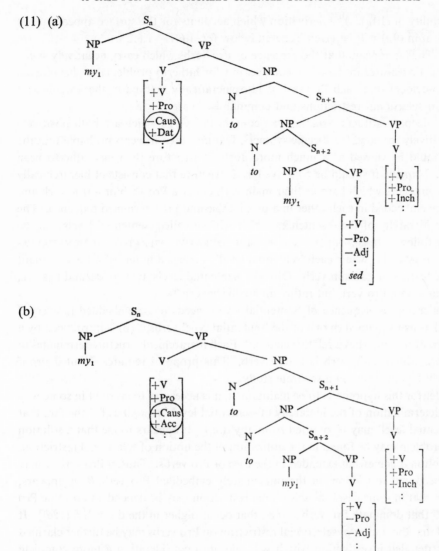

(b)

These two structures are identical up to the circled features. The Pro verb in (9b) which carries the feature specification [+ Caus] and [+ Acc], *i.e.*, which commands the accusative case, has no selectional restrictions on the Subject NP of the embedded S, with respect to identity, as can be seen from the fact that the NP *my* in S_{n+2} can be replaced by the NP *Petr* with the resulting derivation of (10b). The Pro verb in (9a) which carries the feature specifications of [− Caus] and [+ Dat] must, however, contain the selectional restriction that the Subject NP of the embedded S must be identical to its own Subject NP. This selectional restriction accounts for the non-permissibility of (10a). The derivation which accounts for the surface appearance of the clitic *si* in (9a) will be given in detail below (*cf.* 1.6.1.—1.6.2.).

1.4.3. Thus it appears that the presence of Pro verbs which carry negatively specified syntactic features in the d.c.s. can account for hitherto problematic phenomena. It is also evident that each Pro verb is idiosyncratically marked in the lexicon with respect to selectional restrictions and command of case.

1.5. If deep constituent structure can contain Pro verbs which are both positively and negatively specified for specific syntactic features, then it seems probable that the d.c.s. should be viewed as a much more abstract structure than has hitherto been thought. Namely, it should be conceived as a structure that consists of hierarchically ordered sentences which have as their main verb either a Pro verb or a true verb and which are embedded in each other in a predictable and predetermined sequence. The tentative hierarchy of these sentences which will be called 'sentential levels' can be given as follows: TENSE–FREQUENCY–PASSIVE–DURATIVE–ITERATIVE–ACTION–CAUSATION–INCHOATIVITY, where each 'sentential level' is labelled in terms of the dominant syntactic feature of its main verb. Of these 'sentential levels' two, TENSE and PASSIVE, do not contain a Pro verb but rather an auxiliary verb.[9]

This hierarchical sequence of 'sentential levels' needs to be embedded in every S that (a) has as its main verb one of the 'sentential type' verbs,[10] (b) is introduced by a true verb, or (c) underlies a relative clause.[11] Each hierarchical structure terminates in a sentence whose main verb is a true verb. This proposal requires detailed proof which will be attempted in a separate study.

In order for this hypothesis to be maintained, it is necessary to account in some way for the determination of the hierarchy of 'sentential levels' as well as for the fact that no 'sentential level' may be omitted from any d.c.s. It appears to me that a solution to this problem may be found in the utilization of the notion of selectional restriction, if that notion is somewhat extended in the case of Pro verbs. Thus, a Pro verb *A* may place selectional restriction on the immediately embedded Pro verb *B*; it appears, however, that in some cases the selectional restriction may be dependent on some Pro verb(s) *C* that dominate Pro verb *A*, *i.e.*, that occur higher in the d.c.s. [*cf.* (12e)]. It is hoped that the notion of selectional restriction on Pro verbs may be further clarified by more detailed investigation which will take into consideration a more complete feature specification of these verbs. At this point, the following selectional restrictions on those Pro verbs which are under immediate consideration in this study may be tentatively given in a schematized form in (12), where A, B, C refer to the above specified Pro verbs.

[9] For discussion of these two 'sentential levels' see A.L.Vanek, "The Tense Auxiliary Verb in Czech". University of Illinois:1967 (mimeo, Eric/Pegs), and A.L.Vanek, "The Passive Auxiliary Verb" (in preparation).

[10] Cf. Jerrold M. Sadock, "A Note on Higher Sentences", University of Illinois, 1967 (mimeo: Eric/Pegs).

[11] The hypothesis that relative clauses are introduced by a special verb that bears the feature [Relative] will be treated in Vanek, *Syntactically Oriented Phonological Analysis*.

(12)

	A	B	C
(a)	± Dur ± Compl	± Act	
(b)	+ Act	± Caus	
(c)	− Act	− Caus	
(d)	+ Caus	+ Inch	
(e)	− Caus	α Inch	α Compl α Dur − Act

The selectional restrictions in (12) permit us to delimit the 24 possible permutations (if the Pro verb which contains the feature specification [− Dur, − Compl] has already been eliminated at a higher level) to 10 permissible ones, the others being rejected on the basis of selectional restrictions.

1.6. In 1.3. it was stated that introduction of the syntactic features of causation and/or inchoation into a verb that does not contain these features inherently in its lexical entry could be effected by postulation of a T-rule which would transfer a duplicate of the syntactic features of a Pro verb to the verb of the embedded S that bears the feature specification [− Pro]. If Pro verbs may contain both positively and negatively specified syntactic features, then it is possible to formulate the following general feature changing rule:

(13) (a)

$$
to \quad {}_{s}\!\left[X \begin{bmatrix} +V \\ -Cop \\ \pm Adj \end{bmatrix} Y \right]_{s} \begin{bmatrix} +V \\ +Pro \\ F_1 \\ \vdots \\ F_n \end{bmatrix}
$$

$$
\quad 1 \quad 2 \quad 3 \quad 4 \quad\quad 5 \quad \Rightarrow 1\ 2 \begin{bmatrix} 3 \\ -Adj \\ F_1 \\ \vdots \\ F_n \end{bmatrix} 4\ 5
$$

(b)

$$
X \begin{bmatrix} +V \\ +Pro \\ F_1 \\ \vdots \\ F_n \end{bmatrix} to \ {}_{s}[Y\ V\ Z]_{s}
$$

$$
\quad 1 \quad\quad 2 \quad 3 \quad 4\ 5\ 6 \ \Rightarrow 1\ 2\ 3\ 4 \begin{bmatrix} 5 \\ F_1 \\ \vdots \\ F_n \end{bmatrix} 6
$$

Both alternatives, (a) and (b), have to be stated to account for transitive and intransitive Pro verbs. The specification $F_1 \ldots F_n$ permits this rule to be stated with variables, making it generally applicable. The rule applies cyclically to any structure that contains a Pro verb and an embedded S. It should be noted that (13a) accounts for the change of the feature [+ Adj] in term 3 to [− Adj], thus accounting for the fact that (6b) and (6c) do not contain in their surface structure the adjective *hluchý* but rather the verbs *ohluchnul* and *ohlušil*, although their d.c.s. do contain the adjective, as can be seen in (7c).

1.6.1. It is now possible to consider the derivation of sentences (6c) and (9a), taking as the starting point of derivation the more complete approximate underlying structures (14a)[12] and (14b), respectively, which contain four 'sentential levels', namely DURATIVE, ACTION, CAUSATIVE, and INCHOATIVE.

(14) (a)

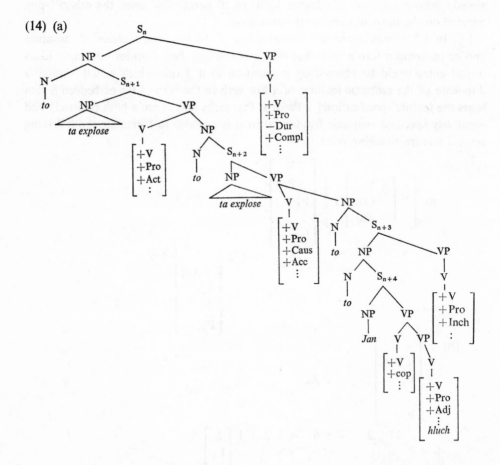

---

[12]   The adverb *přechodně* 'temporarily' is not considered here mainly because it is not clear what the derivation of this constituent is. It is probable that the adverb is derived from a higher sentence.

(b)

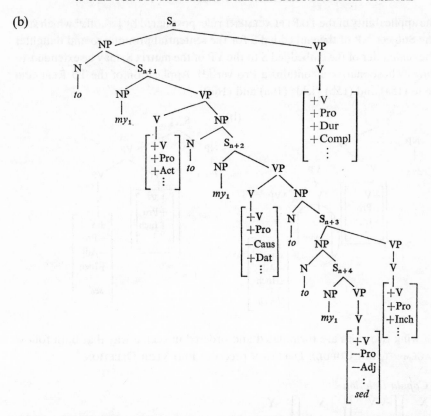

(14a) and (14b) differ with respect to positive and negative specification of the durative Pro verb of S_n, the causative Pro verb of S_{n+2}, and the feature [Adj] of the true verb of S_{n+4}. If rule (13) applies to (14a) and (14b) at the S_{n+3} cycle, we obtain the following derived structures:

(15) (a)

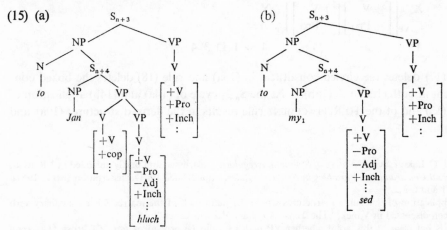

1.6.2. The applicability of the To Replacement rule, postulated by Lakoff,[13] which substitutes the Subject NP of the embedded S for the sentential pronoun *to* and daughter adjoins the remainder of the embedded S to the VP of the matrix S, may be extended to all structures whose matrix S contains a Pro verb.[14] Application of the To Replacement rule to (15a) and (15b) yields (16a) and (16b):

(16) (a)   (b)

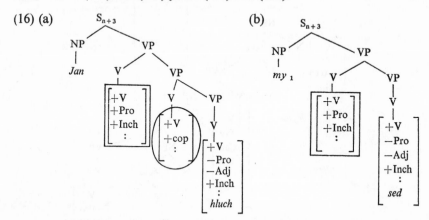

If the following two rules are formulated and ordered in such a way that both follow To Replacement, but Copula Deletion precedes Pro Verb Deletion

(17)   *Copula Deletion*

$$X \quad _{VP}\left[\left[\begin{array}{l}+V\\+cop\end{array}\right]\left[\begin{array}{l}+V\\-Adj\end{array}\right]\right]_{VP} \quad Y$$
$$1 \qquad 2 \qquad 3 \qquad 4 \Rightarrow 1\ \varnothing\ 3\ 4$$

(18)   *Pro Verb Deletion*

$$X \quad _{VP}\left[\left[\begin{array}{l}+V\\+Pro\end{array}\right]\left[\begin{array}{l}+V\\-Pro\end{array}\right]\right]_{VP} \quad Y$$
$$1 \qquad 2 \qquad 3 \qquad 4 \Rightarrow 1\ \varnothing\ 3\ 4$$

rule (17) deletes the circled constituent in (16a) and rule (18) deletes the boxed constituent in both (16a) and (16b).[15] At the S_{n+2} cycle of (14a) and (14b) application of rule (13) and of the To Replacement rule results in the derived structures (19a) and (19b):

---

[13] Cf. G. Lakoff, *On the Nature of Syntactic Irregularity*; discussed and partly amended in J. R. Ross, *Universal Constraints on Variables in Syntactic Rules*, unpublished Ph. D. Dissertation (MIT, 1967), 5.1.1.1 and 6.3.2.

[14] Application of this rule to structures where the main verb of the matrix S is an auxiliary verb has been discussed in Vanek, "The Tense Auxiliary Verb in Czech".

[15] It is not clear at this point whether VP nodes should be pruned or not. Cf. Ross, *Universal Constraints*, 3.2.

(19) (a)

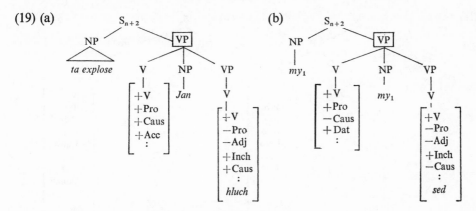

Before the rule of PRO VERB DELETION can apply to (19a) and (19b), the rule of CASE ASSIGNMENT must transfer a duplicate of the case feature of the Pro verb to the NP which is immediately dominated by the same VP, *i.e.* the boxed VP. Moreover, REFLEXIVIZATION must apply to the second occurrence of my_1 in (19b) under identity, since both NP are within a 'simplex sentence'.[16] It is not clear to me at this time whether identity implies also identity of case feature; if that is the case, then REFLEXIVIZATION must apply before CASE ASSIGNMENT. It is clear, however, that REFLEXIVIZATION must apply after the TO REPLACEMENT rule. Rules of CASE ASSIGNMENT and PRO VERB DELETION apply then both to (19a) and (19b), and REFLEXIVIZATION applies to (19b), yielding (20a) and (20b):

(20) (a)

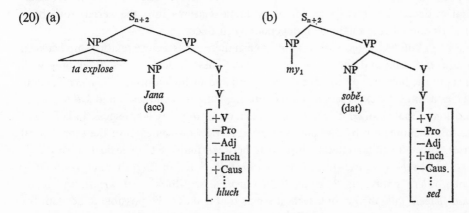

The reflexive pronoun *sobě* in (20b) undergoes a reduction rule to clitic *si*. At the S_{n+1} and S_n cycles of (14a) and (14b), rules (13), EQUI NP DELETION, TO REPLACEMENT, TO DELETION and PRO VERB DELETION apply cyclically in that order, deriving structures (21a) and (21b):

---

[16]   Cf. R. B. Lees and E. Klima, "Rules for English Pronomalization", *Language* 39 (1963) 17-28.

(21) (a)   (b)

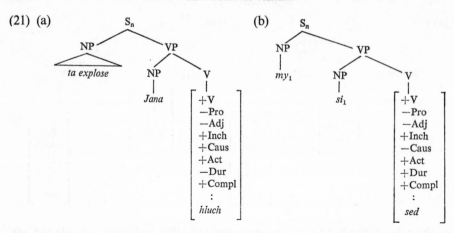

1.7. Rule (13) incorporates the syntactic features of Pro verbs into the lexical entry of the embedded true verb, *i.e.*, into the verbal root. Since in 1.2. it was shown that the information about the presence of causation and/or inchoation seems to be contained not in the root, but in the 'verb-forming suffix', we may question whether the syntactic features should be introduced into the verbal root at all, and whether it might not be indicated that they should instead be directly adjoined to the verbal root as a suffix segment. This approach has been explored in the original version of this paper with the result that a number of separate suffixation rules had to be postulated which were required to be variously constrained.[17] Rule (13) permits a more general statement of the phenomenon of feature introduction into true verbs. There is, moreover, additional evidence that incorporation of syntactic features into the verbal root by a transformational rule might be independently justified.

1.7.1. Lakoff has suggested[18] that in English there exists a close relationship between the adjective *dead* and the verbs *die* and *kill*. These lexical entries differ only with respect to the presence or absence of causation and/or inchoation. Thus, *dead* merely specifies a state, *die* expresses a change into the state of 'deadness', and *kill* expresses causation of that change. Similar phenomena occur in many languages. Lakoff deals with this phenomenon by designating special restrictions on each of the three lexical entries. Since a similar relationship exists between many sets of lexical entries, *e.g.*, *hear–listen, see–look, eat–feed, learn–teach, fall–throw* in English, *voir–regarder* in French, *videt'–smoret'* in Russian, *viděti–dívati se* 'see–look', *jísti–krmiti* 'eat–feed', *padati–házeti* 'fall–throw' in Czech, it seems that it should be possible to account for this phenomenon on the basis of the presence of positively or negatively specified syntactic features of causation and/or inchoation which are introduced into the lexical entry by rule (13) from Pro verbs.

This analysis would necessitate, however, a change in the concept of lexical inser-

---

[17] Vanek, "On Some Problems in the Phonology of Czech Conjugation", rules (T-1) through (T-4).
[18] Lakoff, *On the Nature of Syntactic Irregularity*, Chapter IX.

tion. Chomsky[19] has specified that lexical insertion rules insert not only semantic and syntactic features but also phonological matrices (PMs). If the lexical insertion rule is limited to the insertion of semantic and syntactic features, and the PMs are inserted at the conclusion of the transformational component when rule (13) has incorporated syntactic features of the Pro verbs into the lexical entry of the true verb, *i.e.*, if the lexical insertion rule is limited to the extent of specifying the lexical entry only basically with respect to syntactic features and does not insert any PMs, and the transformational component in turn fully specifies each lexical entry with respect to syntactic features, then it would be possible to limit the lexicon significantly. The lexicon would need to contain only a single lexical entry for each related set of such verbs as *listen–hear*, *dead–die–kill*, etc.

1.7.2. If each set of related verbs shared a common lexical entry, it would be necessary to state only a single selectional restriction for that lexical entry, while when these verbs are assigned separate lexical entries, their selectional restrictions may differ. Thus, while the separate lexical entries *dead*, *die* and *kill* would need to be restricted to a living Subject in the two former cases and a living Object in the latter case,[20] if they shared a common lexical entry only a single selectional restriction would be required, namely 'has to take a living Subject', since the Subject NP would be automatically converted into Object NP at the 'sentential level' of causation. Transitivity and intransitivity would be at least partially accounted for in a similar manner.

1.7.3. In so far as I have been able to determine, there exists no T-rule that refers to phonological matrices. As a matter of fact, the apparent reference to phonological matrices in trees can be viewed as a mnemonic device, as an abbreviation for the set of features that comprise the lexical entry. Those T-rules which do refer to the sentential pronoun *to* 'it' and to the complementizers *that* and *for-to* could well be reformulated so as to refer to a set of syntactic features.[21] There is therefore no apparent reason why phonological matrices should be introduced into the lexical entry at the same time as semantic and syntactic features.

1.8. The above discussion indicates that postulation of rule (13) can be supported by independent motivation. If this rule is included in the grammar, we are still faced with the necessity of postulating a rule which transfers a duplicate of the syntactic features which have been introduced into the verb by rule (13) to a sister-adjoined suffix.[22] I venture to propose the following rule (22):

---

[19]   Chomsky, *Aspects*, Chapter 2, Section 2.

[20]   It appears that the semantic feature [Living] rather than the semantic feature [Animate] plays a role here, since for instance a tree which is [—Animate] but [+ Living] can be said to be dead, to die, and to be killed while this cannot be said of a stone which is [—Living].

[21]   In my forthcoming dissertation I will put forth the hypothesis that complementizers derive from a special type of verbs which introduce sentences that have hitherto been viewed as being headed by complementizers *that* and *for-to* in English. These verbs, together with the relative verb that introduces the relative clause, form a special class of verbs which might be thought of as 'subordinate connective verbs'.

[22]   For discussion of suffixation as an instance of sister adjunction, see Vanek, "The Tense Auxiliary Verb in Czech".

(22)   *Suffix Adjunction*

$$X \begin{bmatrix} \begin{bmatrix} +V \\ -Pro \\ F \end{bmatrix}_v + Y \end{bmatrix}_v Z$$

$$1 \qquad 2 \qquad 3 \Rightarrow 1\ 2 + F\ 3$$

where '+' signifies sister-adjunction and the symbol *F* represents a set of syntactic features which will be specified below [see 1.8.3.; *cf.* (24)].

1.8.1. All languages whose nouns are inflected with respect to gender and number, *i.e.*, whose nouns have a phonetically realized gender/number suffix, *e.g.*, *puer–puella*, *pūpillus–pūpilla* in Latin, *ami–amie*, *cousin–cousine*, *citoyen–citoyenne* in French, *školák–školačka* 'schoolboy–schoolgirl' in Czech, must contain some transformational rule that transfers a duplicate of the syntactic features of gender and number from the lexical entry to a sister-adjoined suffix. It appears that the syntactic features of gender and number are inherently contained in the lexical entry. They are not necessarily correlated with the semantic features [sex] and [set][23] (*e.g.*, in English, *scissors* contains the feature [− set] as well as the feature [+ Plural]; in German *das Mädchen* contains the features [+ sex] and [+ female], and [− Gender]; in Czech *žabec* 'tomboy' contains the features [+ sex] and [+ female], [+ Gender] and [+ Masculine]), which indicates that they cannot be predicted. Moreover, the specification of a noun as to its syntactic features of gender and number appears to be language-specific, as may be illustrated by the fact that the gender specification of the lexical entry 'the table' differs in various languages although the semantic specification remains unchanged, containing the feature [− sex], *e.g.*, in English *table* is specified as [− Gender], in French *la table* is specified [+ Gender, + Feminine], and in German *der Tisch*, in Czech *stůl* and in Russian *stol* are all specified [+ Gender, + Masculine].

The rule that transfers a duplicate of the gender/number features into a suffix that is sister-adjoined to the nominal root parallels rule (22), differing only in term 2; it seems that these two rules could in some way be collapsed if this is not prevented by different ordering.

1.8.2. In Slavic languages all adjectives contain a suffix segment which is absent in participial forms. This segment accounts for the long final vowel in Czech adjectives, *e.g.*,

(23) (a) *Každá matka, která je milována svými dětmi, dostane dárek na Svátek Matek*
      (Every mother who is loved by her children gets a gift on Mothers' Day)
   (b) *Každá matka milovaná svými dětmi dostane dárek na Svátek Matek*
      (Every mother loved by her children gets a gift on Mothers' Day)

While in (23a) the passive participle *milována* contains the feature [− Adj], in the course of relative clause reduction the specification of this constituent is changed to

---

[23] Cf. J. McCawley, "How to Find Semantic Universals in the Event that There Are Any", Texas Conference on Language Universals, 1967 (mimeo, Eric/Pegs).

[+ Adj] (becoming a verbal adjective *milovaná*), and a suffixation rule adjoins a duplicate of this feature to the verbal root, creating a suffix whose phonological realization
accounts for the length of the final vowel. This suffixation rule which must be ordered
after rules that account for relative clause reduction could also be collapsed with rule
(22) if ordering permits it.

1.8.3. These facts indicate that the notion of a suffixation rule such as (22) which
creates an inflectional suffix is well motivated for inflected languages. It should be
stressed that rule (22) is NOT a 'segmentalization rule'. Segmentalization implies
destruction of the original input set of syntactic features; rule (22) does not alter the
feature composition of the verbal root, but takes duplicates of some of the features
and adjoins them to the input constituent.

The specification of the symbol F in rule (22) raises the question of whether this
rule operates at every cycle, adjoining each syntactic feature individually, or whether
the features are adjoined in specified sets. The features that underlie the person/
number suffixes, and to some extent perhaps also those that underlie the gender/
number suffixes, appear to constitute cohesive sets.[24] The same relationship appears
to exist between the features [Duration] and [Completion], and possibly [Iteration]
as well, and between the features [Inchoative], [Causative], and [Action]. This close
relationship is reflected in the fact that completion cannot coexist with iterativity,
that causation implies inchoation, and that causation implies action, or rather non-
stativity. No such relationship obtains for example between features [Inchoative] and
[Iterative] or between [Duration] and [Action].

In view of these facts I assume that syntactic features form specified interrelated
sets, and that rule (22) transfers syntactic features not individually, but in sets. Consequently, the symbol F can now be specified as follows:

(24)

$$\text{where } F = \left\{ \begin{bmatrix} \alpha\,\text{Inch} \\ \beta\,\text{Caus} \\ \gamma\,\text{Act} \\ \alpha\,\text{Iter} \\ \beta\,\text{Dur} \\ \gamma\,\text{Compl} \end{bmatrix} \right\}$$

This specification may be extended to account for the suffixation of those syntactic
features which are introduced into the verbal lexical entry from other Pro verbs and
from Auxiliary verbs.

1.8.4. If the specification of the variable F in (22) is that given in (24), then rule (22)
will apply to (14a) and (14b) at the S_{n+1} and S_n cycles only. Its ordering cannot be

---

[24] The phonological matrices assigned to the gender/number suffixes (29b) appear to contain a
uniform phonological segment a which might be thought of as a separate 'suffix of number'. If that
were the case, however, this suffix would have to appear likewise as a part of the person/number
PM's in (29a). In view of the absence of such parallel phenomenon in (29a), I feel at this time that
both the sets of gender/number and person/number features have to be treated as cohesive units.

determined precisely at this time, but it is certain that it must apply after rule (13). If this rule is applied to (14a) and (14b) at the specified cycles, we obtain structures (25a) and (25b), respectively:

(25)   (a)   (b)

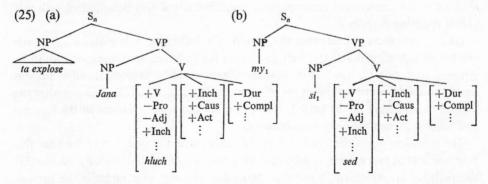

If a more complete d.c.s. is given for (14a) and (14b), one that takes into account the tense sentential level, rule (22) will sister-adjoin to the lexical entry also the suffixes specified by the features [+ Tense] or [+ Past] and the rules of SUBJECT NP-VERB AGREEMENT[25] will sister-adjoin to it duplicates of the gender/number and person/number feature sets, yielding the derived structures (26a) and (26b) which underlie (14a) and (14b), respectively:

(26)   (a)

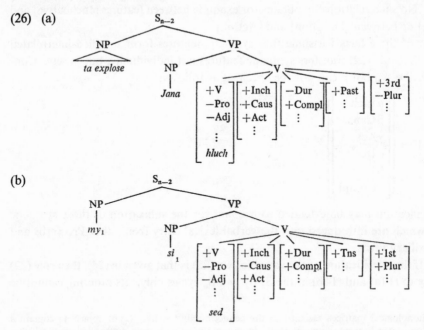

(b)

1.9. The following table presents a schematized output of the transformational com-

[25] Cf. Vanek, "The Tense Auxiliary Verb in Czech".

ponent for selected verbal forms which will be discussed below, with respect to phonological analysis (*cf.* 2.1., 3.1.1., and 3.1.2.).

(27)

Orthographic representation	Root	1st suffix			2nd suffix		Tns suff.	Person/number suffix	
		Inch	Caus	Act	Dur	Comp	Tns	1st	Plur
(a) *sedím*	sæd	—	—	+	+	—	+	+	—
(b) *sedíme*	sæd	—	—	+	+	—	+	+	+
(c) *sedneme*	sæd	+	—	+	—	+	+	+	+
(d) *sedáme*	sæd	+	—	+	+	+	+	+	+
(e) *posazujeme*	sæd	+	+	+	+	+	+	+	+
(f) *posadíme*	sæd	+	+	+	—	+	+	+	+
(g) *hloubíme*	glanb	+	+	+	+	—	+	+	+
(h) *prohlubujeme*	glanb	+	+	+	+	+	+	+	+
(i) *prohloubíme*	glanb	+	+	+	—	+	+	+	+
(j) *odvádíme*	væd	+	+	+	+	+	+	+	+

a. 'I am sitting'
b. 'we are sitting'
c. 'we will sit down'
d. 'we are sitting down'
e. 'we are seating'

f. 'we will seat'
g. 'we are deepening'
h. 'we are deepening'
i. 'we will deepen'
j. 'we are leading away'

2.0. As stated previously, the primary goal of this study is to ascertain the relationship of the output of the syntactic component to the input into the phonological component, and in particular to establish the relationship between the derived sets of syntactic feature configurations that constitute the verbal suffixes and the underlying phonological representations (UR) of these suffix segments. Thus, the problem at hand concerns the introduction of appropriate phonological matrices (PM) into these 'grammatical formatives'. The proposal put forth here concerns the introduction into the theory of grammar of the notion PHONOLOGICAL MATRIX INSERTION RULE (PMIR) which supplies appropriate PM's for each set of features that constitute a 'grammatical formative' and ADDS them to that set of features. As the input into these rules is the sets of features derived by T-rules, these rules operate, as far as I have been able to ascertain at this time, at the conclusion of the transformational component.

In the original version of this paper I had taken the stand that the PMIR's might be restricted to 'grammatical formatives', *i.e.*, to those sets of features not containing a category feature. It has been pointed out to me by Bierwisch,[26] however, that the notion of PMIR should not be conceived as a sort of late 'lexicon' with the accompanying characteristic of an unordered set of rules, roughly paralleling the lexical insertion rule postulated by Chomsky, but that it should be viewed as a set of partially ordered rules.

Reconsideration of the above notion, and the evidence of a basic dissimilarity between lexical entries and 'grammatical formatives' led me to conclude that Bierwisch's suggestion might be correct. Even if the notion of PMIR should be generalized to encompass the insertion of PM's into lexical entries at the conclusion of the transformational component, as has been suggested above (*cf.* 1.7.1.—1.7.3.), a distinction would still have to be made between PMIR's which would have as their input lexical entries and those whose input is the set of features comprising a 'grammatical formative', a transformationally derived entity. In the latter case partial ordering of the PMIR's is clearly indicated, for if for instance (PMIR-3) applied before (PMIR-1) [*cf.* (28)] we would obtain a PM realization for suffixes that do not seem to have any.

2.1. The sets of syntactic features of the verbal suffixes schematized in (27) may be assigned PM's by the following partially ordered PMIR's which are tentative, pending further investigation:

$$
\begin{align}
(28)\ (a)\ &\ (PMIR\text{-}1) \\
(b)\ &\ (PMIR\text{-}2)
\end{align}
\left.\begin{matrix}[[+CAUS]] \\ [[-INCH]]\end{matrix}\right\} \rightarrow
\begin{bmatrix} +syll \\ -cmp \\ -grv \end{bmatrix}
$$

$$
\begin{align}
(c)\ &\ (PMIR\text{-}3) \\
(d)\ &\ (PMIR\text{-}4)
\end{align}
\left.\begin{matrix}[[+INCH]] \\ [[-DUR\ ]]\end{matrix}\right\} \rightarrow
\begin{bmatrix} -syll \\ -grv \\ -cnt \\ +nas \end{bmatrix}
\ /\ \left\{\begin{bmatrix} \underline{\quad\quad} \\ +ACT \\ \underline{\quad\quad} \end{bmatrix}\right\}
$$

$$
(e)\ (PMIR\text{-}5)\ \ [+DUR\ ] \rightarrow
\begin{bmatrix} +syll \\ +cmp \\ +grv \end{bmatrix}
\ /\ \begin{bmatrix} \underline{\quad\quad} \\ +COMPL \end{bmatrix}
$$

$$
(f)\ (PMIR\text{-}6)\ \ [+TNS\ ] \rightarrow
\begin{bmatrix} +syll \\ +cmp \\ -grv \end{bmatrix}
$$

$$
(g)\ (PMIR\text{-}7)\ \ [+PAST\ ] \rightarrow
\begin{bmatrix} -syll \\ -grv \\ +cnt \\ -nas \end{bmatrix}
$$

The output of PMIR's for the gender/number and person/number suffixes which have been discussed elsewhere may be summarized as follows:

(29)

Person ↓	−PLUR	+PLUR
+1st	mu	mæ
+2nd	xi	tæ
+3rd	t	nt

Gender ↓	−PLUR	+PLUR
+MSC	aC	ai
+FEM	aa	aaC
+NEUT	a	aa

In (29) the phonological segments have no independent status but are merely abbreviations for redundancy-free phonological matrices.

It is now possible to approximate the input into the phonological component, *i.e.*, the UR's, for the verbal forms (27 b, d, e, i), which is directly correlated to the output of the syntactic derivation of these forms:

(30)

Orthographic representation (OR)   *Underlying phonological representation (UR)*

(a) *sedíme* 'we are sitting'

$$\#\begin{bmatrix} +V \\ : \\ \hline sæd \end{bmatrix} + \begin{bmatrix} -INCH \\ -CAUS \\ +ACT \\ \hline i \end{bmatrix} + \begin{bmatrix} +DUR \\ -COMPL \\ : \\ \hline \emptyset \end{bmatrix} + \begin{bmatrix} +TNS \\ : \\ \hline æ \end{bmatrix} + \begin{bmatrix} +1st \\ +PLUR \\ : \\ \hline mæ \end{bmatrix}\#$$

(b) *sedáme* 'we are sitting down'

$$\#\begin{bmatrix} +V \\ : \\ \hline sæd \end{bmatrix} + \begin{bmatrix} +INCH \\ -CAUS \\ +ACT \\ \hline \emptyset \end{bmatrix} + \begin{bmatrix} +DUR \\ +COMPL \\ : \\ \hline a \end{bmatrix} + \begin{bmatrix} +TNS \\ : \\ \hline æ \end{bmatrix} + \begin{bmatrix} +1st \\ +PLUR \\ : \\ \hline mæ \end{bmatrix}\#$$

(c) *posazujeme* 'we are seating'

$$\#\begin{bmatrix} +V \\ : \\ \hline sæd \end{bmatrix} + \begin{bmatrix} +INCH \\ +CAUS \\ +ACT \\ \hline i \end{bmatrix} + \begin{bmatrix} +DUR \\ +COMPL \\ : \\ \hline a \end{bmatrix} + \begin{bmatrix} +TNS \\ : \\ \hline æ \end{bmatrix} + \begin{bmatrix} +1st \\ +PLUR \\ : \\ \hline mæ \end{bmatrix}\#$$

(d) *prohloubíme* 'we will deepen'

$$\#\begin{bmatrix} +V \\ : \\ \hline glanb \end{bmatrix} + \begin{bmatrix} +INCH \\ +CAUS \\ +ACT \\ \hline i \end{bmatrix} + \begin{bmatrix} -DUR \\ +COMPL \\ : \\ \hline n \end{bmatrix} + \begin{bmatrix} +TNS \\ : \\ \hline æ \end{bmatrix} + \begin{bmatrix} +1st \\ +PLUR \\ : \\ \hline mæ \end{bmatrix}\#$$

The OR's of (27 a-f, g-i) show alternations in the vowel segment of the root, *i.e.*, the lexical entry segment, *e.g.*, *sed–sad–sáz*, *hloub–hlub*, as well as alternations in the final consonantal segment of the root. Traditionally, the vocalic alternation has been referred to as 'gradation' or '*ablaut*'.

2.2. I venture to propose that certain phenomena, of which the '*ablaut*' is a salient example, are not the product solely of those phonological rules which take into consideration segmental (phonological) and non-segmental (constituent boundary) information, but that they depend crucially on those phonological rules which take into consideration syntactic features and possibly other, as yet undetermined, lexical information as well. That is to say, these phenomena are directly dependent on the output of the syntactic component.

It is necessary to clarify the relationship between the syntactic features and the phonological features that constitute each UR. While each phonological segment contains only specific phonological features and is independent of all other segments that adjoin it, the syntactic features range over the entire set of phonological matrices associated with the suffix. Thus reference to a phonological feature affects only the phonological segment of which that feature is a part, but reference to a syntactic feature in a phonological rule affects the entire sequence of phonological segments over which the syntactic feature ranges. This condition is subject to further modifications.

In the following sections I will discuss several cases which point to the fact that the utilization of syntactic features in phonological rules results in a considerable simplification of these rules and tends to express more naturally the intuitively felt relationship that exists between the verbal forms that undergo them.

2.2.1. The first case in question can be illustrated by a Russian example. There exist Russian verbs where dental stops are deleted before the past tense suffix -*l*. But there also exist Russian verbs where this suffix is deleted in word final position after a consonant, *e.g.*,

(31)

	Inf.		*Root*	*1 sg.*	*msc.sg.past*	*fem.sg.past*
	vesti	'lead'	ved	vedu	vel	vela
	mesti	'sweep'	met	metu	mel	mela
	nesti	'carry'	nes	nesu	nes	nesla
	vezti	'transport'	vez	vezu	vez	vezla
	oslepnut'	'become blind'	slep	oslepnu	oslep	oslepla
	peč	'bake'	pek	peku	pek	pekla

To ascertain that the suffix -*l* is not deleted in masculine short adjectives, *e.g.*, *odutl*, *podl*, Lightner[27] formulates the following rules to account for the consonant deletion in the past tense forms on the basis of their constituent structure.

(32)   (dl : l) $\begin{bmatrix} +\text{obstr} \\ -\text{grave} \\ -\text{contin} \end{bmatrix} \rightarrow \emptyset / \underline{\hspace{1cm}} l)_{\text{PS}}$

          (l : ∅) l $\rightarrow \emptyset / C \underline{\hspace{1cm}})_{\text{V}}$

The above phenomenon of deletion is not limited to Russian. In other Slavic languages, as for example Czech, there are dialects in which the past tense suffix -*l* is always deleted in masc. sg. forms if it is preceded by an obstruent, *e.g.*,

[27]   T. M. Lightner, *Segmental Phonology of Modern Standard Russian*, p. 82.

(33) a. *dialect A*   b. *dialect B*

lezl –lezla	les –lezla	'he/she crawled'
tekl –tekla	tek–tekla	'he/she flowed'
vedl–vedla	vet–vedla	'he/she led'
blbl –blbla	blp–blbla	'he/she was becoming idiotic'

To account for this phenomenon in dialect B of (33), the following rule can be formulated:

$$(34) \quad \begin{bmatrix} -\,\text{obstr} \\ +\,\text{cns} \\ -\,\text{nas} \end{bmatrix} \rightarrow \emptyset \,/\, [+\,\text{obstr}] \underline{\quad\quad})_{\text{Verb}}$$

the constituent boundary $)_{\text{Verb}}$ being specified to prevent deletion of the final liquid in nouns, *e.g.*, *hadr* 'rag', *bratr* 'brother', *lotr* 'rascal', *mysl* 'mind', *mandl* 'mangle', *Litomyšl*, *smysl* 'sense'. But the reference to the constituent boundary in (34) can be dispensed with if reference is made to the syntactic feature $[+\,\text{PAST}]$; moreover, if this feature is utilized, the phonological specification of the liquid can be dispensed with as well, due to the fact that the syntactic feature refers to the entire suffix segment, which in this case consists of a single phonological segment *l* (*cf.* 2.2. above), allowing us to state the rule in a much simpler manner, as in (35), and allowing us to capture the intuitively felt generality of the phenomenon.

$$(35) \quad [+\,\text{PAST}] \rightarrow \emptyset \,/\, [+\,\text{obstr}] \underline{\quad\quad} \#$$

Lightner's rules (32) can be reformulated analogously, utilizing the syntactic feature $[+\,\text{PAST}]$ with the resulting considerable simplification:

$$(36) \quad (\text{dl}:\text{l}) \begin{bmatrix} +\,\text{obstr} \\ -\,\text{grv} \\ -\,\text{cnt} \end{bmatrix} \rightarrow \emptyset \,/\, \underline{\quad\quad} [+\,\text{PAST}]$$

$$(\text{l}:\emptyset) \, [+\,\text{PAST}] \rightarrow \emptyset \,/\, [-\,\text{syll}] \underline{\quad\quad} \#$$

2.2.2. Another case where the utilization of syntactic features in a phonological rule leads to simplification is rule (P-17) which is repeated below in (37) for reference:

$$(37) \quad (\text{P-17}) \underset{1}{\begin{bmatrix} +\,\text{TNS} \\ -\,\text{long} \end{bmatrix}} \underset{2}{[+\,\text{nas}]} \underset{3}{\left\{ \begin{bmatrix} +\,\text{grv} \\ +\,\text{syll} \\ -\,\text{grv} \end{bmatrix} \right\}} \Rightarrow \left\{ \begin{matrix} 1 \quad 3 \quad 2 & \text{(a)} \\ 1 \quad 2 \begin{bmatrix} 3 \\ +\,\text{diff} \end{bmatrix} & \text{(b)} \end{matrix} \right\}$$

This rule accounts for the presence or absence of the final segment *-m* in 1 sg. and of the final segment *-e* in 1 pl. forms of Czech verbs, *e.g.*,

(38) (a) *vedu –vedem*   'I am leading–we are leading'

    (b) *sedím–sedíme*   'I am sitting –we are sitting'

The UR's of *vedu* and *vedem* given in (39a) and (39b), respectively, differ only with regard to the person/number suffix:

(39)

(a) *vedu*:

$$\text{UR: } \# \begin{bmatrix} +V \\ -\text{Pro} \\ : \\ \hline \text{væd} \end{bmatrix} + \begin{bmatrix} +\text{INCH} \\ +\text{CAUS} \\ +\text{ACT} \\ \hline i \end{bmatrix} + \begin{bmatrix} +\text{DUR} \\ -\text{COMPL} \\ : \\ \hline \emptyset \end{bmatrix} + \begin{bmatrix} +\text{TNS} \\ : \\ \hline æ \end{bmatrix} + \begin{bmatrix} +1\text{st} \\ -\text{PLUR} \\ : \\ \hline \text{mu} \end{bmatrix} \#$$

(b) *vedem*:

$$\text{UR: } \# \begin{bmatrix} +V \\ -\text{Pro} \\ : \\ : \\ \hline \text{væd} \end{bmatrix} + \begin{bmatrix} +\text{INCH} \\ +\text{CAUS} \\ +\text{ACT} \\ : \\ \hline i \end{bmatrix} + \begin{bmatrix} +\text{DUR} \\ -\text{COMPL} \\ : \\ \hline \emptyset \end{bmatrix} + \begin{bmatrix} +\text{TNS} \\ : \\ \hline æ \end{bmatrix} + \begin{bmatrix} +1\text{st} \\ +\text{PLUR} \\ : \\ \hline \text{mæ} \end{bmatrix} \#$$

The applicable rules (RR-1) through (P-16) (for all references to redundancy rules RR and phonological rules PR see 3.2.2. and 3.3.) as well as an as yet unformulated rule that deletes the suffix -*i*- under certain conditions: convert the UR of (39b) to the partially derived structure # ved + e + me #. Rule (P-17a) does not apply, but rule (P-17b) changes the final segment to *i*: # ved + e + mi #, and rule (P-19) deletes this final segment, yielding the desired form *vedem*. Similarly, application of rules (RR-1) through (P-16), together with the deletion rule mentioned above, to (39a) gives the partially derived structure # ved + e + mu #. The output of rule (P-17a) is # ved + e + um #, rule (P-17b) does not apply, and rule (P-18) deletes the final segment *m*, yielding # ved + e + u #, whereupon rule P-20) yields the correct derived form *vedu*.

The fact that the final segments *m* in *sedím* and *e* in *sedíme* in (38b) [*cf.* (27a, b)] are retained is directly related to the fact that rule (P-17) cannot apply to the partially derived structures of these forms since the tense suffix [+TNS] has been subject to the application of rule (P-12) and is long at the point when rule (P-17) is to apply.

Rule (P-17) is not a Czech-specific rule. The extent of its application varies in different Slavic languages, as does its ordering with respect to other phonological rules. For example, in Russian, rule (P-17) applies to every verb with the exception of *dat'* and *est'* which have the phonetically realized final segment -*m* in 1 sg. forms *dam* and *em*. It appears, then, that these two verbs must be idiosyncratically marked as not undergoing this general rule in Russian.

In Lusatian, rule (P-17) has wider application than in Czech and Bulgarian and is slightly modified. It seems that the grammars of Slovak and Serbocroatian do not contain this rule, for every verb in these languages retains the segment *m* in 1 sg. forms and has a realized segment sequence *me* and *mo*, respectively, in 1 pl. forms. Elsewhere I will investigate the possibility whether or not this rule might not have wider application in Slavic languages, *i.e.* whether or not it is limited solely to 1 sg. and 1 pl. forms of verbs.

Were we not to utilize the syntactic feature information which is present in the input into the phonological component in phonological rules, the phenomena that are accounted for by rule (P-17) could at best be accounted for by the following rule, or any variant of it:

(40)

$$\begin{bmatrix} +\text{syll} \\ -\text{long} \end{bmatrix} \begin{Bmatrix})\,\text{Future} \\ )\,\text{Present} \end{Bmatrix} [+\text{nas}] \begin{Bmatrix} \begin{bmatrix} [+\text{grv}] \\ [+\text{syll}] \\ -\text{grv} \end{bmatrix} \end{Bmatrix}_{\mathbf{v}} \Rightarrow \begin{Bmatrix} 1 & 3 & 2 & & 4 \\ 1 & 2 & 3 \begin{bmatrix} +\text{diff} \end{bmatrix} & 4 \end{Bmatrix} \begin{array}{l} (a) \\ (b) \end{array}$$

$$\quad\quad\quad 1 \quad\quad\quad\quad 2 \quad\quad 3 \quad\quad 4$$

which, in comparison to (37), is unquestionably complicated. Moreover, (40) is unable to account for the generalization that present tense forms of imperfective verbs and future tense forms of perfective verbs are subject to it equally, *e.g., nesu–nesem* 'I/we are carrying', *ponesu–ponesem* 'I/we will carry', *sednu–sednem* 'I/we will sit down' in Czech, without recourse to the specification of both constituent boundaries, $)_{\text{Future}}$ and $)_{\text{Present}}$ in term 1. The syntactic component already accounts for this generalization by introducing into the suffix the feature [+TNS] in all cases where verbs do not utilize the tense auxiliary;[28] the fact that (37) does utilize the syntactic feature [+TNS] signifies that it makes use of the generalization effected at the syntactic level.

2.3. The introduction of syntactic features into phonological rules appears to eliminate the need to refer to constituent boundaries, as has been shown in 2.2.1. and 2.2.2. In fact, the syntactic analysis of inflection presented in skeletal form in 1. as well as other relevant studies of inflection[29] do not seem to indicate any motivation for the postulation of innermost constituent boundaries. Since cyclic application of phonological rules has been conceived as depending crucially on the notion of innermost constituent boundaries, I do not find any motivation to assume that phonological rules must apply cyclically in Czech, as Lightner has postulated for Russian and Old Church Slavonic.[30]

Although limited by the scope of this paper, the above facts seem to indicate that consideration of syntactic features in phonological rules results in considerable simplification of these rules and enables us to capture certain intuitively felt generalities of natural languages. Especially, the fact that reference to a single syntactic feature implies reference to the entire sequence of PM's associated with that feature (*cf.* 2.2.) might permit a greater insight into the relationship between the syntactic content of some verbs and their phonetic realization. For example, it might explain why so-called 'motion verbs' which in all probability share some syntactic feature that is absent from all other verbs, such as [Locomotion][31], have traditionally been treated as a special verbal class.

---

[28] Cf. rule of *AUX Replacement* in Vanek, "The Tense Auxiliary Verb in Czech".
[29] Cf. Vanek, "The Tense Auxiliary Verb in Czech"; Vanek, "The Passive Auxiliary Verb" (in preparation); Vanek, *Syntactically Oriented Phonological Analysis* (in preparation).
[30] T. M. Lightner, *Segmental Phonology of Modern Standard Russian*; T. M. Lightner, "O cykliče-skix pravilax v russkom sprjaženii", *Voprosy Jazykoznanija* 2, 45-54 (1965); T. M. Lightner, "On the Phonology of Old Church Slavic Conjugation", *International Journal of Slavic Linguistics and Poetics*, X (1966).
[31] Cf. Note 7.

3.0. The specific problem which I intend to touch upon in this section is the '*ablaut*' mentioned in 2.1. The '*ablaut*' is not exclusively a Slavic phenomenon. It occurs, for example, in German (*sitzen–setzen*), in Dutch (*zitten–zetten*), in English (*sit–seat*), and in numerous other languages. Due to space limitations I will concentrate on this phenomenon in Czech, restricting my discussion to a few salient examples, as my primary purpose is not to account for the entire grammar of Czech but merely to illustrate the principle as to what criteria play a role in this phenomenon. Even the limited analysis given below, however, has a wider application in Slavic languages.

3.1. In 2.1. and 2.2., phonological rules were discussed in which a syntactic feature triggers either a change or deletion of a phonological feature, or segment permutation. I venture to propose below that '*ablaut*' is likewise not solely the product of those rules which utilize segmental or non-segmental information exclusively, but that vowel alternation in the root segment is triggered by phonological rules which take into consideration syntactic features that are an integral part of the UR.

3.1.1. Examination of the surface realizations of verbal forms (27b-f) together with the syntactic feature configuration of their suffixes shows that those forms which contain the feature [− CAUS] have a phonetically realized vowel *e* in their root, *e.g.*, *sedíme–sedáme–sedneme*, while those which contain the feature [+ CAUS] have in their root the phonetically realized vowel *a*, *e.g.*, *posazujeme, posadíme*. In order to determine whether the change of *e → a* is accountable for by a single or by more phonological rules, and in order to determine what triggers the application of the rule(s), it is necessary to consider the small caps portions of the following examples:

(41) (a) *šEl* – CHO*dil* – *při*CHÁ*zel*   '(he) went – was going – was coming'
      (b) *začnul – začínal*   '(he) began – was beginning'
      (c) *o*HNUL – *o*HÝ*bal*   '(he) bent – was bending'
      (d) *vEdl* – *v*O*dil* — *odv*Á*děl*   '(he) led – was leading – was leading away'

In (41a) *š* occurs before a [− grv] vowel, while the velar *x* (ch) remains unchanged before [+ grv] vowels. A number of cases of which (41a) is a salient example, lead me to postulate velars as basic segments from which some palatals are derived by rules (P-2) and (P-5). Consequently, it follows that *č* in (41b) must be followed by a [− grv] vowel which in fact is apparent in *začínal* but not in *začnul*. I am thus led to postulate that this vowel is present in the UR of *začnul* as well as in the UR of *začínal*, but that it is deleted at some point in the derivation, after rule (P-2) has applied, changing *k → č*. Moreover, it appears that since the non-deleted vowel in *začínal* is [+ long], the deleted vowel in *začnul* is in all probability [− long], and the deletion rule applies only to [− long] vowels. If this rule did not apply, we would derive **začinul*. It is therefore necessary to assume that there exists a rule that changes a short vowel to a long vowel. This change is apparent in *přicházel* (41a), *začínal* (41b), *ohýbal* (41c) and *odváděl* (41d).

3.1.2. In (41a) and (41d) we can observe another change in the root vowel, namely the change *e → o*, *e.g.*, *šel–chodil* and *vedl–vodil* which is independent of the above lengthening rule. That the rules which introduce gravity and length into the root vowel segment cannot depend on solely phonological environment is apparent. We could perhaps claim that there exist three separate lexical entries for the roots for instance of *vedl–vodil–odváděl* '(he) led–was leading–was leading away', *ved–vod–vád*, respectively, instead of a single lexical entry which is assigned the PM *ved* by PMIR. But this claim is counterintuitive from the semantic point of view, as the semantic content of these verbs is virtually identical. Moreover, there is strong evidence, as has been suggested in 1.7.1. above, that many semantically related verbs share a common lexical entry which is modified during derivation by the addition of syntactic features by rule (13). Even if the PM's are inserted into lexical entries at the conclusion of the transformational component, the multiplication of PM's that would result if closely related lexical entries were assigned PM's that differed only with respect to root vowel seems to ignore the fact that the change in root vowel can be predicted.

It appears therefore that some other criterion needs to be found which would account for the change in vowel gravity and vowel length. If we consider the verbal forms *posazujeme*, *posadíme*, and *odvádíme* (27e,f,j) we see that while the root vowel in the two former cases is short, it is long in the latter case, *i.e.*, *saz* versus *vád*. The laxness of the root vowel in *saz* is due to the application of a vowel shortening rule that applies to *saz* after the above mentioned vowel lengthening rule. Examination of the syntactic feature make up of the suffixes of (27a-f) shows that the verbal forms which contain the vowel *e* in their root segment have the feature specification $[-\text{CAUS}]$ in the first suffix segment while those forms which have in their root segment the vowel *a* contain in their first suffix segment the feature specification $[+\text{CAUS}]$. It seems therefore that it is the syntactic feature specification $[+\text{CAUS}]$ that triggers the gravity change. Similarly, the lengthening change appears to depend on the presence of the feature specification $[+\text{COMPL}]$ in the second suffix. I propose therefore the following tentative rules which account for the change in the root vowel from *sed* to *sad* in *posazujeme* and *posadíme*:

$$\begin{array}{ll} (42) & (\text{P-6}) \\ (43) & (\text{P-7}) \end{array} \ [+\text{syll}] \rightarrow \begin{Bmatrix} [+\text{grv}] \\ [+\text{long}] \end{Bmatrix} / \underline{\quad} [+\text{obstr}] \ [+\text{CAUS}] \begin{Bmatrix} \text{X} \\ [+\text{COMPL}] \end{Bmatrix}$$

The derived forms of *posazujeme* and *posadíme* are then subject to an additional rule (P-14) which has been independently motivated.

Rules (42) and (43) (which may be subject to reformulation once a more detailed analysis of the syntactic feature composition of the suffix segments is available) indicate that consideration of syntactic features in phonological rules may be capable of adequately accounting for such phenomena as *ablaut* and that it may not be necessary to postulate different PM's for lexical entries that are related semantically (*i.e.*, have a common basic specification) and differ only with respect to the syntactic features that have been introduced into them by rule (13) (*i.e.*, with respect to the syntactic features that fully specify them) and whose PM's would differ only as to root vowel. Considerable investigation remains to be undertaken, however.

3.2. In order to be able to give a sample derivation of selected verbal forms it is necessary to consider some general theoretical notions and to give the necessary phonological rules. Analysis of Czech has led me to postulate a greatly simplified specification of the basic inventory of phonological segments for this language, together with a set of redundancy rules. Moreover, I venture to propose that the phonological component should make no strict segregation of redundancy rules and phonological rules, but that the former should be interspersed among the latter (*cf.* 3.2.3.).

3.2.1. The redundancy-free basic segmental inventory for Czech (which may prove to be Slavic general) is summarized in (44) below:

(44)

Vowels				
	i	æ	a	u
syll	+	+	+	+
cmp	−	+	+	−
grv	−	−	+	+

Sonorants				
	m	n	l	r
syll	−	−	−	−
grv	+	−	−	−
cnt	−	−	+	−
nas	+	+	−	−

Obstruents					
	kg	x	pb	td	sz
obstr	+	+	+	+	+
cmp	+	+	−	−	−
grv	+	+	+	−	−
cnt	−	+	−	−	+
vd	±	−	±	±	±

Thus vowels need to be basically specified for only three features, sonorants for four, and obstruents for five. Only the above PM's occur in the UR's. All other phonological feature specifications are introduced into the PM's of the individual segments by redundancy rules during the course of derivation from the UR to the phonetic derived representation.

3.2.2. The redundancy rules RR which fully specify the PM's of the phonological segments are given below:

$$(RR\text{-}1) \quad [-\text{syll}] \rightarrow [-\text{cmp}]$$

$$(RR\text{-}2) \quad [\alpha\,\text{syll}] \rightarrow \begin{bmatrix} -\alpha\,\text{cns} \\ -\text{obstr} \end{bmatrix}$$

$$(RR\text{-}3) \quad [+\text{obstr}] \rightarrow \begin{bmatrix} -\text{syll} \\ +\text{cns} \end{bmatrix}$$

$$(RR\text{-}4) \quad [-\text{syll}] \rightarrow [-\text{strid}]$$

$$(RR\text{-}5) \quad [+\text{syll}] \rightarrow [+\text{cnt}]$$

$$(RR\text{-}6) \quad [-\text{obstr}] \rightarrow [+\text{vd}]$$

$$(RR\text{-}7) \quad [+\text{syll}] \rightarrow [-\text{long}]$$

$$(RR\text{-}8) \quad [+\text{grv}] \rightarrow [-\alpha\,\text{flt}] \quad /[\overline{\alpha\,\text{long}}]$$

$$(RR\text{-}9) \quad [-\text{cmp}] \rightarrow [+\text{strid}] \quad / \begin{bmatrix} +\text{obstr} \\ +\text{cnt} \end{bmatrix}$$

(RR-10) $[\alpha \text{ cmp}]$ → $[-\alpha \text{ diff}]$

(RR-11) $[-\text{long}]$ → $[-\text{cmp}]$

(RR-12) $[-\text{grv}]$ → $[-\text{flt}]$ / $[\overline{+\text{syll}}]$

(RR-13) $[\alpha \text{ syll}]$ → $[-\text{nas}]$ / $[\overline{-\alpha \text{ obstr}}]$

(RR-14) $[+\text{syll}]$ → $[-\text{stress}]$

Notice that the feature [syll] is used in basic segmental inventory as well as in redundancy rules and that the feature [vocalic] is not mentioned. The introduction of the feature [syll] has been motivated by rules of syllabification and desyllabification, (P-22 and P-9), together with the stress assignment rule (P-23), as well as by acoustic[32] and other considerations.[32a]

Moreover, the fact that the lengthening rule (P-7) discussed in 3.1.1., rule (P-12) which changes two or more identical adjacent vowels to a single long vowel, and rule (P-16) which lengthens a vowel if it is followed by a nasal, deleting the nasal if that nasal is immediately followed by an obstruent or a boundary segment, account for some instances of vowel length led me to propose that the basic segmental inventory of vowels need not include length specification and that length is a derived feature. Elimination of length specification in the basic segmental inventory reduces the vowels to four. If this reduction can be maintained then it follows that Czech is a four-vowel system[33] and, consequently, is a mora counting syllabic language.[34]

In view of the fact that the choice between the feature [diffuse] and the feature [compact] appears to be arbitrary, I have chosen to utilize here the latter while the original version of this study utilized the former. My present choice might be supported by recent phonological studies by Chomsky and Halle.[35]

3.2.3. The phonological matrix insertion rules discussed in 2.0. and 2.1. are feature adding rules. The redundancy rules postulated in 3.2.2. are also feature adding rules with the exception of (RR-9) and (RR-11). It is possible that more complete phonological analysis of Czech and other Slavic languages will show that these two redundancy rules might in fact be phonological rules.

The PMIR's are strictly constrained as to their input which can refer only to syntactic features and as to their output which is restricted to redundancy free PM's. Since the output of these rules are the underlying phonological representations, it is evident that PMIR's have to apply before all redundancy and phonological rules (*cf.* Condition A in 3.2.4.).

[32]   A.L.Vanek, "Positional Variants of Liquids in Czech: a Spectrographic Analysis", *Czechoslovakia Past and Present*, II, (The Hague, Mouton & Co.,1968), in press.

[32a]   Cf. J.McCawley, "The Role of a Phonological Feature System in a Theory of Language", University of Chicago (mimeo, Eric/Pegs).

[33]   N. Chomsky and M. Halle, *Sound Pattern of English*, Chapter IX (New York, Harper & Row, 1968).

[34]   N.Trubetzkoy, *Grundzüge der Phonologie*, 3rd ed., (Göttingen, Vandenhoek and Ruprecht,1962); J.McCawley, *The Accentual System of Standard Japanese*, unpublished Ph.D.Dissertation (MIT, 1965); C.E.Bidwell, "The Czech Verb", University of Pittsburgh,1967 (mimeo).

[35]   Chomsky and Halle, *Sound Pattern of English*, Chapter IX.

Redundancy rules (RR) and phonological rules (PR) are not restricted as to their input and output. Both may refer to either basic or redundant features. If we were to specify, however, that all RR's had to apply either before or after all phonological rules, we would encounter the following difficulties. If all RR's applied after all PR's, then they would automatically undo many of the changes effected by PR's and would yield many undesirable forms. If, on the other hand, RR's applied before all PR's, and if the output of RR's would constitute the input into PR's, then (RR-8) could not apply successfully unless we want to claim that Czech (and possibly Slavic languages in general) is an eight-vowel system instead of a four-vowel system as mentioned in 3.2.2., and the phonological rules given below in 3.3. would have to be drastically changed with resulting complication and the necessity of postulating many additional rules and repetition of phonological feature specifications.

If RR's are interspersed among PR's and ordered not only with respect to other RR's but with respect to phonological rules as well, then we are able to account for basically related phonological changes in a general way. For instance, (P-1) through (P-5), which apply to not fully specified segments, are capable of capturing the generality of the successive and simultaneous changes of dental stops to dental stridents and velars to palatals, and in addition are capable of accounting for the change of voiced velars and voiced stridents from stops to continuants. If all segments were fully specified in the input into PR's that account for these changes, it would be necessary to postulate several rather complicated rules, and the generality that can be captured if RR's and PR's are ordered with respect to each other would be missed.[36]

3.2.4. On the basis of the above discussion we may impose the following conditions on the ordering of PMIR's, RR's, and PR's:

(45)   *Condition A*: No RR or PR may apply to a segment which has not undergone PM specification by a PMIR.

(46)   *Condition B*: No PR which refers to a feature *a* may apply to segment *A* if segment *A* has not previously been specified for feature *a* by an RR or PM1R.

3.3. The following phonological rules and redundancy rules (*cf.* 3.2.2.) account not only for the sample derivation given in 3.4. but have much wider application. It should be stressed here that these rules do not constitute the entire set of rules of Czech grammar. Such an extensive set of rules requires a much more detailed analysis.

(RR-1) through (RR-6)

(P-1) $[-\text{grv}]$ $\rightarrow [+\text{cmp}] / \left[\dfrac{}{+\text{obstr}}\right][+\text{CAUS}][+\text{DUR}]$

---

[36] Cf. T. M. Lightner, "Russian Phonology, Chapter VIII", University of Illinois, 1967, (mimeo, Eric/Pegs) for a similar argument. Lightner argues, however, against redundancy rules and in favor of the notion of markedness.

(P-2) $[+\text{cmp}] \rightarrow [+\text{strid}] / \left[\dfrac{\rule{1cm}{0.4pt}}{+\text{obstr}}\right]\left[\begin{array}{c}+\text{syll}\\-\text{grv}\end{array}\right]$

(P-3) $[-\text{grv}] \rightarrow [-\text{cmp}] / \left[\begin{array}{c}\rule{1cm}{0.4pt}\\+\text{obstr}\\-\text{cnt}\end{array}\right]$

(P-4) $\left\{\begin{array}{c}[+\text{cmp}]\\ [+\text{strid}]\end{array}\right\} \rightarrow [+\text{cnt}] \ / \left[\dfrac{\rule{1cm}{0.4pt}}{+\text{vd}}\right]$

(P-5) $[+\text{strid}] \rightarrow [-\text{grv}]$

(*RR-7*)

(P-6)
(P-7) $[+\text{syll}] \rightarrow \left\{\begin{array}{c}[+\text{grv}]\\ [+\text{long}]\end{array}\right\} / \rule{0.8cm}{0.4pt}[+\text{obstr}][+\text{CAUS}]\left\{\begin{array}{c}X\\ [+\text{COMPL}]\end{array}\right\}$

(P-8) $[+\text{CAUS}]\left[\begin{array}{c}+\text{DUR}\\+\text{COMPL}\end{array}\right] \Rightarrow 2\ 1$
              1   2

(P-9) $[-\text{obstr}] \rightarrow [-\text{syll}] / \left\{\begin{array}{c}\#\\ [+\text{syll}]\end{array}\right\}\left[\dfrac{\rule{1cm}{0.4pt}}{-\text{cmp}}\right][+\text{syll}]$

(P-10) $[+\text{nas}] \rightarrow \emptyset \ \ / \left\{\begin{array}{c}[+\text{CAUS}]\\ [-\text{INCH}]\end{array}\right\}\rule{0.8cm}{0.4pt}$

(P-11) $[+\text{syll}] \rightarrow \left[\begin{array}{c}\alpha\text{cmp}\\ \alpha\text{grv}\end{array}\right] / \left[\begin{array}{c}\alpha\text{cmp}\\ \alpha\text{grv}\end{array}\right] \rule{0.8cm}{0.4pt}$

(P-12) $[+\text{syll}][+\text{syll}] \Rightarrow \left[\begin{array}{c}+\text{long}\\ 1\end{array}\right]$
              1   1

(*RR-8*) *through* (*RR-9*)

(P-13) $[-\text{grv}] \rightarrow [+\text{cmp}] / \left[\begin{array}{c}\rule{1cm}{0.4pt}\\+\text{obstr}\\-\text{strid}\end{array}\right]\left[\begin{array}{c}-\text{grv}\\+\text{long}\end{array}\right]$

(P-14) $[+\text{flt}] \rightarrow [-\text{cmp}] / \rule{0.8cm}{0.4pt} + \left[\begin{array}{c}-\text{syll}\\-\text{cns}\\-\text{grv}\end{array}\right]$

(*RR-10*) *through* (*RR-12*)

(P-15) $[+\text{syll}] \rightarrow [-\text{long}] / \rule{0.8cm}{0.4pt}[+\text{seg}] + [+\text{syll}]\left[\begin{array}{c}-\text{obstr}\\-\text{nas}\end{array}\right]$

(*RR-21*)

(P-16) $[+\text{syll}][+\text{nas}]\left\{\begin{array}{c}[+\text{obstr}]\\ \#\end{array}\right\} \Rightarrow \left[\begin{array}{c}+\text{long}\\ 1\end{array}\right]\ \ \emptyset$
              1   2   3   1   2   3

(*RR-13*)

(P-17) $\begin{bmatrix} +\text{TNS} \\ -\text{long} \end{bmatrix} [+\text{nas}] \begin{Bmatrix} \begin{bmatrix} +\text{grv} \end{bmatrix} \\ \begin{bmatrix} +\text{syll} \end{bmatrix} \\ -\text{grv} \end{Bmatrix} \Rightarrow \begin{Bmatrix} \begin{matrix} 1 & 3 & 2 \\ & & +\text{diff} \\ 1 & 2 & 3 \end{matrix} \end{Bmatrix}$ (a)

(b)

1   2   3

(P-18) $[-\text{syll}] \rightarrow \emptyset \, / \, \underline{\quad} \,\#$

(P-19) $[+\text{syll}] \rightarrow \emptyset \, / \, [-\text{syll}] \begin{bmatrix} \underline{\quad} \\ +\text{diff} \\ -\text{long} \end{bmatrix} \#$

(P-20) $[+\text{syll}] \, [+\text{syll}] \Rightarrow \emptyset$
        1   2   1   2

(P-21) $\bar{o} \rightarrow ou$

(P-22) $[-\text{obstr}] \rightarrow [+\text{syll}] \, / \, [-\text{syll}] \begin{bmatrix} \underline{\quad} \\ +\text{cns} \end{bmatrix} \begin{Bmatrix} \# \\ [-\text{syll}] \end{Bmatrix}$

(*RR-14*)

(P-23) $[+\text{syll}] \rightarrow [+\text{stress}] \, / \, \# \, [-\text{syll}]_o \, \underline{\quad}$

3.4. The derivations in this section are given for the purpose of illustrating the role of the syntactic features in the derivation of verbal forms, and consequently of stressing the necessity of direct correlation between the output of the syntactic component and the input into the phonological component.

(47)
sedíme:

UR: $\#\begin{bmatrix} +V \\ : \\ \underline{\quad} \\ \text{sæd} \end{bmatrix} + \begin{bmatrix} -\text{INCH} \\ -\text{CAUS} \\ +\text{ACT} \\ \underline{\quad} \\ i \end{bmatrix} + \begin{bmatrix} +\text{DUR} \\ -\text{COMPL} \\ : \\ \underline{\quad} \\ \emptyset \end{bmatrix} + \begin{bmatrix} +\text{TNS} \\ : \\ \underline{\quad} \\ \text{æ} \end{bmatrix} + \begin{bmatrix} +1\text{st} \\ +\text{PLUR} \\ : \\ \underline{\quad} \\ \text{mæ} \end{bmatrix} \# \rightarrow$

RR1-6 → YES → P3 → VACUOUS → P5 → VACUOUS → RR-7 → YES →
P11 → sæd+i+i+mæ → P12 → sæd+i+mæ → RR-9 → YES →
P13 → sæǵ+i+mæ → RR10-14 → seǵ+i+me → P23 → séǵ+i+me

DR: *séǵīme*
        where ǵ = d′, and ′ over vowel in the derivation stands for stress,
        while ′ in orthographic representation stands for length.

(48)
sedáme:

UR: $\#\begin{bmatrix} +V \\ : \\ \underline{\quad} \\ \text{sæd} \end{bmatrix} + \begin{bmatrix} +\text{INCH} \\ -\text{CAUS} \\ +\text{ACT} \\ \underline{\quad} \\ \emptyset \end{bmatrix} + \begin{bmatrix} +\text{DUR} \\ +\text{COMPL} \\ : \\ \underline{\quad} \\ a \end{bmatrix} + \begin{bmatrix} +\text{TNS} \\ : \\ \underline{\quad} \\ \text{æ} \end{bmatrix} + \begin{bmatrix} +1\text{st} \\ +\text{PLUR} \\ : \\ \underline{\quad} \\ \text{mæ} \end{bmatrix} \# \rightarrow$

PR1-6 → YES → P3 → VACUOUS → P5 → VACUOUS → RR7 → YES →

P11 → sæd + a + a + mæ → P12 → sæd + ā + mæ → RR 8-14 → sed + ā + me → P23 → séd + ā + me

DR: *sédāme*

(49)
posazujeme:

UR: $\#$ $\begin{bmatrix} +V \\ : \\ \overline{\quad} \\ sæd \end{bmatrix}$ $+$ $\begin{bmatrix} +INCH \\ +CAUS \\ +ACT \\ \overline{\quad} \\ i \end{bmatrix}$ $+$ $\begin{bmatrix} +DUR \\ +COMPL \\ : \\ \overline{\quad} \\ a \end{bmatrix}$ $+$ $\begin{bmatrix} +TNS \\ : \\ \overline{\quad} \\ æ \end{bmatrix}$ $+$ $\begin{bmatrix} +1st \\ +PLUR \\ : \\ \overline{\quad} \\ mæ \end{bmatrix}$ $\# \rightarrow$

RR1-6 → YES → P1 → sæǵ + i + a + æ + mæ → P2 → sæǯ + i + a + æ + mæ → P3 → sæʒ + i + a + æ + mæ → P4 → sæz + i + a + æ + mæ → P5 → VACUOUS → RR7 → YES → P6 → saz + i + a + æ + mæ → P7 → sāz + i + a + æ + mæ → P8 → sāz + a + i + æ + mæ → P9 → sāz + a + j + æ + mæ → RR8-9 → sāz + ɔ + j + æ + mæ → P14 → sāz + u + j + æ + mæ → RR10-11 → sāz + u + j + e + me → P15 → săz + u + j + e + me → RR12-14 → YES → P23 → pó + săz + u + j + e + me

DR: *pósazujeme*

(50)
prohloubíme:

UR: $\#$ $\begin{bmatrix} +V \\ : \\ \overline{\quad} \\ glanb \end{bmatrix}$ $+$ $\begin{bmatrix} +INCH \\ +CAUS \\ +ACT \\ \overline{\quad} \\ i \end{bmatrix}$ $+$ $\begin{bmatrix} -DUR \\ +COMPL \\ : \\ \overline{\quad} \\ n \end{bmatrix}$ $+$ $\begin{bmatrix} +TNS \\ : \\ \overline{\quad} \\ æ \end{bmatrix}$ $+$ $\begin{bmatrix} +1st \\ +PLUR \\ : \\ \overline{\quad} \\ mæ \end{bmatrix}$ $\# \rightarrow$

RR1-6 → YES → P4 → hlanb + i + n + æ + mæ → RR7 → YES → P10 → hlanb + i + æ + mæ → P11 → hlanb + i + i + mæ → P12 → hlanb + i + mæ → RR8, 10-11 → hlanb + ī + me → RR12 → YES → P16 → hlōb + ī + me → RR13 → YES → P21 → hloub + ī + me → RR14 → YES → P23 → pró + hloub + ī + me

DR: *próhloubīme*

E. WEIGL

A NEUROPSYCHOLOGICAL CONTRIBUTION TO THE PROBLEM OF SEMANTICS

For some decades the problem of meaning has become of increasing interest to various sciences apart from linguistics, particulary to psychology (*cf.* Osgood and Miron, 1963). In the course of this development it is the problem of SEMANTIC FIELDS (systems) which is given primary attention.

Only vaguely similar to the use of this term in linguistics (*e.g.*, by Trier), we define 'semantic fields' (systems) as ontogenetically developed systems of meaning, comprising not only logical and linguistical but also psychological and social relations and, therefore, differing from individual to individual (*cf.* Luria and Vinogradova, 1959, p. 89).

A number of investigators, such as Razran (1936 and 1949), Riess, (1949), Branca (1957), Luria (1959), a.o. are carrying through successfully experiments pertaining to the structure and dynamics of these systems.

With the help of a neuropsychological method, developed by the author (1961, 1964, 1967), investigations are carried through in connexion with the study of disturbances of decoding, encoding and recoding (Jakobson, 1964, 1966) of paradigmatic and syntagmatic relations of meaning in cases of cerebral damages.

With most aphasics, the capability for decoding, encoding and recoding verbal information is not completely obliterated. The above processes are more or less disturbed via certain 'channels', while, via others, they are completely or almost completely intact, depending on the localization of the brain lesion, *i.e.*, on the 'type' of aphasia. While, *e.g.*, an alexia patient understands without difficulty the meaning of a certain word when hearing it, he fails to do so when reading it; *vice versa*, the patient with sensory aphasia remains 'deaf' towards the meaning of a word spoken to him, while he is able to understand the same word as soon as it is shown to him in writing.

Similar conditions as in disturbances of decoding, underlie disturbances of encoding and recoding. A patient suffering from disturbances in naming objects, may well be able to read a certain word aloud, whereas he fails when asked to name the respective object, *i.e.*, in the expressive use of the same word; patients with expressive alexia disturbances can react quite normally when requested to name objects, while reading the very same word aloud proves to be an insurmountable difficulty, etc.

Elaborating our deblocking-method, we proceeded from these relations between intact and disturbed functions of speech. The deblocking effect is attained through using the intact channel leading to a certain 'meaning', in order to eliminate the 'blocking' in cases where this meaning cannot be decoded, encoded or recoded via other channels. If a word-deaf patient, *e.g.*, is requested to read several words, among them the 'critical' word, he is able to understand its meaning also auditorily, when this same word is spoken to him afterwards. The fact, that the patients do neither directly nor consciously engage in this process of deblocking, indicates the automatized, stereotype character of these processes.

In this way, we succeeded in eliminating experimentally disturbances like arepetition, alexia, agraphia, anomia, verbal deafness, *etc.*, in various types of aphasia. The deblocking effect is attained through linking two semantically related performances of a preserved and a 'blocked' function, evoking the unimpaired PRIOR to the disturbed performance.

In other words: disturbed auditive or lexic understanding of a certain word can only be deblocked through intact copying, repeating, naming, *etc.*, OF THE SAME OR A SEMANTICALLY RELATED WORD, LYING IN THE RESPECTIVE SEMANTIC FIELD. This makes the specificity of the deblocking effect, its selective character, apparent. The verbal stimuli which we used do not lead automatically to a 'general functional readiness' of the impaired component part of the language system. The functional readiness is, in fact, connected with the SEMANTIC FIELD to which the particular verbal deblocking stimulus belongs. The selective character of deblocking, therefore, is primarily determined by THE FACTOR OF MEANING. Due to this basic fact, it is possible to carry through experimental studies of semantic fields with aphasiacs, and investigate systematically quantitative and qualitative relations between words and categories of words (nouns designating objects, activities, synonyms, antonyms, homonyms, generic nouns, *etc.*).

As the deblocking effect depends on the words given in the 'prestimulation phase', the receptive and expressive speech performances of the patients can be experimentally directed. In the course of this, it becomes apparent that in certain cases 'deviations' can be provoked instead of the adequate reactions. An anomic woman aphasiac, for example, after having read the word *shoes* among several different words calls a picture of stockings *shoes*, being firmly convinced of having used the proper word.

Apart from studying the structural relations existing within certain semantic fields, we also investigate with the help of deblocking method the DYNAMIC RELATIONS between more or less heterogeneous semantic systems, especially in connection with polysemics. For instance the German homonym *Feder* has three concrete meanings: 'pen', 'feather', and 'spring'. In one of our experiments we asked an anomic patient to repeat several words among them the word *Feder*. After this we showed him different pictures, among them a pen, a feather and a spring. And now, the patient was able to name all these three pictures correctly. Thus, it is possible to deblock with a single word stimulus, several meanings, contained in different heterogenous semantic fields. 'Conflicts' between heterogeneous semantic fields can be provoked experimentally, for instance, if during the prestimulation phase one reinforces only one of the meanings of a hononym, and then offers a picture for naming, showing the object carrying the other meaning. In such cases, either the deblocking effect is inhibited, or a deviation in the sense of the dominating semantic fields appears.

The deblocking method referred to pertains primarily to certain SINGLE performances of one and the same disturbed verbal function (*e.g.*, expressive reading, repetition, *etc.*). It is possible, however, to deblock successively a 'chain' of single performances instead of only ONE through the use of one or several deblockants, provided all intact or disturbed functions involved are connected with one and the same semantic field (Weigl, 1967b). An example: Patient *H.*, an aphasiac whom we examined, disposes of receptive reading, repetition, and copying of simple words, while expressive reading, reading of words written by himself, oral and written naming, and writing on dictation are disturbed to various degrees. Immediately, after the patient has read receptively, repeated and understood, and copied the critical among other words, he is able to read the same word aloud, to name it orally and in writing, and to write it on dictation. Generally, however, the order of the performances to be deblocked cannot be arbitrarily changed. In most cases, the 'best possible' order can be ascertained statistically, *i.e.*, an order which permits the relatively highest D-effect to be achieved in relation to every single performance of the various functions. Occasionally, it also happens that the performances of a certain function can be deblocked only within the 'chain' and, furthermore, only at a certain point within the order of that chain. In the case of one of our patients, *M*, for instance, expressive reading could be deblocked only at the end of a relatively long 'chain', after repetition, writing on dictation, oral and written naming had been deblocked.

Examples of some of our chain-deblocking experiments (see Fig. 1) illustrate clearly the POLYFUNCTIONAL effect of the deblocking stimuli. This is due to the fact that under certain conditions the effect of semantic information radiates over the language-functional system as a whole. This means that through hearing a word for example, all other forms of decoding, encoding and recoding, such as receptive understanding, repetition, reading, aloud, writing, *etc.*, this word, are simultaneously put in a state of readiness. This process of radiation is to be regarded as a form of simultaneous prestimulation of the 'blocked' channels, which favours the deblocking of the respective impaired speech performances. The interrelations existing within the 'chain' seem to indicate a certain HIERARCHY among the functions involved, concerning both the possibility of their being deblocked and the possibility of their additionally inducing positive effects.

The assumption of polyfunctional effects of this kind can, of course, not be restricted to the pathological sphere, but must be regarded as a characteristic feature of the language-functional system. In the view of the author, the gradual development of cooperation with linguists interested in semantic problems could provide a chance for

	Intact functions	Disturbed functions				
	copying	repetition	writing on dictation	oral naming	written naming	reading aloud
I	Hänge Gürtel Spagai	"krieg ich nicht"	Per Pagen	legaex	Pagel	nicht möglich
II	Stirn Angel Klammer	nicht möglich	a S Klapper	fange	nicht möglich	Kanne
III	Marawen Tulpe Palme	"saleweinger"	Mali Mali	lege	nicht möglich	trase
IV	Pinsel War Sahne	nicht möglich	nicht möglich	lame schekin	S Maltn Malen Pipe Pinsel	Pinsel
V	h Art Kekse Amsel	Keks	Ar Kekor Kohse	Kekse	Kehse	Kense
VI	Rote hose Decke	Decke	Deche	'ne Decke	Decke	Decke
VII	Sand Nadeln Maus	Nadel	hadel	Feder.....Stege	Nadel	Ladel
VIII	Dackel Bank Falte	'ne Dacke·	Dackel	Deckel, Dackel, Deckel	Dackel	Deckel..Dacker
IX	Lilie s Regal Blite	Dicks	Bitte Böb	Iiks	Blite	Bix
X	globus Rose Buch	Globus	globus globus	der lege..legök	Globub	ein lebes
XI	Stein Schlauch Raupe	'n Strauch...: Strauss	l Schlauch	'n Stauch...... Schlauch	Schlauch	Schlauch
XII	Wolf Fuss hast.	Nest	hest	Nest	Nest	Nest
XIII	Krebs Seide gas	Krebs	Krebs Kröber Krebs	'n Krebs	Krebs	Krebs
XIV	Kette Fuchs Linde	Füchs	Fuchs	Füchs	Fuchs	Füchs
XV	Motte Bier Kragen	streiger Krischen	Kragen	Krägen	Kragen	Krägen

Fig. 1   "Chain" deblocking in a case of sensory aphasia[1]

applying fruitfully, beyond the field of neuropsychology, his studies — only briefly outlined here — which he carried through with his collaborators.

REFERENCES

Branca, A. A.,
  1957 "Semantic generalization at the level of the conditioning experiment", *Am. J. Psychol*, 70, 541.
Jakobson, R.,
  1964 "Towards a linguistic typology of aphasia impairments", in: *A CIBA Foundations Symposium* (London, Churchill Ltd.), p. 21.
Luria, A. R. and O. S. Vinogradova,
  1959 "An objective investigation of the dynamics of semantic systems", *Brit. J. Psychol*. 50, 89.

[1]   From Weigl (1968), p. 152.

Razran, G.,

1936　"Salivating and thinking in different languages", *J. Psychol.* 1, 145.

1949　"Semantic, syntactic and phonetographic generalization of verbal conditioning", *J. Exp. Psychol.*, 39, 642.

Riess, B. P.,

1949　"Semantic conditioning involving the Calvanic skin reflex", *J. Exp. Psychol.*, 26, 238.

Weigl, E.,

1961　"The phenomenon of temporary deblocking in aphasia", *Z. Phonetik, Spr. Komm.*, 14, 337.

1964　"The experimental deblocking of aphasic verbal defects, a method of investigation about processes of cerebral dynamics", *Voprosy Psichologii*, p. 149 (russ.).

1968　"On the problem of cortical syndroms. Experimental studies", in: *The reach of mind. Essays in memory of Kurt Goldstein*, (Springer Publishing Company).